READING
from this
PLACE

READING
from this
PLACE

Volume I

Social Location and
Biblical Interpretation
in the United States

Fernando F. Segovia
and
Mary Ann Tolbert,
Editors

Fortress Press   **Minneapolis**

READING FROM THIS PLACE
Volume 1: Social Location and Biblical Interpretation in the United States

Unless otherwise noted, scripture quotations are from the New Revised Standard Version Bible, copyright © 1989 by the Division of Christian Education of the National Council of the Churches of Christ in the United States of America. Used with permission.

Other credits are listed in the Acknowledgments on p. xi

Cover design: Brad Norr Design
Interior design: ediType

Library of Congress Cataloging-in-Publication Data

Reading from this place / Fernando F. Segovia and Mary Ann Tolbert, editors.
    p.   cm.
    Papers originally presented at conferences on Social Location and Biblical Interpretation and on Globalization and Theological Education, the first held at Vanderbilt University, Jan. 21–24, 1993.
    Includes bibliographical references and index.
    Contents: v. 1. Social location and biblical interpretation in the United States.
    ISBN 0-8006-2812-8 (v. 1 : alk. paper)
    1. Bible—Hermeneutics—Congresses. 2. Theology—Study and teaching—Congresses. 3. Bible as literature—Congresses. Religious pluralism—Christianity—Congresses.   I. Segovia, Fernando F.   II. Tolbert, Mary Ann, 1947–
BS476.R42   1995
220.6′01—dc20   94–33208
                                             CIP

The paper used in this publication meets the minimum requirements of American National Standard for Information Sciences—Permanence of Paper for Printed Library Materials, ANSI Z329.48-1984. ∞™

Manufactured in the U.S.A.   AF 1–2812

3   4   5   6   7   8   9   10

Contents

Part Two
CONTESTATIONS: SOCIAL LOCATIONS IN CONFLICT

Part Three
SOCIAL LOCATION AND ACCOUNTABILITY

Preface _____

The present volume represents the first stage of a multidimensional project entitled "Reading from This Place: Social Location and Biblical Interpretation." This project was first conceived by the editors in the spring of 1991, as a response to certain major and momentous developments taking place in the theory and practice of biblical criticism at the end of the twentieth century: on the one hand, the emergence of the crucial issue of perspective or standpoint in the reading and interpretation of the biblical texts; on the other hand, the increasing diversity and globalization of the discipline, as more and more new voices, more and more new perspectives and standpoints, entered the field of biblical studies.

Thus, having remained in the background for the greater part of the century, biblical criticism was now, at the end of the century, beginning to take seriously into account the role of the reader in interpretation and hence the relationship between interpretation and the social location of the interpreter. In fact, a number of movements in biblical criticism—such as feminist criticism, literary criticism, sociological analysis, and liberation and contextual theologies—had begun to call into question older, established exegetical and theological methods, which had often claimed for themselves universality and objectivity under the construct of an objective and scientific reader, a universal and informed reader. These newer movements all involved a shift of critical focus toward the interpreter or theologian, bringing the issue of standpoint or perspective to the forefront of concern, with a view of the interpretive task as directly influenced by the social location of the individual in question. Thus, factors traditionally left out of consideration were now becoming areas of exploration—for example, gender, race, ethnic origins, class, sexual orientation, religious affiliation, and sociopolitical contexts—with a focus on real, flesh-and-blood readers who were always and inescapably situated both historically and culturally and whose reading and interpretation of the texts were seen as affected by their social location.

The editors formulated, therefore, a threefold project consisting of the following stages. First, the issue of the relationship between interpretation and the social location of the interpreter would be pursued at the national level. A first volume, then, would address this question from the perspective of the diversity present within U.S. society and draw on scholars from a wide variety of the U.S. cultural spectrum. The book would call upon voices long present and active in the field as well as on those that had remained absent or silent until quite recently but that were now making themselves heard for the first time. Thus, the work would involve men and women from a wide variety of ethnic and racial backgrounds. Second, the same issue would be pursued at a global level, involving scholars from outside the United States. This second volume would be quite inclusive as well, involving the traditional and active voices from Europe and Canada as well as the more recent voices from the Third World—Africa, Asia, and Latin America. Again, the work would involve men and women from a wide variety of sociopolitical backgrounds. Finally, in the light of such discussions, the consequences of this issue for theological education in general and biblical pedagogy in particular would be addressed in a third volume, involving a broad variety of representatives from both volumes as well as a number of experts in theological education.

Once the project had received its initial formulation and launching, we approached the Lilly Endowment for a grant that would make it possible to bring together the invited participants for face-to-face discussions. For logistical purposes two such gatherings were proposed: a national conference and an international conference. Our proposal to the Lilly Endowment, under the title of "Social Location and Biblical Interpretation: The Challenge of Pluralism and Globalization in Theological Education," was positively received and graciously approved in the fall of 1991, making both envisioned conferences possible. Once such funding had been received, we approached the Association of Theological Schools in the United States and Canada for a grant—under their awards program entitled "Globalization and the Classical Theological Disciplines," funded by the Pew Charitable Trusts—that would allow us to expand the contours of the third and final stage of the project. Once again, the proposal, entitled "Globalization and Theological Education: Towards New Paradigms in Biblical Pedagogy," was positively received and graciously approved in the spring of 1992. Finally, when the project as a whole was presented to Fortress Press, it was immediately accepted for publication.

The present volume represents, therefore, the results of the first stage of the project: the papers presented at the national conference, which took place at the Vanderbilt Divinity School on January 21–24, 1993. The introduction by Fernando F. Segovia and the conclusion by Mary Ann Tolbert were written after the conference and in the light of its presentations and proceedings. The volume is meant as a contribution to the fundamental question regarding the role of the interpreter in the light of a very different world within biblical criticism—a world of increasing and irreversible diversity and pluralism, the world of the twenty-first century.

Acknowledgments

The editors would like to express their profound gratitude to all those individuals and institutions who have made this volume possible.

First, to the Lilly Endowment and Dr. Craig Dykstra, Vice President for Religion, for the strong support of the project and the generous funding that made possible bringing together all these individuals for the first and national conference entitled "Reading from This Place."

Second, to Dr. Joseph C. Hough, Jr., Dean of the Divinity School at Vanderbilt University, for his kind and invaluable assistance in all the different areas and dimensions of the project.

Third, to Dr. Marshall Johnson, Director of Publishing, Fortress Press, who made the project his own from its very inception, and to the editorial staff of Fortress Press, especially Michael West, who brought it to completion, offering sharp and judicious advice throughout.

Fourth, to all the students in the area of New Testament and early Christian literature within the graduate department of religion at Vanderbilt University whose kind assistance and participation proved invaluable during the course of the conference itself. Two deserve special recognition and gratitude: Ms. Vicki Phillips, who undertook the task of editing and formatting the papers for publication; and Mr. Francisco Lozada-Smith, who served as overall manager for the conference and whose peerless attention to detail and organization made the conference a resounding success.

Finally, to all those scholars and friends who kindly accepted our invitations and whose contributions to the project grace the pages that follow. To them we are specially indebted.

Contributors _____

Randall C. Bailey, Associate Professor of Old Testament, Interdenominational Theological Center, Atlanta.

Walter Brueggemann, Professor of Old Testament, Columbia Theological Seminary, Decatur, Georgia.

Justo L. González, Adjunct Professor of Church History, Columbia Theological Seminary, Decatur, Georgia.

Norman K. Gottwald, Professor of Biblical Studies, New York Theological Seminary.

Ada María Isasi-Díaz, Associate Professor of Theology and Ethics, The Theological School, Drew University, Madison, New Jersey.

Chan-Hie Kim, Professor of New Testament, School of Theology at Claremont and Claremont Graduate School, Claremont, California.

Amy-Jill Levine, Professor of New Testament and Early Christianity, The Divinity School, Vanderbilt University.

Daniel Patte, Professor of Religious Studies, Department of Religious Studies, and Professor of New Testament and Early Christian Literature, The Divinity School, Vanderbilt University.

Tina Pippin, Assistant Professor of Bible and Religion, Agnes Scott College, Decatur, Georgia.

Sharon H. Ringe, Professor of New Testament, Wesley Theological Seminary, Washington, D.C.

Fernando F. Segovia, Professor of New Testament and Early Christianity, The Divinity School, Vanderbilt University.

Abraham Smith, Assistant Professor of New Testament, School of Theology, Boston University.

Mary Ann Tolbert, George H. Atkinson Professor for Biblical Studies, Pacific School of Religion, Berkeley, California.

Herman C. Waetjen, Professor of New Testament, San Francisco Theological Seminary, San Anselmo, California.

Vincent L. Wimbush, Professor of New Testament, Union Theological Seminary, New York.

Antoinette Clark Wire, Professor of New Testament, San Francisco Theological Seminary, San Anselmo, California.

Gale A. Yee, Associate Professor of Old Testament, University of St. Thomas, St. Paul, Minnesota.

"And They Began to Speak in Other Tongues": Competing Modes of Discourse in Contemporary Biblical Criticism

_____ Fernando F. Segovia _____

The world of biblical criticism today is very different from that of the mid-1970s. In the last few decades, the field has undergone a fundamental and radical shift of such magnitude and consequences that it cannot be reasonably compared to any other in the century. This shift, moreover, is by no means over; in fact, its impact has only just begun. Among its manifold and far-reaching consequences, it has allowed for incredible diversity in models of interpretation as well as for a thoroughgoing reformulation of the role of culture and experience in the task of criticism, two issues with which I shall be specifically concerned in this introduction. The shift to which I am referring concerns the long dominance and swift demise of the historical-critical model of interpretation, in unquestioned control for the first three-quarters of the century but in broad retreat during its last and present quarter.[1] In what follows I will set forth my own overview of this change and hence of the overall course of biblical criticism in this century. I undertake such a seemingly grandiose project for a variety of reasons, all of which I regard as ultimately interrelated and interdependent.

First, the shift is thoroughly intertwined with my own life as a critic, with autobiography and discipline going hand in hand. In effect, I have experienced the shift firsthand, having moved myself through the various interpretive paradigms of historical criticism. I began just as redaction

---

1. The first notes of concern or warning begin to appear in the 1970s. In the United States, for example, N. R. Petersen speaks of "a process of potentially revolutionary change" with the future of the method as a "lively question" (*Literary Criticism for New Testament Critics* [Guides to Biblical Scholarship; Philadelphia: Fortress Press, 1978] 9–10). Similarly, in Germany, P. Stuhlmacher speaks of the method as "involved in a war on many fronts," with its "relevance...in part subject to serious doubt in theological and ecclesiastical circles" (*Historical Criticism and Theological Interpretation of Scripture: Toward a Hermeneutic of Consent* [Philadelphia: Fortress Press, 1977; German original, Göttingen: Vandenhoeck und Ruprecht, 1975] 19–21).

criticism was about to change into composition criticism; then came literary criticism, which gradually ran the course of the interpretive spectrum from text-dominant to reader-dominant approaches; next was cultural criticism, which has shifted from sociological to anthropological models, increasingly addressing the question of the reader's sociocultural context and stance. Such experience yields the benefit of analysis from within, from the point of view of the insider and practitioner—highly informed and self-critical. Such experience also yields the advantage of analysis from without, from the point of view of the outsider and former adherent—profoundly aware of social location in terms of intellectual currents of thought and hence of oneself as forming part, as reader and critic, of much wider modes of discourse involving different reading strategies and underlying theoretical orientations. This is not to say, of course, that such experience confers on the proposed overview any sort of privileged or unassailable status, for it is and remains, as with any such analysis, a construction on my part and from my perspective; such experience, however, does lend the overview a certain sense of commitment and authenticity. To recount the course of the discipline represents for me, therefore, a coming to terms with my own socioeducational life.

Second, for me the proposed overview of both shift and discipline is also closely linked to the growing sense that the twentieth century is coming to an end. There is something about the end of certain time periods—such as a year, a decade, or a century—whereby they become inevitably laden with profound significance and symbolism, despite the fact that such time delimitations are ultimately as arbitrary as any other.[2] Such periods elicit, in effect, a greater than usual desire for order and coherence, as a searching and reflective glance is cast backward as well as forward. Such periods call, in effect, for the imposition of a plot on what would otherwise remain a totally unwieldy and deeply frustrating mass of details. With the approaching close of the century, thoughts of the discipline come readily to mind and call for an account of its recent trajectory and future directions, especially in the light of the profound shift that marks the last quarter of the century. For me, therefore,

---

2. For similar ruminations and a similar analysis of a discipline in terms of a time period, see the use of the decade by N. K. Miller in approaching feminist criticism from a personal perspective ("Decades," *Writing Cultural Criticism* [ed. M. Torgovnick; *The South Atlantic Quarterly* 91 (1992) 65–86]). On the power of the concept of an ending century, witness the number of sociopolitical studies beginning to appear already: Z. Brzezinski, *Out of Control: Global Turmoil on the Eve of the 21st Century* (New York: Scribner's, 1993); P. Kennedy, *Preparing for the 21st Century* (New York: Random House, 1993); J. Lukacs, *The End of the 20th Century and the End of the Modern Age* (New York: Ticknor and Fields, 1993). From a more popular point of view, see D. Richards, "Counting Down to the Year 2000," *The New York Times,* June 27, 1993, national ed., H5; and F. Haskell, "Art and the Apocalypse," *The New York Review of Books,* July 15, 1993, 25.

to recount the course of the discipline means also to come to terms with my own sociohistorical context.

Third, I find the shift to be closely intertwined with certain global developments in the sociopolitical arena, developments within which I have found myself inextricably implicated from birth. Indeed, in my own case this yearning for order and organization is directly propelled by the conviction, pointedly reinforced by the recent implosion and collapse of the Soviet Empire, that a predominant characteristic of the century has been the gradual but steady process of liberation and decolonization in the world at large, as the colonial powers of the Northern Hemisphere have lost their sociopolitical grip—though by no means their socioeconomic grip—on the colonized peoples of the Southern Hemisphere. This is a process that I presently see as reaching a climactic stage, as the voices of the colonized come increasingly to the fore. It is also a discourse into which I find myself, as a subject of a number of layers of colonialism,[3] *arrojado* (thrown), with not much choice regarding participation or abstention.[4] As I reflect, as we near the turn of the millennium, on the sociopolitical course of the century and the outlook for the future, I find it impossible not to see an analogous process at work in the classical theological disciplines, including biblical criticism, and hence not to use the same categories of analysis in the formulation of the proposed overview—a process of decolonization and liberation at work in and through the shift. For me, therefore, to recount the course of the discipline means to come to terms with my own sociocultural context as well.

Finally, this shift is, to be sure, directly responsible for the present volume as well. I believe that such an overview of the discipline will serve as a proper introduction to the essays that follow, all of which re-

---

3. Indeed, I come from a country (Cuba) that has lived under three very different colonial powers in the course of the century and still finds itself, with but a few years to go to the centenary of its independence, under the aegis of one such power, even when the imperial center itself has collapsed—the ultimate irony of the colonized mentality! To wit: Spanish colonialism, from the very first year of the era of conquest through the conclusion of the long War of Independence at the turn of the century (1492–1898); American colonialism and neocolonialism, encompassing respectively the period of the occupation (1898–1902) and the period of the republic, at least in name (1902–59); and Soviet colonialism (1959–), covering not only the emergence of a Socialist-Leninist state in alliance with the Warsaw Pact (1959–90) but also its present continuation as a committed outpost or redoubt of Socialism-Leninism even after the demise and breakup of the center itself (1990–).

4. The Indian critic G. C. Spivak describes the space she occupies as having been "written" for her by history and thus as ineluctable; see, for example, her "The Post-Colonial Critic," *The Post-Colonial Critic: Interviews, Strategies, Dialogues* (ed. S. Harasym; New York: Routledge, 1990) 67–74, esp. 68. I much prefer the Spanish term, *arrojar* (to be thrown), as reflecting the unpredictable and turbulent nature of the discourse imposed by colonization; indeed, I find the further connotation of the term ("to be vomited") not altogether out of place.

flect and address in one way or another the state of anomie—permanent anomie, perhaps—that has come to characterize the discipline at this critical though enormously creative juncture in its life.[5] These essays, as we mentioned in the preface, represent the first part of a threefold project entitled "Reading from This Place: Social Location and Biblical Interpretation." In this first part of the project, a number of participants from the broad mosaic of life in the United States were asked to reflect on the relationship between biblical interpretation and the social location of the interpreter, however defined.[6] Both the present collection and the project as a whole can be best understood in the light of the proposed overview of the discipline in this century. The specific question addressed—with its explicit focus on real readers and communities of readers—is one that has remained submerged for most of the century but is now beginning to come to the forefront of the discussion, pressed as it is by those who had remained in the margins for most of the century but who are now beginning to enter the ranks of the discipline in ever greater numbers. Indeed, it is only at this point, when the shift in the discipline has reached a certain level of methodological and theoretical maturity, that such a question can be properly raised and pursued from an informed and sophisticated point of view. Finally, therefore, for me to recount the course of the discipline is to account for the present volume and its encompassing project.

The title I have chosen for this essay—"And They Began to Speak in Other Tongues"—is meant to reflect the proposed course of the discipline; in so doing, however, it also gives away the main lines of the plot. One day as I reflected upon the present situation of the discipline, on the verge of becoming truly global for the first time, this statement from the Lukan scene of Pentecost (Acts 2) came suddenly to mind. It is certainly not my intention to produce an elaborate allegorical reading of this narrative event in the light of the developments in question nor to claim any sort of spiritual guidance or sanction from above for such developments; all I wish to do is to engage in a bit of constructive intertextual encounter.

Indeed, while the present state of the discipline does remind me of a number of elements from the Lukan scene, it also requires a fundamental revisioning of that scene. What I have in mind is a "speaking

---

5. I borrow such a description of the discipline from the article by S. Ortner in which she describes the present state of anthropological theory in such terms ("Theory in Anthropology since the Sixties," *Comparative Studies in Society and History* 26 [1984] 126–66, esp. 126–27).

6. The second volume addresses the same question from a global perspective, with contributors from all continents, while the projected third volume deals with this question from the point of view of biblical pedagogy and theological education; in other words, it addresses the implications of the shift for the teaching of biblical criticism and its role in the theological curriculum.

in other tongues," to be sure, but of a very different kind. Thus, it is not that one and the same group now speaks in other tongues to the multitudes at large—in fact, a rather accurate description of the situation up to this point—but rather that the multitudes at large have begun to speak in other tongues, their own tongues. Given such a revisioning of the scene, a number of analogous observations are in order (Acts 2:4-5): "men" (men and women, readers and critics) "from every nation under heaven" (from all corners of the world and all configurations of social location in the world) "began to speak in their own tongues" (to read and interpret the biblical texts out of their own contexts, addressing not only one another but also the world at large). The result of such "speaking in tongues" is no longer a discourse controlled by the center, as the Lukan narrative would have it (though in effect any translation of such a discourse would immediately serve to decenter the center), but a discourse with no center or with many centers, hence the reason for my subtitle, "Competing Modes of Discourse in Contemporary Biblical Criticism." Such, in my opinion, is where the discipline presently stands, with a beginning moment in the shift involving methodological and theoretical diversity now giving way to a second moment involving sociocultural diversity as well. I would argue, therefore, that what is occurring is actually the reverse of the Lukan agenda: not at all a movement emanating from "Jerusalem" out to the world at large, but rather one decentered away from "Jerusalem" (for "Jerusalem" no longer exists) and in the world at large. I see it as a process of liberation and decolonization, away from the Eurocentric moorings and concerns of the discipline, not in complete abandonment of such discourse but in search of other discourses heretofore bypassed and ignored. I begin my overview of this process with an exposition of the main structural components to be used in the construction and deployment of its plot.

Competing Modes of Discourse in Biblical Criticism

In the plotting of the shift in the discipline that follows, I have recourse to three structural principles: first, I would argue that the process has so far involved three distinct paradigms or umbrella models of interpretation, each involving a variety of interpretive approaches; second, I would describe such a process in terms of liberation and decolonization, although for different reasons at different times; finally, I would argue that, at this point in the process, these three paradigms need not be seen as mutually exclusive but rather as subject to creative interaction.

Competing Interpretive Paradigms

As the discipline has shifted, three different and competing paradigms in contemporary biblical criticism have emerged, each involving a distinctive mode of discourse.[7] First, there is traditional historical criticism broadly conceived, the dominant type of criticism through the mid-1970s, encompassing such different methodological approaches or strategies as literary or source criticism, history-of-religions criticism, tradition criticism, form criticism, redaction criticism, and composition criticism. As an umbrella model or paradigm, historical criticism may be summarized in terms of the medium or text as means, with an emphasis on the signified—the text as a means to the author who composed it or the world in which it was composed. From the point of view of culture and experience, the model calls for a radical contextualization of the text but for universality and objectivity on the part of the reader.

Second, there is literary criticism broadly conceived, an umbrella-type of criticism that first began to dislodge traditional historical criticism from its position of dominance in the 1970s, rapidly establishing itself as a solid alternative in the discipline through the 1980s and into the 1990s. It includes such different approaches as narrative criticism, structuralism, rhetorical criticism, psychological criticism, reader-response criticism, and deconstructionism. As a paradigm or umbrella model, literary criticism may be described in terms of the medium or text as medium, with an emphasis on the signifier—the text as a message from author to readers, with an emphasis on the principles governing the formal aspects of this communication. It is a development that reflects, rather belatedly, the modernist impulse. In terms of culture and experience, the emphasis on the contextuality of the text may or may not diminish, depending on the specific approach in question; however, even when such emphasis continues, its course of direction does undergo a fundamental change. On the one hand, such emphasis tends to disappear considerably when the text is approached as a self-standing and independent object, divorced from world/author and reader. On the other hand, such emphasis shifts direction when contextuality is pursued from a mostly aesthetic or formalist perspective, along the lines for example of generic studies or literary history. At the same time, universality and

---

7. By "paradigm" or "umbrella-model of interpretation" I mean a certain sharing of values and practices, of theory and criticism. I do not mean to imply uniformity or close agreement among the different practitioners, nor do I wish to create hard-and-fast distinctions. Indeed, differences and variations are not only the norm but also quite profound within each proposed paradigm; similarly, the different paradigms advanced also reveal a variety of features in common. Nevertheless, at a certain level of abstraction, a grouping of values and practices is helpful in critical analysis. On this point, see A. Easthope, *Literary into Cultural Studies* (New York: Routledge, 1991) 3–21.

objectivity clearly remain the order of the day with regard to the reader of the text.

Finally, there is cultural criticism broadly conceived, an umbrella-type of criticism that arose alongside literary criticism in the mid-1970s and played a major role as well in the dislodging of historical criticism from its entrenched position in the discipline, firmly establishing itself as a viable alternative through the 1980s and into the 1990s. It encompasses such different lines of inquiry as socioeconomic and ideological analysis along neo-Marxist lines; sociological approaches, mostly informed by the sociology of religion, as with millenarian theory and sectarian theory, but also involving such other approaches as cognitive dissonance, the sociology of knowledge, and the analysis of social dynamics and roles; and anthropological approaches, informed in large measure by cultural anthropology, as in the case of Mediterranean studies, cross-cultural analysis of purity codes, and comparative societal studies in terms of group and grid. As a paradigm, cultural criticism may be summarized in terms of the medium or text as both medium and means, but with a much greater emphasis on the signified than on the signifier—the text as a message from author to readers within a given context, with an emphasis on the codes or principles governing the sociocultural aspects of such communication; hence, the text as a means to that world in which it was produced. As such, it is a development that continues the traditionalist impulse, with its focus on the text as a period construction and remnant. From the point of view of culture and experience, the model calls for an even more radical contextualization of the text; it may also call, though not necessarily, for a contextualization of the reader, as in the case of neo-Marxist approaches and less so in the case of anthropological approaches.

Even a cursory look at the discipline in action, in any of its institutionalized channels—such as annual meetings, faculty composition, book reviewing, and the like—readily shows the presence of all three modes of discourse at work, both in terms of practice and theory.[8] However, while historical criticism may be said to be on the decline, both literary and cultural criticism are clearly on the ascendancy.[9]

---

8. On a similar use of paradigms, see, from the point of view of literary theory, T. Eagleton, *Literary Theory: An Introduction* (Minneapolis: University of Minnesota Press, 1983) 74; from the point of view of biblical criticism, E. Schüssler Fiorenza, " 'For the Sake of Our Salvation...' Biblical Interpretation and the Community of Faith," *Bread Not Stone: The Challenge of Feminist Biblical Interpretation* (Boston: Beacon, 1984) 23–42.

9. Indeed, the historical-critical model may even be described as defunct from a theoretical point of view but not from a practical point of view. From a theoretical perspective, the method is so defunct that it has been unable to mount a serious and informed defense of its own methodological principles or reading strategy and underlying theoretical orientation. From a practical perspective, the method is alive, though at

8 *Fernando F. Segovia*

A Process of Liberation and Decolonization

I regard the emergence of these models of interpretation as a gradual process of liberation and decolonization. On the one hand, the stranglehold of one particular and institutionalized model of interpretation, historical criticism, has been broken. For a long time all biblical critics were trained in this model, with all faculties eventually dominated by its adherents and representatives. Consequently, its grip on both the academy and the church was close to total.[10] On the other hand, this change has not led to the enthronement of any one model of interpretation but has given rise instead to enormous diversity—not only two other interpretive paradigms but also each with a wide repertoire of interpretive approaches much more diverse among themselves than the different methodologies of historical criticism ever were.[11] At first, with the advent of literary criticism and cultural criticism, such diversity was largely methodological and theoretical, with a focus on texts and models for the reading of such texts. More recently, with certain developments in literary criticism and cultural criticism, such diversity has become sociocultural as well, with a focus on readers and their models for reading. Such a process can be appropriately described in terms of liberation

---

various stages of health: while its grasp in the United States has slipped considerably, its dominance in Europe is still very much in evidence, though with dangerous cracks beginning to appear here and there as well. For example, the recent launching of a new journal, *Biblical Interpretation: A Journal of Contemporary Approaches*, by such a publisher as E. J. Brill is quite telling. Indeed, the first paragraph of its "Editorial Statement," as published in its first issue (1 [1993] i–ii), provides, subtly but surely, a thoroughly political rationale for its appearance: "The recent burgeoning of new and sometimes competing approaches to textual interpretation is only sporadically reflected, and reflected upon, in the leading journals of historical, biblical criticism. The need for an international vehicle for both modes of study, practical and theoretical, is acute." In effect, the rationale argues—with recourse even to the liberation language of center and margins—that control of the leading journals in the field by historical critics has prevented the publication of manuscripts reflecting the newer interpretive currents, making a new outlet for such voices imperative.

10. One must be careful to observe in this regard that, from a socioreligious or ecclesiastical point of view, there were many religious bodies for which historical criticism was never an option, let alone the dominant type of biblical criticism; for others, moreover, such as the Roman Catholic church, historical criticism did become, with time, an option and eventually the dominant method but only after a period of considerable struggle. The grip I am talking about has to do primarily with the so-called mainline churches, including Roman Catholicism by this time, and their institutions of higher learning.

11. It would not be at all difficult for a historical critic to shift, say, from a form-critical to a redaction-critical perspective or from redaction criticism to composition criticism; in the end, the overall mode of discourse would remain very, very similar. It would be much harder, however, for a literary critic to go from narrative analysis to psychological criticism or deconstruction or for a cultural critic to go from neo-Marxist criticism to anthropological or sociological criticism. In both instances, while the mode of discourse does possess a certain undeniable common character, the body of theory underlining each particular approach within the given mode of discourse is quite different, extensive, and demanding.

and decolonization: first, in the sense of self-determination regarding the choice of interpretive model; second, in the sense of calling into question the myth of objectivity and universality required of the critic.

Creative Interaction

Finally, from the particular position I occupy, working out of a postmodernist context, I do not regard these three competing modes of discourse as mutually exclusive. I believe that they can and should be used creatively. First, the historical impulse of traditional criticism—its sense of the distance of the text—should not be bypassed. In many ways these texts represent an "other" to us. Second, the formalist impulse of literary criticism—its regard for the principles of narrative—should also not be ignored. These texts do follow certain conventions that are foreign to us. Third, the hermeneutical impulse of cultural criticism—its regard for the context of both text and reader—should be greatly enhanced. To be sure, these texts constitute an "other" to us and follow principles and conventions of another time and culture; at the same time, such "otherness" is always apprehended through our own lenses as readers, socially and historically located as we are. As such, from a postmodernist perspective, reading and interpretation always involve construction on the part of the reader, and the reader proceeds to engage in such a construction knowing that it is in the end a construction. Thus, both the historical and the formalist impulses are followed and put to good use, but in so doing one is always aware that the reconstruction of history and the reconstruction of the text are constructions, also dependent on the social context of the readers.

With these three structural principles fully in mind, I can now proceed with the plotting of the shift in the discipline, following the three interpretive paradigms outlined above.

Historical Criticism: The Text as Means

Though the general sequence as well as the aims and tools of the various methodological movements within historical criticism are well known, its basic strategy for reading and underlying theoretical orientation are not, since the paradigm itself did not require much theoretical sophistication of its adherents, only practical expertise. In other words, the model had little critical self-consciousness, either of itself as a paradigm or of its relationship as model to other modes of interpretation. Though clearly a form of literary criticism, involving the criticism of ancient texts, historical criticism did not require an informed and thorough grounding in the wider world of literary theory, whether European or American. Thus, how this particular approach to texts stood within the history of literary theory or how it conformed to or differed from other contemporary approaches was never considered a subject of interest or discussion; as a result, the question of why it did what it did in the way that it did it was never addressed explicitly, much less in a critically comparative fashion.[12] An overview of the basic principles underlying the model and its strategy for reading a text is therefore in order and will serve in turn as a basis for comparison with the two paradigms that emanated from it.[13]

Basic Principles

1. The historical-critical model approached the biblical text primarily as a means, as historical evidence from and for the time of composition. As such, the text was to be read and analyzed within its own historical context and regarded as a direct means for reconstructing the historical situation that it presupposed, reflected, and addressed. Such a task was broadly conceived, involving extensive knowledge of the period and area under consideration, for example, historical framework, social institutions, cultural conventions, forms of religious expression, and literary production and forms. Within this overall historical conception of the text, its character as a religious document was especially emphasized, with a corresponding focus on its theological content and message.

For the model, therefore, the meaning of the text resided either in the world represented by it or in the intention of the author, or both.[14] Consequently, an analysis of the text as text never really formed part of its methodological repertoire until the very end, and then the entire

---

12. Such theoretical myopia had inevitable consequences. For example, its concentration on acquiring the basic methodological tools for interpretation allowed it to think of itself, quite unreflectively and uncritically, as *the* method, as the one view of criticism shared by all without any realization of its own theoretical and ideological foundations. Likewise, its failure to enter into critical exchange with other interpretive models, varied as they were during the course of the century, not only reinforced this provincial view of itself as *the* method but also prevented it from responding satisfactorily to the theoretical challenges that eventually emerged, adding thereby to the consternation and frustration of its practitioners. Its focus on the wherewithal of exegesis rendered any concern for its theoretical rationale unnecessary, and, as such, devoid of theoretical sophistication, it was left basically defenseless.

13. For an overview of its historical development, its main figures and concerns, see R. F. Collins, *Introduction to the New Testament* (Garden City, N.Y.: Doubleday, 1983) 41–69 (chap. 2: "Historical-Critical Methodology"); and Stuhlmacher, *Historical Criticism,* 22–60.

14. In terms of M. H. Abrams's still useful typology of critical theories, historical criticism would qualify as a combination of mimetic and expressive theory; see Abrams, *The Mirror and the Lamp: Romantic Theory and the Critical Tradition* (New York: Oxford University Press, 1953) 3–29; see also idem, "Types and Orientations of Critical Theories," *Doing Things with Texts: Essays in Criticism and Critical Theory* (New York: W. W. Norton, 1989) 3–30.

model began to collapse. In addition, an analysis of the world or the author behind the text, learned and detailed as it was, never availed itself consistently of any type of social or cultural theory, remaining throughout at a rather impressionistic level. Finally, only the intended readers of the text, usually conceived in terms of the rather loose concept of "community," were of any interest; the task of contemporary readers was to search and recover the original audience of the text, along with its original message and intention.

2. Since the model did not regard the biblical text as an artistic, rhetorical, and ideological production in its own right, there was little conception of the text as a literary, strategic, and ideological whole. In fact, as it presently stood, the text was often regarded as quite problematic and even unintelligible, full of *aporias*—textual unevennesses, difficulties, or contradictions—of a stylistic, logical, or theological sort. The presence of such *aporias* led to a view of the text as the result of a long process of accretion and redaction and an analysis of such a text in terms of an excavative reading involving the separation and reconstruction of its constitutive literary layers, often in conflict with one another. In fact, it was the juxtaposition of such layers that created the *aporias,* which served in turn as guideposts for the process of composition and analysis.[15] The reading involved was, therefore, a reading from the ground up rather than from beginning to end.[16]

3. The model had a strong positivistic foundation and orientation. The meaning of the text was regarded as univocal and objective, and thus it could be retrieved if the proper methodology, scientific in nature, was rigorously applied. Further, since the text presupposed, reflected, and addressed a historical situation, the path of history itself, likewise univocal and objective in nature, could be scientifically reconstructed as well. To be sure, disagreements in such retrievals and reconstructions were constant and profound, leading to criticism of works other than one's own as somehow defective in conception or application. Intrinsic

---

15. For a recent and sophisticated exposition of this procedure in the area of Gospel studies, see R. T. Fortna, *The Fourth Gospel and Its Predecessor: From Narrative Source to Present Gospel* (Minneapolis: Fortress Press, 1988) 1–11. Interestingly enough, this technical term of historical criticism becomes very important as well for deconstruction, with *aporia* as that point where the self-contradictory meanings of the text can no longer be resolved. While in historical criticism the *aporia* leads to earlier versions of the text, with varying degrees of reconstruction, in deconstruction the *aporia* leads to a view of the meaning of the text as undecidable.

16. For the evolutionary theory of literature underlying the model, see Petersen, *Literary Criticism,* 11–20. I believe this reading was informed from the ground up by an operative though implicit theological principle to the effect that what comes earlier is better. In other words, the separation and reconstruction of layers were undertaken not only as a critical exercise but also as a theological imperative, with an underlying view of the earlier layers or traditions as somehow closer to the source, whether that source be Jesus himself or earliest Christianity, and hence more historically secure or accurate.

to historical criticism was the methodological exposé or demolition of previous scholarship, usually carried out at the beginning of any work in a section generally known as the *status quaestionis,* the history of scholarship. Scholarship was thus seen as ultimately progressive and evolutionary in principle, though subject to serious deviations and aberrations, rather than in terms of different strategies of reading with their corresponding theoretical orientations.

4. Given its proposed scientific basis and approach, the model called for a very specific kind of reader—the reader as a universal and informed critic. The biblical critic assumed a position of neutrality and impartiality with regard to the text through a careful application of the proper methodological tools of the discipline; as a result, the critic brought nothing to the text in the process of interpretation. Thus, in order to recover the objective meaning of the text, the critic assumed an air of objectivity, involving a complete divestiture of all presuppositions, whether theological or sociocultural. It was the function of such a disinterested critic to approximate the meaning of the text, unpack it, and make it available to untrained readers. In the process, to be sure, the position of the critic emerged as highly authoritative and powerful, within a hierarchical system consisting of text–critic–readers.

5. The model was profoundly theological in orientation. Given its overriding concern, as noted above, for the religious content and message of the texts, it pursued a decidedly idealistic approach to them with a strong emphasis on biblical theology and on the theological positions, conflicts, and developments of the early Christian movement. Despite its claims to scientific distance, the model also possessed a strong underlying theological stance, with two distinct variations. On the one hand, interpretation could be regarded as radically divorced from theology, as an exercise in the history of religion yielding facts or data for the theologians to work with in their respective contexts. On the other hand, Christian doctrine and life could be seen as ultimately subject to the guidance and judgment of the Word of God, a "word," however, that could be appropriated only indirectly, via historical criticism itself, rather than directly, as in traditional dogmatic theology. While for both variations the task of theology was independent of the task of historical reconstruction, in the first variation reconstruction was regarded as an exercise in itself, while for the second variation reconstruction became a propaedeutic. Both positions were highly theological, to be sure, but not regarded and much less analyzed as such.

Since for historical criticism the text as means possessed a univocal and objective meaning and since this could be retrieved via a properly informed and conducted scientific inquiry, the meaning uncovered was for all times and cultures. Consequently, a proper hermeneutical appropriation and application of the text could ultimately be based on such a meaning and interpretation of it. In other words, the original meaning of the text, properly secured and established, could dictate and govern the overall boundaries or parameters of the Christian life everywhere and at all times.

6. The model presupposed and entailed a very specific and universal pedagogical model: all readers, regardless of theological persuasion or sociocultural moorings, could become such informed and universal critics if the right methodological tools were properly disseminated and acquired. This was a pedagogical model of learned impartation and passive reception, highly hierarchical and authoritative in character, with strong emphasis on academic pedigree (who studied under whom) and schools of thought (proper versus improper approximations to the text). Readers had to learn how to read texts correctly but did not have to read themselves, except of course for a mandatory surfacing of theological presuppositions so that these could be duly obviated. Not surprisingly, such an educational model closely paralleled the interpretive model, with students/readers dependent on teachers/critics for an account of the text and its meaning.

Concluding Comments

In terms of theory and methodology, the historical paradigm was remarkably inbred and thoroughly hegemonic. The theoretical discussion, such as it was, consisted mostly of an in-house affair conducted within certain well-established parameters: acquaintance with the various stages of historical criticism and a reading of previous exegesis on the area of research in question. Dialogue with other critical models and disciplines was largely nonexistent. As regards experience and culture, the model was mixed: while it took into account the social location of the work under analysis, it deliberately bracketed the social location of those who read and interpreted the work. Thus, while the culture and experience underlying the texts themselves were regarded as essential for sound scholarship and proper interpretation, as something to be avidly pursued, the culture and experience informing the readers of these texts were looked upon as intrusive and unscholarly, as something to be avoided at all cost, so as not to vitiate or contaminate the whole process of interpretation. The proper task of the critic was to engage in *exegesis,* not *eisegesis*—a reading of the text, not a reading into the text; allowing the text to speak on its own terms rather than inserting one's words into the text.[17]

---

17. See in this regard the introduction to a recent handbook on biblical exegesis for the American student: J. R. Hayes and C. R. Holladay, *Biblical Exegesis: A Beginner's Handbook* (Atlanta: John Knox, 1982) 5–29. Here the language of exegesis/eisegesis, proper scientific tools, and meaning of the text still predominate. The authors do specify

In the end, historical criticism collapsed from within when its methodological development was no longer able to address the emerging new questions, concerns, and challenges. On the one hand, with the change from redaction criticism to composition criticism in the 1970s, a turn to literary theory became inevitable.[18] Once a consideration of the role of the author shifted from an analysis of the changes introduced into the received tradition (the heart of redaction criticism) to an examination of the finished product in terms of its overall (theological) arrangement and development (the goal of composition criticism), the need for literary theory soon became obvious. It no longer proved sufficient to see the composition of the text as text in terms of overall sequence or its meaning in terms of the author as theologian. On the other hand, with the pronounced interest of both redaction and composition criticism on the community and context behind the text, a turn to social theory—of whatever sort, whether economic, sociological, or anthropological—became imperative as well. It was no longer sufficient to address the text as a social construct in an impressionistic fashion; the need for a theoretical framework became evident. The traditional tools of the discipline were simply no longer able to address such challenges satisfactorily; new tools were very much in order, and they began to be imported en masse into the discussion. Out of historical criticism, then, emerged literary criticism and cultural criticism, although, to be sure, for many historical criticism remained the operative model of interpretation.

---

that the meaning of the text is virtually inexhaustible and hence only partially available to any particular kind of exegesis; at the same time, the role of the reader as reader is almost completely bypassed. In the end, eisegesis is described in terms of either asking the wrong questions of the text or answering the right questions wrongly. See also the beginning remarks to an introduction to New Testament exegesis meant originally for the German student: H. Conzelmann and A. Lindemann, *Interpreting the New Testament: An Introduction to the Principles and Methods of N.T. Exegesis* (Peabody, Mass.: Hendrickson, 1988) 1–5. Once again, the language of exegesis/eisegesis, scientific study and criteria, and proper understanding of the text are very much in evidence. The authors do point out that the exegete must be aware of his own presuppositions, conceived in purely theological terms; however, such awareness is seen as necessary in order to avoid reading such presuppositions in and into the text. A focus on the reader as reader, therefore, remains at a very minimal level indeed.

18. Redaction criticism begins in the 1950s, solidifies in the 1960s, and begins to yield to composition criticism in the 1970s. For a brief account of redaction criticism, see Collins, *Introduction*, 196–230; N. Perrin, *What Is Redaction Criticism?* (Guides to Biblical Scholarship; Philadelphia: Fortress Press, 1969). For composition criticism, see idem, "The Evangelist as Author: Reflections on Method in the Study and Interpretation of the Synoptic Gospels and Acts," *Biblical Research* 17 (1972) 5–18.

Literary Criticism: The Text as Medium

When a prevailing interpretive paradigm begins to collapse in a discipline, there is usually a concomitant and vigorous turn to theory—a turn to first principles, as it were. Biblical criticism in this last quarter of the twentieth century was no exception in this regard. As the absence of and disregard for theory became emblematic of traditional historical criticism, reflecting its longstanding and institutionalized entrenchment, so did a pronounced and sophisticated theoretical discussion mark the rise of the "new" literary criticism (as opposed to the "old" literary criticism or source criticism), likewise reflecting its character as a movement from the margins of the discipline with a serious challenge to the established center. Moreover, such theoretical reflection turned directly outward for grounding and inspiration—away from the traditional in-house discussion and theological moorings of the discipline toward a variety of other fields in the humanities, such as literature and psychology; its dialogue partners thus became literary theory, psychoanalytic theory, structuralist theory, and rhetorical theory.[19]

In effect, a new mode of discourse was beginning to emerge: armed with its own tools of analysis and corresponding terminology; by no means monolithic but rather highly diverse and highly dependent on the particular theoretical grounding in question. As a result, any discussion between historical critics and literary critics became well-nigh impossible, despite the cautious stance of the latter at first, grounded as they were in traditional historicism. From a theoretical point of view, historical critics proved no match for literary critics. A new umbrella model of interpretation was gradually coming into being, demanding of its practitioners a very different type of reading and practice.

Basic Principles

1. The literary model envisioned the biblical text primarily as a medium, as a message or communication between a sender and a receiver, an author and a reader. As a result, the text as text began to receive an attention it had never garnered before, with the text now gradually emerging as a literary and rhetorical product in its own right. The main focus of inquiry was no longer on the world behind the text or on the

---

19. For examples of such early work and concern with theory, see D. O. Via, *The Parables: Their Literary and Existential Dimension* (Philadelphia: Fortress Press, 1967); and idem, *Kerygma and Comedy in the New Testament: A Structuralist Approach to Hermeneutic* (Philadelphia: Fortress Press, 1975); D. Patte, *What Is Structural Exegesis?* (Philadelphia: Fortress Press, 1976); Petersen, *Literary Criticism;* and M. A. Tolbert, *Perspectives on the Parables: An Approach to Multiple Interpretations* (Philadelphia: Fortress Press, 1979).

author who conceived it, but rather on the aesthetic or artistic character of the text, with a corresponding emphasis on its formal features. Such analysis encompassed, for example, questions of genre and generic theory; questions of structure and architecture, whether at the surface or a deep level; and questions of anatomy and texture, ranging from the study of ancient rhetoric to modern narratology. Consequently, for literary criticism the artistic features of the text drew far more attention than its religious or theological aspects. In turn, while the analysis of author and reader focused on the concepts of implied author and implied reader (on the author and reader as derived from the text as a whole) rather than real authors and real readers, the analysis of the world centered on such concepts as levels of narration, characterization, and above all point of view—on the world as depicted in and through the text.[20]

In retrospect, such a turn in biblical studies was quite logical and not at all surprising. It followed rather closely, in fact, a pattern already set in the wider realm of critical theory, though approximately forty years later. Just as the stranglehold of historicism in literary studies in the early part of the century eventually gave way to the roughly contemporary though largely independent movements of New Criticism in the United States and formalism in Europe, with their similar emphasis on the text as an independent aesthetic object, so was historical criticism in biblical studies replaced in part by the new literary criticism in all of its various forms: the text, submerged as it had been under the critical focus on the world and author, had now come fully to the surface.[21] This is not to say, however, that critical attention to the world and author behind the text were now altogether abandoned; rather, such analysis now perceived the text, as medium, as a primary and unavoidable filter in any such inquiry.

With the benefit provided by twenty years of hindsight, it is now possible to trace the overall course of literary criticism. In an interpretive spectrum ranging from a text-dominant pole to a reader-dominant pole, the path of analysis gradually wound its way from the former to the latter pole: from a focus on the text as text to a focus on the reader of the text; that is, from textual analysis in the form of narrative or rhetorical analysis to reader-response criticism.

2. With the new literary criticism, the highly atomistic approach of

---

20. Within Abrams's typology, literary criticism would represent an example of an objective critical theory, with an increasingly pronounced though always subordinate expressive emphasis as it began to shower more and more attention on the reader; see n. 14 above. For a concise contrast with literary criticism in biblical studies, see M. A. Powell, *What Is Narrative Criticism?* (Guides to Biblical Scholarship; Minneapolis: Fortress Press, 1990) 1–10.

21. On the character and context of formalism in literary theory, see Eagleton, *Literary Theory*, 17–53; V. B. Leitch, *American Literary Criticism from the Thirties to the Eighties* (New York: Columbia Univ. Press, 1988) 24–59.

historical criticism, with its sustained emphasis on textual ruptures, gave way to an analysis that viewed the text as a literary and rhetorical whole. Instead of regarding the text as suffused with all types of *aporias,* the text was increasingly seen as a unified and coherent whole, a harmony and unity often ascribed to authorial intention itself, with such expressions as "carefully prepared" or "consciously crafted" much in vogue. As a result, the vertical reading of historicism, that inevitable sifting and reconstruction of literary layers necessary for a proper reading of the text from the ground up, began to yield to a horizontal reading, a reading from beginning to end for which development and temporality became of the essence. The *aporias* of the past, over which there had never been much agreement, were now either altogether dismissed, disregarded from a methodological point of view, or ironically revisioned as examples of literary techniques. Even if excavative work was granted in principle, as it often was, the age of the *aporia* had basically come to an end.

3. The age of positivism or empiricism, however, had by no means come to an end. For literary criticism, above all in its text-dominant varieties but also in many of its reader-dominant expressions, the meaning of the text still tended to be regarded as univocal and objective and hence as retrievable on the basis of a rigorous application of proper and scientific methodology, now derived from literary or psychoanalytic theory. By and large, the literary and rhetorical features of the text, the concepts of implied author and implied reader, and the view of the world advanced by the text were regarded as present in the text and rather passively received or activated by the reader. With time such objectivism did begin to recede in the light of other theoretical developments. For example, as regards the text, the polysemic nature of all signs, including language, was increasingly acknowledged, giving rise to the concept of a plurality of interpretations based on the text itself; no one interpretation, it was now argued, could exhaust the meaning of the text. Similarly, a much more active role was gradually assigned to the reader in the production of meaning, insofar as the text began to be seen as replete with gaps or lacunae that were to be filled in by the reader. Again, the notion of a plurality of interpretations, now grounded in the reader, began to come to the fore, insofar as different readers would supplement such gaps in different ways. In the end, however, the principle of a plurality of interpretations was always fairly circumscribed, with a view of such interpretations as ultimately subject to the constraints imposed by the text.

On the whole, therefore, disagreements over the identification and interpretation of the literary or rhetorical features of a text were still common and sharp, with criticism of works other than one's own perceived as somehow deficient in grounding or application. At the same

time, the methodological exposé of the *status quaestionis* within historical criticism was replaced by a beginning section with a dual thrust: on
the one hand, the sense of demolition still prevailed, though now with
a twofold focus on the methodological shortcomings of historical criticism and the radical difference entailed by the new literary approach
to be adopted; on the other, a sense of pedagogy entered the scene, as
the theory that was to underpin the particular approach in question was
paraphrased at great length and without much critical acumen. As such,
scholarship was still basically regarded as progressive and evolutionary
in principle, with the light of literary criticism leaving behind the darkness of historical criticism. Only with time and to a rather limited extent
did the possibility of different readings begin to be granted within the
literary model, but the consequences of such a position were left largely
undeveloped.

4. It is fair to say that for the new literary criticism the reader remained faceless, even when the reading process became in and of itself a
focus of attention—the reader as a universal and informed critic. In its
text-dominant expressions, the biblical critic was called upon to master
a specific body of theory, so that it could be applied correctly, from a
technical point of view, to the biblical text and yield the desired results:
this was a reader whose voice remained largely in the background. In
its reader-dominant expressions, the biblical critic was also called upon
to become self-conscious about the various strategies available for reading (for example, a recourse to the implied reader; the assumption of a
naive, first-time reading; the assumption of a sophisticated reader, with
the advantage of multiple readings; any combination thereof) and proceed accordingly: this was a reader whose voice was duly foregrounded,
with constant use of such expressions as "now the reader does this"
and "then the reader does that." In either case the identity of the reader
in question remained of little interest: this was a technically proficient
reader devoid of all presuppositions, theological or sociocultural. Even
when most active, therefore, such a reader remained fundamentally
neutral and impartial. In the end, the basic function of such a reader
consisted in activating the meaning of the text, whether in a mostly passive way or more actively so, and making it available to uninformed
and untrained readers. The position of the critic thus remained highly
authoritative and powerful, maintaining that important mediating role
within the text–critic–reader hierarchy.

5. As literary criticism veered away from the traditional moorings of
historicism, its theological concerns and underlying theological stance
shifted accordingly. On the one hand, following a course of action not
unlike that adopted by those historical critics who saw their task as radically divorced from the larger theological enterprise, there was a move
to focus on the newly highlighted literary and rhetorical features of the

text to the detriment of that religious or theological dimension that had been so dear to historical criticism. Interpretation could be seen thereby as an exercise in literary formalism or even literary history, providing data for the theologians to apply in their respective situations. On the other hand, akin to those historical critics who did see in their work a necessary foundation for a proper hermeneutical appropriation and application of the Word of God, such a newfound interest in the formal features of the text could also be invested with a more explicit theological function. It could be argued that by bringing such features to the surface, literary criticism made possible not only a better appreciation of the craft and beauty of the Word of God but also a better feel for its power and hold upon readers. Again, both positions were theological to the core, but were neither regarded nor analyzed as such.

Since for literary criticism the meaning of the text resided by and large in the text as medium, it could be argued that a more enlightened approach to the text—an approach with due sensitivity to its literary features—would ultimately bring such meaning with greater clarity and force to the surface. In turn, such a meaning—a meaning for all readers and hence for all times and cultures—could still dictate and govern, in a far more effective way, the overall boundaries and parameters of the Christian life.

6. The pedagogical implications of literary criticism were, at least to begin with, not all that different from those of historical criticism: all readers, regardless of their respective sociocultural contexts or theological positions, could become informed and universal critics if the right theoretical and methodological apparatus was properly learned and propagated. In this regard the model was still, by and large, one of sophisticated impartation and passive acquisition. The model continued to be highly authoritative and hierarchical as well, with a strong emphasis now on theory (position within the interpretive spectrum) and theoretician (external authority to be read). Even when readers began to read themselves, they did so only in a highly formalistic way; the real readers remained strangely absent. As in historical criticism, therefore, the pedagogical model closely followed the interpretive model, with students/readers still ultimately dependent on teachers/critics for an account of the text and its meaning. To be sure, such a position gradually weakened: once the concept of a plurality of interpretations found its way into the discussion, no matter how constrained or circumscribed, the question of authority and hierarchy became a problematic.

Concluding Comments

From the point of view of theory and methodology, the literary paradigm represented a profoundly liberating step in biblical studies. Not only did it break with historicism, which had had a stranglehold on critical practice, exposing along the way the largely unspoken and seemingly natural assumptions of the historical model; but it also, in critical theory, opened the way for a new direction of research involving an enormous diversity of interpretive approaches and hence a myriad of new ways in which to read and interpret the biblical texts. What had been, despite the differences in methodologies, a rather tight common discourse was now replaced by a variety of different discourses—related, to be sure, but quite distinct nonetheless. In terms of experience and culture, the model was also a mixed model, though with less emphasis than the historical model on the context of the text. While attention continued to be bestowed on the social location of the text, such attention was now largely literary or formalist, with much less regard for the socio-cultural dimensions of the text. In addition, while attention did focus on the reader for a change and the notion of a plurality of interpretations gradually entered the discussion, such attention also remained largely formalist in tone, with little regard if any for the social location of the reader. For the model, therefore, the identity of the reader was of no importance whatsoever, totally unrelated to the analysis and interpretation of the biblical texts, even if the language of *exegesis* and *eisegesis* was no longer employed.

In more recent times, however, as the model has expanded into the reader-dominant pole of the interpretive spectrum, from an analysis of the features of the text to an analysis of the role of the reader in the production of meaning, and as the notion of a plurality of interpretations has been increasingly contemplated, whether based primarily on the text or on the reader, an encounter with the fundamental issue of flesh-and-blood readers has become inevitable. In other words, literary criticism must come to terms with the fact that lying behind the identification and interpretation of the formal features of a text in text-dominant approaches and lying behind the different reading strategies in reader-dominant approaches is always the real reader—the flesh-and-blood reader, historically and culturally conditioned, with a field of vision fundamentally informed and circumscribed by such a social location. It is such a reader, out of such social locations, that engages in the reading and interpretation of texts, arguing for certain literary and rhetorical reconstructions of the text and employing in the process a variety of interpretive model-constructs.

Cultural Criticism: The Text as Means and Medium

The explosion of theory that served to mark the breakdown of the historical-critical paradigm was actually twofold, though with not much interaction between these two different currents even to this day. Alongside literary criticism there emerged another line of inquiry variously characterized by its own practitioners as sociological, social-world, or social-scientific criticism—what I prefer to call cultural criticism.[22] As in the case of literary criticism, its vigorous and sophisticated turn to theory was indicative of both its marginal beginnings in the discipline and its profound challenge to the established center. Like literary criticism, moreover, such theoretical activity turned outward for grounding and inspiration—away from the in-house, largely theological discussion of the discipline, toward other fields in the humanities, like economics, sociology, and anthropology; its partners in conversation became as a result neo-Marxist theory, sociological theory with an emphasis on the sociology of religion, and anthropological theory with a focus on cultural anthropology.[23]

A new mode of discourse was again in the offing: while possessing once again its own analytical apparatus and accompanying vocabulary, the movement was not at all uniform but quite wide-ranging, since such vocabulary and apparatus were directly dependent as well on the specific theoretical basis employed. For the discipline the result was the same: dialogue between cultural critics and historical critics proved largely futile, again despite the cautious positions of the cultural critics at first, trained as they had been in historical criticism. From a theoretical point of view, historical critics were again at a deep disadvantage. At the same time, dialogue between literary critics and cultural critics proved to be largely nonexistent, with each movement going in its own direction. For the literary critics, the cultural critics remained mired in a different form of historicism, with little sense for the character of the text as text; for the cultural critics, the literary critics remained hopelessly immersed in an ahistorical exercise in aestheticism, with a disembodied

---

22. See, for example, H. C. Kee, *Christian Origins in Sociological Perspective* (Philadelphia: Westminster, 1980); R. Scroggs, "The Sociological Interpretation of the New Testament: The Present State of Research," *New Testament Studies* 26 (1980) 164–79; J. G. Gager, *Kingdom and Community: The Social World of Early Christianity* (Englewood Cliffs, N.J.: Prentice Hall, 1975); J. H. Neyrey, ed., *The Social World of Luke-Acts: Models for Interpretation* (Peabody, Mass.: Hendrickson, 1991); J. H. Elliott, ed., *Social Scientific Criticism of the New Testament and Its Social World* (*Semeia* 35; Decatur, Ga.: Scholars Press, 1986); and B. J. Malina and R. L. Rohrbaugh, *Social-Science Commentary on the Synoptic Gospels* (Minneapolis: Fortress Press, 1992).

23. For examples of such early work and involvement with theory, see, from a neo-Marxist perspective: J. P. Miranda, *Marx and the Bible: A Critique of the Philosophy of Oppression* (Maryknoll, N.Y.: Orbis Books, 1977), and idem, *Being and the Messiah: The Message of St. John* (Maryknoll, N.Y.: Orbis Books, 1977), as well as F. Belo, *A Materialist Reading of the Gospel of Mark* (Maryknoll, N.Y.: Orbis Books, 1981); from a sociological perspective, Gager, *Kingdom and Community* and G. Theissen, *The First Followers of Jesus: A Sociological Analysis of Early Palestinian Christianity* (Philadelphia: Fortress Press, 1978); from an anthropological perspective, B. J. Malina, *The New Testament World: Insights from Cultural Anthropology* (Atlanta: John Knox, 1981).

view of the text as text. Neither set of critics engaged in metatheory, despite the fact that their own supporting disciplines were fast becoming at this time increasingly interrelated and interdependent.[24] As a result, yet another umbrella model of interpretation was gradually coming into being, requiring of its adherents a very different type of orientation and application.

Basic Principles

1. With regard to the location of meaning, the cultural model was much closer in spirit to historical criticism than to literary criticism. Despite a view of the text as medium somewhat similar to that of literary criticism—a message or communication between a sender and a receiver, an author and a reader—the primary focus of cultural criticism lay not on the text as text, as medium or message, but on the text as means, as evidence from and for the time of composition. Such evidence, however, was now approached not so much in terms of its historical uniqueness or specificity, as in historical criticism, but rather in terms of its broader social and cultural dimensions. The emphasis was on the text as a product and reflection of its context or world, with specific social and cultural codes inscribed, and hence as a means for reconstructing the sociocultural situation presupposed, reflected, and addressed. Such analysis involved, for example, questions of social class and class conflict—applicable across time and cultures and hence addressed from a broad comparative perspective; questions of social institutions, roles, and behavior—again widely ranging across time and cultures and thus analyzed from a similarly broad comparative position; and questions of cultural matrix and values—deliberately culture-specific in orientation and hence examined from a more self-conscious crosscultural perspective. For cultural criticism, therefore, the economic, social, or cultural dimensions of the biblical text proved far more attractive than its theological or religious character. The meaning of the text was seen as residing primarily in the world behind it, with analysis of text, author, and readers undertaken in terms of their relationship to and participation in that world.[25]

---

24. See, for example, J. Culler, *On Deconstruction: Theory and Criticism after Structuralism* (Ithaca, N.Y.: Cornell Univ. Press, 1982); C. Geertz, "Blurred Genres: The Refiguration of Social Thought," *Local Knowledge: Further Essays in Interpretive Anthropology* (New York: Basic Books, 1983); J. Clifford, "Introduction: Partial Truths," *Writing Culture: The Poetics and Politics of Ethnography* (ed. J. Clifford and G. E. Marcus; Berkeley: Univ. of California Press, 1986) 1–26; and, more recently, R. Rosaldo, "The Erosion of Classical Norms," in *Culture and Truth: The Remaking of Social Analysis* (Boston: Beacon, 1989) 25–45.

25. From the point of view of Abrams's fourfold typology, cultural criticism should be seen as a mimetic type of theory, though with some expressive as well as objective elements here and there; see nn. 14 and 20 above.

In retrospect, this second turn in biblical studies was also quite understandable and to be expected. Indeed, a similar pattern can again be discerned in the wider field of literary theory with the breakdown of historicism: alongside the rise of formalism, one witnesses as well the emergence of cultural criticism, whether in the form of neo-Marxist criticism, with its emphasis on the socioeconomic context of the text and on the text as an ideological product, or along the lines of either the New York Intellectuals movement or myth criticism, with a view of the text as a broad cultural phenomenon.[26] Thus, the impressionistic approach of historical criticism to the world behind the text gave way to a much more rigorous and systematic analysis of that world. Forty years later, the same development could be observed in biblical studies.

With two decades of hindsight, it becomes possible here also to trace the overall course of cultural criticism: a gradual movement away from sociological models to anthropological models, with a persistent neo-Marxist emphasis on economics and ideology throughout; that is to say, a movement away from more universal to more culture-specific models, with a continuing concern throughout for the socioeconomic and ideological dimensions of the text.

2. From a practical point of view, the discussion between a reading founded in *aporias* and a holistic reading, a vertical reading and a horizontal reading, proved largely inconsequential for cultural criticism, with examples of both approaches in evidence within the model. The emphasis was neither on the need for a diachronic reading of the text, with a view of the text as consisting of different and conflicting literary layers, nor on the need for a synchronic reading, with a view of the text as a unified and coherent whole. What now mattered above all was the proper decoding of the economic, social, or cultural codes contained in the text, whether such codes were approached diachronically or synchronically. By and large, however, cultural criticism did tend to work with the text as a whole, as a sociocultural entity within a larger sociocultural context, but not so much as a matter of principle and thus without the same reverence for the formalist canons of anatomy, development, and temporality so dear to literary criticism. One way of describing the difference between the two models is to say that whereas literary criticism emphasized plotting and texture (the text as a literary and rhetorical whole), cultural criticism focused on story and codes (the text as an ideological whole). In any case, though excavative work was indeed pursued from time to time, the age of the *aporia* had once again, for all practical purposes, come to an end.

---

26. On the emergence and development of Marxist criticism, see T. Eagleton, *Marxism and Literary Criticism* (Berkeley: Univ. of California Press, 1976; Leitch, *American Literary Criticism*, 1–23; on the rise of cultural criticism, see Leitch, *American Literary Criticism*, 81–114, 115–47.

3. The same could not be said, however, for the age of positivism and empiricism. For cultural criticism as a whole, regardless of its specific variation, the meaning of the text was still seen as largely univocal and objective and, as such, retrievable. Indeed, cultural criticism saw in the borrowing of models from the social sciences a much more scientific and rigorous way of approaching and recovering the meaning of the biblical text in the fullness of its context, going far beyond the simplistic and unstructured impressionism of historical criticism. In fact, the principles of historical criticism were turned directly against it: without a proper and informed theoretical foundation, historical criticism had been engaging in *eisegesis*. The goal of cultural criticism was true *exegesis,* objectivity in approach and results. Thus, the codes of the world behind the text, no longer in use or even understood, were regarded as preserved in the text, as if in a repository or time capsule; such codes could, moreover, be properly decoded through the use of appropriate models.

To be sure, sharp debate ensued as to which models constituted the right ones: models that found their point of departure in a world very different from that of the ancient Mediterranean Basin and did not reflect self-consciously on the gulf created by such profound differences, as in the case of neo-Marxist analysis or the sociology of religion; or models that attempted to take seriously into account the crosstemporal and crosscultural character of any such enterprise, as with cultural anthropology. The result, once again, was sharp disagreement regarding the reconstruction of the world that lay behind and informed the text, with opposing critics charging that one another's works were flawed in grounding. In terms of composition, the *status quaestionis* of historical criticism was replaced by the same twofold thrust of demolition and pedagogy observed in literary criticism: a beginning exposé of the profound methodological inadequacies of historical criticism alongside praise for the benefits of the new approach, followed by an extensive and largely uncritical exposition of the particular model to be adopted. Consequently, scholarship was still looked upon as progressive and evolutionary in principle, even more so than in literary criticism insofar as the possibility of a plurality of interpretations was little entertained; with the light of cultural criticism, the shadows of historical criticism would be left behind.

4. With regard to the readers behind the models, a number of distinctions are in order within cultural criticism. First, within the socioeconomic approach represented by neo-Marxist criticism, the reader did by no means remain faceless. Just as the text was considered an ideological product and hence a site of struggle in the class conflict, so was the critic: the task of criticism was similarly regarded as ideological to the core, a site of struggle. Thus, in effect, only a sophisticated *and* committed critic would be able to perceive and evaluate the socioeconomic,

ideological dimension of the text and hence its position within the class struggle—the reader as an informed and interested critic. In a sense objectivism was now born out of both theoretical sophistication and political commitment: only the properly trained and *engagé* critic could arrive at the deep meaning of the text. At the same time, consideration of all other sociocultural dimensions of the text was regarded as distracting and ultimately apolitical.

Second, within the sociological approach informed by the sociology of religion, the reader did remain faceless—the reader as a universal and informed critic. The new models from the social sciences allowed the biblical critic to assume an even greater position of neutrality and impartiality vis-à-vis the text. No critical analysis of the reader was called for and none was undertaken. Finally, within the anthropological approach rooted in cultural anthropology, the reader was called upon to become self-conscious with regard to his or her own sociocultural world, so that the world of the text could be more sharply differentiated and its reconstruction more clearly articulated. A combination of such self-awareness and the models in question was regarded as affording a more secure position of neutrality and impartiality with regard to the text—the reader as informed and culture-specific, but able to transcend the acknowledged limitations of culture. In other words, when properly accounted for, the sociocultural location of the biblical critic could be not only methodologically obviated but also put to good use in the search for the meaning of the text, insofar as the gulf between text and reader would be properly acknowledged as a point of departure.

In all three variations it remained the function of the reader—interested or disinterested, *engagé* or distant—to search for the meaning inherent in the text, bring it to the surface, and make it available to untrained and unsophisticated readers. As such, the position of the critic remained highly authoritative and powerful, with the hierarchy of text–critic–reader still very much in place.

5. As in the case of literary criticism, the shift of cultural criticism away from the theoretical moorings of historicism brought about a clear change in theological concerns and underlying stance. At this point, an important distinction is in order between the socioeconomic approach, on the one hand, and sociological and anthropological approaches, on the other.

From the perspective of neo-Marxist criticism, the view of the text as an ideological product, of the world behind the text as a site of struggle, and of the critic as committed and hence as a further factor in the struggle ultimately led to the belief that proper criticism is criticism on the side of the oppressed and with liberation in mind. Thus, to engage in the recovery of the deep, socioeconomic meaning of the text was to take sides in the struggle for liberation and against oppression; that choice became, in turn, the fundamental theological motivation of the critic, carried out in practice either by rejecting that which is oppressive in the biblical text or adopting that which is liberating. In this case the theological commitment of the critic was neither denied nor bypassed but roundly affirmed, with theology itself conceived not just as worldview but as engagement.

From the point of view of sociological and anthropological criticism, a twofold theological direction may be observed, following the basic pattern outlined in historical criticism and then traced also by literary criticism. On the one hand, criticism was regarded as radically divorced from any type of theologizing, with emphasis placed on the newly highlighted sociocultural dimensions of the text to the detriment of its religious or theological aspects so central to historical criticism. Interpretation could thus be seen as an even more sophisticated exercise in the history of religion, yielding far more rigorous data for the theologians to work with in their respective applications of the text. On the other hand, interpretation could also be seen as laying an even more solid foundation for a proper hermeneutical appropriation and application of the Word of God—the focus on the sociocultural dimensions of the text yielding a much more realistic reading of the Word of God and hence a greater grasp of its flesh and power. Yet again, although both positions were deeply theological, neither was properly regarded or analyzed as such.

Since for cultural criticism the meaning of the text resides in the text as a product of its context, it could readily be argued that a more enlightened approach to the text would bring out such a meaning more securely and forcefully. Such a meaning then—a meaning for all times and cultures—could still be used to dictate and govern, again in a far more effective way, the overall boundaries or parameters of Christian life in the world.

6. The pedagogical implications of cultural criticism were very similar to those of historical criticism: all readers, regardless of their respective theological beliefs or sociocultural contexts, could become informed as well as universal or committed readers if the right methodological tools and theoretical apparatus were properly acquired and taught. Learned impartation and passive reception thus remained the order of the day. Insofar as the untrained reader had to be trained in order to read the biblical text correctly, the model also remained highly authoritative and hierarchical, with a twofold emphasis on which model (what discipline to use) and which authority (whom to read) to follow. Although readers were now reading themselves, such readings either remained quite circumscribed, limited to the question of socioeconomic class, or, even when more broadly pursued, were regarded as somehow separable and distinct from the task of interpretation. As in the other

two paradigms, the educational model followed thereby the interpretive model, with students/readers looking to teachers/critics for an account of the text and its meaning.

Concluding Comments

As regards theory and methodology, the cultural paradigm constituted, as in the case of literary criticism, another profound liberating step in biblical studies. In terms of critical practice, the model pointed out certain salient weaknesses of the historical paradigm: not only the lack of a well-informed and articulated theory regarding the study of texts from a very different time and culture, but also the largely idealistic character of the enterprise with its heavy emphasis on theological positions, developments, and conflicts. In terms of critical theory, the model also brought into the discipline a refreshingly wide variety of interpretive approaches, giving rise once again to many new ways of reading and interpreting the biblical texts. In so doing, the stranglehold of historical criticism was further loosened: what had been a fairly compact common discourse yielded once again to a number of different discourses—ultimately related, of course, but also quite distinct in their own right.

With regard to culture and experience, the cultural paradigm was a mixed model as well, though with more emphasis than the historical model on the context of both text and reader. On the one hand, the social location of the text was more radically emphasized, with a systematic and sustained emphasis on its economic, social, and cultural aspects and ramifications. On the other hand, the social location of the reader received varying degrees of attention: from no analysis whatsoever, as in the case of studies employing sociological models; to analysis in terms of socioeconomic and ideological aspects, as with neo-Marxist models of interpretation; to analysis from a broad cultural perspective, as in the case of studies informed by anthropological theory. However, even when the reader was taken into consideration, such analysis still remained quite limited. In the case of neo-Marxist models, for example, since a clear relationship was acknowledged between the ideological commitment of readers and their interpretation of the text, analysis concentrated on the socioeconomic dimensions of the readers to the exclusion of all other sociocultural aspects. Similarly, in the case of anthropological models, the broader sociocultural dimensions of the readers were addressed, but the relationship between context and interpretation was largely bypassed if not altogether denied. In both cases, the goal remained the proper retrieval of the meaning of the text, not the vision that social location bestows on the results of such retrievals as well as on the very process of retrieval itself.

More recently, given the persistent focus of neo-Marxist interpretations on readers and readings as ideological products and sites of struggle and the turn toward readers and readings as sociocultural products on the part of anthropological approaches, an encounter with the full complexity of the issue of flesh-and-blood readers has become inevitable as well. Again, cultural criticism must come to terms with the fact that lying behind the identification and interpretation of the sociocultural codes present in the text, the reconstructions of the world behind the text, and the interpretive models employed in such reconstructions is always the real reader—the flesh-and-blood reader, historically and culturally conditioned, with a field of vision fundamentally informed and circumscribed by such a social location. It is such a reader, immersed in such social locations, that engages in the reading and interpretation of texts, arguing for certain economic, social, and cultural reconstructions of the world of the text and employing in the process a variety of interpretive model-constructs.

Cultural Studies: The Text as Construction

The distinct turn toward the real reader observed within both literary and cultural criticism represents, in my opinion, the beginning of another major development within the profound shift affecting biblical criticism since the 1970s. Indeed, such a development, I would venture to say, represents the beginning of a fourth paradigm or umbrella model of interpretation, with its own mode of discourse in which historical, formalist, and hermeneutical questions and concerns become closely interrelated and interdependent.

It is a development that calls into question the construct of a neutral and disinterested reader presupposed by historical criticism and followed in large part by both literary and cultural criticism—the universal and informed reader whose different variations can be readily outlined: the reader of historical criticism, steeped in theological presuppositions but able to put them aside in the task of interpretation through proper self-awareness; the reader of literary criticism, forthcoming with regard to reading strategy in the process of interpretation but only at a formalist level; the reader of cultural criticism, whether forthcoming with regard to socioeconomic class and ideological stance, or quite unaware of the processes of socialization and acculturation informing readers and readings, or properly aware of such processes but able to transcend them in the task of interpretation through the use of appropriate comparative and crosscultural models. This new development posits instead a very different construct, the flesh-and-blood reader: always positioned and interested; socially and historically conditioned and unable to transcend such conditions—to attain a sort of asocial and ahistorical nirvana—not only with respect to socioeconomic class but also with regard to the many other factors that make up human identity. As such, it is a development that carries the ongoing process of liberation and decolonization in the discipline a step further: from enormous diversity in the realm of theory and methodology to enormous diversity in the sociocultural realm. It is a development that I would describe in terms of "cultural studies"—a joint critical study of texts and readers, perspectives and ideologies—thereby distinguishing it from cultural criticism and at the same time showing its affinity with similar developments in other disciplines and critical practices.

To be sure, the enduring construct of a universal and informed reader, the reader who would attain to impartiality and objectivity through the adoption of scientific methods and the denial of particularity and contextuality, was a praiseworthy goal but also quite naive and dangerous. It was praiseworthy because it did realize, however faintly, the effects of social location on all reading and interpretation. It was naive because it thought that it could really avoid or neutralize such effects by means of an acquired and hard-earned scientific persona. It was dangerous because in the end what were in effect highly personal and social constructions regarding texts and history were advanced as scholarly retrievals and reconstructions, scientifically secured and hence not only methodologically unassailable but also ideologically neutral. Indeed, given the origins and development of such constructions on both sides of the North Atlantic, the construct remained inherently colonialist and imperialistic. It emerged out of a Eurocentric setting, and, as such, it was and remained thoroughly Eurocentric at every level of discourse and inquiry.[27] As a result, the construct unreflectively universalized its bracketed identity, expecting on the surface all readers everywhere to become ideal critics, informed and universal, while in actuality requiring all readers to interpret like Eurocentric critics. In fact, the entire discussion, from beginning to end and top to bottom, was characterized and governed by the fundamental concerns, questions, and horizons of this particular group, uncritically disguised as the fundamental questions, horizons, and concerns of the entire Christian world. To become

---

27. This is not to say that there were not profound differences and rivalries among the different Eurocentric traditions. In fact, the discipline was often quite provincial in character, as even a cursory survey of notes and bibliography readily shows: the Germans, the English, and the French dominated the discussion by far and in that order, with each group basically reading and interacting with members of the same group. North American scholars (leaving Mexico out), reflecting that peculiar combination of former colonials/empire builders, were far more eclectic in their reading and dialogue partners but always rather servile in their attitude toward and estimation of their European colleagues.

the ideal critic, therefore, was to enter into a specific and contextualized discussion, a Eurocentric discussion.[28]

In retrospect, one may say that the use of such a construct, under the guise of neutrality and impartiality, dehumanized the reader, asking for divestiture of all those identity factors that constitute and characterize the reader as reader—for example, gender, ethnic or racial background, socioeconomic class, sociocultural conventions, educational attainment, and ideological stance. On another level, such divestiture was not a dehumanization at all but a rehumanization, insofar as objectivity and impartiality were cover terms for Europeanization, given the thoroughly Eurocentric contours and orientation of the discipline. Thus, while the experience and culture of readers and critics were seemingly sacrificed in the pursuit of truth, in effect it was the experience and culture of some critics and readers that were sacrificed to the experience and culture of other critics and readers. The result was a classic case of neocolonialism, where the interests of the colonized or the margins were sacrificed, subtly but surely, to the interests of the colonizers or the center.

This situation of neocolonialism began to come apart with the emergence and solidification of the literary and cultural paradigms in the mid-1970s. Liberation came largely by way of diversity in methodological principles and theoretical orientation. Although in and of itself an important step in the process of liberation and decolonization, the construct of a universal and informed reader still remained largely in place, however. Such neocolonialism now threatens to come apart altogether with the recent developments described above within both cultural and literary criticism. Slowly but surely the foundations behind such a construct have been eroded. Ongoing developments in a wide number of disciplines as well as in theological studies itself, involving a focus on theory as perspective with its own sociocultural and ideological foundations, made any claims for a disinterested objectivity in reading and interpretation increasingly untenable and subject to critical exposé. In large part such developments were the result of outsiders coming into the different disciplines for the first time. In the theological world, for example, the validity and ideology of such claims came under increasing attack from a wide variety of quarters, as more and more silent/silenced voices entered the discipline, both in the North Atlantic world and the Third World, laying claim to their own voices and vision in theology

---

28. On this point, with a specific focus on African American students and critics in graduate programs and academic institutions governed by Eurocentric interests, see the interesting essay by W. H. Myers, "The Hermeneutical Dilemma of the African American Biblical Student," *Stony the Road We Trod: African American Biblical Interpretation* (ed. C. H. Felder; Minneapolis: Fortress Press, 1991) 40–56. See also the beginning remarks by R. S. Sugirtharajah in a volume he edited, *Voices from the Margin: Interpreting the Bible in the Third World* (Maryknoll, N.Y.: Orbis Books, 1991) 1–6 and 434–44.

and interpretation. Most prominent among such voices were the liberation theologians from the colonial world, feminist theologians in the First World, and minority theologians residing in the First World.[29]

Thus, with readers now fully foregrounding themselves as flesh-and-blood readers, variously situated and engaged in their own respective social locations, the process of liberation and decolonization moves into the sociocultural domain itself. Different readers see themselves not only as using different interpretive models and reading strategies but also as reading in different ways in the light of the multilevel social groupings that they represent and to which they belong. Such a way of reading ultimately looks upon all interpretive models, retrievals of meaning from texts, and reconstructions of history as constructs—formulated and advanced by positioned readers, flesh-and-blood persons reading and interpreting from different and highly complex social locations.[30] It is a reading highly influenced by postmodernist theory, with its ironic realization that all is construction and that one has no choice but to engage in such construction.[31] Such a reading calls for a "speaking in other tongues," in one's own tongue, because otherwise such a "speaking" would be usurped and carried out—as it often has been—by other tongues. Such a reading also calls for critical dialogue among the many tongues, in the course of which the foundations, contours, and ramifications of all such constructs would be addressed and weighed. Such a reading takes competing modes of discourse for granted, renounces the idea of any master narrative as in itself a construct, and looks for a truly global interaction. Such a reading, I would add, is both the inevitable result and mode of a postcolonial Christian world and a postcolonial biblical criticism.

---

29. In fact, it would be very interesting indeed to trace the relationship of these three movements to the paradigms described above, to analyze the different reading strategies and theoretical orientations adopted along the way, but that task lies beyond the scope of the present study.

30. For different applications of such an approach, see the following recent works: with regard to Greece and classical antiquity, R. and F. Etienne, *The Search for Ancient Greece* (Discoveries; New York: Harry N. Abrams, 1992); with regard to the Middle Ages, N. F. Cantor, *Inventing the Middle Ages: The Lives, Works, and Ideas of the Great Medievalists of the Twentieth Century* (New York: Morrow, 1991); with regard to tradition, E. Hobsbawm and T. Ranger, eds., *The Invention of Tradition* (Cambridge: Cambridge Univ. Press, 1983).

31. For a fine overview of postmodernism, see C. Jencks, *What Is Post-Modernism?* (3d. ed.; New York: St. Martin's, 1989); for this and other definitions of postmodernism, see L. Hutcheon, *The Poetics of Postmodernism: History, Theory, Fiction* (New York: Routledge, 1988), and idem, *The Politics of Postmodernism* (New Accents; New York: Routledge, 1989); for the ramifications of postmodernist thought, see V. B. Leitch, *Cultural Criticism, Literary Theory, Poststructuralism* (New York: Columbia Univ. Press, 1992).

Reading from This Place

It was with such developments and intentions in mind that the project "Reading from This Place: Social Location and Biblical Interpretation" was conceived and undertaken. The project represents an attempt, in the light of the emerging sociocultural pluralism and globalization in the theological world in general and biblical interpretation in particular, to address in a systematic and sustained fashion such fundamental issues as the role of the reader in biblical criticism, the complex relationship between the task of interpretation and the social location of the interpreter, and the consequences of such discussions for the future of biblical pedagogy and theological education.

The essays that follow represent the contributions to the first stage of the project, dealing with diversity in the American scene as such. They represent that "speaking in other tongues" within the United States itself that, I argued above, characterizes the most recent development in biblical criticism and reflects the postmodernist turn at large: a world in which readers become as important as texts and in which models and reconstructions are regarded as constructions; a world in which there is no master narrative but many narratives in competition and no Jerusalem but many Jerusalems; a world in which the fundamental problem lies not in the translation and dissemination of a centralized and hegemonic message into other tongues but rather in having the different tongues engage in critical dialogue with one another. Such a world, I would submit, is the direct and inevitable result of any process of liberation and decolonization, as the center is decentered and its controlling discourse displaced: a world where conversation becomes both exciting and fragile, imperative and hard to achieve, understanding and critical—in short, a world of "speaking in other tongues."

Part One

Social Location and Hermeneutics

1

Acknowledging the Contextual Character of Male, European-American Critical Exegeses: An Androcritical Perspective

_____ Daniel Patte ____

We male, European-American, critical exegetes,[1] readily acknowledge that we contextualize our critical exegeses, although we prefer to speak of pedagogy or hermeneutics. We contextualize our teaching by making "relevant" for our students the results of our critical exegeses. For this, we reexpress scholarly works in terms and categories understandable to our students and emphasize what we believe is of "interest and concern" to them. Such practices demonstrate that, in our view, our critical exegeses are _not_ in and of themselves contextual—since they need to be contextualized.

In this essay, I want to argue the opposite: in and of themselves our male, European-American critical exegeses _are and have always been_ contextual; they are thus "interested,"[2] even though we contend that

---

1. This essay prolongs the many months of intensive reflections on ethical responsibilities and practices in biblical criticism that Gary Phillips and I shared as we formulated, led, and interpreted the results of a project on this issue sponsored by the Lilly Endowment (including a conference held at Vanderbilt University in March 1991). Since this essay is grounded in these joint reflections (so "joint" that it soon became impossible to distinguish the insights contributed by each of us), it owes much to Gary Phillips. Of course, each of us has a distinct perspective, related to the more specific contexts out of which we speak and write. Thus, I go beyond these joint reflections in that I try to conceptualize their implications for the issue of contextualization from my own perspective. However, Gary Phillips also contributed to this essay by his critical comments on a first draft of it. Similarly, this essay owes much to the participants of the above-mentioned conference and in particular regarding the issues discussed below, to Elisabeth Schüssler Fiorenza, Ada María Isasi-Díaz, and Sheila Briggs.

2. "Interested" is one of the few technical terms I shall use in this essay, in which I avoid theoretical discussions; I use the term because this is a matter concerning a paradigm shift (from traditional, male, European-American positions to what I call an "androcritical" position). What brings about such a shift is the confrontation with concrete problems that one faces in one's contextual practices (rather theoretical arguments). Yet I need to clarify at the outset the theoretical background of some of the concepts I use. Thus, "interested," "interest," "concern," and "group" are to be understood against

our use of rigorous critical methods ensures that they would be disinterested—a self-evident point for feminist, African-American, and other liberation biblical scholars who call them androcentric and Eurocentric. Furthermore, I want to emphasize, on the basis of reflections on our pedagogical practices and their (often unintended) effects, that it is urgent and essential that we acknowledge and affirm that our critical exegeses are contextual and interested, that is, that they have been developed with the interests and concerns of European-American males at heart. Recognition and acknowledgment of this epistemological reality is urgent and essential because without it we forsake our very vocation as critical exegetes and teachers. Most of us are committed either to promote the freedom from alienation and oppression[3] that the Bible promises or alternatively to denounce its alienating and oppressive character; but our research and pedagogical practices have the material effect of alienating and oppressing others and of teaching our students to become oppressors themselves.

This acknowledgment of the contextual character of our critical exegeses that I advocate is itself contextual. To begin with, although the understanding of contextualization that I propose is in tension with the traditional, male, European-American one, it remains that of a male, European-American critical exegete. Whether I like it or not, it is out of this context that I think, speak, write, and teach. The four qualifications—male, European-American,[4] critical, exegete—characterize those persons who dominate(d) the field of critical biblical studies, including by means of the institutions we control (for example, academic institutions, the guild). Our group exerts its power, protects its "interests," and addresses its "concerns" by means of a "morality of

---

the background of a semiotic theory of interpretation and reading—more specifically a theoretical model concerning "enunciative contract" and "social semiotics." In brief, the "interests" and "concerns" of an interpreter are never his or her own alone, but actually that of a "group." This "group" is a social entity, which might eventually be institutionalized. But it is first of all defined as a "discourse space"; persons participate in this group by virtue of sharing a common kind of discourse; they abide by a certain discourse-interpretation contract characterized by a "morality of knowledge" and "codes" through which they protect or address the interests and concerns of the group. This is a formulation in terms of Greimas's semiotics (see A. J. Greimas and J. Courtés, *Semiotics and Language: An Analytical Dictionary* [Bloomington: Indiana Univ. Press, 1982]) of the analysis of "social semiosis" by J. Habermas (*Knowledge and Human Interests* [Boston: Beacon, 1971]) already largely expressed by M. Bal (*Femmes imaginaires: L'Ancien Testament au risque d'une narratologie critique* [Paris: Nizet, 1986]). For a convenient summary, see M. Bal's discussion of "codes" in *Murder and Difference: Gender, Genre, and Scholarship on Sisera's Death* (Bloomington: Indiana Univ. Press, 1988) 3–11.

3. I refer to all kinds of alienation and oppression, be they personal, social, religious, or cultural.

4. "European-American" designates persons of North Atlantic origins and cultures, including, therefore, Europeans.

knowledge"[5] ("criticism") that authorizes certain biblical interpretations and prohibits others. Yet this morality of knowledge is not stable and is always in a process of transformation—so the diversity of methodologies—because our group is heterogeneous and because its interests and concerns evolve. Consequently, there is a plurality of male, European-American critical exegetical perspectives (as there is, for example, a plurality of feminist perspectives). Yet each of these perspectives remains male and European-American; somehow, it reflects our group's interests and concerns. Thus, my conception of contextualization remains thoroughly male and European-American, even though it is different from the traditional one. This difference is due to the more specific context from which I write.

My own context is delimited by the more specific groups (discourse spaces)[6] with which I associate, each of these groups being defined by its relations to other groups (and thus, for example, in terms of class and relative political power) and/or by its ideological stance. My conception of contextualization is particularly marked by my identification with one specific group:[7] an emerging and diversified group of male European-American biblical scholars that I call *androcritical.* Though dispersed throughout the world and thus very different from each other, androcritical biblical scholars share a common twofold experience: that of having been fundamentally challenged in our interpretive and pedagogical practices by feminist, womanist, *mujerista,* African-American, Hispanic-American, Native-American, and/or Third World liberation theologians and biblical scholars, among others; and that of striving to respond constructively to this challenge by radically transforming our practices as critical exegetes and teachers. Since this kind of twofold experience is relatively new, the androcritical group is best described as "emerging." Yet it does exist. I stumbled into it, surprised to discover that what I thought was a personal struggle is shared by so many other European-American men.[8] In so doing, I changed con-

---

5. See V. Harvey, *The Historian and the Believer: A Confrontation between the Modern Historian's Principles of Judgment and the Christian's Will-to-Believe* (New York: Macmillan, 1966). The laws of this morality of knowledge (an exclusively historical one, when Harvey wrote his book) are comparable to the "codes" described by Bal in *Murder and Difference,* 5–11. Thus, I interpret Harvey's concept of "morality of knowledge" in terms of Bal's concept of "codes" and the above-mentioned theoretical background.

6. See above, n. 2.

7. To a lesser degree, it is also marked by my identification with other male, European-American groups that I will discuss below.

8. The group of androcritical biblical scholars is, of course, related to the growing "men's movement" and more specifically to its trends that conceive it as parallel to (not antagonistic with) feminism, trends that include S. Keen, *Fire in the Belly: On Being a Man* (New York: Bantam Books, 1991). Yet an important difference is that, in my understanding, androcritical biblical scholars do not mimic the feminist liberation

text, and my old conceptions of contextualization were transformed. Instead of viewing contextualization as a secondary issue, we androcritical exegetes view it as a central issue in biblical interpretation and teaching, in the same way that feminists and other liberation theologians and biblical scholars do.[9] But because of our particular perspective as male, European-American critical exegetes, our emerging androcritical conception of contextualization remains different from theirs.

In what follows, I attempt to conceive of "contextualization in biblical studies" from an androcritical perspective—my version of androcritical perspective that owes its specificity to other aspects of my personal context, and especially to the fact that I am a Protestant (active in and committed to the church) and a semiotician (member of another guild). I first describe what are for me the most relevant characteristics of an androcritical perspective, which takes shape primarily in the practical effort of developing pedagogical practices in biblical studies informed by such a perspective. I will argue that an androcritical reflection upon contextualization ultimately demands that we male, European-American exegetes reconceive our task as critical exegetes and teachers, especially its relationship to "ordinary readings."

An Androcritical Understanding of Contextualization

An androcritical perspective distinguishes itself from other male, European-American perspectives foremost by the acknowledgment that all biblical interpretations, including any critical exegeses, are contextual. This means admitting that all critical exegeses offered by us male, European-American scholars have been and are "interested." Despite our denials and claims to the contrary, these critical exegeses have been or are performed to meet needs, concerns, and interests of male European Americans—in the same way that feminist, African-American, and other advocacy biblical interpretations seek to meet needs, concerns, and interests of women, African Americans, and other groups. The term "androcritical" expresses, among other things, that we are male European Americans (hence "andro") who quite consciously and conscientiously "criticize" the lack of acknowledgment and denial by other male, European-American biblical scholars that we perform critical exegeses that are "interested" and thus contextual.

---

approach, as Keen does, by claiming ourselves as victims of oppression. Rather we acknowledge that our current practices are oppressive and thus must be "criticized" in this light.

9. Who see their task as "contextual," as is made explicit in the names of various liberation theology groups in South Africa: Institute for Contextual Theology (Johannesburg; out of which came the *Kairos Document*); Institute for Context Theology (Braamfontein); Center for Contextual Hermeneutics (Stellenbosch).

Yet, for me, criticizing this denial does not mean rejecting the exegeses that embody it or putting into question their "critical" character.[10] On the contrary, for me, being an androcritical biblical scholar involves both (1) making explicit the contextual character of these exegeses, and (2) *affirming the legitimacy and validity of these interpretations*— something that becomes possible when they have been stripped of those features that result from the denial of their contextual character. From this androcritical perspective, the affirmation of the legitimacy and validity of male, European-American critical exegeses as contextual interpretations becomes a necessary condition for truly acknowledging the legitimacy and validity of other contextual interpretations.

These statements need to be clarified through a detailed description of the contexts that give rise to the androcritical group and of the way in which these contexts contribute to a shaping of our understanding of contextualization. To be brief, however, I simply list what are, in my view, the main characteristics of an androcritical perspective.[11] These include:

- an acknowledgment of the pluralistic character of the situation in which we male European Americans practice critical biblical scholarship (teaching and research);

- a commitment to pursue this endeavor in a way that would be accountable to the plurality of groups that are directly or indirectly affected by our work;[12]

- the conviction that this professional accountability is in the interest of our group (male European Americans) because it is a metaphor for the kind of relationship that our group needs to have in society with other groups, for its own sake as well as for the sake of others;[13]

- the conclusion that such an accountability can be conceived and achieved only by "speaking with" those whom our traditional practices of biblical scholarship have marginalized, excluded, or

10. An androcritical exegetical practice remains "critical." The affirmation of the legitimacy and validity of "critical" studies is part of the andro*critical* perspective.

11. As will become clear from the footnotes, I became aware of these characteristics in dialogue with male, European-American biblical scholars in Europe, South Africa, and North America.

12. Accepting the challenge of E. Schüssler Fiorenza in her Society of Biblical Literature presidential address, "The Ethics of Interpretation: De-Centering Biblical Scholarship," *Journal of Biblical Literature* 107 (1988) 3–17.

13. A series of points exemplified for me by the efforts by male, Western biblical scholars in South Africa to transform radically their practices of biblical studies as a part of the struggle to bring about a "new South Africa" (that is, a postapartheid society).

oppressed,[14] rather than "speaking for them" or "listening to them";[15]

- the awareness that "speaking with others," in a dialogue in which each respects the otherness of the others,[16] is possible only insofar as we not only acknowledge but also affirm our own otherness as male, European-American critical biblical scholars,[17] and thus acknowledge and affirm the interests and concerns of our group (the context out of which we speak) that "encode" our exegetical practices.[18]

---

14. This point is based upon my theological convictions as a Protestant formed in the ecumenical movement in a secularized and Catholic France and by the memory of Jews hidden by our Protestant community during World War II. Those people that we marginalize, reject, and/or oppress, because they are different from us, are precisely those who are Christ-for-us. When Christ enters our idolatrous world in order to free us from it, our first reaction is to crucify him, to reject her as a blasphemer, to marginalize and oppress her; liberation occurs for us when we acknowledge that the one we had rejected is Christ. I already expressed these convictions in D. Patte, *L'athéisme d'un chrétien ou un chrétien à l'écoute de Sartre* (Paris: Nouvelles Editions Latines, 1965), which concludes with a confession of faith.

15. The three analytical categories, "speaking for others," "listening to them," and "speaking to them" (or, better, "speaking with them"), were proposed by Spivak in her study of the "representations" (either political "speaking for" [*vertretung*] or artistic or philosophical re-presentation [*darstellung*] following a "listening to") of women as sub-altern subjects in Colonial India by British authorities or artists and philosophers (as undeconstructed subjects). "Speaking with" does not exclude representation, but takes place when the process of subject-construction (both that of the speaker and that of the one who is spoken to) and the "interests" involved are made explicit. See G. C. Spivak, "Can the Subaltern Speak?" *Marxism and the Interpretation of Culture* (ed. G. Nelson and L. Grossberg; London: Macmillan, 1988) 271–313, esp. 295. See also, Spivak, *In Other Worlds* (New York: Methuen, 1987), esp. "French Feminism in an International Frame," 134–53. Spivak's categories are used by Western biblical scholars in South Africa, especially J. Arnett, "Feminism, Post-Structuralism and the Third World: An Assessment of Some Aspects of the Work of Gayatri Spivak" (paper, Critical Studies Group, University of Natal at Pietermaritzburg) and G. O. West in several papers, among them "The Presence of Power in the Joseph Story" (paper presented at the Ideological Criticism of Biblical Texts Consultation, 1991 SBL meeting). See also G. O. West, *Biblical Hermeneutics of Liberation: Modes of Reading the Bible in the South African Context* (Pietermaritzburg: Cluster, 1991).

16. See the discussion of the different types of relation to the "other" in E. Dussel, *Philosophy of Liberation* (Maryknoll, N.Y.: Orbis Books, 1985); see esp. chap. 2, "From Phenomenology to Liberation," 16–66. The author challenges the "centeredness" and the structure of "sameness" of North Atlantic (European-American) ontology. However, these are not "necessary" characteristics of the male, European-American way of thinking, as he shows by his own discourse and sources (including Sartre).

17. This is another way of expressing Spivak's point (see n. 13). Several of us male European Americans learned this point the hard way from the conference on "ethical responsibilities and practices in biblical criticism" in which our failure to acknowledge and affirm our otherness was confronted by feminist, womanist, *mujerista,* African-American, Hispanic-American, and Jewish scholars in biblical criticism and ethics. I fully understood this point with the help of Gary Phillips, as we reflected on the implications of this conference—a watershed event for both of us.

18. See the discussion of the role of "codes" in critical interpretation by Mieke Bal, who emphasizes their "interested" character (Bal, *Murder and Difference,* 3–11).

This brief description begins to explain why, for me, androcritical practices of biblical criticism must start with the acknowledgment, elucidation, and *affirmation* of the contextual character of our own critical interpretations as male, European-American biblical scholars.

Such a conclusion is in direct conflict with the traditional understanding of critical exegesis that, not so long ago, I shared with many other male, European-American scholars, but also in tension with what we read and hear about ourselves from many feminist and other liberation biblical scholars. Thus, each of the features of the androcritical understanding of contextualization summarized above needs to be explained. For this purpose, I shall discuss, somewhat autobiographically, key features of the journey from the traditional perspective that I held to the androcritical perspective that I now hold. I shall speak of the different stages of this journey in the present (rather than the past) tense because they are still in the present tense for many European-American biblical scholars, and also for me, whenever I "forget myself" and revert to old patterns. It is not easy to abandon old habits!

Aspects of the Traditional Male, European-American Understanding of Contextualization: "Speaking for Others"

Traditionally, we male, European-American critical exegetes acknowledge the role of contextualization in biblical interpretation in two distinct ways: as preunderstandings and as hermeneutics.

When we acknowledge the role of "preunderstandings" in critical exegesis, we are admitting that our exegeses are somehow contextualized, since our preunderstandings reflect our interests and concerns in a specific context (be it personal or collective). But as long as we conceive the task of critical exegesis as the establishment of *the* (single, true) meaning of a text—be it conceived as "what the text meant," as "*the* literary effect of the text," or in any other way—we perceive preunderstandings (as a type of contextualization) *in a negative light*: either as limitations or as obstacles to a proper critical exegesis, which we hope the collective work of scholars will overcome.[19] From this perspective, contextualization (preunderstandings) in a critical exegesis of a text is illegitimate. It is denounced as a fault that the guilty exegete should confess or at least acknowledge as a severe limitation of his or her work.

Yet this does not mean that we do not recognize the need for contextualizing the message of the biblical text. This is what we commonly

---

19. This negative conception of "preunderstandings" is the one we implement in our exegetical practices, even though our theoretical conception of it might be quite different and much more sophisticated (for example, following R. Bultmann, M. Heidegger, H. G. Gadamer).

conceive of as the pedagogical task or more generally the hermeneutical task (by contrast with the "exegetical" task). When *the* meaning of a text in its original cultural context has been at least provisionally established through critical exegesis, it needs to be made available to people in other cultural contexts, through a hermeneutical process that can take the form, for instance, of a demythologization (Bultmann) and a return to discourse (Ricoeur). Thus, this type of contextualization is envisioned as a process to be performed for the sake of other groups (exegetes already understand the text!). It takes the form of "speaking for others"; "translating" the message of the text (which we have established and which we have decided they need) into cultural terms that are relevant for them.

The patronizing effect of this view of hermeneutics and of contextualization understood as the task of contextualizing the biblical message for the sake of others cannot be ignored.[20]

Male, European-American Exegetes "Listening to Others"

A first step away from this view of the practice of critical exegesis and of contextualization occurred to me and other male, European-American exegetes when we agreed "to listen to" feminists and other "minority"(!) scholars. But, for us, even this small step, insufficient as it turns out to be if taken alone, is not easy to take. Our initial response to feminist, African-American, and other "minority" biblical scholarship is one of ambivalence: both negative and positive.

For many of us, this response turns out to be more negative than positive. It is important to understand why. Because of the rich legacy of hermeneutical and social consciousness that characterizes male, European-American biblical scholarship, we are ready to join feminist and other "minorities" in "their" struggle against sexism, patriarchalism, racism, and all other forms of exclusion, marginalization, oppression, and alienation. Thus, we readily commit ourselves to focus our scholarship and teaching of the Bible in such a way that they might contribute to the

---

20. Even though this traditional view of the practice of critical exegesis was developed over against fundamentalist interpretations (are not fundamentalists reading into the text their dogmatic preunderstandings?), it is striking that it follows the same pattern. Thus, from their evangelical perspective, D. J. Hesselgrave and E. Rommen open their book *Contextualization: Meanings, Methods, and Models* (Leicester, England: Apollos, 1989) with these words: "The missionary's ultimate goal in communication has always been to present the supracultural message of the gospel in culturally relevant terms" (1). See also part 4, "Authentic and Relevant Contextualization: Some Proposals" (197–257). For them also, there is *the* true meaning of a text: what they call its "supracultural" or "divine element in biblical interpretation." Contextualization is then envisioned as expressing *the* meaning of the text "in culturally relevant terms" for the sake of other people.

amelioration of theses problems. We are even prepared to acknowledge as a "sin of omission" (our mea culpa) that our practices as traditional critical biblical scholars have failed to be accountable toward "minorities" and others—an absence of accountability that Elisabeth Schüssler Fiorenza made explicit in her Society of Biblical Literature presidential address. But because of our ideological commitment to the task of hermeneutics and to social justice, we are shocked and outraged to hear the charge that we male, European-American exegetes and our exegetical works are part of the problem. The charges of "androcentrism"[21] and "Eurocentrism"[22]—which carry with them the implication, at times made explicit, that we are patriarchal, sexist, and racist—are in nonsensical contradiction with all that we stand for. We are deeply hurt and troubled by such accusations, even though we dismiss them as originating from "radical feminist and minority activists." Are these accusations not reminiscent of Malcolm X's denunciation of all white people as "white devils" (a denunciation that, in our interpretation, is at best an obvious rhetorical overstatement)? We are ready to concede that, unfortunately, there are always some rotten apples in a barrel. But this cannot possibly mean that all of us and everything that we do are racist, sexist, and/or patriarchal! We "do not hear" what feminists and other liberation biblical scholars are saying to us because we perceive these as personal accusations that contradict our personal commitments that we strive to implement in our exegetical work.

For some of us (indeed a growing number of us), the response to feminist, African-American, and other "minority" biblical scholarship is more positive than negative. Thus, we hear what liberation biblical scholars say, yet, as it turns out, without really hearing them. At this point, we adopt a "positive" attitude toward "minorities" (analogous to the attitude of European-American liberals participating in the civil rights movement)[23] out of a sense of guilt. We are indeed deeply disturbed by their accusations. Yet on further reflection we have to confess that they are accurate. We cannot deny the ways in which our critical exegetical works affect women, African Americans, and other "minorities"(!); our exegetical practices do exclude and alienate them, because they are androcentric and Eurocentric.

This acknowledgment is facilitated by certain liberation scholars who emphasize that these accusations are not personal attacks: androcen-

---

21. See, for instance, E. Schüssler Fiorenza, *In Memory of Her: A Feminist Theological Reconstruction of Christian Origins* (New York: Crossroad, 1983) 3–64.

22. As the authors have emphasized in C. H. Felder, ed., *Stony the Road We Trod: African American Biblical Interpretation* (Minneapolis: Fortress Press, 1991) 6–7.

23. That James H. Cone, following Malcolm X and Martin Luther King, Jr., denounces. See Cone, *Martin and Malcolm and America: A Dream or a Nightmare* (Maryknoll, N.Y.: Orbis Books, 1991) 94–97, 232–43, passim.

trism and Eurocentrism, and the patriarchalism and racism associated with them, are *structural* and *collective* problems.[24] With their help, we recognize that our collective ethical failure as male, European-American biblical scholars is a pervasive and serious problem. Thus, it appears to us that the only appropriate response is "repentance": a radical transformation of our practices, which demands a radically new vision of our task as biblical scholars. And so it is. Yet in light of this recognition, our first impulse is to conclude that our "maleness" and our "Europeanness" are fundamentally problematic. In order to transform our practices in biblical studies so that they might be ethically responsible, we believe that we must totally abandon our male, European-American perspective and adopt the perspective of feminist, African-American, and other liberation biblical scholars. We need to learn from them, to "listen to them." We envision practicing with them a feminist or African-American hermeneutic, or at least practicing a biblical interpretation that would be "interested" (contextualized) through the adoption of a preferential option for the poor and the oppressed. In this way, we would hopefully participate with them in "their" struggle against patriarchalism, racism, and oppression embedded in biblical studies. Instead of being part of the problem, we would then be part of the solution.

Yet to our surprise, liberation biblical scholars do not welcome our efforts to "listen to them" and to learn from them what would be an ethically responsible practice of biblical studies by male, European-American biblical scholars.[25] This is once again an attitude arising out of a misconception of contextualization. By proposing to listen to "minority" biblical scholars, we treat them precisely as "minorities" for the sake of whom we need to contextualize our work in biblical studies; in so doing, we imagine that we will help them resolve "their" problem (for example, patriarchalism, racism).

In sum, contextualization, even from an enlightened liberal position, is still conceived as something we need to do for the sake of others; this view of contextualization carries with it the same patronizing attitude as before—compounded, in the present case, by a co-opting of the works of liberation biblical scholars. Furthermore, by pretending that, somehow, we could abandon our male, European-American perspective, we continue to refuse to acknowledge that our critical exegetical

---

24. For instance, Schüssler Fiorenza underscores that it is a matter of "paradigm" and "paradigm-shift" (see *In Memory of Her,* xx–xxiv; see also 3–95). Malcolm X made a similar point in his explanation of his denunciation of "white devils." See Cone, *Martin and Malcolm,* 103, where he quotes Malcolm X: "Unless we call one white man, by name, a 'devil,' we are not speaking of any *individual* white man. We are speaking of the *collective* white man's *historical* record."

25. It is one of the things Gary Phillips and I "learned" at the Lilly conference on ethical responsibility. It took us long months of joint reflections to understand the extraordinary significance (for us) of this conference.

work is interested and contextual, that is, encoded by the concerns and interests of our group, male European Americans. We are still involved in a quest for a disinterested and a-contextual interpretation of the Bible, as we were when proposing traditional "academic" (if not "objective") interpretations that would be valid in any cultural and social situation, and therefore that would be "universally" legitimate.[26] The generous(!) project of "listening to others" in order to adopt their perspective and become one of them duplicates what is, according to liberation theologians and biblical scholars, the most problematic aspect of our traditional practices of critical exegesis.

Affirming the Legitimacy and Validity of Our European-American Perspective as a Condition for "Speaking with Others"

As male European Americans, we must assume responsibility for the exclusionary, alienating, and oppressive effects of our critical biblical scholarship. These negative effects—more or less subtle forms of patriarchalism, racism, classism, and cultural hegemony (the more subtle, the more insidious they are)—are our problems, and we must address them. Furthermore, we have to acknowledge the accuracy of the diagnostic proposed by liberation scholars: the fundamental issue is our androcentrism and Eurocentrism, that is, the *universalizing of our perspective as male European Americans.* In theological terms I can describe androcentrism and Eurocentrism as *idolatries*—taking as absolute (universal) what is particular. For me an androcritical perspective is "critical" of traditional, male, European-American practices of exegesis in that it strives to overcome the idolatries of androcentrism and Eurocentrism.

My theological formulation[27] shows that what is wrong with an-

---

26. From a theoretical standpoint, those of us who have studied semiotics, deconstructionism, and/or reader-response criticism can readily recognize that the above practices of biblical studies, conceived of in terms of either "speaking for others" or "listening to others," are problematic because the constructed character of the subjects involved—and especially us male European Americans as critical biblical scholars—is not accounted for (as Spivak emphasizes in "Can the Subaltern Speak?"). But this recognition by itself does not prevent us (contrary to what would be expected) from seeking to abandon our male, European-American perspective in an interpretive project that we conceived by "listening to others." At least, this was my own experience, as well as that of several other male European Americans, as I witnessed in several situations.

27. This formulation is based upon my own theological convictions. In brief, for me, an idolatry is the perversion of a true partial revelation (or gift from God) that is taken as absolute (as God, as a complete revelation, as a universal truth). This idolatry is a destructive bondage for (bringing death to) the idolaters and the partial revelation and transforms both the idolaters and the partial revelation into oppressors, bringing death to others. The knowledge of our condition as idolaters does not provide liberation from idolatry (see Romans 7 and the case of the Corinthians). It takes the intervention in our idolatrous world of a Christlike person (or group) who does not conform to

drocentrism and Eurocentrism is *not* our male, European-American perspective in itself, *but its absolutization.* Overcoming androcentrism and Eurocentrism necessarily includes acknowledging the relative and contextual character of our perspective. But this is not enough! More than a simple acknowledgment is needed, since we often acknowledge the relative character of our perspective and of our critical work even as we "speak for others" or "listen to others" (with disastrous consequences, as noted above). For me, by itself this acknowledgment—which can be very refined through a rigorous analysis of our condition in terms of our sophisticated, male, European-American theories—does not free us from our idolatry; it can serve actually to reinforce it (note the theories that are used to bring it about). Thus, despite our acknowledgment of the relative character of our perspective, we still absolutize it. This is what happens in our practices when we "speak for others" or "listen to others."

The problem is that we apologize for the relative and contextual character of our work; it is a limitation, a "sin" that tarnishes our critical work, and therefore something that we must strive to overcome. For me, in order to avoid duplicating the problematic attitudes involved in "speaking for" and "listening to" others, we need to adopt a positive critical attitude toward our own distinctive perspective as male European Americans. We must not only acknowledge it but also *affirm its legitimacy and validity as a perspective.* This acknowledgment and affirmation are possible only insofar as we "speak *with* others" in a genuine dialogical relationship, that is, as we acknowledge and affirm the legitimacy and validity of the "otherness" of others. My statement that we male, European-American critical exegetes must affirm the legitimacy and validity of our own perspective will certainly be read with "suspicion" by liberation biblical scholars. So let me underscore that as long as we apologize for the contextual character of our works, our practices of biblical studies and our other actions are necessarily characterized by a universalizing attitude, since they involve a denial and/or rejection of the particularity of our perspective. On the contrary, by affirming the legitimacy and validity of our peculiar perspective, we would put ourselves in a position of acknowledging the contextual character of our exege-

---

our idolatrous world and is therefore truly "other" than us. We reject (marginalize, oppress) that person in the name of our God or Truth (= idol). Liberation occurs when we recognize the one whom we "crucified" as "sent by God" (or bearer of truth) in his/her otherness. This Christlike person is then a sign of contradiction that breaks the power of bondage of our idol. In the process the partial revelation that was also in bondage is itself freed. We can then affirm the legitimacy and validity of this revelation *as partial revelation* (that is, as contextual truth)—rejecting it would be falling into another idolatry. This is, in very brief, my contextual (and legitimate!) interpretation of Paul's view of idolatry; see D. Patte, *Paul's Faith and the Power of the Gospel: A Structural Introduction to Paul's Letters* (Minneapolis: Fortress Press, 1984) 256–95.

ses even as we practice them; thus, our exegetical practices would no longer make implicit or explicit universal claims. This is what it means practically to adopt an androcritical practice, which includes *affirming* our otherness as male, European-American scholars. Yet what does this mean for our reading and teaching practices in biblical studies?

Adopting an androcritical practice entails affirming without reservations that all male, European-American critical exegeses, past and present, are contextual in character. This is also affirming that all these exegeses have been and are governed by concerns and interests of male European Americans. Such an affirmation is possible only insofar as we recognize the legitimacy and validity of our male, European-American critical exegeses. Recognizing their "legitimacy" and recognizing their "validity" are, however, quite different processes.

The Affirmation of the Validity of Our Critical Exegeses

Affirming the validity of our critical exegeses involves recognizing that they have "value"—of course, a contextual value. Our exegeses have value in that they seek to address our concerns (for certain problems) and our interests (to promote certain things that we view as "good") as male, European-American exegetes. This "interested" character of our exegeses as well as their validity should be made explicit as we develop new exegeses according to an androcritical practice. Yet our (former) androcentric and/or Eurocentric exegeses[28] should not be viewed as disinterested[29] or as without value. The fact that we hide and deny (because of our androcentrism and Eurocentrism) that our critical exegetical works are "interested" and are driven by certain concerns and

---

28. I use this vocabulary in the specific sense defined above. "Androcentric and Eurocentric exegeses" is the designation for those exegeses that absolutize and universalize these perspectives, by contrast with "androcritical exegeses," which would not. Androcritical exegeses would still be performed from a male, European-American perspective, but without absolutizing and universalizing it. It remains that we are like recovering alcoholics; we will always remain in danger of backsliding into androcentrism and Eurocentrism. The best we can do is constantly to resist and criticize our androcentrism and Eurocentrism. This is what the term "androcritical" also tries to convey. So the parenthetical "(former)."

29. As G. O. West implies, in an otherwise excellent book, when he writes: "The challenge is to move away from the notion of biblical studies as the pursuit of disinterested truth" (*Biblical Hermeneutics of Liberation*, 173). See also J. W. Rogerson, "What Does It Mean to Be Human? The Central Question of Old Testament Theology," *The Bible in Three Dimensions* (ed. D. Clines, S. Fowl, and S. E. Porter; Sheffield: Sheffield Academic Press, 1990), and C. Rowland and M. Corner, *Liberating Exegesis: The Challenge of Liberation Theology to Biblical Studies* (London: SPCK, 1990). These works ultimately advocate abandoning current critical exegeses so as to develop "interested" biblical studies, hermeneutics for the sake of the poor, the oppressed, and so on. In this sense they have not really moved away from the attitudes of "speaking for" or "listening to" others.

interests does not make them less so. Making explicit the concerns and interests that govern such exegetical works involves an analysis aimed at elucidating the morality of knowledge they presuppose and the meanings (readings) that they authorize and prohibit, and how these are related to institutional and social concerns and interests.

We male, European-American critical exegetes often make explicit these concerns and interests in the very process of hiding them. In order to recognize this, it is enough to remember that our distinction between exegesis and hermeneutics was (is) made in order to protect the objective or academic (and thus universal) character of our exegeses; we express(ed) the concerns and interests, which implicitly govern our exegeses, by qualifying them as "hermeneutical." Thus, typical male, European-American concerns and interests can be identified by considering what we say (said) about hermeneutics. In very general terms, I can suggest that they are related (1) to the rejection of obscurantist (fundamentalist, dogmatic, integrist) interpretations and their devastating consequences; (2) to the struggle against secularization; and/or (3) to the promotion of ecumenical dialogue (as a substitute for sectarianism).

These suggestions are enough to show that male, European-American exegetes can affirm and defend the contextual validity of such concerns and interests. Obscurantism, secularization, and sectarianism have such dire consequences for individuals and groups and engender so many social and political evils that we can readily argue for the validity of exegeses attempting to overcome them. Of course, as we do so, we will want to debate among ourselves and with others specific conceptualizations of these concerns and the strategies developed for addressing them. My point is that, by making explicit the interested, and thus contextual, character of our critical exegeses, we European-American males could affirm their validity and also debate their contextual value with the practitioners (liberation scholars) of other kinds of interested interpretations (whose contextual character we would also acknowledge and affirm). Debates concerning strategies, priorities, and the urgency of various kinds of interested interpretations would, of course, have to be expected and welcomed: they would be possible, at last! Because we would affirm (rather than apologize for) the contextual character of our exegeses and of our peculiar perspective as European-American males, we would be in a position to "speak with" others.

The Affirmation of the Legitimacy of Our Critical Exegeses: Reconceptualizing the Task of Critical Exegesis

But for male, European-American critical exegetes, such an affirmation of the contextual validity of our critical exegeses fundamentally contradicts our traditional conception of our task as *critical* exegetes. According to our definition, critical exegeses cannot be interested. Affirming the contextual validity and the contextual legitimacy of our exegeses demands that we envision our critical task then in a different way: in a nonandrocentric and non-Eurocentric way; in an androcritical way.

For this, let us remember that the problem is an absolutization of what is not absolute. From an androcentric-Eurocentric point of view, "critical exegesis" is truly "legitimate" when it is an interpretation that is demonstrably based upon and accounts for *the entire* textual evidence.[30] What is "an absolutization of what is not absolute" in this definition of an ideal critical exegesis? I have highlighted what it is for me.[31] It is the claim that a critical exegesis can be based upon and ac-

---

30. Here, and in what follows, I use the phrase "textual evidence" in its broadest sense to include not only the characteristics and features of the text itself but also everything to which these features refer and allude.

31. Other androcritical scholars (with a reader-response and/or poststructuralist perspective) disagree with me on this point because they identify the problem with the claim that "critical" studies are based upon "textual evidence." I agree with them that what critical exegesis studies is always a text already read (see below the discussion of the relationship between critical exegesis and ordinary readings). But, though indirectly, critical studies do deal with textual evidence in order to establish their legitimacy. I also agree with them that the basic problem is that of the "objectification" of the text. But we disagree on what "text" is objectified and absolutized. In my view, it is a "meaningful text" (conceived as having a single true meaning), and therefore the problem is with conceiving the "text" in this way. Thus, I agree that a "meaningful text" does not exist; yet I insist that a text with the power to affect people and to contribute to produce certain meanings (plural!) does exist. Otherwise, why bother to read a text rather than another one? And why strive to write texts ourselves?

My position is, of course, contextual. It is related to my theological convictions: our traditional exegetical practice is idolatrous; but being freed from idolatry involves recovering what is a partial truth in it (so my argument). It is also related to my methodological and epistemological views as a semiotician. In brief, the semiotic epistemology emphasizes that "semiosis," the production (and prohibition!) of meaning, occurs according to similar rules (or structures) in all the domains of human experience (for example, speech, social, psychological, cultural, religious domains), which are, therefore, perceived as necessarily interrelated. From this particular epistemological perspective, I envision any discourse (a production of meaning) as necessarily contextual (it is part of a web of semioses) and as multidimensional—it produces different coherent meaning-effects through the different structures that link it to its multifold context. I thus understand the multiplicity of different readings of a given "text" (the representation of a discourse) as due *both* to the multiplicity of contexts in which these readings take place *and* to the multiplicity of meaning-producing dimensions of the text.

I do not deny the plausibility (and thus legitimacy) of the epistemology and ontology of my poststructural androcritical colleagues (from whom I learned a lot). The debate is one concerning "validity" and thus "praxis." My semiotic epistemology and theological convictions allow me to envision multidimensional critical exegetical practices that, I believe on the basis of classroom experiments, address quite effectively our concerns as androcritical biblical scholars (as further defined by my Protestant position). I believe the "intertextual" pedagogical strategy envisioned by my poststructural colleagues is very effective as well. But I am concerned by the effect of such a teaching: for the students, it shows the contextual character of a given biblical "text" (and not so much, or not at all,

counts for *the entirety* of the textual evidence. But any critical study, however complete and detailed it might be, is based upon and takes into account only *a part* of the textual evidence, never its entirety.

Androcentric and Eurocentric exegetes might want to concede this point by acknowledging that the use of a given critical method (or a set of methods from a given methodology) in an exegetical work limits it to studying a part of the textual evidence.[32] But even when we acknowledge this, we usually object to the above suggestions by appealing to the collective character of the exegetical task: taken together the various exegetical works using different critical methods will ultimately account for the entire textual evidence. In this way, the exegetical task is still conceived as a quest for *the* (true and single) meaning of each given text. This vision of the collective exegetical task, however, is directly challenged by a comparison of the results of the use of different critical methods (especially those based on different methodologies):

- their results are often incompatible and at times contradictory, rather than complementary;[33] I thus conclude that the present methodological diversity confirms that any critical exegesis is based upon and accounts for only a *part* of the textual evidence; to put it a different way, no critical exegesis can claim to provide an explanation of everything;

- yet each of these diverse critical exegeses usually presents a "meaning of the text" that is coherent and is demonstrably based upon and accounts for one kind of textual evidence that is pertinent according to a given method.[34]

How should this situation be understood? One might be content (1) to see in it a proof that critical exegeses are as interested and contextual as any other interpretation (since the meaning of the text they present is always partial, it is biased by the reader-exegete who is contextualized in a particular location) and (2) to deny that critical exegesis has any special status or role (it is like hermeneutical and ordinary readings).

---

of a given interpretation of that text). In other words, the perception of the contextual character of a text is not perceived as a contextual interpretation itself. I am concerned about this confusion, which ends up neutralizing the entire pedagogical project. Thus, the use of the excellent intertextual strategy needs, in my view, to be complemented by an emphasis on the multidimensionality of the text (through the presentation of several legitimate interpretations of the same text).

32. This is an instance of the confession of the "limitations," "sins of omission" by androcentric, Eurocentric exegetes (see above).

33. This problem is resolved by traditional, male, European-American scholars by denying any legitimacy to methods that do not produce results compatible with their own exegetical work.

34. Exegeses that would not have these characteristics (for example, a poor application of a method) are then appropriately labeled as "uncritical."

I fully agree with the first part of this conclusion: any reading, be it a critical reading, an "ordinary reading" (which does not claim to be critical), or a hermeneutical reading, is contextual. But as a male, European-American exegete, I cannot agree with the second part of this conclusion. We male European Americans who have devoted our lives to the task of critical exegesis are convinced of the importance and value of this task—which is for many of us a vocation. We cannot deny that there is a fundamental difference between "critical readings" and "ordinary readings"; for us, this difference should be maintained in all its sharpness, rather than "watered down," as some of us (under the influence of deconstructionism and reader-response criticism) do together with liberation scholars by renaming critical readings "hermeneutical readings." If the distinction between critical exegeses and ordinary readings is not maintained, we lose any sense of our vocation as exegetes and teachers—a vocation that, we are convinced, is legitimate and valid. It is this difference between the two kinds of reading that needs to be accounted for. But in view of the preceding arguments and from my androcritical perspective (which owes part of its specificity to my identity as a Protestant and semiotician), I want to argue that the relationships between ordinary readings and critical readings need to be totally reconceived;[35] we need to envision our task and vocation as critical exegetes in a totally different way.

For me, this reconceptualization of the task and vocation of critical exegesis progressed in two main steps: the acknowledgment of the "polysemy" of any text and the rediscovery of the theological character of the critical exegetical task (as expression of the contextualized character of our exegetical practices). Beyond these two steps (and this essay), much still needs to be clarified, including the relationship between vocation and practice (task), and in our practices (for example, pedagogical practices) our different positions of authority and power as traditional and androcritical exegetes.

Acknowledging the Polysemy of Any Text

The fact that exegeses using different critical methods elucidate "different meanings" for the same text does not make these exegeses less critical. This phenomenon can readily be explained by envisioning any text as polysemic, that is, as having a plurality of coherent semantic dimensions, each of which offers the possibility of being perceived as

35. G. West's work *Biblical Hermeneutics of Liberation* is essential for this purpose. It is devoted to a close examination of the complex interrelations between ordinary and critical readings in a specific context. I am obviously much indebted to his work.

"a meaning of the text."[36] This is conceiving a text as being similar to the well-known black and white picture used in psychological studies of perception, in which one perceives either two persons looking at each other (when focusing on its black features) or a goblet (when focusing on its white features). Both images are demonstrably in the picture. Similarly, any given text includes a plurality of coherent meaning-producing dimensions (more than two!). When we use a given critical method, we perceive one such coherent dimension and reach a certain conclusion regarding the meaning of the text. When using another critical method, we perceive another dimension and a different meaning of the text. And so on. Thus, each of these diverse exegeses can be said to be truly "critical" and thus legitimate readings insofar as it demonstrates that it is based upon a coherent textual evidence—one of the coherent meaning-producing dimensions of the text.[37]

This view of text, which is at least as plausible as others, opens the possibility of acknowledging simultaneously that an exegesis is critical and legitimate (based upon a coherent meaning producing dimension), and that it is *partial* and thus not universal. Then, other interpretations, with different conclusions regarding the meaning of the text, can also be recognized as potentially legitimate. This conclusion applies to other critical exegeses (using different methods), but also to ordinary readings.

Critical Exegesis and Ordinary Readings

This view of the text opens the possibility of envisioning the task of critical exegesis vis-à-vis ordinary readings in a very different way. Rather than being aimed at correcting these uncritical and "wrong" ordinary readings, the critical task can be envisioned as aimed at elucidating the meaning-producing dimensions upon which these ordinary readings are based. The critical task would involve presupposing that ordinary read-

---

36. This multidimensionality of any text can be theoretically explained by considering the epistemological theories upon which the different methods are based. This is what I attempted to do by considering the semiotic theory that is the basis for many literary, semiotic, and structural exegetical methods, while suggesting that historiographical theories also presuppose a plurality of meaning-producing dimensions for each text. See D. Patte, *The Religious Dimensions of Biblical Texts: Greimas's Structural Semiotics and Biblical Exegesis* (Atlanta: Scholars Press, 1990). See also M. Bal, *Murder and Difference*.

37. In my view, the meaning-producing dimensions are not to be limited to those defined by a single theory or methodology. Each methodology, because of its contextual character, perceives only a limited number of dimensions! As I will suggest below, certain ordinary readings might refer to textual dimensions not accounted for by any existing methodology (so the need to develop new methodologies).

ings are basically legitimate[38] (based upon actual textual features that form a coherent meaning-producing dimension of the text) and seeking to demonstrate it, if necessary by developing new critical methods.

This view of ordinary readings involves acknowledging that reading is an interactive process between (1) readers with specific contextual concerns and interests and (2) a text with the power to constrain the reading (despite the contextual character of reading, it makes a difference which specific text is read) and also, positively, to contribute to the production of meaning by *affecting readers in certain ways*. Much would need to be said on this important point. Be it enough here to say that the multiplicity of ordinary readings can then be explained without negating their respective legitimacy: readers with specific concerns and interests are affected by different meaning-producing dimensions of the text.[39]

Rediscovering the Theological Character of Critical Exegesis

The relationship of this view of ordinary readings and of the task of critical exegesis with theologies of liberation became clear to me at the Faculté de Théologie of the University of Neuchâtel (Switzerland). There, colleagues and students insisted that, as a critical exegete, I am as much a "theologian" as the specialists in dogmatics and constructive theology. I was at first surprised by this insistence. But on second thought, it became clear to me that our denial that we are "theologians" is simply the way in which so many of us male, European-American critical exegetes deny the interested character of our critical exegetical task. Affirming that critical exegesis is a theological task is one way (among others) of acknowledging its contextual character. I find it particularly helpful because it further clarifies the relationship between critical exegetical readings and ordinary readings.

Albert Nolan's insightful effort to inscribe the theologies of liberation within the traditional understanding of theology (Anselm)—faith seeking understanding (*fides quaerens intellectum*)—provides a model for understanding how ordinary readings are related to critical exegesis as a theological task.[40] As theology is contextual in that it brings

---

38. I write *"basically* legitimate" (and not simply "legitimate") because in my view ordinary readings can themselves be distorted by making absolutizing claims. Then, I would call them "dogmatic readings" or "ideological readings."

39. These different dimensions can be called "different texts" (read by different readers). See, for example, Stanley Fish, *Is There a Text in This Classroom? The Authority of Interpretive Communities* (Cambridge, Mass.: Harvard Univ. Press, 1980). While this vocabulary is very helpful to shock us out of our one-dimensional view of a text, I do not find it particularly helpful in developing a constructive proposal.

40. A. Nolan and R. Broderick, *To Nourish Our Faith: Theology of Liberation for South Africa* (Hilton, South Africa: Cornerstone Book, 1987) 10–29, passim. See also,

to (critical) understanding the *sensus fidei* of the people in a certain context (oppressed people, in the case of theologies of liberation), so critical exegesis can be conceived as bringing to critical understanding the "faith-interpretations" or "ordinary readings" of people in certain contexts. As a theology of liberation affirms the legitimacy and validity of the specific *sensus fidei* and faith-experience of ordinary believers, so critical exegesis can be conceived as affirming the basic legitimacy and validity of the faith-interpretations of specific ordinary readers[41] that it brings to critical understanding.

In this perspective, I want to propose that any critical exegesis, whether or not it acknowledges it, is based upon a "faith-interpretation" (ordinary readings of the exegete and of his or her group) that it brings to critical understanding and affirms by making explicit the textual evidence that legitimizes this faith-interpretation.[42] The contextual characteristics of our critical exegeses as male European Americans are manifested by the faith-interpretations that they bring to critical understanding and by the specific critical method used for this purpose.

In this perspective, our task as androcritical exegetes would therefore be twofold: (1) to elucidate the faith-interpretations that existing exegeses by male, European-American scholars bring to critical understanding by focusing in each case on a certain meaning-producing dimension of the text through the use of a specific critical method; (2) to make explicit the faith-interpretations that our new critical exegeses bring to critical understanding through the use of one or another method. This twofold endeavor would require that we proceed to the critical analysis of existing male, European-American exegeses and of faith-interpretations (including our own). This analysis would seek to identify the interests and concerns (of a specific group) that our interpretations embody, and thus also the power structures that authorize such interpretations and prohibit others. In other words, such an androcritical exegetical practice would first of all be a critical interpretation of male, European-American interpretations aimed at elucidating the legitimacy of each (that it is based upon a certain coherent dimension of a given text, despite its claim to deal with the entirety of the textual evidence) and its contextual validity (the kinds of interests and concerns of a specific group it

A. Nolan, *Jesus before Christianity* (2d ed.; Cape Town: David Philip Publisher, 1986); and idem, *God in South Africa: The Challenge of the Gospel* (Cape Town: David Philip Publisher; Grand Rapids, Mich.: Eerdmans, 1988).

41. The faith-interpretations of specific ordinary readers is legitimate and valid because, as ordinary readings, they express how certain readers have been affected by the text (or more specifically, by one of its meaning-producing dimensions) without making universal or normative claims. Thus, I distinguish them from "ideological readings," which make such claims.

42. Which can be religious or secular, positive or negative, an affirmation or a rejection of "what the text says."

seeks to address). Then we would be in a position to debate among ourselves, but also with feminist and other liberation critics, regarding the greater or lesser validity of each of these interpretations.

The analytical procedures that would be most appropriate for this endeavor remain to be determined. Since in all this our goal would no longer be to present a critical interpretation that should be accepted as universal or normative by others (other male European Americans in other contexts, as well as members of other groups), our presentation of critical exegeses should be in most instance "multidimensional": the presentation of several critical readings as equally legitimate and potentially valid.[43] Furthermore, as could be expected from a proposal based on reflections on our pedagogical practices, this androcritical perspective would also demand from us a totally different pedagogical strategy. Here again, despite a few experiments, I can only say that the appropriate pedagogical strategy remains to be determined.[44] I can only suggest that instead of asking our students to abandon their ("wrong") ordinary readings or faith-interpretations in order to adopt *the* correct critical interpretation that we teach them, we should teach them how to bring to critical understanding *their own* faith-interpretations (whatever they might be), so that in turn they might acknowledge and affirm their legitimacy and *contextual* validity, and thus might be in a position to debate with others their appropriateness in the present concrete situations.

In sum, acknowledging the contextual character of our male, European-American exegeses is the first order of business for us. It is clear that this acknowledgment entails from us quite different practices in all aspects of our work. But we just begin to envision these practices: androcritical exegetical practices.

---

43. "Potentially valid" and not "equally valid" because we, personally, will always want and need to acknowledge and affirm the validity of a single type of reading— our specific male, European-American reading. But, as debates regarding the respective validity of different readings take place (see above), we might agree to change our minds!

44. An issue that Gary Phillips and I pursue as we develop a project entitled "Teaching the Bible Otherwise: Can We Be Responsible and Critical in a Pluralistic Context?"

2

Toward a Hermeneutics of the Diaspora:
A Hermeneutics of Otherness and Engagement

Fernando F. Segovia

As the title for the present essay indicates, I believe that the time has come to introduce the real reader, the flesh-and-blood reader, fully and explicitly, into the theory and practice of biblical criticism; to acknowledge that no reading, informed or uninformed, takes place in a social vacuum or desert; to allow fully for contextualization, for culture and experience, not only with regard to texts but also with regard to readers of texts, with a view of all readings as constructs proceeding from, dependent upon, and addressing a particular social location, however circumscribed.

I see this irruption of the flesh-and-blood reader into biblical criticism as a harbinger not of anarchy and tribalism, as many who insist on impartiality and objectivity often claim, but rather of continued decolonization and liberation, of resistance and struggle against a subtle authoritarianism and covert tribalism of its own, in a discipline that has been, from beginning to end and top to bottom, thoroughly Eurocentric despite its assumed scientific persona of neutrality and universality.[1] In

---

1. It is amazing how resistant, sometimes bordering on the hysterical, male biblical critics from the world of the North Atlantic can be to any admission of contextuality in their own work, despite the fact that the concept of the *Sitz im Leben* ("the situation in life" or the social context) has been liberally applied from within the paradigm of historical criticism itself to the texts and authors in question. Such reactions, familiar to any individual not from that world or of minority status in that world, tend to be quite similar as well. The following stand out: (1) a reaffirmation of the hermeneutical model involving the retrieval of a meaning "back then" and its application "for today," not as a model, however, but as an unquestioned and unquestionable reality or modus operandi; (2) an ad hominem (or "ad feminam") argument to the effect that the proposed hermeneutical enterprise in effect abandons the realm of scientific and scholarly objectivity for that of subjective and political advocacy, without any critical analysis of the argument itself, that is, of the presuppositions involved in arguing that a particular hermeneutical stance is not politicized and, in effect, lacks any agenda of advocacy; and (3) an overall formulation of such argumentation in strong theological terms, derived either from the Protestant or the Catholic tradition (as the case may be), without any corresponding recognition of the undeniable and sometimes overriding theological foundations and agenda of their own critical work and hermeneutical stance. It should be

effect, I regard the admission and intromission of real readers, of the contextuality and particularity of all readings, as an acceptance of the world for what it is, in the richness and fullness of its diversity, especially in this time of increasing and irreversible globalization in every sphere of life, including the theological and the interpretive—an acceptance of the other not as an imposed or defined "other" but as independent and self-defining.[2]

In this essay I should like to propose, therefore, the beginnings of a hermeneutical framework for taking the flesh-and-blood reader seriously in biblical criticism, not so much as a unique and independent individual but rather as a member of distinct and identifiable social configurations, as a reader from and within a social location.[3] The proposed framework is not conceived in essentialist terms, as a master or totalizing narrative derived from the human condition and calling for universal applicability, but as a contextual stance that is directly grounded in and informed by my own social location as a member of the diaspora, by which I mean specifically the massive dispersion of the children of the Third World, the world of the politically and/or economically colonized, in the First World, the world of the colonizers, of the political and/or economic center. In my own case, furthermore, such a location in the diaspora can be more specifically described in terms of my sociopolitical status as a Hispanic American, a readily identifiable and distinct social configuration within U.S. society. It is a framework that I refer to as a hermeneutics of the diaspora, a Hispanic-American hermeneutics of otherness and engagement, whose fundamental purpose is to read the biblical text as an other—not to be overwhelmed or overridden, but acknowl-

---

noted that, for the most part, such reactions and arguments tend to lack a thorough and sophisticated theoretical foundation.

2. In this essay I shall be using the term "the other" in two ways: in a negative or pejorative way, when the definition of the other is imposed from the outside without taking the other into consideration; in a positive and constructive way, when the other is allowed to surface and describe itself as the other. While in the former case, a situation of overwhelming and overriding imposition, the term will be found in quotation marks, in the latter, a situation of respect and engagement, the term will appear without quotation marks.

3. I certainly do not mean to deny the presence of independence and uniqueness to individuals within such social groupings, but rather to focus on those aspects that characterize individuals as members of specific social groupings. In any case such a relationship should never be conceived or formulated in terms of an either/or: individuals undergo a sustained, complex, and differentiated process of socialization; the process itself may be questioned, resisted, and altered by individuals. Likewise, I by no means wish to present such a framework as the sole and definitive framework for approaching and interpreting the biblical texts; it is but one strategy. For a number of other frameworks emerging out of the Hispanic-American experience in the diaspora, see F. F. Segovia, "Hispanic American Theology and the Bible: Effective Weapon and Faithful Ally," *We Are a People! Initiative in Hispanic American Theology* (ed. R. S. Goizueta; Minneapolis: Fortress Press, 1992) 21–50.

edged, respected, and engaged in its very otherness. It is a framework that is ultimately grounded in a theology of the diaspora (a Hispanic-American theology of otherness and mixture) and that gives rise to a specific methodological approach—the reading strategy of intercultural criticism.

I see such a framework as forming part of that paradigm or umbrella model of interpretation within biblical criticism that I have characterized in terms of cultural studies.[4] Thus, for example, the proposal calls into question the enduring and beloved construct of a neutral and disinterested reader in biblical criticism (a universal and informed reader) and opts instead for the construct of a flesh-and-blood reader (a real reader who is always situated and engaged, socially and historically conditioned, reading and interpreting from a variety of different and complex social locations). Such a reader is not universal and may or may not be informed, that is to say, may or may not possess sophisticated training in criticism and theory of whatever sort. Moreover, the proposal also calls for engagement in a joint critical study of texts and readers of texts, for analysis of textual as well as interpretive perspectives and ideologies. As such, it looks upon a critical analysis of the biblical texts to be as important as a critical analysis of their readers and readings. Furthermore, the proposal regards all models of interpretation and strategies for reading, all retrievals of meaning from texts, and all reconstructions of history behind texts as constructions, formulated and advanced by flesh-and-blood readers. In other words, no model, retrieval, or reconstruction is seen as beyond interpretation and controlling interpretation. Finally, the proposal forms part of a much larger process of decolonization and liberation taking place in the discipline since the mid-1970s; in fact, it extends such a process from the realm of theory and methodology into the realm of human diversity. As such, it continues to break down the traditional and fundamental Eurocentric moorings and boundaries of the discipline in favor of a multidimensional and decentered mode of discourse, a global discourse in which all readers have a voice and engage one another out of their own respective social locations, out of their own otherness.

In what follows, then, I begin with an analysis of the social location of the diaspora and my own position within the diaspora as a Hispanic American; then, I proceed to outline the basic contours of the proposed hermeneutics of the diaspora.

---

4. For what follows see my introduction to the present volume.

The Diaspora as Social Location

The Context of the Diaspora

Diasporas are not all the same: they are highly complex and multidimensional realities. A beginning distinction in this regard is, I believe, in order and helpful. At its most general level, the diaspora represents the sum total of all those who presently live, for whatever reason, on a permanent basis in a country other than that of their birth. Diasporas involve migration, therefore, and are, at their very core, political phenomena, involving changes in sociopolitical status and/or affiliation. As such, they affect the world as a whole: the First World; the Second World, or the former communist bloc; and the Third World. At the same time, the reasons for expatriation and the resultant status of the expatriates vary enormously in each case.

Thus, for example, with regard to the first two types of diaspora, the reality of expatriation for academicians or highly trained professionals of the United States or Western Europe who choose to live their lives in the other continent is very different from the reality of the former political refugees from behind the Iron Curtain who fled to and settled in the West or the reality of the unemployed masses of workers from the former Eastern Europe now seeking employment in Western Europe. I belong to neither one of these realities and cannot speak for them, although I suspect that the ongoing diaspora involving the former denizens of the communist bloc has a great deal in common with the diaspora of the Third World; after all, such a situation can ultimately be described as well in terms of a colonizer/colonized relationship, given the hegemonic role and power of the former Soviet Union in these countries and the devastating economic conditions left behind by the imperial center after its collapse and withdrawal.

It is with the third type of diaspora mentioned above, therefore, that I am specifically concerned, that is, with that large and growing segment of people from the Third World who are forced to live—for whatever reason, though usually involving a combination of sociopolitical and socioeconomic factors—in the First World, whether in Europe, Japan, or the United States.[5] By and large, these are the children of colonialism and neocolonialism: people from the world of the colonized who now have to live in the world of the colonizers, from the world of the poor and undeveloped/developing South who now have to live in the world of the rich and developed North. Given the traditional relationship between colonizers and colonized—a relationship profoundly marked by a

---

5. On the political dynamics involved in such diasporas, see the excellent study by M. J. Esman, "The Political Fallout of International Migration," *Diaspora* 2 (1992) 3–41.

set of binary oppositions ultimately grounded in those of center/margins and civilization/primitivism—such a reality is global and comprehensive. At the same time, to be sure, within such a reality, distinctions have to be made, based on a number of different factors: despite overall similarities, it is far different to be a farm worker than to be an accountant or engineer, to have "colored" skin rather than "white" skin, and to be male rather than female. It is this diaspora in which I find myself "thrown" (*arrojado*) as a human being, as a critic, and as a theologian; it is this diaspora, therefore, that serves not only as a fundamental constitutive factor for my social location but also as a point of departure for my critical and theological voice.[6]

In what follows I proceed to analyze my own position within such a diaspora as a Hispanic American, with an emphasis on the general characteristics or similarities of this reality rather than on its distinguishing features or characteristics.[7] Such a diaspora is, of course, a diaspora of the Western Hemisphere: the children of Latin America and the Caribbean who are forced to live in the North for a variety of interrelated and interdependent reasons. Within such a diaspora, those of us from the Spanish-speaking countries of Latin America have become known as Hispanic Americans. It is from such a corner of the diaspora that I set out to construct a hermeneutics of the diaspora, a hermeneutics of otherness and engagement.

The Context of the Hispanic-American Diaspora

As a Hispanic American, I belong to a large group of people for whom biculturalism constitutes a fundamental and inescapable way of life.[8] Such biculturalism reveals two essential dimensions. On the one hand, we live in two worlds at one and the same time, operating relatively at ease within each world and able to go in and out of each in an endless exercise of human and social translation; on the other hand, we live in

---

6. Just as I find myself "thrown" by birth into a discourse of colonialism and neocolonialism, I also find myself "thrown," as a result of such a discourse, into the further discourse of the "diaspora." In other words, the triple-layered colonial subject by birth becomes through migration and exile a minority subject within an alien and alienating culture; see the introduction to this book.

7. For descriptions of the social location of Hispanic Americans, see, for example, V. Elizondo, *Galilean Journey: The Mexican American Promise* (Maryknoll, N.Y.: Orbis Books, 1983) 5–46; A. Figueroa Deck, *The Second Wave: Hispanic Ministry and the Evangelization of Cultures* (New York: Paulist Press, 1989) 9–25; J. L. González, *Mañana: Christian Theology from a Hispanic Perspective* (Nashville: Abingdon, 1990) 31–53; and idem, "Hispanics in the United States," *Listening: Journal of Religion and Culture* 27 (1992) 7–16.

8. The following working definition of Hispanic Americans is operative throughout: individuals of Hispanic descent, associated in one way or another with the Americas, who now live, for any number of reasons, on a permanent basis in the United States. For the rationale and attendant problems, see my "Hispanic American Theology," 25–30.

neither one of these worlds, regarded askance by their respective populations and unable to call either world home. Thus, our biculturalism results in a very paradoxical and alienating situation involving a continuous twofold existence as permanent strangers or aliens, as permanent "others." It is a situation that I have described elsewhere as having both two places and no place on which to stand.[9] This situation of double and reinforced otherness may be further delineated as follows:[10]

1. As Hispanic Americans, our present, permanent, and everyday world is that of the United States, whether we are born or naturalized citizens, legal or illegal aliens. In this world we immediately find—much to the surprise of those of us who are immigrants, given our image of the country from the outside as a bastion of freedom, justice, and opportunity[11]—that there is a script ready for us to play and follow, outside of which we dare venture only against great odds and with considerable opposition. This script involves a name, a pattern, and a value judgment.

First, the name does vary, with Hispanics, Hispanic Americans, and Latinos as recurrent options; the important point in this regard, however, is that we use none of these names for ourselves. The names are given to us and thus form part of the script itself. Second, the pattern

9. F. F. Segovia, "Two Places and No Place on Which to Stand: Mixture and Otherness in Hispanic American Theology," *Listening: Journal of Religion and Culture* 27 (1992) 26–40.

10. Again, though Hispanic Americans constitute a distinct and identifiable social configuration, the group does encompass a variety of similarly distinct and identifiable subgroups. To be sure, any description of the Hispanic-American experience and reality will bear the imprint of the describer, even when the explicit aim of the description is to focus on the common characteristics rather than the distinguishing features. From a methodological point of view, therefore, it is important to describe this angle of vision, given the diversity that characterizes the group: the voice and perspective that follow are those of a first-generation immigrant of Caribbean descent, a naturalized citizen and original refugee from the Cuban experience of neocolonialism and colonialism, of political convulsion and exile.

11. Such an image is not at all surprising. It is a direct product of colonialism and neocolonialism. The colonized believe—and have been taught to believe—that the world of the colonizers is a superior world, where civilization, however conceived, has reached its zenith and now reaches out to the rest of the world. As a result, whatever is autochthonous or indigenous is regarded as ultimately inferior to what lies at the seat of the empire. This image has of course its counterpart among the colonizers: to lead and guide the inferior and the primitive to civilization, with contempt and derision going hand in hand with authoritarianism and paternalism. Given this bipolar view of the world on both sides, one can begin to understand the shock of the colonized within the womb of the colonizer: the exported image of civilization is very different from the everyday reality, especially with regard to their own perception within that civilization. On the contrast between colonizer and colonized, see the classic study by A. Memmi, *The Colonizer and the Colonized* (New York: Orion Press, 1965). For a sharp description of the relationship between the dominant and the subordinate from a feminist perspective, see J. Baker Miller, *Toward a New Psychology of Women* (2d ed.; Boston: Beacon, 1986) 3–12; for a very interesting view of this relationship on the part of a Protestant Hispanic American, see González, *Mañana*, 21–30.

behind the name is consistent and inflexible: regardless of geographical
or social origins, we are all seen in terms of a rather monolithic and
undifferentiated mass. Again, we have but little choice in this regard,
with no amount of explanation seemingly capable of altering the established pattern. Third, the value judgment that underlies the pattern
is not only similarly rigid and unchanging but also quite disparaging
and destructive. Its overall contours encompass such attributes as lazy
and unenterprising, carefree and sensual, undisciplined and violent, vul-
gar and unintelligent; its corresponding images in popular culture come
readily to mind: the Puerto Rican gangs of the film *West Side Story;*
the Mexican outlaws or *bandidos* of countless Westerns; the drug lords
and pushers of *Miami Vice* and a host of other television programs; the
happy-go-lucky Carmen Mirandas and Ricky Ricardos of this world.
Thus, the name and the pattern are by no means neutral but reveal and
convey a dominant perception of the group as primitive, inferior, and
uncivilized. Once again, we find ourselves tightly locked into this external view of ourselves, with protestation or enlightenment as a seemingly
useless enterprise. In our present, permanent, and everyday world, therefore, we begin as strangers and we remain strangers throughout—the
undesirable "others," the ones who do not fit.

2. As Hispanic Americans, directly or indirectly, our former, traditional, and distant world is that of Latin America, even for those whose
world was annexed by the United States, as is the case with Puerto
Rico and the formerly Mexican territories of the Southwest. Contrary
to popular perception in the United States, this former world of ours
is a world of profound differences, incredible diversity, and great richness. First, in direct contrast to the homogeneity ascribed to us via
name and pattern in our present world, we hail from many and enormously diverse quarters—many countries and areas, each with its own
distinctive history, traditions, and culture—and we call ourselves mainly
by our place of origin, for example, Dominicans, Puerto Ricans, Sal-
vadorans. Similarly, in direct contrast to the judgment rendered against
us, we represent, in varying degrees and configurations, a new *raza,* a
rich mixture of races and cultures, encompassing European, African,
Amerindian, and even Asian components. Ironically, such elements have
perhaps never interacted before to the extent that they now do in the
United States, especially given our present numbers as the equivalent of
the fifth most populous nation in Latin America, so that in effect the
emerging Hispanic-American reality in the United States may in the end
give rise to an even greater degree of biological and cultural mixture
than ever before.[12]

_____

12. On this point, see the sharp remarks by González, "Hispanics in the United
States," 11–14.

Yet with each passing year in our present world, we realize that our traditional world is no longer ours: our association with it has become remote, at best intermittent, and passive. In fact, from the point of view of our former world, we encounter yet another script ready for us to play and follow, outside of which we can venture but not very far. The script has a name: the (willing or unwilling) emigrant or expatriate, such as the Mexican-American *pocho* or the Puerto Rican *neorican;* an ironic pattern: getting ahead in the land of freedom, justice, and opportunity; and an even more ironic value judgment: culturally disconnected but economically superior. This script, however, is far more understandable, given our absence and distance, and much more benign, given an abiding sense of ultimate, even if conditioned, acceptance. In our former, traditional, and distant world, therefore, we gradually and inevitably become and remain aliens as well—the distant "others," the ones who left.

3. We are thus always strangers or aliens, the permanent "others," both where we came from and where we find ourselves. As such, we find ourselves always defined by somebody else—in our traditional world by those whom we left behind and in our present world by those with whom we live; silenced and speechless—without an autochthonous, self-conscious, and firm voice; and without a home of our own—excluded and condemned by such external definitions and such lack of voice. On the one hand, we know and understand, however regretfully and painfully, the definition of those we left behind—a permanent and living association elsewhere does remove one slowly but surely from one's traditional world. On the other hand, we suffer and fail to comprehend the definition of those with whom we live—our permanent and every-day association is disdained and rejected. Such "otherness," bestowed upon us and defined for us, overwhelms and overrides us, depriving us not only of a present, past, and future but also of self-definition, self-appropriation, and self-direction.

Such a constitutive and alienating "otherness" can be, as is often the case, internalized and lived out, resulting in the classic pattern of the colonized—passivity, submission, obedience. To be sure, this process of internalization can and does range anywhere from the truly constitutive or existential (the full acceptance of the external definition as the self-definition) to the purely strategic or tactical (the surface adoption of the external definition as a way of survival). Such "otherness," however, can also be turned into a point of departure for the formulation of our own voice, a voice that not only makes explicit the spirit of independence, resistance, and rebellion that so often lies beneath the surface of the friendly and hospitable colonized but also gives rise to the classic pattern of the colonizer, the pattern of manifest destiny—self-confidence, self-expression, and self-determination. For me it is precisely this latter option that gives rise to the voice behind the theology of otherness and mixture, the hermeneutics of otherness and engagement, and the interpretive strategy of intercultural criticism.

Toward a Hispanic-American Voice

Given this social location of ours as Hispanic Americans, we must claim our *otherness* and turn it precisely into what it is, our very identity, using it constructively and creatively in the interest of liberation, not only on our behalf but on behalf of others as well.[13] I would argue, therefore, that our theological and hermeneutical voice must be grounded in and grow out of this identity of otherness.

1. To begin with, this otherness does indeed have another and much more positive dimension. While our paradoxical situation does mean having no place to stand, it also means having two places on which to stand, a second fundamental dimension that cannot be overlooked or bypassed. The very source of our alienation becomes thereby the very source of our identity. While regarded as "others" in both worlds of our existence, the fact remains that we do live in both worlds and that we do know how to proceed, at a moment's notice, from one world to the other. In other words, we know both worlds quite well from the inside and the outside, and this privileged knowledge of ours gives us a rather unique perspective: we know that both worlds, that all worlds, are constructions, rather solid and firm constructions to be sure, but constructions nonetheless. We know from our very experience that "nature" is itself a construction and its "laws" conventions. We know what makes each world cohere and function; we can see what is good and bad in each world and choose accordingly; and we are able to offer an informed critique of each world—its vision, its values, its traditions.

This privileged knowledge allows us in the end to see our own reality as others in terms of construction—understanding thereby the attributes of and rationale for our perception as "others"; to use this reality to our own advantage—giving such otherness a voice of its own; and to do so critically, not in terms of "nature" and "laws" but rather in terms of our own power to construct ourselves and others—avoiding thereby all semblance of a new romanticism or a new imperialism, a utopian or messianic interpretation of our otherness, whereby such otherness becomes idealized or exclusionist. In the end, any such glorification of our

---

13. To do so does not imply a rejection of our tradition of mixture. Given our historical racial, cultural, and theological rejection by the mainstream or dominant culture, liberation becomes self-affirmation in the face of the mainstream—resisting colonization, so to speak. In a fundamentally segregationist culture, the very possibility of a continued mixture demands, for the mixture to be voluntary and not forced, sustained opposition and resistance, a decentering of the center, a valuation of the margin in the face of the center. Thus, quite ironically, self-affirmation becomes not at all a rejection of mixture but an option for proper and respectful mixture in the face of cultural annihilation.

otherness would only serve to define and silence those who are others to us, doing thereby unto others what others have done to us.

2. Giving a voice to this otherness of ours entails a threefold critical process of self-affirmation: (*a*) self-appropriation, or a revisioning of our past and our history with our own eyes; (*b*) self-definition, or a retelling of our present reality and experience in our own words; and (*c*) self-direction, or a reclaiming of our future and self-determination in terms of our own dreams and visions. Thus, the process entails, on the one hand, an active refusal to be bound by our imposed definitions, with a corresponding commitment to understand, expose, and critique such definitions; on the other hand, the process also entails an active determination to offer our own self-definitions, with a corresponding commitment not only to the self-affirmation of others but also to a critical exchange with such others and their own corresponding self-affirmations. As such, the process of self-affirmation envisioned is one that confers dignity, liberation, and openness not only on the group itself but on all other groups—a manifest destiny that goes against the very grain of manifest destiny, that redefines and reenvisions the very notion of manifest destiny.

3. In this process of self-affirmation, we must fully acknowledge, embrace, and integrate the fundamental characteristics of our otherness. First, we do well to remember our sociocultural past in a world where mixture is regarded as highly problematic and indeed offensive. We are a hybrid people, with biological and/or cultural miscegenation at our very core. This indiscriminate mixture, this *mezcolanza*,[14] brings together in many and varied ways the heritage of Europe via Mediterranean and Catholic Spain, of Africa and America, as well as of Asia (though to a much lesser extent). Though it is in large part because of such mixture that we find rejection in our present world, we must emphasize and embrace mixture: for us mixture is life and gives life. Second, we do well to remember our sociohistorical and sociopolitical past. Our mixture is by no means the result of an irenic encounter and coexistence but rather of a harsh and cruel tradition of colonialism and neocolonialism. Such a tradition has given rise to a history of violence and oppression, tyranny and corruption. Yet, despite such history and tradition, we have also manifested an enduring commitment to freedom, life, and dignity. We must emphasize and embrace such a commitment: in the very midst of chaos and death, we struggle for life and enjoyment of life. Third, we do well to remember our sociocultural present. We find ourselves not

---

14. I deliberately employ the term *mezcolanza* rather than *mezcla,* the proper translation for "mixture," to convey the highly indiscriminate—motley; unplanned; haphazard—character of the mixture; its meaning is best captured perhaps by the English terms "hotchpotch" or "jumble."

only the target of sustained discrimination, socially and culturally rejected at all levels of life, but also in a situation of widespread social devastation—politically powerless, economically deprived, and educationally fragile. At the same time, we struggle to make a home under the democratic principles of the nation, hoping that our commitment to life can ultimately take root and grow. We must emphasize and embrace this struggle as well: despite often unbearable conditions, we continue to believe in and strive for our dream of freedom, justice, and opportunity in a new home.

This embrace of mixture, life, and struggle should ultimately provide us with an identity that recognizes the others but refuses to define them, as we ourselves have been and continue to be defined; that allows such others to speak and to define themselves, in contrast to our own silencing and silence; that is committed not to a placid exchange of views with these others but to hard critical exchange, including the very construction of others as others. Thus, the voice of our otherness becomes a voice of and for liberation: not afraid to expose, critique, and provide an alternative vision and narrative; grounded in mixture as something not to be eschewed and marginalized but valued and engaged; and committed to the fundamental principles of freedom and justice. From such a voice emerges a profound commitment not to overwhelm or override the other but rather to acknowledge it, value it, engage it—a theology of mixture and otherness, a hermeneutics of otherness and engagement, and a reading strategy of intercultural criticism.

Toward a Hermeneutics of the Diaspora: The Text as Other

The voice of *otherness* begins with contextualization and aims for it. In reference to biblical criticism, it argues that contextualization is imperative with regard to the biblical texts as well as with regard to their readers and critics.[15] In effect, it sees a genuine exchange with otherness—the otherness both of the text and of other readers of the text—as impossible without a preliminary renunciation of presumed universality and objectivity and a corresponding admission and acceptance of contextuality. It is a voice that seeks not a dehumanization or rehumanization of the reader but a liberating and empowering humanization of

---

15. The question is not, therefore, whether there should be historical criticism; it is a point I readily grant. The question rather is what kind of historical criticism should there be. What is rejected is historical criticism as traditionally practiced. On the fundamental questions involved, see L. Hutcheon, *The Politics of Postmodernism* (New Accents; New York: Routledge, 1989) 62–92; and H. White, "The Fictions of Factual Representation," *Tropics of Discourse: Essays in Cultural Criticism* (Baltimore: Johns Hopkins Univ. Press, 1978) 121–34.

the reader, of all readers, by taking fully into account the experience and culture of readers in the act of reading and interpretation. Such is the basis for a diaspora hermeneutics of otherness and engagement, from which emerges the proposed reading strategy of intercultural criticism.

Its theoretical foundation in literary criticism is that of reader-response criticism, involving a fundamental position to the effect that no text is read, understood, or interpreted without a reader and a corresponding view of meaning as the result of interaction between the reader and the text. Within this overall theoretical orientation, a broad interpretive spectrum can be readily outlined, ranging from a reader-dominant pole (with meaning coming primarily from the reader either as an individual subject or as a member of an interpretive community) to a text-dominant pole (with meaning coming primarily from the text in terms of its own strategies and constraints).[16] Within this theoretical spectrum, I would locate intercultural criticism to the left of center, toward the reader-dominant pole, with a view of meaning as the result of interaction between a socially and culturally conditioned reader and a socially and culturally conditioned text, with such a reader as an inevitable and ever-present filter in the reading and interpretation of such a text. In what follows I should like to explore these three basic dimensions of intercultural criticism.

First, the text is to be regarded, like any contemporary social group, as a socially and culturally conditioned other. The question of access is crucial. Rather than positing any type of direct or immediate entrance into the text, the hermeneutics of otherness and engagement argues for distantiation from it as a working desideratum, emphasizing thereby the historical and cultural remoteness of the text. Such a hermeneutics begins, therefore, by recognizing that the biblical text comes from a very different historical situation and cultural matrix, a very different experience and culture; that all texts, including the biblical texts, are contextual products; and that no text—not even the biblical text—is atemporal, asocial, ahistorical, speaking uniformly across time and culture.

---

16. On reader-response criticism, see V. B. Leitch, *American Literary Criticism from the Thirties to the Eighties* (New York: Columbia Univ. Press, 1988) 210–37; J. P. Tompkins, "An Introduction to Reader Response Criticism," *Reader Response Criticism: From Formalism to Post-Structuralism* (ed. J. P. Tompkins; Baltimore: Johns Hopkins Univ. Press, 1980) ix–xxvi; S. Suleiman, "Introduction: Varieties of Audience-Oriented Criticism," *The Reader in the Text: Essays on Audience and Interpretation* (ed. S. Suleiman; Princeton, N.J.: Princeton Univ. Press, 1980) 3–45. On reader-response criticism in biblical criticism, see R. S. Fowler, "Who Is the 'Reader' in Reader-Response Criticism?" *Reader Response Approaches to Biblical and Secular Texts* (ed. R. Detweiler; Semeia 31; Decatur, Ga.: Scholars Press, 1985) 5–23; B. Lategan, "Introduction: Coming to Grips with the Reader in Biblical Literature," *Reader Perspectives on the New Testament* (ed. E. V. McKnight; Semeia 49; Atlanta: Scholars Press, 1989) 3–20.

This operative attitude of distantiation grows out of our bicultural reality as Hispanic Americans. First, this experience shows us that all reality is construction and, as such, profoundly historical and cultural. Second, this experience further shows us that external perceptions of ourselves as "others" revolve around the stereotypical and fail to respect our otherness, readily overriding and overwhelming our sense of identity, with disastrous and long-lasting consequences for us both as a group and as individuals. Out of such experience emerges a key element in the theology of mixture and otherness: a commitment to understand those who function as others to us—the many social groups with whom we relate and coexist, even within our own social configuration—in terms of their own words and visions, by allowing them to speak on their own, to create their own narrative, and to define their own identity. Out of this experience emerges as well a key element in the hermeneutics of otherness and engagement: a commitment to understand the biblical text—or any other text for that matter—as an other to us, with its own words and visions, allowing it to speak on its own, to unravel its own narrative, and to define its own identity. In effect, if contemporary and coexisting social groups prove to be so different from and so puzzling to one another, then one is justified in calling into question any type of immediate and unqualified identification with texts that come from a very different historical situation and cultural framework.

For intercultural criticism, therefore, the contextuality and otherness of the text must be acknowledged, valued, and analyzed. This process of distantiation is helped immensely by a view of the text as a literary, rhetorical, and ideological product in its own right: an artistic construction with underlying strategic concerns and goals in the light of its own point of view, its own vision of the world and reality, within a given historical and cultural matrix. As such, a consideration of the text as other should avail itself of any variety of literary and sociocultural methodologies that allow us to bring this multidimensional character of the text to the fore. The ultimate aim of such an enterprise would be an understanding of the text as a whole, as a world of its own, as a construct within a more comprehensive historical-cultural framework—no matter how strange or remote.

Second, the reader is also to be regarded as socially and culturally conditioned, as an other to both text and other readers. The question of critical honesty is crucial. Rather than seeking after impartiality or objectivity, presuming to universality, and claiming to read like anyone or everyone, the hermeneutics of otherness and engagement argues for a self-conscious exposition and analysis of the reader's strategy for reading, the theoretical foundations behind this strategy, and the social location underlying such a strategy. This hermeneutics further begins, therefore, by recognizing that the reader, like the text, comes from a specific historical situation and cultural matrix, a specific experience and culture; that all readers are contextual products and that such different social locations can and do influence the process of reading and interpretation; and that no reader—not even an ideal or highly informed one—is atemporal, asocial, or ahistorical, speaking uniformly for all times and cultures.

This attitude of self-conscious reflection grows out of our bicultural reality as Hispanic Americans. First, this experience shows us that all reality, as construction, has its own way of seeing and acting and that such vision and behavior have in turn their own historical and cultural roots. Second, this experience also shows us that it is possible to live and function with relative ease in more than one reality, putting on and removing the proper lenses of each reality or world as the occasion warrants. From such an experience, once again, an important element in the theology of otherness and mixture comes to the fore: a commitment to acknowledge and allow for the voice of otherness in a world of incredible diversity. From such an experience, furthermore, an important element in the hermeneutics of otherness and engagement comes to the fore: a commitment to see readers, all readers and readings, as distinct and autonomous voices within such a rich diversity. In effect, if we ourselves know how to "read" reality with more than one lens, then one is fully justified in positing an enormous variety of such lenses and readings, both in the present and in antiquity.

For intercultural criticism, therefore, the contextuality and otherness of readers must also be acknowledged, valued, and analyzed. This process of conscious self-reflection is helped immensely by a view of the reader as a product, a "text" as it were, in his or her own right: a historical and cultural construction involving a view of the past, the present, and the future. Consequently, a consideration of the reader as other should avail itself of any variety of social and cultural methodologies that would bring to the fore this multidimensional identity of the reader, with a systematic and sustained analysis of such factors as socioreligious tradition and affiliation, ideological stance, sociopolitical status and affiliation, socioeconomic class, gender, racial or ethnic background, sociocultural conventions, and socioeducational attainment. The ultimate aim of such an analysis would be an understanding of the reader as a whole, as a world of his or her own, as a construct within a more comprehensive historical and cultural matrix—again no matter how strange or remote.

Finally, the interaction between such a text and such a reader is to be regarded not as a neutral encounter between two independent, socially and culturally conditioned entities or worlds, but rather as an unavoidable filtering of the one world or entity by and through the other, of the text by and through the reader. In this regard both the question of access and the question of critical honesty are crucial. Despite the attitude of distantiation from the text, the hermeneutics of otherness and engagement argues that the historical and cultural remoteness of the text as an other is in itself not a reconstruction but a construction of the past on the part of the reader. Despite the attitude of conscious self-reflection, this hermeneutics further argues that such a construction of the past is dependent as well on the reader's own social location. The hermeneutics of otherness and engagement continues, therefore, by recognizing that the very process of distantiation ultimately comes out of a specific historical situation and cultural matrix, a specific experience and culture; that the results of such a process are likewise contextual products, influenced by the social location of the reader in question; and that no process of distantiation—not even a properly informed and self-conscious one—is in itself atemporal, asocial, or ahistorical.

This attitude regarding the interaction between the reader and the text again grows out of our bicultural reality as Hispanic Americans. First, this experience shows us that all reality, though construction, is quite resistant to change, that it is not at all easy to go against or deviate from historical and cultural roots. Second, this experience further shows us that the external perception of ourselves as "others" stubbornly resists any type of critical questioning or enlightenment, often turning the whole exercise of conscientization into a frustrating Sisyphean task. Third, this experience also shows us that such a fundamental sense of reality as construction is very difficult to attain within a monocultural matrix. Out of this experience emerges a key element in the theology of mixture and otherness: a commitment to critical dialogue and exchange with the other, subjecting our respective views of one another and the world to critical exposure and analysis. Out of this experience emerges as well a key element in the hermeneutics of otherness and engagement: first, a commitment to critical dialogue and exchange with the text as other, subjecting our respective views of the world to critical exposure and analysis; second, a commitment to critical dialogue and exchange with other interpreters of the text, both historical and contemporary, again subjecting our respective views of the text and its world to critical exposure and analysis. In effect, if contemporary and coexisting social groups prove so resistant to change with respect to one another, even in the face of sharp critique and protestations, then one is fully justified in seeing all reconstruction of the past as another form of construction, no matter how well-informed or self-conscious it may be, especially given the inability of the text to engage in a similar process of critique and protestation.

For intercultural criticism, therefore, the interchange between the reader and the text must be seen in terms of both construction and engagement. On the one hand, the process of distantiation is helped immensely by a view of all reconstruction as construction. In other words, even when attempting to understand the text as an other to us, historically and culturally removed, we ultimately play a major role in the construction of such otherness; thus, even when considering the text as a literary, rhetorical, and ideological product, we ultimately have a major hand in the very identification and articulation of its literary structure and development, its rhetorical concerns and aims, its ideological thrust, and its relationship to its historical and cultural matrix. On the other hand, the process of self-reflection is helped immensely by a comprehensive and critical engagement both with the text as other and with others regarding their own constructions of the text. First, an understanding of the text as an other to us demands critical engagement with it—a thorough evaluation of its world, strategy, and applicability in terms of the reader's own historical and cultural context; the goal of such an engagement is none other than that of liberation itself. Second, in attempting to understand the text as an other to us, it is necessary to understand as well how the text has been interpreted by others, by readers in a variety of different historical situations and cultural frameworks. Such an understanding also demands critical engagement with these others—a thorough evaluation of reading strategies, theoretical orientations, social locations, as well as interpretive results, reception, and aftereffects; again, the goal of such engagement is none other than liberation itself.

Concluding Comments

Such then are the essential characteristics of the envisioned hermeneutics of the diaspora, a hermeneutics of otherness and engagement, and the basic principles for its proposed methodological approach, the reading strategy of intercultural criticism.

I see this hermeneutics of the diaspora—specifically grounded in and informed by the social location of Hispanic Americans—as having a manifest destiny of liberation and decolonization. Thus, it begins with and aims for contextualization—it puts aside and calls into question any claim to be objective and scientific, neutral and impartial, universal. Likewise, it opts for humanization and diversity—it resists both dehumanization, any divestiture of all those identity factors that constitute and characterize the reader as reader, and rehumanization, any attempt to force all readers into one and the same particular and contextualized discussion. Finally, it seeks to acknowledge, respect, and engage the other—it opposes any attempt, implicit or explicit, to overwhelm or override the other, to impose a definition upon it, to turn the other into an "other."

I also see the reading strategy of intercultural criticism not as the sole, proper, and definitive strategy for reading from within the diaspora of the Third World or even the diaspora of Hispanic Americans in particular, but as one such strategy among many, as one way of approaching and interpreting the biblical texts, with a similar dream and task of liberation in mind. Indeed, were I to argue otherwise, the results would be distinctly counterproductive: I would be going directly against the enormous diversity to be found not only within the diaspora itself but also among Hispanic Americans in particular; I would end up advancing yet another master or totalizing narrative, universalizing my own strategy and project for all and thus effectively ruling out other such strategies and projects arising out of the same social location; and I would be defeating the whole project of liberation and decolonization, preventing others from speaking out in their own voices and thus in the end overwhelming the very otherness I set out to rescue and foreground. At the same time, I would argue that all such strategies should strive to engage one another as well as other strategies in critical dialogue. In fact, were I to argue otherwise, the consequences would be, once again, distinctly counterproductive: I would be ultimately abetting a gradual and inevitable absolutizing or totalizing of such strategies into master narratives, through both an avoidance of much-needed criticism and a failure to benefit from the voices and perspectives of others.

In conclusion, I believe that a hermeneutics of otherness must go hand in hand with a hermeneutics of engagement, and that I see as the very essence of the proposed hermeneutics of the diaspora.

3

Social Location and the Hermeneutical Mode of Integration

"Reading from this place" implies *Dasein,* a "being-there" at a particular time and place in history.[1] It presupposes the limitations of finitude that predetermine the understanding that is generated by the process of reading. The historicity of understanding, therefore, is distinguished by the distinctive cultural horizon into which one has been socialized; the establishment of an identity structure that is dialectically a production of a particular society and the individual self; and systems of signs, including language, that both constitute and communicate the unique reality of the world that is inhabited.[2] Not the least, the understanding of *Dasein* also involves ideologies and creeds that have been shaped by the realities of class, gender, race, and religion within that society, along with the perceptions and prejudices that they generate.[3]

In the finiteness and historicity of "being-there"—distinguished by its comprehensive process of socialization—understanding, the objective of reading, like understanding in general, is made possible by the operations of a preunderstanding. Consisting of structures of meaning, which function as preconceptions and prejudgments—or prejudices!— and which are continuously being enlarged and reshaped, reason and its preunderstanding project expectations of meaning into the realities of everyday experience. When the projections correspond to "the things

---

1. For an analysis of *Dasein,* see M. Heidegger, *Being and Time* (New York: Harper and Row, 1962) 78–90. Although Heidegger denies that his analysis of *Dasein* should be interpreted ontically in historical terms, the word itself, apart from a Heideggerian sense, is useful in this context. Moreover, as A. Megili states, "Certain aspects of *Being and Time* do suggest precisely the sort of view that Heidegger disavows" (*Prophets of Extremity* [Berkeley: Univ. of California Press, 1987] 125).
2. See P. Berger and T. Luckmann, *The Social Construction of Reality* (Garden City, N.Y.: Doubleday, 1966) 119–68.
3. See, for example, D. M. Lowe, *History of Bourgeois Perception* (Chicago: Univ. of Chicago Press, 1982).

themselves," that is, the realities that are to be grasped, the potentiality of understanding is actualized.[4]

Understanding, therefore, is subject to the boundedness and limitations of "being-there." The neutrality of scientific objectivity is unattainable. A Cartesian purification of the mind is impossible! The preconceptions and prejudices of the preunderstanding cannot be bracketed or removed; indeed, in actuality they facilitate understanding. Of course, not all of them promote openness and enable understanding. Hans-Georg Gadamer differentiates between "blind prejudices" and "justified prejudices productive of knowledge" and breaks with the tradition of the Enlightenment by associating the latter with the authority of both reason and tradition. "If the prestige of authority displaces one's own judgment, then authority is in fact a source of prejudices. But this does not preclude its being a source of truth, and that is what the Enlightenment failed to see when it denigrated all authority."[5] Thus, tradition or authority, like reason, can promote openness to the world and advance understanding and truth. As a matter of fact, the structures of reason are determined by tradition and its predispositions and cannot function without them. Indeed, tradition and the predispositions that it embodies may in fact constitute a unified-field theory, a paradigm, a configuration of interconnections that builds world and simultaneously facilitates understanding.[6]

Accordingly, the structures and meanings of preunderstanding, which to one extent or another include tradition and all of its prejudices and predispositions, initiate the hermeneutical circle of understanding. Living within this bounded circle is the fundamental character of being-in-the-world, of *Dasein;* and it is within this circle that meaning is generated.

Reading as an activator of meaning naturally participates in this hermeneutical circle. Its material cause, like the activity of understanding in general, is always an "other"; in the case of reading, of course, it is the alterity of a text. As the "thing itself," which marks the beginning and the end of every hermeneutical enterprise of reading, the written word, whatever its age or character, "is the intelligibility of mind transferred

---

4. As H.-G. Gadamer asserts, "Every hermeneutical understanding begins and ends with the 'thing itself' " ("The Problem of Historical Consciousness," *Interpretive Social Science: A Reader* [ed. P. Rabinow and W. M. Sullivan; Berkeley: Univ. of California Press, 1979] 159. Also: "Interpretation begins with fore-conceptions that are replaced by more suitable ones. This constant process of new projection constitutes the movement of understanding and interpretation" (*Truth and Method* [2d ed.; New York: Crossroad, 1989] 267).

5. Gadamer, *Truth and Method,* 279. See idem, "Prejudices as Conditions of Understanding," in *Truth and Method,* 277–85.

6. On paradigms, see T. S. Kuhn, *The Structure of Scientific Revolutions* (2d ed.; Chicago: Univ. of Chicago Press, 1970) 43–51, 174–210.

to the most alien medium."[7] Needless to say, the Bible is no exception to this principle. Its texts, torn from their original contexts, require some kind of historical mediation, even though their historical distance is overcome—to some degree at least—by their meaningful presence as authoritative tradition, namely, a body of Scripture that is considered to be a bearer of the word of God.

Reconstruction and *integration* are two hermeneutical modes of interpretive understanding that have been employed to mediate the historical distance between the biblical texts and contemporary readers.[8] Modern hermeneutics was inaugurated with the mode of reconstruction. According to Friedrich Schleiermacher, understanding is the art of reexperiencing the mental processes of the author. It is both a comparative and an intuitive/divinatory activity combining the objective, grammatical operation of moving from the part to the whole *and* the subjective/ psychological reconstruction of the author's thought by "transforming oneself into the other person in order to grasp his individuality directly."[9] Meaning resides in the recovery of the author's intellectual activity as it is expressed in and through the language of the text. "Grammatical interpretation comes first because in the final analysis both what is presupposed and what is to be discovered is language" (70). "One should construe the meaning from the total pre-given value of language and the heritage common to the author and his reader, for only by reference to this is interpretation possible" (70). The illumination that is provided by the text's context adds precision to the determination of meaning, for "the richness of meaning depends on when and where a work arose" (70). This includes an identification of the original addressees, so that "if one knows who these people were and what effect these passages were to have on them, then, since these factors determine the composition of the work, the interpreter knows everything that is necessary" (109).

Schleiermacher's hermeneutics of reproduction fostered the progression of historical consciousness and promoted the somewhat earlier development of historical criticism and its application to the biblical texts. The reconstruction of the texts' original contexts; the deciphering of the language of the biblical authors through linguistic parallels; the elucidation of such religious and cultural phenomena of antiquity as cult, magic, and myth, which had been denigrated by a scientifically oriented Western culture—all are considerable achievements of this hermeneutical methodology. The historical-critical method, source

---

7. Gadamer, *Truth and Method,* 163.
8. See ibid., 167.
9. F. Schleiermacher, *Hermeneutics: The Handwritten Manuscripts* (ed. H. Kimmerle; Atlanta: Scholars Press, 1977) 150; see also 64, 69.

criticism, the old and new quests of the historical Jesus, the literary-critical methods of form, tradition, and redaction criticisms—these are among its evolutionary derivatives by which historical mediation has been attempted.[10]

Integration is another hermeneutical mode of historical mediation. In contrast to reconstruction, however, it endeavors to secure the interiorization of textual meaning by a direct and immediate application to contemporary life. The interpretation of biblical texts, simply by reconnecting them to the organic vitalities of the context that produced them, cannot produce undistorted understanding. For the restoration of the past into the present is nothing more than a lifeless reproduction, existentially biased and incomplete at best. "Putting [the texts] back in their historical context does not give us a living relationship with them but rather a merely ideative representation."[11] Readers of the present cannot situate themselves in the place of the original addressees, nor can they achieve a personal or definite identity with the author.[12] The understanding of any text that has been separated from its original context and consequently has become a piece of universal tradition requires integration into the readers' contemporary situation.

The so-called New Criticism rejected both reconstruction and integration. Understanding is produced by a "close reading of the text" that concentrates on all the internal features of language, structure, coherence, style, and representation of reality. Form and content may be differentiated, but they are not separable. External realities, such as historical context, biographical information, causality, psychoanalytic or sociological data, are irrelevant to the determination of meaning.[13] Historical analysis is not entirely repudiated but limited to the elucidation of the text's language. Literary works should be treated as autonomous and objective texts, and their explication is achieved by a literary-critical analysis of the collaboration and modification of their individual parts in the formation of a comprehensive aesthetic unity.[14] The meaning that is construed is independent of the reader's affectations and is essentially a re-presentation of the human values of attitude, feelings, tensions, paradox, ambiguity, and irony communicated by the text: "What is immediately meant by words and [not] what is evoked by the meaning of words" determines interpretation.[15] Application or integration into the

---

10. See K. Stendahl, "Biblical Theology, Contemporary," *Interpreter's Dictionary of the Bible* (ed. G. A. Buttrick; Nashville: Abingdon, 1962) 418–31.

11. Gadamer, *Truth and Method,* 168.

12. Ibid., 266 n. 187.

13. See W. K. Wimsatt, "The Intentional Fallacy," *The Verbal Icon: Studies in the Meaning of Poetry* (Lexington: Univ. of Kentucky Press, 1967) 3–18.

14. See W. K. Wimsatt, "Explication as Criticism," *The Verbal Icon,* 235–51.

15. W. K. Wimsatt, "The Affective Fallacy," *The Verbal Icon,* 24.

reader's own context is a separate undertaking and is not to be confused with exegesis.

For Russian formalism, fundamentally oriented toward literary structure and technique, the hermeneutical mode of integration is achieved by the communicative instrument of form, the "how" rather than the "what" of literature. Since literary works must be considered to be autonomous, the subject of literary study is the distinctive nature of literary art in general, namely, the distinguishing features of literary texts and not those of their authors. Formalism is preoccupied with "images and all other purely literary devices such as phonetic patterns, rhyme, rhythm, meter, the use of sound not to represent sense but as a meaningful element in its own right."[16] The objective of these structural features is "to counteract the process of habituation, to deform the normal, to restructure the human perception of reality, to generate a heightened awareness."[17] Accordingly, a literary work is not to be treated simply as a text that has been torn from its context. In its very nature it functions to reverse the anesthetizing effects that language exerts on human perceptions and to make strange the reality structures of being-in-the-world. Historical mediation, therefore, is not achieved by a reproduction of the past but by the internalization of the subject-object division and its coincidental experience of alienation. Understanding, therefore, is the actualization and intensification of self-awareness through an encounter with the otherness of the text, specifically its distinctive literary qualities.

For literature, according to the formalists, has its own self-sufficient being. It is not a window through which other entities can be perceived. In spite of any pretensions toward realism that it might have, even when it attempts to be representative of the empirical world, it is determined by its own norms and conventions, as well as those of the language it employs.[18] It is self-contained and self-justifying; it has its own rules and requires no external validation. The words that are used in both poetic and narrative discourses have no external reference. Wolfgang Iser, proceeding from Charles Morris's essay "Esthetics and the Theory of Signs," summarizes:

> The symbols of literary language do not "represent" any empirical reality, but they do have a representative function. As this does not relate to an existing object, what is represented must be language itself. This means that literary speech represents ordinary speech, for it uses the same symbolic mode, but as it is without any of

---

16. T. Hawkes, *Structuralism and Semiotics* (Berkeley: Univ. of California Press, 1977) 62.

17. Ibid.

18. See J. Mukarovsky, "Standard Language and Poetic Language," *Critical Theory since Plato* (ed. H. Adams; San Diego: Harcourt Brace Jovanovich, 1971) 1050–57.

> the empirical references, it must increase the density of instructions
> to be imparted by the symbolic arrangement. . . . Fictional language
> provides instructions for the building of a situation and so for the
> production of an imaginary object.[19]

The signs that an author employs to build a narrative world constitute an arrangement of signifiers that do not refer to external objects,
but instead designate instructions for the production of the signified
by the reader.[20] Consequently, by the creative structuring of a plotline
accompanied by a calculated selection of content the traditional view
that a literary work of art is mimesis is negated. Historical mediation
through hermeneutical reconstruction is debarred. Integration is more or
less immediate. For both narrative and poetic discourse, as has already
been observed, convey their meaning by engendering the experiences of
defamiliarization and reconstruction of the human perception of reality.

Structural criticism is also oriented to the hermeneutical mode of integration. The text alone, and not the text placed into a reconstructed
context, is regarded as the sole source of meaning. But the text is a kind
of formless space whose shape is determined by structured modes of
reading. At the same time the preunderstanding with its forestructures
and prejudices is a social construct formed by the conventions of the
institution of literature in which both readers and authors participate.
"One can think of these conventions not simply as the implicit knowledge of the reader but also as the implicit knowledge of authors."[21]
Consequently, there is no useful distinction between reading and writing a text, for the linguistic and literary norms of a particular society
are equally operative in both. The semantic and pragmatic dimensions
of communication acts, namely, the relationship of sign to referent and
the relationship of sender and receiver respectively, play no role in the
production of meaning. Signification is limited to the generational ca-
pabilities of the infrastructure of the text, specifically the syntagmatic
and paradigmatic dimensions of language (*langue*). That is, on the one
hand, the relations of contiguity and the accompanying principles of
combination, and, on the other hand, the accompanying principles of
selection.[22]

---

19. W. Iser, *The Act of Reading: A Theory of Aesthetic Response* (Baltimore: Johns
Hopkins Univ. Press, 1978) 64. See also C. Morris, "Esthetics and the Theory of Signs,"
Journal of Unified Science 8 (1939) 131–50.

20. For an analysis of the difference between poetic and narrative modes of discourse,
see R. Jakobson, "The Metaphoric and Metonymic Poles," *Critical since Plato*, 1113–16.

21. J. Culler, *Structuralist Poetics: Structuralism, Linguistics and the Study of
Linguistics* (Ithaca, N.Y.: Cornell Univ. Press, 1975) 116.

22. S. Wittig, "A Theory of Multiple Meanings," *Polyvalent Narration* (ed. J. D.
Crossan; *Semeia* 9; Decatur, Ga.: Scholars Press, 1977) 81.

Integration, therefore, is a natural occurrence since the text is assumed to be "the product of perceptual structures which operate in the creator's mind at an unconscious level, rather than at a consciously artistic level." And concomitantly the semantic universe of the reader is presumed to be "conditioned to receive and decode the message at this unconscious level."[23] What is appropriated is not a system of ideas but rather "a system of deep values presupposed by conscious intellectual activity."[24] Essentially self-evident, "these deep values are truths that impose themselves upon us with such power that no further proof is needed in order to perceive their validity and reality."[25]

Of all the current literary-critical and hermeneutical theorists, reader-oriented critics operate in the hermeneutical mode of integration by concentrating their analysis of understanding on the effects that the reading process has on the reader. Although they represent a wide spectrum of theoretical orientations on the role that readers play in the determination of meaning, they are united in their rejection of the New Criticism's differentiation between "what is immediately meant by words and what is evoked by the meanings of words," between descriptive meaning and emotive meaning. For reader-response criticism the two are inseparable; understanding and significance are identical experiences. Through the process of reading, literature fundamentally communicates experience, not a detachable message, not meaning as a thing that can be extracted from the text as a kernel from a shell and exist independently of it.[26] The experience of reading produces the experience of meaning, and "meaning has no effective existence outside of its realization in the mind of a reader."[27] The understanding of texts, therefore, is determined by *Dasein*.

What divides reader-response critics are the issues of the objectivity of the text and the location of meaning. Walker Gibson's "mock reader," conceived analogously on the basis of literary criticism's earlier identification of a textually conveyed speaker (an implied author), distinguishes the reader in the production of meaning and initiates the gradual subver-

---

23. Ibid., 82. Also Culler, *Structuralist Poetics*, 118–21.

24. D. and A. Patte, *Structural Exegesis: From Theory to Practice* (Philadelphia: Fortress Press, 1978) 101.

25. Ibid. See also E. S. Malbon, "Structuralism, Hermeneutics, and Contextual Meaning," *Journal of the American Academy of Religion* 51/2 (1983) 213–15.

26. Extracting meaning as a thing, that is, a set of truths, from the text, is the modus operandi of redaction criticism, as the titles of various redactional-critical publications indicate. For example: H. Conzelmann's *The Theology of St. Luke* (New York: Harper and Row, 1961); and J. D. Kingsbury's *Matthew, Structure, Christology and Kingdom* (Philadelphia: Fortress Press, 1975). But see W. Iser's analysis of Henry James's story "The Figure in the Carpet" for a critical analysis of this activity (*The Act of Reading*, 3–19).

27. J. P. Tompkins, ed., *Reader-Response Criticism: From Formalism to Post-Structuralism* (Baltimore: Johns Hopkins Univ. Press, 1980) ix.

sion of the objective text.[28] As a textual reality the "mock reader" draws the real reader into a role that will actualize the effects that the text is intended to produce.[29] While meaning for Gibson is embedded in the text, its activation shapes the understanding that is generated. Accordingly, understanding and significance are one and the same experience, determined by the extent to which the actual reader has succeeded in playing the role of the "mock reader."

Integration operates dynamically in Wolfgang Iser's theory of aesthetic response. For in his view meaning exists neither in the text nor in the reader but originates in the interaction between them: "The literary work has two poles, which we might call the artistic and the aesthetic: the artistic pole is the author's text and the aesthetic is the realization accomplished by the reader."[30] The words of a text, therefore, which designate instructions for the production of the signified, are only potentially significant; like the notes of a musical composition that must be played or sung to make music, they must be read in order to actualize meaning and fulfill the being of the text. "Thus, the meaning of a literary text is not a definable entity but, if anything, a dynamic happening."[31] The reader and the text are partners collaborating as cocreators in an aesthetic event of understanding that, by generating an experience of meaning, originates something that did not exist before. Here the ontology of play, so central to Gadamer's philosophical hermeneutics, is operative. While this is generally true of the reader's interaction with the text, it applies particularly to the resolution of the indeterminacies of the texts, the "gaps," by the construction of signifieds that are not denoted by any signifiers.[32] The creative play of interpretation, however, is never divorced from the constraints of the text. "The reader's activity is only a fulfillment of what is already implicit in the structure of the work."[33]

Stanley Fish's reader-oriented theory stands at the opposite end of the spectrum of affective criticism; here the objectivity of the text disappears. Meaning resides in the reader, for it is the *experience* of an utterance that is its meaning. What a word or sentence *does* is what it means, but always in a specific context. Consequently, no text can mean anything in particular until it is read, and then the meanings that are produced may be as many as its readers. The norms of interpretation are not embedded in the utterance but in the public and constituting

28. W. Gibson, "Authors, Speakers, Readers, and 'Mock Readers,'" *Reader-Response Criticism*, 3–6.

29. Ibid., xi.

30. Iser, *The Act of Reading*, 21.

31. Ibid., 22, 67.

32. Ibid., 65–67. See also W. Iser, *The Implied Reader: Patterns in Communication in Prose Fiction from Bunyan to Beckett* (Baltimore: The Johns Hopkins Press, 1974) 279–82. An apt biblical example of this is the Greek text of Mark 14:54.

33. Tompkins, *Reader-Response Criticism*, xv.

conventions of language and understanding, and it is the situation or context of the utterance that imposes constraints on the determination of meaning.[34] Because the reader's mind is the location of "the developing responses of the reader to the words as they succeed one another on the page," "literature... [becomes] a sequence of events that unfolds within the reader's mind."[35] Given the instability of the text and the unavailability of determinate meanings, interpretation operates within systems of intelligibility that have been appropriated through socialization and education in particular communities. And that experience of meaning is also the very moment of integration.

Unfortunately no method can be formulated for this operation. "Its results are not transferable because there is no fixed relationship between formal features and response (reading has to be done every time); and its skills are not transferable because you don't hand it over to someone and expect him at once to be able to use it."[36] Competent reading and its attendant experience of meaning are developed by participation in "interpretive communities," and as readers "experience more and more of the varieties of effect and subject them to analysis, they also learn how to recognize and discount what is idiosyncratic in their own responses."[37]

Although biblical interpretation generally continues to pursue and practice the hermeneutical mode of reconstruction in order to generate understanding, its gradual approbation of reader-oriented criticism,[38] and to a lesser extent of structural criticism,[39] chronologically following the limited sanction of "the New Hermeneutic" during the 1960s[40] and the even more restricted utilization of the New Criticism,[41] appears to signal a gradual reorientation to the mode of integration. Of course,

---

34. S. Fish, *Is There a Text in This Class? The Authority of Interpretive Communities* (Cambridge, Mass.: Harvard Univ. Press, 1980) 305–7.

35. Tompkins, *Reader-Response Criticism,* xvii.

36. S. Fish, "Literature in the Reader," in *Reader-Response Criticism,* 98.

37. Ibid., 99.

38. See R. A. Culpepper, *Anatomy of the Fourth Gospel: A Study in Literary Design* (Philadelphia: Fortress Press, 1983); M. A. Tolbert, *Sowing the Gospel: Mark's World in Literary-Historical Perspective* (Minneapolis: Fortress Press, 1989); H. C. Waetjen, *A Reordering of Power: A Socio-Political Reading of Mark's Gospel* (Minneapolis: Fortress Press, 1989); R. M. Fowler, *Let the Reader Understand: Reader-Response Criticism and the Gospel of Mark* (Minneapolis: Fortress Press, 1991). For a survey of biblical literary criticism in the poststructuralist mode, see E. McKnight, *The Post-Modern Use of the Bible: The Emergence of Reader-Oriented Criticism* (Nashville: Abingdon, 1988), and S. D. Moore, *Literary Criticism and the Gospels: The Theoretical Challenge* (New Haven: Yale Univ. Press, 1989).

39. See D. Patte, *The Gospel according to Matthew: A Structural Commentary on Matthew's Faith* (Philadelphia: Fortress Press, 1987).

40. See J. M. Robinson, *The New Hermeneutic: New Frontiers in Theology* (New York: Harper and Row, 1964).

41. See D. O. Via, Jr., *The Parables: Their Literary and Existential Dimension* (Philadelphia: Fortress Press, 1967) 70–107; and more recently, to some extent, D. Rhoads and

historically oriented biblical interpretation never ignored the mode of integration; it simply differentiated between reconstruction and integration as two discrete hermeneutical operations. The hermeneutics of reconstruction produced understanding; the hermeneutics of integration engaged in application. This difference is classically illustrated in the hermeneutics of E. D. Hirsch Jr.'s *Validity in Interpretation* and its differentiation between understanding and significance.[42] The former was the domain of biblical scholarship; the latter belonged to practical or systematic theology.

The paradigm of historical reconstruction presupposes a subject-object relationship between the interpreter and the text. As a model derived from the natural sciences, it requires the detachment of the interpreter and the attendant application of theories and methods. On the one hand, the understanding that is actualized within such a supposedly ahistorical matrix is equated epistemologically with knowledge and truth. On the other hand, relativity, the obverse side of the objectivity that this subject-object scheme reputedly establishes, claims that all concepts or norms of rationality, reality, truth, knowledge, ethics, and aesthetics are historically limited to and determined by the realities of society, culture, gender, class, race, and framework. The truth that understanding embraces in one context may be false in another.

Beyond this paradigm of historical reconstruction and its operations of the subject-object relationship that generate understanding is the model of the ontology of play, which Gadamer derived from Kant's aesthetics and which he applies to the hermeneutical mode of integration: "[Play] is neither the orientation nor even the state of mind of the creator or of those enjoying the work of art, nor the freedom of a subjectivity engaged in play, but the mode of being of the work of art itself."[43] In other words, it is the *experience* of art. The players are not the subjects of play, and the game is not its object. Play itself is the subject with its own rhythm and structure, and, as Gadamer says, "play...reaches presentation (Darstellung) through the players" (103). "The mode of being of play does not allow the player to behave toward the play as if toward an object. The player knows very well what play is, and that what he is doing is 'only a game'; but he does not know what exactly he 'knows' in knowing that" (102).

An apt illustration is that of a drama enacted on a stage. As a work

---

D. Michie, *Mark as Story: An Introduction to the Narrative of a Gospel* (Philadelphia: Fortress Press, 1982).

42. See E. D. Hirsch Jr., *Validity in Interpretation* (New Haven: Yale Univ. Press, 1967) 127–63. Of "descriptive biblical scholarship," Krister Stendahl says, "The question about relevance for present-day religion and faith was waived, or consciously kept our of sight" ("Biblical Theology," 419).

43. Gadamer, *Truth and Method* 101–2.

of art it has its true being in its performance. The drama will occur only if it is acted out. Those who produce it are not its subjects, and the drama that is produced is not the object that stands over against them. The subject of the performance is the performance itself in which the drama is enacted and the roles of the various characters are played. The actors fulfill their purpose only if they lose themselves in the play (102). As a work of art completes itself when it becomes an experience that changes the person who has interiorized it, a drama accordingly attains to its being in its performance by actors who coincidentally may be transformed by their very act of performance.

Similarly the being of biblical texts—or indeed any texts!—is play, and their true being is realized in the performance of reading and understanding. Interpretation is not a representation of objects that have been manipulated by an application of methods and theories, but a presentation of understanding through the performance of an interpreting reader. Engaged in this ontology of play, the latter, like the actors of a drama, interacts with the biblical texts and actualizes their meaning. Just as "being read belongs to literature by its nature," being understood belongs to the reading of a text (161, 164).[44] Accordingly, biblical texts—or any texts—are not to be construed as objects but events, indeed ontological events.

As a participant who loses herself or himself in this event of play, the reader is existentially affected by the performance of interpretive understanding. That, of course, implies an openness to the biblical texts, a requirement of their being understood through the act of reading. However, the realities of *Dasein* and its existential condition of "thrownness" into a particular system of sociocultural traditions, with all of its sedimentations, impose the operations of both openness and closedness, operations attributable to the prejudices and structures of the preunderstanding. Consequently, the hermeneutical play of interpretation engaging the structures and prejudices of the preunderstanding, as well as the conventions of reading, is facilitated as well as impeded in its performance of understanding. Therefore, as Gadamer says,

> That is why a hermeneutically trained consciousness must be, from the start, sensitive to the text's alterity. But this kind of sensitivity involves neither "neutrality" with respect to content nor the extinction of one's self, but the foregrounding and appropriation of one's own fore-meanings and prejudices. The important thing is to be aware of one's own bias, so that the text can present itself in all its otherness and thus assert its own truth against one's own fore-meanings. (269)

---

44. A slight revision of Gadamer's similes.

In order to promote the openness of "being-there," particularly in order to mediate historical distance in the operation of the hermeneutical mode of integration, an "effective historical consciousness" that is aware of its entanglement in "the web of historical effects" is "necessary for scientific consciousness" (300–301). An awareness of what is historically pregiven is an indispensable element in the act of interpretive understanding. It is the reality of the reader's situation, which Gadamer calls "horizon," "the range of vision that includes everything that can be seen from a particular vantage point" (302). Because the projection of meaning originating from the horizon of the preunderstanding also includes prejudices and presuppositions that obstruct the performance of understanding, the "effective historical consciousness" of the reader must be oriented to the correction and expansion of that horizon. That necessarily involves the reader in a critical analysis of the world of that "horizon" and the linguistic and sociocultural realities that have constituted it. The domains of semiotics, the sociology of knowledge, and psychology can contribute significantly to the scrutiny of that "horizon" and the conscious-raising process of self-examination.[45]

The hermeneutical mode of integrating biblical texts into the horizon of the reader also presupposes the horizon of the biblical texts. Speech acts, as Iser asserts, "are linguistic utterances in a given situation or context, and it is through this context that they take on meaning."[46] While the prejudices and presuppositions of the preunderstanding that are operative in the hermeneutical circle of understanding will mediate historical distance and promote interpretation, the alien linguistic and sociocultural aspects of the texts and the horizon that they reflect will remain unintelligible. Moreover, the blinding prejudices, the erroneous presuppositions, and the historically limited structures of the preunderstanding will produce inadequate, distorted, even incorrect readings and consequently poor performances of meaning. The determination of meaning and its integration into the experience of the interpretive reader, particularly within the framework of formalist and reader-oriented theories, and more explicitly by Iser's aesthetic interaction of the reader with the text or by Fish's "informed reader," requires some knowledge of the culturally determined signs of the text as well as of the sociocultural realities of their context. The utilization of the social sciences will enable the act of "reading from this place" to oper-

---

45. For example, see Berger and Luckmann, *The Social Construction of Reality;* P. Berger, *The Sacred Canopy* (Garden City. N.Y.: Doubleday, 1967); N. Abercrombie, *Class, Structure and Knowledge* (Oxford: Basil Blackwell, 1980); T. Luckmann, *Life-World and Social Realities* (London: Heinemann, 1983); and Lowe, *History of Bourgeois Perception.* Also R. Barthes, *Elements of Seminology* (New York: Hill and Wang, 1978); and idem, *Mythologies* (New York: Hill and Wang, 1975).

46. Iser, *The Act of Reading* 55.

ate within the same system of intelligibility as that of the biblical texts and to facilitate the transference of meaning from the contemporaneity of the author to that of the reader.[47]

Macrosociology, the study of human societies, offers a foundational analysis of advanced agrarian society, the specific type of society in which the biblical texts originated. Integrating structural functionalism and conflict theory with their own ecological-evolutionary approach, Gerhard and Jean Lenski provide an indispensable paradigm for the investigation of the systemic structures and their disposition of power and wealth in biblical Palestine.[48] T. F. Carney's "handbook of models," *The Shape of the Past: Models and Antiquity,* expands the analyst's power by explaining and illustrating various kinds of models for the investigation of the multiple institutions and economic systems that operated and determined life in antiquity.[49] The texts and contexts of Jewish apocalypticism and its derived categories of the *basileia tou theou* (kingdom of God) and *huios tou anthropou* (Son of Man) in the New Testament are elucidated by the sociology of millennialism.[50] The code of honor/shame, which served as "the boundary markers [of]... power, sexual status and religion" throughout the Mediterranean world of antiquity and which is more or less implicit in the biblical texts, is explicated by cultural anthropology.[51]

All of these socioeconomic and cultural actualities of antiquity are reflected in the biblical texts, more explicitly by the textual realities of "the implied author" and "the implied reader." The repertoire or content of the texts, consisting of the social norms and traditions of

---

47. See D. M. May, *Social Scientific Criticism of the New Testament: A Bibliography* (Macon, Ga.: Mercer Univ. Press, 1991).

48. See G. and J. Lenski, *Human Societies: An Introduction to Macrosociology* (5th ed.; New York: McGraw-Hill, 1987), and G. Lenski, *Power and Privilege: A Theory of Social Stratification* (Chapel Hill: Univ. of North Carolina Press, 1981). Also G. Sjoberg, *The Preindustrial City, Past and Present* (New York: Free Press, 1960), and E. R. Wolf, *Peasants* (Englewood Cliffs, N.J.: Prentice-Hall, 1966).

49. T. F. Carney, *The Shape of the Past: Models and Antiquity* (Lawrence, Kans.: Coronado Press, 1975). For a review and application of some of these models, see J. H. Elliott, "Social-Scientific Criticism of the New Testament and Its Social World: More on Method and Models," *Social-Scientific Criticism of the New Testament and Its Social World* (ed. J. H. Elliott; *Semeia* 35; Decatur, Ga.: Scholars Press, 1986) 1–33.

50. See, for example, K. Burridge, *New Heaven–New Earth: A Study of Millenarian Activities* (New York: Schocken Books, 1969). S. L. Thrupp, ed., *Millennial Dreams in Action: Studies in Revolutionary Movements* (New York: Schocken Books, 1970); P. Worsley, *The Trumpet Shall Sound: A Study of "Cargo Cults" in Melanesia* (New York: Schocken Books, 1968).

51. See B. J. Malina, *The New Testament World: Insights from Cultural Anthropology* (Atlanta: John Knox, 1981); also his book, *Christian Origins and Cultural Anthropology: Practical Models for Biblical Interpretation* (Atlanta: John Knox, 1986). An example of how the categories of cultural anthropology can dominate and distort the interpretation of a biblical text is J. H. Neyrey's *An Ideology of Revolt: John's Christology in Social-Scientific Perspective* (Philadelphia: Fortress Press, 1988).

the environment selected by the authors—and therefore to be included among the textual perspectives that constitute "the implied author"—conveys realities familiar to the originally intended readers, realities that corresponded to their own contemporaneous world. The social sciences provide crosscultural models and theoretical frameworks for the contemporary interpretation of this alien territory of repertoire. More significantly, the concomitant illumination of the sociocultural realities of biblical contexts, which the repertoire mirrors, will enable the contemporary reader to recognize the authorial strategies of the rearrangement of the social norms and traditions that were intended to produce defamiliarization and to restructure the perception of reality.[52] Confronted by the predispositions of "the implied reader," the role offered by the text to the originally intended reader, the contemporary reader is compelled to embrace or reject the textually communicated experience of deformation and estrangement. Such a contemporizing of "the implied reader" will result in integration and coincidentally in the transformation of the reader.

Since the literary work of the author is more than the text—in as far as the meaning of its sign system, which conveys the textual realities of "the implied author" and "the implied reader," must be actualized by the performance of a reader—the production of multiple meanings is inevitable. The interaction between the reader and the text necessarily generates polyvalence, not only because of the *Dasein* of the reader but also because of the virtuality of the text. The indeterminacy of the so-called gaps, the signifieds not denoted by any textual signifiers, fosters the interpretive activity of play and naturally engenders multisignification. Similarly the functions of figurative language in the literary devices of parables, illustrations, allegories, metaphors, and symbols constitute "a duplex sign system which operates denotatively and connotatively at the same time, and which has at least two signifieds: a stated and an unstated signified, a *denotatum* and a *designatum*."[53] The first order of meaning, the stated signified, activates the structure of play in order to construe the second order of meaning, that which must be drawn from the reader's system of values and beliefs. The *designatum,* the unstated signified, is the resulting dynamic experience; and it, like the first order of signified, requires the indispensable illumination of understanding that the social sciences offer.

Multiple meanings may also arise from texts that are "immoderately 'open' to every possible interpretation." According to Umberto Eco, texts that can be read in many different ways, that potentially speak

52. See W. Iser, "The Referential System of the Repertoire," *The Act of Reading,* 68–85.

53. Wittig, "A Theory of Multiple Meanings," 75.

to everyone, or that can easily be decoded in contradiction to the intention of the author will invariably generate invalid productions of meaning. Such "open" texts are considered to be closed because there are no structural elements that guide the generative process of reading.[54] In contrast, texts that are genuinely open are well-organized texts that presuppose a competent reader, yet at the same time also develop the competence that is presupposed (8). Eco claims:

> An author can foresee an ideal reader...able to master different codes and eager to deal with the text as with a maze of many issues. But in the last analysis what matters is not the various issues themselves but the maze-like structure of the text. You cannot use the text as you want, but only as the text wants you to use it. An open text, however "open" it be, cannot afford whatever interpretation. (9)

Unfortunately, biblical texts are all too frequently "closed"—in Eco's sense of the term—because the structural elements that are intended to guide the performance of meaning are imperceptible to its readers. Nevertheless, the generative structures of meaning that they constitute can be activated by readers who embody the competence that the texts presuppose and that the texts by authorial will are determined to develop (10–11). The narrative criticism of formalist theory, with its orientation toward the literariness of literature, the "how" of meaning rather than the "what" of meaning, is as indispensable here as the social sciences. For like prose in general, biblical narrative has its own self-sufficient being. It is not engaged in historical mimesis; it does not offer a window through which the past can be viewed. It is self-contained and self-justifying, it has its own techniques and is determined by its own rules, and it requires no external validation.[55] Such a morphological approach, with its revolutionary goal of defamiliarization, can enlarge the reader's capacity to activate the generative structures of meaning that are latent in the biblical texts and in turn to be enlarged in that capacity by the texts themselves.

This comprehensive orientation toward the hermeneutical mode of integration, including the utilization of the social sciences, contradicts the games that deconstruction, and perhaps especially Jacques Derrida, play with texts. In his book *Against Deconstruction*, John Ellis critiques deconstruction according to the linguistics of Ferdinand de Saussure:

---

54. U. Eco, *The Role of the Reader: Explorations in the Semiotics of Texts* (Bloomington: Indiana Univ. Press, 1984) 8–9.

55. As examples, see Tolbert, *Sowing the Gospel*, 1–34, 90–126; Waetjen, *A Reordering of Power*, 1–26; and Fowler, *Let the Reader Understand*, 1–58. For a diachronically critical, holistic reading of a limited narrative unit inside of a larger narrative complex, see F. F. Segovia, *Farewell to the Word: The Johannine Call to Abide* (Minneapolis: Fortress Press, 1991).

> In the conceptual system of a language, its concepts are not simple, positive terms that achieve their meaning by corresponding to reality or to non-linguistic facts; instead, they achieve their meaning by the place they take within the system of concepts of the language and, in particular, by their function in differentiating one category of things from another.[56]

The signifier is a "slice of sound" that is arbitrarily chosen to name a given concept (a signified). While the bond between them is also arbitrary, the sign that they constitute has its own distinctive place in a linguistic system that makes meaning and communication possible.[57] "The community is necessary if values that owe their existence solely to usage and general acceptance are set up; by himself the individual is incapable of fixing a single value."[58] The structure and stability of the linguistic system, therefore, determined both by the place each sign occupies in that system and the community that has established it, deter the randomness and indeterminacy of meaning. This is no less true of individual signs in their defining relationship to each other in poetic and narrative discourses. Consequently, linguistic signs are not subject to infinite play and the deference of meaning.[59] If a text's explicit formulations undermine its implicit aspects, as deconstruction claims, it can only be attributable to either the inferiority of the author's work or the experience of the reader who has not yet succeeded in operating within the text's system of intelligibility. Polyvalence is generated by other factors, as already indicated, and not by the infinite play of signification.

In spite of various objections from within the domain of literary criticism, interpretation continues to be the goal.[60] For biblical scholarship, however, no other *telos* seems legitimate. Yet Jane Tompkins's critique of reader-response criticism is also valid for the enterprise of biblical studies, particularly that movement within it that operates in the hermeneutical mode of integration:

> When the literary work is conceived as an object of interpretation, response will be understood as a way of arriving at meaning, and not as a form of political and moral behavior. The distinction

---

56. J. Ellis, *Against Deconstruction* (Princeton, N.J.: Princeton Univ. Press, 1989) 46.

57. F. de Saussure, "Course in General Linguistics," *Critical Theory since 1965* (ed. H. Adams and L. Searle; Tallahassee: Univ. Presses of Florida and Florida State, 1986) 649.

58. Ibid.

59. As an example of this kind of play in a poststructuralist, deconstructive mode of reading the Gospels of Mark and Luke, see S. D. Moore, *Mark and Luke in Poststructuralist Perspectives: Jesus Begins to Write* (New Haven: Yale Univ. Press, 1992).

60. See J. Culler, *The Pursuit of Signs: Semiotics, Literature, Deconstruction* (Ithaca, N.Y.: Cornell Univ. Press, 1981) chap. 1.

between response conceived as meaning, and response conceived as action or behavior, separates the current conception of literary response not only from the classical one but from the way responses to literature have been understood by most critics before the twentieth century.[61]

If the hermeneutical mode of integration is appropriate to the interpretation of biblical texts, the experience of meaning that is generated should be directly relevant to the reader's location. By projection this would include all the circumstances of that location: social, economic, political, religious, and cultural. In contrast, the mode of reconstruction presupposes a kind of *techne,* for its techniques culminate in the production of a "thing," the thought of a text or an author, which, in as far as it is "detached from any particular kind of being," may be considered *episteme,* the type of objective knowledge that is universal.[62] The outcome of such an approach to the Bible would be, as Bruce Malina deduces from his utilization of the social sciences, "increased understanding of the behavior" of people and God as described in the texts, of the Bible as "a record of the 'religion of persons' and their theocentric and christocentric successes and failures that lie at the source of our Judaeo-Christian tradition," and "of our flesh and blood ancestors in faith and the dimensions of their quest for an adequately meaningful human existence."[63] To what extent that kind of historical information can be extracted from the Bible depends on the evaluation of the legitimacy of the hermeneutical mode of reconstruction.

The biblical texts themselves presuppose the mode of integration. While it can also be employed to reconstruct historical and sociocultural realities by means of critical methods, the outcome will always be a fusion of horizons and therefore an understanding determined by the interpreter's social location. Given the traditionally ascribed character of the biblical texts as "the word of God," the interaction with them and the resulting process of understanding as meaning-coming-into-being may actualize the potentiality that they incarnate as the word of God. The reader, who has temporarily turned away from the contextual realities of "being-there" and in whom coincidentally the subject-object division is being internalized, is confronted by an "other" and its claim

61. J. Tompkins, "The Reader in History: The Changing Shape of Literary Response," *Reader-Response Criticism,* 206. At the same time Tompkins's insinuation that reader-oriented critics present themselves as a kind of high priesthood of interpretation should be contradicted. Fish insists that no method can be formulated for his theory of meaning as experience, and Iser offers a phenomenology of reading to enable the reader in the activity of interacting with a text.

62. Gadamer, *Truth and Method,* 314–17.

63. B. Malina, "The Social Sciences and Biblical Interpretation," *Interpretation* 36/3 (1982) 241–42.

to truth. Not to be identified with the text of the Bible nor with the doctrines and dogmas that are extracted from the Bible, this experience of an "other" and its claim to truth is a dynamic event of illumination and self-disclosure.

But the production of meaning and the coincidental happening of the word of God are not the *telos* of biblical interpretation. For if, as Gadamer contends, interpretation, understanding, and application are essentially one and the same activity, the natural result, as Gadamer himself realized, is *praxis,* not simply the experience of meaning.[64] And in as far as application is more than the experience of meaning, the ultimate outcome of the mode of integration, therefore, must be practical activity linked to the realities of *Dasein,* specifically the practical activities of ethical and political conduct. Consequently, when attention is shifted from the experience of meaning and its divine revelation back to the circumstances of everyday life, the objectification of that experience must be translated into concrete deeds of justice and love.

Hermeneutical activity, therefore, that is true to the mode of integration culminates in moral action. For Gadamer, understanding as application to social location is *phronesis,* a mediation between the moral knowledge that has been gained from textual interpretation and the particular situation of the reader, for "the purpose of this knowledge is to govern...action."[65] Richard J. Bernstein shows how Gadamer employs Aristotle's category of *phronesis* as a model—differentiating it from *episteme,* scientific knowledge, and *techne,* knowledge that results in the production of a "particular thing" that can be detached from a human being—in order to clarify the relationship between understanding and social location.[66] *Phronesis* is the process of applying the moral knowledge that has been gained through interpretation into the "being-in-motion of *Dasein,*" the very concrete circumstances of historical existence:

> The interpreter seeks no more than to understand this universal, the text—i.e., to understand what it says, what constitutes the text's meaning and significance. In order to understand that, he must not try to disregard himself and his particular hermeneutical situation. He must relate the text to this situation if he wants to understand at all.[67]

---

64. Gadamer, *Truth and Method,* 307–11.
65. Ibid., 314.
66. Ibid., 315–17; see R. J. Bernstein, *Beyond Objectivism and Relativism: Science, Hermeneutics, and Praxis* (Philadelphia: Univ. of Pennsylvania Press, 1991) 144–50. In Bernstein's book, this use of *phronesis* plays a central role in his philosophical endeavor of moving beyond objectivism and relativism.
67. Gadamer, *Truth and Method,* 324.

If the biblical text is the incarnation of the potentiality of the word of God, the actualization of that potentiality may be identified with the performance of meaning. Beyond that, however, is the *telos* that the biblical texts themselves witness to: the actualization of the potentiality of the incarnation of the word of God in the social location of flesh-and-blood existence. In this vein Jeremiah prophesies, " 'This is the covenant I will make with the house of Israel after that time,' says Yahweh. 'I will put my law in their minds and write it on their hearts. I will be their God, and they will be my people' " (31:33; my trans.). Additionally, but in an affirmation of fulfillment, the apostle Paul writes to the Corinthian Christians: "You are an epistle of Christ delivered by us, written not with ink but with the Spirit of the living God, not on stone tablets but on tablets of fleshly hearts" (2 Cor 3:3). Both Testaments offer a vision of a universal actualization of the kind of incarnation of the word of God that manifests itself in world reconstruction and its accompanying realities of social and economic justice for all human beings.

When that eschatological objective is reached, the operation of the hermeneutical mode of integration in and through the biblical texts will have achieved its fulfillment. Accordingly, if the social construction of reality is also a product of the activity of interpretation, which hermeneutical mode and which interpretive system prevail has profound implications for the future of human being.[68]

---

68. An expanded revision of Tompkins's closing remarks in "The Reader in History," 226.

4

Reading Texts as Reading Ourselves:
A Chapter in the History of African-American
Biblical Interpretation

Vincent L. Wimbush

I

Literature, especially religious literature, ideally aims to trigger degrees
of empathy in readers who share a particular universe of meaning, with
the goal of entertaining, provoking, challenging, and persuading.[1] The
literary text that has achieved something of the status of a "classic"
is one that has consistently—that is, "beyond its time...beyond its
space"—proved to be engaging and empathetic, consistently challenging
and inspiring the spirit, provoking thoughts and arresting the imagination of those generally sharing a universe of meaning, or culture.[2]
But such texts, precisely because of their empathy-producing qualities,
should also inspire among readers again and again over time a certain suspicious posture, the cultivation of certain critical sensibilities
and faculties—such faculties that will allow them to see themselves as
chronologically and ideologically distant and different from both "the
tyranny of the present" and the texts and text-worlds if only in order to
return to these texts with a grasp of cultural or communal clarity of interpretive history.[3] The distancing and the recognition of difference are
imperative in order that "classics" or "canonical" texts not be "defined"

---

1. See P. J. Cahill, *Mended Speech: The Crisis of Religious Studies and Theology*
(New York: Crossroad, 1982) 126, for reference to R. Bultmann's understanding of
religious literature as "form of direct address," and the general argument that religious
literature makes use of imagery, symbolism, and metaphor in order to "evoke...a wide
range of imaginative response" (127).
2. K. Stendahl, "The Bible as a Classic and the Bible as Holy Scripture," *Journal of
Biblical Literature* 103/1 (1984) 4.
3. J. Goody and I. Watt, "The Consequences of Literacy," *Literacy in Traditional
Societies* (ed. J. Goody; Cambridge: Cambridge Univ. Press, 1964) 53, quoting Oswald
Spengler.

or made meaningful solely by one interpreting group within a culture or by one interpreting generation for all time.

Such cultural protection or culture defensiveness is also important because the reading of empathy-inducing texts is at the same time the reading of "world" and of a position of the self and culture in the world. Aesthetically induced empathy must never take away any cultural group's or generation's responsibility to discover for itself what it is about a text that is inspiring and challenging, beautiful and noble, trivial and destructive.

Our general (so-called First World) situation in a postindustrial, late capitalist, postmodern society at the end of the twentieth century would seem to demand for all peoples a rethinking—especially regarding authoritative, self-defining, and world-orienting traditions. Transnational corporations, the global reach of technologies from military-strategic uses to entertainment, the frightfully rapid and global dissemination of information and noninformation (regarding fashions, music, and so on) would seem to include—if not in fact to induce—what Fredric Jameson refers to as innumerable ongoing "changes and modifications," tremendous sociocultural, economic, political, and ideological conflicts, a great deal of confusion and alienation, and constant institutional restructuring and repositioning of loyalties and ideologies. The smaller world created by advanced networks and technologies (CNN, global faxing, and so on) puts absolutes, totalities, and traditions of all types under some suspicion.[4]

The search for identity, for belonging, for wholeness and understanding in this situation has propelled many of a religious bent toward a hardening and tightening, toward an effort to freeze in time that which is judged to be self-defining, good, and meaningful in a world perceived to be moving too fast, spinning out of control. Thus, we witness the resurgence of fundamentalisms—worldwide—not merely in reaction to modernity[5] but as a complicated and paradoxical part of and response to postmodernism. Jameson states:

> In the gentler atmosphere of an uncontested postmodernism, more effortlessly secular than any modernism could have wished,... religious traditionalisms [namely, "mainline" churches] seem to have melted away without a trace... while the wildest and most unexpected forms of what is now called "fundamentalism" flourish, virtually at random and seemingly obedient to other climac-

---

4. F. Jameson, *Postmodernism: Or, The Cultural Logic of Late Capitalism* (Durham, N.C.: Duke Univ. Press, 1991) ix.

5. See G. Marsden, *Fundamentalism and American Culture: The Shaping of Twentieth Century Evangelicalism, 1870–1925* (New York: Oxford Univ. Press, 1980); B. Lawrence, *Defenders of God: The Fundamentalist Revolt against the Modern Age* (San Francisco: Harper and Row, 1989).

terics and ecological laws.... The "fundamental" question seems to... be the one about tradition and the past, and how the new [fundamentalist] religions compensate their irreplaceable absence in the depthlessness of the new social order.[6]

Just short of what may be called fundamentalism we witness among some in more "respectable" circles an awkward revisiting of "old landmarks," a flirtation with long-discarded premodernist leanings and rhetorics all in the effort now to compete with fundamentalist communities and hold on to dwindling numbers of communicants. These efforts seem to serve only to frustrate and confuse all the more the small pool of the class-specific faithful, and they generally fail to recruit class-specific outsiders looking for more than the lukewarm, middle-of-the-road sensibilities of respectable and world-embracing religion. Fundamentalism is clearly a trap: it lures communities into believing that a tight hold on and freezing of tradition makes them socially, culturally, and politically critical and even socially, culturally, and politically transcendent when they are in fact no more than weak tradents of a class-specific ideology. Respectable religion, since it by definition comes out of, legitimizes, and lives (for the most part) among the socioeconomic and sociopolitical middle to upper classes, by tradition and sensibility cannot fully accommodate itself to the agenda of those on the periphery. Clearly, other options need to be considered.

II

For those whose lives are played out on the periphery of power and influence—whether political-economic, social, or religious/ideological—neither fundamentalism nor reformed religious respectability holds much profit. The majority of African Americans—Africans in the New World that became the United States—have nonetheless consistently embraced religion in order to be affirmed and to have their world be reshaped and redefined—as is consonant with African sensibilities.[7] They manipulated the religions they embraced until such religions became their own and began to reflect their views about themselves and the world to which they were brought. The major turning points in the history of their engagement of religion in North America, especially but not limited to Protestantism, reflect religion's significant and complex role in the development of African America.

---

6. Jameson, *Postmodernism*, 387–88.
7. N. Q. King, *African Cosmos: An Introduction to Religion in Africa* (Belmont Calif.: Wadsworth, 1986) 112–13.

Almost from the beginning of their experience in "America," the Africans heard the powerful narratives of the Bible and moving hymns; some of them responded to the preachings of white evangelists and exhorters representing respectable and not so respectable religion. By the middle of the nineteenth century, in solidarity with the wave of populist democratized religion, many more of them responded to the exhortation of already "converted" Black evangelists and exhorters; they joined local white churches and helped to build historic, large denominational groups; they founded their own separate local churches and denominational groups in protest against racism and in advancement of racial solidarity. In the early part of the twentieth century in the urban areas of the North and South they founded splinter groups— "cults" and "sects"—in protest against the worldliness and apostasy of both ("mainline") African-American religious ways and respectability and white American racism and perfidy. More recently, in the late twentieth century in many places, the attraction to Black and white fundamentalist communities, institutions, and orientations has been noted (but not yet documented and analyzed).

These different religious responses or turns among African Americans need to be more clearly sorted out, explained, and qualified. No one response represents the sensibilities and orientations of all African Americans. And any comprehensive explanation and schema will certainly need to address the matter of the functions of the Bible in the formation, nature, articulation, and justification of responses made. Because the Bible has figured so prominently in the history of American cultural and religious self-definitions (and this is especially so as regards the Protestant-evangelical, dominant culture), including literature and art, all aspects of popular culture, education at all levels, politics and political rhetoric, and jurisprudence,[8] it must be considered in any serious effort to address and influence the thinking and orientations of a still-large segment of African Americans.

It has been argued that the Bible has functioned as something of an icon in the founding, growth, and rise to world power of the United States,[9] first providing the fledgling nation its ideological and principled stance against British rule, then providing justification for its brutalities against natives and enslavement of Africans, its expansionist policies, and its long-held traditions and policies of racism, racial

---

8. See N. O. Hatch and M. A. Noll, eds., *The Bible in America: Essays in Cultural History* (New York: Oxford Univ. Press, 1982); and A. S. Phy, ed., *The Bible and Popular Culture in America* (Philadelphia: Fortress Press; Chico, Calif.: Scholars Press, 1985).

9. M. Marty, *Religion and Republic: The American Circumstance* (Boston: Beacon, 1987) chap. 7.

brutality, and apartheid.[10] Ironically, precisely because these and other hallmarks of the making of America were articulated through and justified by readings of the Bible, African Americans embraced the latter, recognizing in it a source of socioreligious and sociopolitical power. Although at first it was viewed as a rather strange source or locus of power by peoples steeped in rich oral cultures,[11] the Bible quickly came to be embraced as a powerfully arresting and large language world that included poignant, memorable stories, breathtaking visions, pithy sayings and riddles, haunting prophecies, adventures of heroes and heroines, the pathetic travails and great triumphs of a rootless people, and a savior figure who is mistreated and abused but who ultimately overcomes.

During the times leading up to and just after the Civil War, the Bible functioned as an ideological and rhetorical weapon on an ideological and rhetorical playing field. Different regions of the country, different religious and cultural groups, and different racial and ethnic groups and classes turned to the Bible both to articulate and to justify their views on the great controversial topic of the times—slavery. In the period just after the Second Great Awakening (early nineteenth century), African Americans who had become evangelical Christians saw the opportunity to enter the rhetorical, ideological playing field. They saw themselves as *hermeneutically* free: they sang, preached, exhorted, prayed, joked, and debated issues in biblical terms and categories. And their expressions were, of course, self-focused and self-affirmative, at times pathetic, but always hopeful.

For African Americans these were times of hermeneutical innocence and playfulness. Because in an evangelical culture they were to an extent free to discern the will of God for their collective lives as they could discern it in the Bible, their engagement of the latter, reflective of their African origins, was primarily oral and therefore somewhat fluid. Since the written text of the Bible could not be engaged by very many African Americans throughout the eighteenth and nineteenth centuries,[12] a strict literalism did not characterize their engagement of the Bible. This situation led to the laying of the foundations of a rich tradition of a culture-specific reading of the Bible. There was, after all, little that white evangelical Christians could do to check the hermeneutical exercises of the Africans turned Christians. The Book had been opened and read and

10. For the early period, see D. G. Mathews, *Religion in the Old South* (Chicago: Univ. of Chicago Press, 1977) chap. 4.

11. See S. D. Gill, "Nonliterate Traditions and Holy Books: Toward A New Model," *Beyond "The Primitive": The Religions of Nonliterate Peoples* (ed. S. D. Gill; Englewood Cliffs, N.J.: Prentice Hall, 1982) 226–27.

12. See J. D. Cornelius, *"When I Can Read My Title Clear": Literacy, Slavery, and Religion in the Antebellum South* (Columbia: Univ. of South Carolina Press, 1991) chap. 4.

heard. And the Africans knew themselves to be free to mine the Book for those stories and oracles that spoke to their situation. They knew they were free—in accordance with African sensibilities—even to manipulate the biblical stories in ways that would guarantee their continuing relevance and poignancy.

Such hermeneutical freedom was psychological/ideological freedom, not, as many have argued, passivity, even if the expressions or transcripts of that freedom were somewhat veiled or hidden.[13] It was freedom in the playfulness, whimsicalness, and release of the collective cultural imagination in the engagement of the Bible that was translated into psychic affirmation and power—the power to imagine the other, something other than the given of slavery and disenfranchisement, the power to imagine the "by and by," a future situation better than, if not altogether a reversal of, the status quo. The imagination arrested and exercised in such manner inspires liberating and strategic survival responses.

African Americans' hermeneutical and ideological freedom as defined here obtained for a long time. The nature of the dominant religious tradition embraced by them—its evangelical Bible-centeredness, its loose, relatively nonhierarchical structures and polities—and the perception on the part of many whites that the Africans' religious ways are naive and innocent contributed to the longevity of the situation that allowed the cultivation of such freedom.

However, plenty of signs point to the serious threat to, if not actual loss of, such freedom among African Americans. The early twentieth-century rise and late twentieth-century resurgence of fundamentalism in the United States as part of the resurgence of fundamentalisms worldwide (as mentioned above) should be seen as an attempt to freeze and hold fast to certain inherited (interpretations of) traditions. This attempt was very likely inspired by crises in thinking, cultural displacement or disorientation, and loss of confidence. Although most African Americans have a long history of the use of fundamentalist-like rhetoric, they have not consistently or evenly or without equivocation embraced fundamentalist institutions and positions. The racialism and racism of the United States have prevented them from totally and consistently embracing fundamentalism. That is, until recent times.[14]

---

13. See J. C. Scott, *Domination and the Arts of Resistance* (New Haven: Yale Univ. Press, 1990) chaps. 1, 8

14. Although I argue this point in another essay, it is clear to me that it is yet to be established and explained. Nevertheless, the signs of recent drifts toward acceptance of white fundamentalist camps, their ethos, literatures, use of electronic media, and so on, are dramatically evident.

III

All of the above can be seen as a modest, preliminary, and sketchy effort to put the contemporary African-American religious and sociopolitical situation in historical-interpretive perspective. This perspective does not now explain all that has gone on before; it serves only as an interpretive framework for understanding African-American religious traditions that goes beyond the focus upon histories of institutions, dramatic periods, great men (and women), and ideas. It is intended to function less as a definitive statement than as a conceptual springboard for further more comprehensive, critical-historical, and constructive thinking. The point is that the proffering of an authentic (namely, culture-specific) cultural-critical biblical hermeneutic for African Americans for the end of the twentieth century must respect and therefore critically engage their long and dynamic history of readings of the Bible. It is no longer defensible for contemporaries to offer constructive readings of the Bible that begin from a (conceptual) place that assumes that there is no such tradition of readings among African Americans or—as is most often the case—that perhaps there is such a tradition, but it is not very relevant for the present challenges or critical-constructive considerations.

Consideration of the history of readings of the Bible among African Americans is critical to any effort to offer a particular constructive reading of the Bible among African Americans of the present for a number of reasons. (1) It showcases what is perhaps the clearest and strongest case for the direct linkage between, on the one hand, social location (here in the United States, especially, including racial identity) and cultural identity and perspective, and, on the other hand, readings of the Bible, and thereby establishes its heuristic power. (2) It forces attention upon and makes valuable the rich historical-cultural sources for interpretation. It thereby shifts the focus of interpretation away from objective text toward "world" or culture. (3) It provides a basis upon which continuing criticism and reformulation of African-American and other culturalist readings of the Bible can be carried out. (4) It points to possibilities for a basis for communication across cultural, racial, and religious divides that nonetheless respects the divides.

If what I am urging is embraced, the traditional focus in African-American readings of the Bible, including popular and religious readings and the burgeoning academic readings, would need to shift. The shift would be from the simple, unquestioning acceptance and valorization of "traditional" interpretations—as if whatever anyone claimed was a part of the tradition qualified for such status, and as if whatever is deemed a legitimate part of the tradition always merits continued acceptance or status as part of the tradition—to a willingness to critique the tradition in its historical trajectories of readings, emphases, and meanings. There are, of course, hermeneutical implications beyond African-American culture.

The hermeneutical process assumed in this argument is circular to a degree. There is some correspondence between this process and the reasons provided above for consideration of a history of readings of the Bible among African Americans. First, there must be among African Americans enough of an ongoing conscientization regarding culture-specific or communal construal (reading assumptions, principles of interpretation) of the Bible as reflection of (an important aspect of) cultural self-definition that it can be accepted and embraced without apology or defensiveness, even if (at this and at any point in the process) the specific boundaries, characteristics, and ramifications of such a construal are not clear. Second, this acceptance of a culture-specific construal of the Bible should lead to a highlighting of those biblical texts that seem (at this point or at any point in the process) to speak to or in support of (an aspect of) cultural self-definition, those texts that seem to arrest the collective imagination and strike a chord. Third, such texts need then to be taken up into the history of readings of the Bible among African Americans. This is important in order to tap into the collective cultural wisdom across the generations as evidenced in the selection and engagement of certain texts. The sources would include those genres—sermons, testimonies, speeches of all types, songs, prayers, diaries, and so forth—through which popular sentiment from the very beginning of the African experience in the New World to the late twentieth century was typically registered. Fourth, critical reflection upon contemporary interpretations in light of the history of cultural interpretation should follow. This does not now mean that the single meaning of any text would be established from isolated usage in the history of African-American readings. It does mean that the history of readings provides a broader cultural perspective from which to interpret the biblical text and through the biblical text the world. But ultimately, both past and present readings are held up for critique in this process: the past is critiqued by the present insofar as the former is understood as part of the ongoing engagement of the Bible within the culture, not as the primitive-purist stage in the process; even liberating texts and liberating uses of texts would be required to be critically examined in the present to determine whether they remain so; and every present is critiqued simply by virtue of continuing consciousness of the gravity of the history of witnesses—of interpreters past.

IV

An example of how this interpretive process might work is in order. A culture-specific, African-American reading of the Bible is not only recognized but embraced and celebrated. An easily recognizable and enduring principle of interpretation that has been embraced in a significant, if not dominant, segment of the African-American religious community over a rather long historical period is that of nonracism, or the universal kinship, freedom, and equality of all humanity under God's sovereignty.[15] This nonracist, nondiscriminatory "prophetic principle" has served as a foundational principle for a number of churches, denominations, subdenominational groups, and other groups and institutions. But prior to such usages there was obviously a striking of a communal chord with respect to, some resonance and identification with, and then engagement of certain biblical texts thought to raise the issue of and even valorize the principle.

Many biblical texts have been isolated by African Americans as expressions and legitimizations of the embraced nonracist principle. In reading the New Testament, for example, a pastiche of biblical passages raising the issues behind the principle can be identified in a number of different types of historical sources. The most important passages are found in Galatians and Acts. The King James Version, historically the version made available to, and the adopted favorite of, the great majority of African Americans, should be referenced:

> For ye are all children of God by faith in Christ Jesus. For as many of you as have been baptized into Christ have put on Christ. There is neither Jew nor Greek, there is neither bond nor free, there is neither male nor female: for ye are all one in Christ Jesus. And if ye be Christ's, then are ye Abraham's seed, and heirs according to the promise. (Gal 3:26-29)

In Acts, Peter says:

> Of a truth I perceive that God is no respecter of persons: But in every nation he that feareth him, and worketh righteousness, is accepted with him. (Acts 10:34-35)

And Paul in Athens, on Mars Hill, says:

> And [God] hath made of one blood all nations of men for to dwell on all the face of the earth, and hath determined the times before appointed, and the bounds of their habitation. (Acts 17:26)

---

15. P. Paris, *Social Teaching of the Black Churches* (Philadelphia: Fortress Press, 1985) 10.

In scholarly jargon, these passages can be said to function collectively as a *locus classicus* of an important, if not dominant, African-American religious sentiment, especially regarding the acceptance of all peoples within God's economy. Of course, behind such a sentiment must be identified a particular social location and orientation within African-American culture—that of relatively elite individuals and groups with an accommodationist, integrationist agenda, even if the latter includes blistering prophetic and social critique. The sentiment—in its religious casting—emphasizes a moral imperative, namely, the biblical mandate (as understood in evangelical Protestantism) of the inclusion of all types of peoples, irrespective of social station or origins, in the "household of God." These and related themes were articulated most forcefully or openly beginning in the nineteenth century in non–slave-holding areas of the northern United States often by free Blacks or freedpersons with some formal education.

The importance of the biblical passages cited above in the rhetoric and orientations of many of such African Americans and the multitudes for whom they spoke is great. Space permits only a summary treatment of the engagement of the passages and their corresponding and spin-off themes and motifs in the rhetoric of one highly representative individual—the cleric and social activist Reverdy Ransom, whose career spanned the last part of the nineteenth century and the first half of the twentieth century, the time of the most forceful articulation and institutionalization of the principle under discussion.

Ransom was born in Ohio in 1861. A member of the African Methodist Episcopal Church, he graduated from Wilberforce University in 1886 and accepted the charge of an AME church in Chicago in 1896. He immediately became involved in a number of progressive movements (including the Niagara Movement and the Afro-American Council) committed to the struggle to ameliorate the lot of African Americans. The combination of the negative public-relations spin that his associations received within the African-American community in Chicago, including within the AME hierarchy and politics, and his outspokenness finally led to his "move" to Boston in 1905. His continuing activism and outspokenness did not prevent him from being elected bishop in 1924. This election, his leadership in protest organizations, his work in urban ministry, his editorial leadership of the *AME Review,* and his numerous associations and ties across the country show that Ransom represented the sentiments and orientations of a significant segment of African Americans during his times.[16]

---

16. See D. Wills, "Reverdy C. Ransom: The Making of an A.M.E. Bishop," *Black Apostles* (ed. R. K. Burkett and R. Newman; Boston: G. K. Hall, 1978) 181–212, for more detailed information.

In 1906, just after having moved to Boston, Ransom delivered an address in the Park Street Church. Entitled "The Race Problem in a Christian State, 1906,"[17] it strikes many of the themes that are so familiar in the different genres of expressions—open/public and private; veiled; secular/political and religious—among African Americans during Ransom's career. It certainly should be identified with the prophetic critique that I have elsewhere isolated as one of the historical responses of African Americans to their situation in the United States.[18] This critique made use of biblical rhetoric and images in an effort to excoriate the United States, given its (unofficial) claims to be a Christian nation following biblical principles, with its history of racism and oppression of Africans in its midst. The critique notwithstanding, the agenda behind the rhetoric was for the most part the African integration into mainstream American society. This was to be expected from those leaders who delivered sermons and speeches and who wrote tracts and dissertations of all kinds in opposition to the status quo as far as institutional racism was concerned. They were, after all, the ones somewhat in the middle, with some education, the capacities to negotiate the outside world, with the most to gain from African integration into American society, the most to lose from the status quo. So was Ransom; so spoke Ransom.

"There should be no race problem in the Christian State." This is the first statement in Ransom's address. As it develops it becomes clear that it is actually a haggadic-like exposition of Acts and Galatians—more specifically Acts 10 and 17, with Gal 3:26-28 resonating in the background. The point that Ransom attempts to make is that at its very foundation Christianity was open to all peoples. To this end he offers the following introductions to and loose versions of two biblical texts:

> When Christianity received its Pentecostal baptism and seal from heaven it is recorded that, "there were dwelling at Jerusalem Jews, devout men, out of every nation under heaven, Parthians, and Medes, and Elamites, and the dwellers in Mesopotamia and in Judea and Cappadocia, in Pontus and Asia, Phrygia, and Pamphylia in Egypt, and in parts of Lybia about Cyrene; and strangers

---

17. Reverdy Ransom, "The Race Problem in a Christian State," *Afro-American Religious History: A Documentary Witness* (ed. M. Sernett; Durham, N.C.: Duke Univ. Press, 1985) 296–304.

18. V. L. Wimbush, "The Bible and African Americans: An Outline of an Interpretative History," *Stony the Road We Trod: African American Biblical Interpretation* (ed. C. H. Felder; Minneapolis: Fortress Press, 1991) 81–97; but see also a very different typology of responses ("four traditions of response") in C. West, *Prophesy Deliverance: An Afro-American Revolutionary Christianity* (Philadelphia: Westminster, 1982) 69–91.

in Rome; Jews and Proselytes, Cretes and Arabians." (Acts 2:5, 9-11)[19]

St. Paul, standing in the Areopagus, declared to the Athenians that, "God hath made of one blood all nations of men for to dwell on all the face of the earth." (Acts 17:26a)[20]

The point that Ransom makes with these and other biblical quotations and allusions is that a "Christian state"—"one founded upon the teachings of Jesus"—must adhere to the teachings of Jesus regarding the kinship of all humanity. Ransom declared that the United States, a "Christian nation" (indeed, "the first nation that was born with a Bible in its hands"), has the greatest challenge to follow Jesus' precepts. The obvious fact that it does not do so justifies Ransom's blistering prophetic critique:

> The Race Problem in this country is not only still with us an unsolved problem, but it constitutes perhaps the most serious problem in our country today.... American Christianity will unchrist itself if it refuses to strive on, until this Race Problem is not only settled, but settled right; and until this is done, however much men may temporize and seek to compromise, and cry "peace! peace!" there will be no peace.[21]

The New Testament provided Ransom with the ideological principle that he, as member of an oppressed, marginalized group, could readily embrace, not only in order to name and characterize the racial situation in the United States but also to seek to transcend it, to find a grand perspective from which to relativize racial distinctions. Ransom understood Jesus to have stood for and established the unification of humankind, to have broken down " 'the middle wall of partition,' between man and man,... Jew and Gentile," in order " 'that He might reconcile both unto God in one body by the cross...so making peace.' "[22] In the last paragraph of the address, the application to the racial conflict and oppression in the United States is made crystal-clear:

> As God is above man, so man is above race. There is nothing to fear by forever demolishing every wall, religious, political, industrial, social, that separates man from his brother man. God has given us a splendid heritage upon these shores; he has made us the pioneers of human liberty for all mankind. He has placed the Negro and white man here for centuries, to grow together side

---

19. Ransom, "Race Problem," 296–97.
20. Ibid., 297.
21. Ibid., 298.
22. Ibid., 297; quotation from Eph 2:14-25.

by side. The white man's heart will grow softer, as it goes out in helpfulness, to assist his black brother up the heights whereon he stands, and the black man will take courage and confidence, as he finds himself progressing, by slow and difficult steps upward toward the realization of all the higher and better things of human attainment; thus will these two peoples one at last become the school masters of all the world, teaching by example the brotherhood of man.[23]

The integrationist and accommodationist ethos is clearly evident in this concluding part of Ransom's address. It is also clear that the Bible, especially the New Testament, supplied him with the rhetoric and images needed in order to be persuasive. After all, Ransom could assume that his audience on the occasion of the delivery of the address in the Park Street Church in Boston, or in other settings, of whatever race, accepted the Bible as a legitimate and powerful arbiter in all matters.

The biblically inspired call to unity in Ransom's address must be understood finally as an example of biblical interpretation done from a complicated and relative social and ideological position within African-American communities. Ransom was in the middle: he was of, and considered himself a spokesperson for, a marginalized group that he always understood as being comprised of all African Americans. But he was also an elite within this racial/cultural group. He was an articulate, educated male from the North who was a leading force in a hierarchical association with nonetheless clearly populist origins. He reflected and spoke for the particular views, sensibilities, orientations, and agenda of such a group. The integrationist position held the most promise for members of such a group.

V

This sketchy analysis of Ransom's address is enough to serve as a springboard for final consideration of several issues regarding African-American biblical interpretation. First, African-American readings of the Bible should be considered a type of cultural reading, reflective of a cultural and ideological situation—and social location. Second, such readings have a history; they did not appear first in the late twentieth century, nor in Ransom's era. Such a history of readings reflects different situations in, understandings of, and orientations to the world. Third, these historical readings can and should inform all contemporary African-American culturalist readings of the Bible.

---

23. Ibid., 304.

To ignore these readings is to cut the present off from the rich resources and wisdom of the past, to be deprived of perspectives beyond the givens of the present. To embrace these readings is in turn to provide the general orientation that allows every historical reading to be put in perspective and critiqued accordingly. Thus, even the reading associated with Ransom's address can be critiqued as a historical reading, as a reading that is a response to a time and place and reflective of a particular (social-status) agenda. The aspects of it that may be considered liberating and prophetic for its time may not necessarily be considered so for many in the late twentieth century. Thus, only respect for the long historical trajectory of biblical readings among African Americans will help them come to see a reading as authentically their own, and on what basis such a reading can be engaged for the sake of rereading for the present and the future.

This essay points to the general importance and hermeneutical implications of the consideration of situation in the readings of the Bible. African Americans, perhaps more than any other racial/ethnic group in the United States, by historical tradition and present realities, represent radical otherness—of origins, appearance, speech, orientation to world, and (for most, even today) physical location. Consideration of readings of the Bible among African Americans, then, forces the issue of the imperative for addressing social location in biblical interpretation, and thereby offers dramatic case-study possibilities and challenges for all biblical-historical and constructive work. Full consideration of African-American historical readings of the Bible may now, for example, make it nearly impossible to escape coming to terms with "Scripture" as cultural construction, as having meaning only within the history of construction of world. And so now it would seem that the logical and provocative place from which to begin the critical-interpretive task for the end of this century is not with a focus upon text, but upon construction of world.

5

The Author/Text/Reader and Power: Suggestions for a Critical Framework for Biblical Studies

Gale A. Yee

In his introduction to literary theory, Terry Eagleton states that

> one might very roughly periodize the history of modern literary theory into three stages: a preoccupation with the *author* (Romanticism and the nineteenth century); an exclusive concern with the *text* (New Criticism); and a marked shift of attention to the *reader* over recent years.[1]

One may also observe similar periods with special emphases either on the author, the text, or the reader in the study of the Bible.[2] Historical, form, source, tradition, and redaction criticism all focus on the author, more broadly defined to include not only the composer himself[3] but everything involved in the *production* of his text, for example, the preliterary history of the oral traditions that he takes over, the historical world in which he lived and to which he responded, and so on. The main focus of these methods, comprehensively assumed under the "historical-critical" designation, is the reconstruction of history and religion in the biblical world.

Dissatisfaction with the limitations of the historical-critical method has expressed itself within the past fifteen years in different ways. First, the field has seen a shift from author-centered *historical*-critical methods to text-centered *literary*-critical methods. A move has taken place from inquiries into the preliterary stages seeking the historical setting, the more original saying, the various *Sitze-im-Leben,* the circles of tradents,

---

1. T. Eagleton, *Literary Theory: An Introduction* (Minneapolis: Univ. of Minnesota Press, 1983) 74; emphasis added.
2. J. Barton, *Reading the Old Testament: Method in Biblical Study* (Philadelphia: Westminster, 1984) 198–207.
3. I am assuming that the Bible on the whole is a product of male authorship, particularly in his symbolization of woman as evil.

and so on, to the literary texts themselves. The turn to the text fore-
grounds the aesthetic beauty of the literature and the religious power of
its rhetoric. One encounters firsthand the text and not simply the formative historical situations behind the text. This shift from author to
text, from production to product, from history to literature, has taken
a number of forms, corresponding to the plurality that already exists in
contemporary literary theory.[4]

Second, another trajectory in biblical interpretation remains author-
centered in approach but moves beyond history to the social world of
the biblical text. Scholars here employ the methods and models of cultural anthropology and sociology to shed light on the ancient society
and culture of the biblical world. Focus is put on the interrelationships
of groups organized in social structures, functioning in harmony or in
conflict.[5] The topics of interest from a social-scientific perspective are
many and varied. One may investigate the social structure of ancient Israel as a confederation of tribes, as a nation under a monarchy, or as a
people under a colonial power. Others can examine kinship, marriage,
and inheritance customs; class structures; values systems (for example,
honor/shame, purity/impurity); or the social roles of priesthood, ritual,
and symbol—all in order to illumine the biblical world of both the
Hebrew Bible and New Testament.

Third, along with the move toward text-centered methods, biblical
criticism has witnessed the emergence of reader-centered criticism.[6] As
the name implies, reader-response or reception theories locate meaning
in the experience of the reader and his or her *consumption* of the text:

> The reader makes implicit connections, fills in gaps, draws infer-
> ences and tests out hunches; and to do this means drawing on a
> tacit knowledge of the world in general and of literary conven-
> tions in particular. *The text itself is really no more than a series of
> "cues" to the reader, invitations to construct a piece of language
> into meaning.* In the terminology of reception theory, the reader

4. See, for example, R. M. Schwartz, ed., *The Book and the Text: The Bible and
Literary Theory* (Cambridge, Mass.: Basil Blackwell, 1990). In the turn to the text, one
also observes the rhetorical criticism of J. Muilenburg; the focus on narrative poetics
in M. Sternberg, R. Alter, A. Berlin, and S. Bar-Efrat; on narratology in M. Bal; on
structuralism in D. Jobling; and on deconstruction in P. Miscall.

5. B. J. Malina, "The Social Sciences and Biblical Interpretation," *The Bible and
Liberation: Political and Social Hermeneutics* (ed. N. K. Gottwald; Maryknoll, N.Y.:
Orbis Books, 1983) 11–25. N. K. Gottwald, "Sociological Method in the Study of
Ancient Israel," in *The Bible and Liberation*, 26–37.

6. E. V. McKnight, *Post-Modern Use of the Bible: The Emergence of Reader-
Oriented Criticism* (Nashville: Abingdon, 1988); idem, *The Bible and the Reader: An
Introduction to Literary Criticism* (Philadelphia: Fortress Press, 1985). See *Semeia* 31
(1985) and 48 (1989) for special issues on reader-oriented approaches to biblical texts.

"concretizes" the literary work, which is in itself no more than a chain of organized black marks on a page.[7]

Biblical criticism is still undergoing shifts in paradigm from author, to text, to reader, which parallel similar movements emphasizing literary production, written product, or reader consumption in contemporary literary theory. It is possible and quite legitimate to keep the three elements, author, text, and reader, analytically distinct in biblical criticism. The discipline of biblical studies already manifests this heuristic separation in the different emphases placed on each of these three elements during the course of its history of interpretation.

Problems arise, however, when one views the essential critical act in studying the Bible solely as the determination of its "meaning," whether this meaning is located in the author, the text, or the reader. Critical analysis then becomes primarily *interpretation* of this foundational text, whose ultimate goal is "meaning" (either the author's, the text's, or the reader's meaning). I will first address the problems in privileging one of these three areas where "meaning" is thought to occur. I will then argue for a shift of focus in biblical study that takes seriously the question of power that influences author, text, and reader in the production, product, and consumption of "meaning."

Privileging the Author

One problem in the exclusive focus on the author in traditional historical criticism is the neglect of the text itself. Obvious reaction to this restriction of meaning to the author is seen in the shift away from historical criticism to more literary-critical investigations of the biblical text in recent years.

The modification of author-centered approaches in the present rise of social-scientific criticism is also not immune to the neglect of the text.[8] In a review several years ago, I criticized a social-scientific study on the ancient Israelite woman by Carol Meyers precisely in this regard.[9] Although Meyers's interdisciplinary approach is informed by the social-scientific and archaeological theories that illuminate the social world

---

7. Eagleton, *Literary Theory*, 76; emphasis added. See also the annotated bibliography in J. P. Tompkins, ed., *Reader-Response Criticism: From Formalism to Post-Structuralism* (Baltimore: Johns Hopkins University Press, 1980) 233–72.

8. D. Jobling ("Sociological and Literary Approaches to the Bible: How Shall the Twain Meet?" *Journal for the Study of the Old Testament* 38 [1987] 85–93) has already discussed this problem in his review of N. K. Gottwald's *The Hebrew Bible: A Socio-Literary Introduction* (Philadelphia: Fortress Press, 1985).

9. G. A. Yee, review of *Discovering Eve: Ancient Israelite Women in Context*, by C. Meyers, *Catholic Biblical Quarterly* 52 (1990) 530–32.

of ancient Israel, she has no literary theory to reckon with the biblical text itself. This lack of literary theory accounts for her dismissal of the biblical text in her reconstruction of the ancient Israelite woman. In her endeavor to show that the position of women in ancient Israel was higher than has been appreciated, she overlooks passages in the text itself that would reveal otherwise.

Privileging the Text

The text-centered literary-critical approaches to the Bible are susceptible to the same criticisms lodged against their literary counterparts, New Criticism, formalism, and structuralism. Severing the text from the author and the reader results in an ahistorical analysis that regards literature primarily as an aesthetic object unto itself rather than a social practice intimately connected to a particular history.[10] The valorization of the text, what Mikhail Bakhtin describes as *"the fetishization of the artistic work artifact,"*[11] ignores the workings of ideology in the text. It disregards the fact that ideology is *produced* by a particular author, culturally constrained by historical time, place, gender, class, and bias, among other things.

Besides ignoring its *production,* the valorization of the text, or the *product,* creates problems in the *consumption* of the text by the reader. These problems become particularly acute when reading the Bible, which has a different normative value in different religious communities. Difficulties lie in the location of meaning primarily in "the text" as *the* inspired word of God. The biblical text is vested with an authority that is literally sacrosanct. The major dilemma is that competing claims to truth become very problematic. The same text can be used for diametrically opposed contexts and theological positions. A work like the book of Exodus can be appropriated by both a right-wing fundamentalist and a Marxist liberation theologian. Genesis 1–3 has been taken up by misogynists and feminists alike to diminish or exalt the status of women. Those who locate meaning exclusively in "the text" must reckon with the issue of competing claims to truth, rather than simply dismissing the opposing view as heretical or bourgeois, male-bashing or sexist. One of the insights of modern literary theory is the recognition

---

10. Eagleton, *Literary Theory,* 91.

11. M. Bakhtin, "Discourse in Life and Discourse in Art (Concerning Sociological Poetics)," *Contemporary Literary Criticism: Literary and Cultural Studies* (ed. R. C. Davis and R. Schleifer; 2d ed.; New York: Longman, 1989) 394. See also, Eagleton, *Literary Theory,* 49

of the polyvalent character of the text.[12] In different ways this insight is being taken over by scholars of the Bible.[13] However, religious and denominational constraints often still hinder or preclude the development of a more reader-sensitive doctrine of biblical inspiration.

Privileging the Reader

The term *eisegesis* is one often employed by biblical scholars to refer to what should *not* be done with regard to the Bible, that is, "reading into" the biblical text what one wants it to mean. It is opposed to *exegesis,* ostensibly the correct way of studying the Bible, where, through historical-critical and some varieties of literary-critical exegesis, one is able to draw "out" of the text its meaning.[14] The negative evaluation of eisegesis is related to two assumptions about the nature of "correct" exegesis: first, that an objective, value-neutral inquiry into the text is possible in a proper exegesis of the text, and, second, that there is *one meaning,* primarily the author's own, that exegesis wants to discern. The suspicion of the reader of the biblical text is closely allied to the determination of both religious and academic communities to control the interpretation of such a founding text. Interpretation is put into the hands of elites and specialists who are equipped (either by the laying on of hands or with academic degrees) to grasp *the meaning* of the text.

Although a plurality of reader-centered literary theorists exists, each having different perspectives on the role of the reader,[15] all of them seem to concur in opposing the conviction of New Criticism that meaning is intrinsic to the literary text totally and exclusively. Taking their cues from their literary colleagues, reader-centered biblical scholars challenge historical-critical methods with their so-called objective, value-neutral search for *the* definitive and universal meaning in the biblical text, thought to be located either in the author's intention or in the world represented by the text. The shift of paradigm to the reader underscores the importance of context and a reader's specific social location or place

---

12. This is particularly evident in poststructuralism. See Eagleton, *Literary Theory,* 127–50.

13. See S. Lasine, "Indeterminacy and the Bible: A Review of Literary and Anthropological Theories and Their Application to Biblical Texts," *Hebrew Studies* 27 (1986) 48–80.

14. See J. H. Hayes and C. R. Holladay, *Biblical Exegesis: A Beginners Handbook* (Atlanta: John Knox, 1982) 5.

15. S. R. Suleiman, "Introduction: Varieties of Audience-Oriented Criticism," *The Reader in the Text: Essays on Audience and Interpretation* (ed. S. R. Suleiman and I. Crosman; Princeton, N.J.: Princeton Univ. Press, 1980) 3–45. The first two chapters of S. Mailloux, *Interpretive Conventions: The Reader in the Study of American Fiction* (Ithaca, N.Y.: Cornell Univ. Press, 1982) 19–65, provide a helpful critique of psychological and social models of reading.

of interpretation. The positionality of the reader with respect to factors such as gender, race, class, ethnicity, and religion becomes determinative in answering the question, What does the text mean?[16]

Nevertheless, in an engaging article Jane Tompkins maintains that despite their apparently radical divergence from New Criticism, reader-oriented critics are akin to their New Critical associates in presuming that determining "meaning" is the goal of the critical enterprise:

> The essential similarity between New Criticism and reader-response criticism is obscured by the great issue that seems to divide them: whether meaning is to be located in the text or in the reader. The location of meaning, however, is only an issue when one assumes that the specification of meaning is the aim of the critical act. Thus, although New Critics and reader-oriented critics do not locate meaning in the same place, both schools assume that to specify meaning is criticism's ultimate goal.[17]

Tompkins goes on to show that in the classical period, in the Renaissance, and during the Augustan Age, audience response rather than the determination of meaning was the primary critical concern. In classical antiquity, language was considered a form of power that is exerted upon the world. Hence, literary criticism was absorbed in mastering the rhetorical skills that enabled one to wield that power and in exercising ethical control over literary production. In the Renaissance, when poets became dependent upon an aristocratic class for patronage, poems were regarded as a public form of influence, a means of accomplishing specific class-related social transactions. During the Augustan Age, satire commanded the literary scene, and the literary act was regarded as a weapon to be hurled against an adversary, as a partisan activity whose purpose was to advance individual and factional interest. Thus the social functions of literature and the motives of its users were particularly foregrounded in criticism during this time.

Nevertheless, from the late eighteenth century onward, culminating in New Criticism, literature was gradually severed from its social roles and designated as an aesthetic object of contemplation and study. "Once the

---

16. According to McKnight, *Post-Modern Use of the Bible*, 150: "A reader-oriented approach acknowledges that the contemporary reader's 'intending' of the text is not the same as that of the ancient author and/or the ancient readers....But is there not continuity between the past and the present? Is it not possible that the reader's 'intention' is of a piece with the author's intention and with the meaning and significance found by earlier readers with different views? This will mean not that there is no meaning, but that meanings discovered in different epochs are authentic—that meanings discovered with approaches that are informed by discourse and hermeneutic oriented insights are authentic in the same fashion—not final, but satisfying and authentic."

17. J. P. Tompkins, "The Reader in History: The Changing Shape of Literary Response," *Reader-Response Criticism*, 201.

literary work has been defined as an object of knowledge, as meaning not doing, interpretation becomes the supreme critical act."[18] According to Tompkins, reader-response critics have failed to break out of the New Critical mold that equated criticism with the quest for meaning and explication. She argues for a shift of emphasis "away from the analysis of individual texts toward an investigation of what it is that makes texts visible in the first place." Taking on a political nature in this endeavor, criticism will share a commonality with a long history of criticism prior to formalism in viewing language as a form of power exerted in the world. Questions regarding meaning will be framed more broadly in the complex relationship between discourse and power: "What makes one set of perceptual strategies or literary conventions win out over another? If the world is the product of interpretation, then who or what determines which interpretive system will prevail?"[19]

Discourse and Power

Whatever dangers the term *eisegesis* signal for interpreters should not blind them to the fact that all scholarship on the Bible begins with the *act of reading:*

> Be it from the point of view of philology, historical criticism, textual criticism, or on the literary side, close reading, structuralism, or deconstruction, each and every approach to the Bible starts with readings. Readings always in the plural.[20]

Biblical scholars should therefore repudiate the positivist notion of a value-free investigation. Any investigation into the biblical text through whatever method is a reading by a particular reader.

According to Mieke Bal, the exegetical methods themselves are institutionalized sets of codes, or modes of discourse, structured by readers and imposed upon the text by readers.[21] A particular exegetical method functions like a template to make some sense of the text or give it some coherence. It gathers the codes in the text and correlates them with its own mode of discourse or code. The synthetic ability of interpretive

---

18. Ibid., 222.

19. Ibid., 225–27.

20. M. Bal, "Introduction," *Anti-Covenant: Counter-Reading Women's Lives in the Hebrew Bible* (ed. M. Bal; Bible and Literature Series 22; Sheffield, England: Almond, 1989) 11–12.

21. M. Bal, *Murder and Difference: Gender, Genre, and Scholarship on Sisera's Death* (Bloomington: Indiana Univ. Press, 1988) 2–11. The disciplinary codes, or modes of discourse, that Bal examines are the historical code, the theological code, the anthropological code, and the literary code. The thematic code and the neglected gender code constitute the two transdisciplinary codes.

codes to integrate seemingly diverse and disparate data into a coherent whole accounts for the power of codes as critical instruments. Nevertheless, while acknowledging that codes lead us far into the understanding of the text and its cultural background, Bal argues that "*at the same time* they reveal to what degree their bias imposes, stimulates, or permits a practice of censorship that stems from the restriction and the institutionalization of codes."[22]

The characteristic feature of this censorship in all the exegetical methods paradoxically discloses by way of exclusion the interests, biases, and ideologies of those who utilize them. What is deemed important to study in a particular investigation automatically reveals what is not important to look at. We have already seen how author-centered inquiries invariably neglect the text and reader and how text-centered methods often overlook the author and underestimate the reader. We can expand the author- and text-centered (or production-, product-centered) categories further: examining only powerful men in the biblical world excludes all women and ordinary men. Looking only at elite groups in that world overlooks the common folk, poor people, slaves, and other marginalized populations. A text that recounts only the exploits of great men makes it seem as if these were the only individuals important in the society that produced it. A text told from the perspective of the conquerors will not usually reveal the interests or the pain of the conquered.

By choosing a particular method with which to study a biblical text, a reader automatically sets limits on the kinds of questions that can be asked and on the results of her or his investigation. It therefore behooves a reader to be conscious of what these methodological limitations actually are. Lack of regard to the censorship feature in any exegetical method lulls a reader into a false security that allows "the implicit codes—moral, religious, and aesthetic—to go unnoticed, smuggled in like contraband."[23] It is precisely these implicit codes affecting the conclusions of one's study that divulge one's concerns, prejudices, and ideologies. The real danger in espousing a "value-neutral" perspective in reading is having an ideological agenda without acknowledging it.

At stake in foregrounding the reader is one's ethical responsibility in reading and its concomitant political repercussions. This is especially the case in reading such a foundational work as the Bible, a book that continues to be a powerful standard for people's present-day social, as well as religious, attitudes and behavior. The Bible was not written to be an object of aesthetic beauty or contemplation, but as a persuasive force forming opinion, making judgments, and exerting change. It was a form of power acting upon the world. Hence, Tompkins's sug-

---

22. Ibid., 9.
23. Ibid., 136.

gestion that a shift of critical emphasis focusing on what makes the Bible visible in the first place is particularly relevant. Critical study of the Bible would then be in keeping with the more pragmatic notion of criticism in antiquity that sought to appropriate a text's rhetorical power and to exercise ethical supervision over its uses. Such a criticism poses different questions: How does my reading of the Bible affect my relationships with my spouse, my children, with others in my religious community, my social community, my national community, my global community? Does my reading help in transforming society or does it (sub)consciously affirm the status quo and collude with its sexism, racism, anti-Semitism, classism, and imperialism? Which power groups and interests does my reading serve or not serve? What power groups have a say in determining the "veracity" of my reading?

> However eagerly one attempts to overcome the limitations of reading, every scholar of texts is a reader in the first place. Acknowledging that status, and accounting for the underlying guiding conventions, is a primary ethical responsibility of all scholars. Not only must we acknowledge the relative status of our readings, we also need to analyze the positions of power which underlie the social circulation of readings.[24]

In giving this attention to the reader, I am not advocating a completely reader-centered investigation. In fact, my argument is that one should not privilege any of the three areas author/text/reader as the sole locus of meaning. This includes the reader. Nor am I championing eisegesis, reading into the text what you want it to say. Both the author and the text constrain the reader in some way, just as the reader constrains in some way both the author and the text. Nor am I rejecting meaning as a legitimate pursuit in critical inquiry. Rather, my concern is that the question of meaning be more broadly framed within the relations of discourse and power. What are the social locations of power that make meaning possible in the *production of meaning* in the text and in the *consumption of meaning* by the reader?

In emphasizing the reader, I wish to show three things: first, how all exegetical approaches are a matter of reading; second, how the rejection of the reader, in the mistaken interests of an objective, value-neutral study, makes the reader/investigator unknowingly (or perhaps even knowingly!) complicit in the institutionalized ideologies of the methods, which have for the most part excluded gender, race, and class as specific categories of analysis; and, third, that all readings involve ethical responsibility, particularly in the case of a religiously and socially influential work like the Bible.

---

24. Bal, "Introduction," 15.

I have kept the discussions of author, text, and reader (production, product, consumption) analytically distinct for heuristic reasons. They are, however, very much interconnected, interrelating through the course of history very much like a spiral that is both circular and linear. The ancient biblical writer affects and is affected by the social world in which he lives. In a very real way, he is a product of that world. Nevertheless, he is involved in the production of that world in the production of the literary text. The text that he proffers is his "reading" of the social world he inhabits, a "reading" that describes, legitimates, denounces, satirizes, entertains, and exhorts that social world. In short, through his "reading" of his social world he attempts to create or produce that world. His "reading" becomes a product for consumption by other readers, who themselves are products of their own social world. These later readers utilize the ancient text/reading in the production of their own "readings" of their particular world in order to legitimate, satirize, entertain, exhort, and so on, that world.

In order to get beyond the problems of author-centered, text-centered, or reader-centered methods, one should not privilege any of these areas. A critical task in biblical exegesis is developing a theoretical framework that encompasses all three components, author, text, and reader, as they interface with power. This theoretical framework must be able to bridge the fissures among the author (broadly defined to include everyone and everything involved in the production of the text), the autonomous text, and the specific reader, all three in their historical specificities of gender, race, class, and religion. "Meaning" and "truth" in the biblical text involve a dynamic interplay among these three, with power as the pivotal variable. "Meaning" and "truth" must be critically analyzed to determine the answer to the question: Whose meaning and whose truth?

Part Two

Contestations:
Social Locations in Conflict

6

They're Nothing but Incestuous Bastards: The Polemical Use of Sex and Sexuality in Hebrew Canon Narratives

Randall C. Bailey

The scholarly treatment of sex and sexuality within Hebrew Canon narrative and poetry is becoming a more interesting and complex subject with the rise of feminist, womanist, and ideological criticism.[1] This reexamination in terms of literary motifs has led to some more critical and alternative readings of these passages.[2]

1. Earlier versions of this paper were presented at the 1991 international meeting of the Society of Biblical Literature in Rome and at the annual meeting of the society in Kansas City that same year. Those works were supported through a faculty development grant from the Interdenominational Theological Center.

2. See, for example, R. C. Bailey, "Doing the Wrong Thing: Male-Female Relationships in the Hebrew Canon," *We Belong Together: Churches in Solidarity with Women* (ed. S. Cunningham; New York: Friendship, 1992) 18–29; M. Bal, *Lethal Love: Feminist Readings of Biblical Love Stories* (Bloomington: Indiana Univ. Press, 1987); idem, *Murder and Difference: Gender, Genre, and Scholarship on Sisera's Death* (Bloomington: Indiana Univ. Press, 1988); idem, *Death and Dissymmetry: The Politics of Coherence in the Book of Judges* (Chicago: Univ. of Chicago Press, 1988); J. W. H. Bos, "Out of the Shadows: Genesis 38; Judges 4:17-22; Ruth 3," *Reasoning with the Foxes: Female Wit in a World of Male Power* (ed. J. C. Exum and J. W. H. Bos; Semeia 42; Decatur, Ga.: Scholars Press, 1988) 37–67; F. van Dijk-Hemmes, "Tamar and the Limits of Patriarchy: Between Rape and Seduction," *Anti-Covenant: Counter-Reading Women's Lives in the Hebrew Bible* (ed. M. Bal; Sheffield, England: Almond, 1989) 135–56; D. N. Fewell and D. M. Gunn, "Controlling Perspectives: Women, Men and the Authority of Violence in Jud 4–5," *Journal of the American Academy of Religion* 56 (1990) 389–411; idem, "Tipping the Balance: Sternberg's Reader and the Rape of Dinah," *Journal of Biblical Literature* 10 (1991) 193–211; E. Fuchs, "Structure and Patriarchal Functions in the Biblical Betrothal Type-Scene," *Journal of Feminist Studies in Religion* 3 (1987) 7–13; S. Pace Jeansonne, *The Women of Genesis* (Minneapolis: Fortress Press, 1990); A. Marmesh, "Anti-Covenant," *Anti-Covenant*, 43–58; B. Merideth, "Desire and Danger: The Drama of Betrayal," *Anti-Covenant*, 61–78; C. A. Newsom, "Women and the Discourse of Patriarchal Wisdom: A Case Study of Prov 1–9," *Gender and Difference in Ancient Israel* (ed. P. L. Day; Minneapolis: Fortress Press, 1989) 142–60; S. Niditch, "Eroticism and Death in the Tale of Jael," *Gender and Difference*, 43–57; P. Trible, *God and the Rhetoric of Sexuality* (Overtures to Biblical Literature; Philadelphia: Fortress Press, 1978); idem, *Texts of Terror: Literary-Feminist Readings of Biblical Narratives* (Overtures to Biblical Literature; Philadelphia: Fortress Press, 1984); and R. J. Weems,

Within the prophetic literature one sees a gradual growth of the tradition of the use of sexual innuendo and sexual motifs from simply labeling to more graphic and sexually explicit detailing of actions. Thus, one notes Hosea's charges of apostasy by the people depicted in the imagery of illicit sexual behavior, namely, harlotry:

> Therefore your daughters play the whore
> and your daughters-in-law commit adultery.
> I will not punish your daughters when they play the whore,
> nor your daughters-in-law when they commit adultery;
> for the men themselves go aside with whores,
> and sacrifice with temple prostitutes;
> thus a people without understanding comes to ruin. (4:13b-14)

Similarly, Hosea depicts divine judgment in sexual terms in the statement:

> I will strip her naked
> and expose her as in the day she was born. (2:3a)

Later in the preexilic period the use of rape as a metaphor for divine judgment was further expanded by Jeremiah and Nahum in such statements as:

> And if you say in your heart,
> "Why have these things come upon me?"
> it is for the greatness of your iniquity
> that your skirts are lifted up,
> and you are violated. (Jer 13:22)

> I am against you,
> says the LORD of hosts,
> and will lift up your skirts over your face;
> and I will let nations look on your nakedness
> and kingdoms on your shame.
> I will throw filth at you
> and treat you with contempt,
> and make you a spectacle. (Nah 3:5-6)

During the exilic period Ezekiel developed the use of sexual imagery to a much more explicit and detailed literary level, as can be seen in the following passage:

> And the Babylonians came to her into the bed of love, and they defiled her with their lust; and after she defiled herself with them, she

Just a Sister Away: A Womanist Vision of Women's Relationships in the Bible (San Diego: LuraMedia, 1988).

turned from them in disgust. When she carried on her whorings so openly and flaunted her nakedness, I turned in disgust from her, as I had turned from her sister. Yet she increased her whorings, remembering the days of her youth, when she played the whore in the land of Egypt and lusted after her paramours there, whose members were like those of donkeys, and whose emission was like that of stallions. Thus you longed for the lewdness of your youth, when the Egyptians fondled your bosom and caressed your young breasts. (23:17-21)

Recently this use of sexuality and sexual imagery has come under attack by scholars such as Mark S. Bryan, Renita J. Weems, and Gale A. Yee,[3] who have understood these metaphors to grow out of the everyday experience of the people at the time they were utilized but who find these metaphors of questionable theological value today.[4] What is interesting in this development and expansion of the metaphor of sex for apostasy and the metaphor of sexual violation and violence for divine judgment in the Prophets is that all of it is directed at Israel. It is Israel who is depicted as acting in a sexually deviant or unacceptable fashion and who receives the blame from the Israelite deity. While Ezekiel expands the metaphor to describe the actions of the other nations,[5] it is still Israel and Judah who are the addressees.

In the narrative materials in the Hebrew Canon, the motif of sexuality is developed in a manner similar to that in the Prophets: the depictions of the breaking of sexual taboos move from the less explicit to the more graphic. Unlike the prophetic materials, however, the objects of ridicule in most of these narratives are not Israel and Judah but their neighbors, the foreign nations that surround them. It is only late in her development that such use of sexuality within narratives is directed at the people of

---

3. M. S. Bryan, "The Threat to the Reputation of YHWH: The Portrayal of the Divine Character in the Book of Ezekiel" (Ph.D. diss., Sheffield University, 1992) esp. chap 3; R. J. Weems, "Gomer: Victim of Violence or Victim of Metaphor?" Interpretation for Liberation (ed. K. Canon; Semeia 47; Decatur, Ga.: Scholars Press, 1989) 87–104; G. A. Yee, "Spreading Your Legs to Anyone Who Passed: The Pornography of Ezekiel 16 and 13" (paper presented at the 1990 annual meeting of the Society of Biblical Literature in New Orleans, November 17, 1990).

4. One of the aims of historical-critical scholarship is to situate the text within its own historical context. Thus, many of the texts (such as the ones just cited) of sexual violence perpetrated against women are understood or explained as "fitting" within the context of a patriarchal society. While this may well be the case, such explanations often have either of two effects. One of the effects is "redeeming" the text from the horrors found within it because the reader can say, "Well that's just the way they thought about women then, but in our enlightened state, we don't think of them in this way." The other effect is a desensitizing of the reader to the extreme nature of the objectionable material. While this essay will use aspects of historical-critical methodology, especially source criticism, there will be a conscious attempt to push beyond this limiting Tendenz of the method.

5. See Ezek 16:1ff.

ancient Judah.[6] It is the purpose of this essay, therefore, to examine how this use of sexuality by either innuendo or graphic detail functions literarily as part of an agenda of discrediting these individuals and nations and thereby sanctioning, or sanctifying, Israelite hatred and oppression of these people.[7] My argument will appeal to how the nations so depicted are treated in other parts of the narratives of a certain source. Given the limitation of space, only a few examples found in Genesis will be explored to demonstrate how the literary motif functions.

There are three personal/contextual preliminary remarks that I should share with the reader, since I do not approach this subject without bias. First, within these narratives there is an in-group (generally Israel or an Israelite) and an out-group (the foreigner). I grew up as a fat kid who had no acumen on the basketball court, leaving me always as the unchosen one when teams picked up for sides, and that has left me wary of this kind of "in-group/out-group" hermeneutics.

Second, in the narratives about to be discussed the difference between "in" and "out" is expressed in labeling the other as one who practices a taboo sexual act. As a member of the Black African diaspora, I have lived my life as an outsider in a society that has used sexual stereotyping as a means of sanctioning its racist practices in oppressing my people.[8] This social location has most probably helped me in being repulsed by these texts. My interest in examining these narratives is in demonstrating how this part of the narrative functions as a programmatic piece for the writer.[9] I must admit that finding such polemical works within the canon makes the struggle of exegesis more painful but all the more necessary for liberative efforts.

Finally, what is offered here is *a* reading of the texts. It is not

6. Note for instance the portrayal of the men working for Boaz in Ruth 2 (see D. N. Fewell and D. M. Gunn, *Compromising Redemption: Relating Characters in the Book of Ruth* [Louisville: Westminster, 1990] esp. 76–77, 84–86, and 122–23 n. 11) and the portrayal of Boaz in Ruth 3 (see my treatment in "Doing the Wrong Thing," 26–28).

7. Examples of how this type of discrediting functions literarily are T. Friedman, "Heard Any Good Jews Lately," *Exploring Language* (ed. G. Goshgarian; 6th ed.; New York: HarperCollins, 1992) 311–16; and H. A. Bosmajian, "Defining the 'American Indian': A Case Study in Language," *Exploring Language,* 317–24.

8. For a discussion of the role of sexuality in the formation of white supremacist thought, especially as regards people of African descent, see L. Smith, *Killers of the Dream* (Garden City, N.Y.: Anchor Books, 1963), and A. Hacker, *Two Nations: Black and White, Separate, Hostile, Unequal* (New York: Macmillan, 1992).

9. In this regard I am following M. Sternberg's concept of the "primacy effect"; Sternberg notes that a programmatic text is one that contains early categorization that predisposes the reader to view a particular character or character group in accord with the perspective of the writer (see *Expositional Modes and Temporal Ordering in Fiction* [Baltimore: Johns Hopkins Univ. Press, 1978] 93–96). Similarly, B. Upensky speaks to how the ideological view of the narrator is depicted through characterization as a means of getting the reader on the narrator's ideological side (see *A Poetics of Composition: The Structure of the Artistic Text and Typology of a Compositional Form* [Berkeley: Univ. of California Press, 1973]).

presented as *the only* reading, but as one of many possible readings and interpretations. My hope is to offer an example of a "subversive reading," to use Mary Ann Tolbert's phrase.

Jeopardizing the Matriarch

The earliest strands of the Torah contain narratives depicting the "jeopardizing of the matriarch" (Genesis 12, 20, and 26).[10] In these narratives the patriarch speculates that the foreigners among whom the family is intending to reside are the types of sexual deviants who would kill a man in order to marry his wife. Thus, there is a plan of trickery devised[11] in which the matriarch is to pose as the sister of the patriarch in order to spare his life, which she does. In two of these narratives, Genesis 12 and 20, this action results in her being placed in the harems of the unsuspecting foreign kings. The allusion to sex in these narratives is not graphic. Rather, it is posed as a speculation placed on the lips of the patriarch and alluded to in the enigmatic phrase placed in the mouth of Pharaoh in 12:19a, "so that I took her for my wife."

What is interesting in all three of these narratives is that the foreign monarchs, upon discovering the ruse, show themselves to be more god-fearing and upright than the patriarchs by either returning the wife and paying the husband (12:20 and 20:14) or legislating for the couple's protection (26:11). In this manner the reader may be left with the questions: Who is the sexual deviant—the one smeared by innuendo—in this narrative? Is it the foreign monarch, or the patriarch who places his wife in jeopardy to save his own life and then profits from such deception, or the writers who gave us these stories? As Ann Marmesh correctly notes:

> There is a strange logic in this fabula.... When wife-abduction benefits the patriarchs, it is allowed. If wife-abduction threatens the well-being of the male household, it is disallowed. God intervenes, or one male negotiates with the other, and the patriarch goes off with more riches than before. The logic of the fabula is

---

10. This naming of the literary motif is in line with von Rad's designation (see G. von Rad, *Genesis* [Old Testament Library; Philadelphia: Westminster, 1972] 167). It is offered in place of J. Williams's benign designation of the "wife-sister type scene." Interestingly, Williams's focus in these narratives is the way the "*promise* to the patriarch is *endangered*" as opposed to the matriarch's safety (see J. Williams, *Women Recounted: Narrative Thinking and the God of Israel* [Sheffield, England: Almond, 1982] 46–47; emphasis added). Similarly, Marmesh's designation of "the sister-wife masquerade" focuses on the motivation of the male, without attention to the dire consequences for the female [see "Anti-Covenant," 48–49].

11. Although the foreigners change, Egyptians in Genesis 12 and Philistines in Genesis 20 and 26, this difference does not substantially affect the argument or motif.

twisted in a way that absolves the males from being condemned or condemning themselves for the trading of women for favors.[12]

As one looks at the tradition history of these narratives, one finds, first, that throughout the patriarchal narratives, trickery is a major motif by which the social status of the patriarchs is advanced. Second, in the redacting of the J traditions found in Genesis 12 and 26 by E in Genesis 20, one notes the common tendency to correct ethical problems posed by J in earlier narratives.[13] Thus, in chapter 20 Sarah does not engage in sexual activity while in the harem (v. 4), and Abraham is shown not to have really lied (v. 12 says Sarah was indeed his half sister).[14] Interestingly, E changes neither the sexual innuendo, as regards the foreign leaders, nor the solution of jeopardizing the matriarch. The message is that these parts of the narrative are not problematic for the tradition. Therefore, this threefold repetition of innuendo tends to counteract or skew the reader's perception that in these narratives these foreigners act responsibly and ethically once confronted with the reality of the situation.[15] Instead, many readers accept the veracity of the innuendo and cheer for the patriarch.

Further evidence of these writers' polemical use of sexual innuendo is seen in the fact that this point of contrast between the unrealized fantasy of the patriarch and the moral uprightness of the foreigners is often missed by modern commentators. For instance, in his classic work *The History of Israel,* Martin Noth proclaims:

Above all, however, it was the life and faith of the Canaanites that was alien to the Israelite tribes. They seemed to them to *be morally inferior and degenerate, lustful and unprincipled....* The

---

12. Marmesh, "Anti-Covenant," 50.

13. While R. Alter and others prefer to explain this duplication of narratives in terms of the narrative use of "type scenes" (see R. Alter, *The Art of Biblical Narrative* [New York: Basic Books, 1981] 49–51), an important part of this analysis is the explanation of the polemical use of the motif within its historical and possibly developmental contexts. Thus, in this and the following analyses the dating and naming of sources/writers of these materials will be crucial in identifying the ideological concerns of the writers in giving us the materials in this way.

14. See the discussion of this unit in J. Van Seters, *Abraham in History and Tradition* (New Haven: Yale Univ. Press, 1975) 175–81.

15. Note for example J. Skinner's attempts at rationalizing Abraham's fears (J. Skinner, *Genesis* [International Critical Commentary; Edinburgh: T. and T. Clark, 1930] 248–49). In a similar vein W. Brueggemann argues, "As so often in the Old Testament, in this text we are dealing with minority literature of survival. It is a narrative told by a powerless community to maintain its courage and identity in the face of overwhelming odds and unresponsive power. The story itself *redresses the imbalance between imperial reality and helpless faith* by introducing Yahweh, the new reality which neither the hungry father nor the king had reckoned with.... The story might still serve that function for the faithful community when it is a minority needing to maintain its courage and identity *in the face of overwhelming odds and hostile values*" (W. Brueggemann, *Genesis* [Atlanta: John Knox, 1982] 128; emphasis added).

intention behind the story told in Gen. xxvi, 7-11 is to point out that anyone who comes into the region of a Canaanite city must reckon with the possibility of his wife falling victim to the inhabitants' covetousness and himself, as the woman's husband, running the danger of being treacherously murdered.... For the Israelite tribes, who were used to the strict discipline of a patriarchal society, *all this moral laxity was contemptible and shocking.* It was no doubt bound up to some extent with the special character of the Canaanite cult to the which the Israelites, with the devotion to *the demands of a stern deity,* were particularly antagonistic.[16]

Similarly, Gerhard von Rad argues that "the narrative vividly describes how *accurate* Abraham's forecast was."[17] Again, these narratives contradict such a notion. The foreigners are exonerated in these narratives. The innuendo posed by the fantasy of the patriarch, however, is so strong literarily that the reader, especially the one holding the Israelites to be the "in-group," misses the ending and is fixated at the beginning. Such commentators forget that the one who placed his wife in jeopardy in Genesis comes from the same group who placed their daughters and daughters-in-law into whoredom according to Hosea. By the same token, this stern deity, as Noth refers to YHWH, is one whose just judgment is depicted as divinely sanctioned rape.

What could cause such a polemicizing of the foreign monarch as a sexual deviant?[18] Perhaps the answer can be found in the fact that the only extant narrative from that part of the ancient world in which a monarch kills a foreigner in order to marry his wife is found in 2 Sam 11:2-27, the David-Bathsheba-Uriah complex. This should cause us to wonder whether we have in these jeopardizing-of-the-matriarch narratives Israel's attempt to foist onto foreigners its own foibles. Peter Miscall has noted the comparison not only with 2 Samuel 11 but also with 1 Kings 21, the incident with Naboth's vineyard. He has similarly argued that

---

16. M. Noth, *The History of Israel* (2d ed.; New York: Harper and Row, 1960) 143; emphasis added. It should be noted that this tendency goes back to Josephus, who uses phrases and clauses such as "the Egyptians' frenzy for women" and "The king of the Egyptians, not content with the reports of her, was fired with a desire to see her and on the point of laying hands on her" (*Ant* 1.8.1).

17. Von Rad, *Genesis,* 168; emphasis added.

18. It is most interesting that this is not a question raised by commentators. Most attempts at delineating "intention" speak to the portrayal of Abraham and the intervention of YHWH. They do not, however, examine the function of the ruse in terms of the characterization of the "foreigner." See G. W. Coates, *Genesis with an Introduction to Narrative Literature* (Grand Rapids: Eerdmans, 1983) 112; von Rad, *Genesis,* 169–70; D. Rosenberg and H. Bloom, *The Book of J* (New York: Grove Weidenfeld, 1990) 200–201; and G. Wenham, *Genesis 1–15* (Waco, Tex.: Word, 1987) 291–92.

in comparison with Genesis 12, the two stories of David and Ahab involve royal power and the possible exercise of it in a violent manner. A king or queen may murder simply because he or she wants something and perhaps has already taken it. Other modes of action may be open, but royal power and desire seem to have a close, if not necessary, relation to violence and murder. This statement, in view of Genesis 12, 20, and 26, should not be expressed so generally, since in those passages the kings do not act violently. It is kings and queens of Judah and Israel for whom murder is an automatic recourse, and it is Hebrews, Abraham and Isaac, who assume that desire and murder are necessarily related.[19]

In other words, the polemicists for the monarchy could be deflecting criticism of the sexual practices and appetites of their sponsors by propagandizing that this type of behavior was really that of foreigners. They may be suggesting that the Israelites should not pay attention to the sexual politics of Israel,[20] but rather should worry about the deviant foreign monarchs. Similarly, the negative view of foreign nations in the North, as evidenced by prophetic judgment speeches against depending on these nations,[21] is reinforced by keeping this innuendo going in later centuries. Thus, there is no need for E to correct it in redacting the tradition.

The Incestuous Bastards

As with the prophetic materials, during the exilic and postexilic periods the portrayal of individuals partaking in taboo sexual acts in narratives involving foreigners becomes more explicit. Unlike the earlier narratives, however, the foreigners so depicted are not exonerated.

The earliest of these narratives is the seduction of Lot by his daughters after the destruction of Sodom and Gomorrah (Gen 19:29-38). According to the narrative, after the destruction of the cities by the deity, Lot and his two daughters are directed from Zoar (ṣô'ar) into the mountains, where they settle in a mĕ'ārāh (a cave), which, as David Gunn

---

19. P. Miscall, *The Workings of Old Testament Narrative* (Philadelphia: Fortress Press, 1983) 33–40.

20. For a discussion of the David-Bathsheba narrative as one of political intrigue, where sexuality is a tool of politics, rather than merely a story of sexual lust, see my treatment of these texts in *David in Love and War: The Pursuit of Power in 2 Samuel 10–12* (Sheffield, England: Sheffield Academic, 1990) 84–90.

21. It is most interesting to see how often these prophetic judgment speeches argue against dependence upon Egyptian military might. For a further elaboration of this, see my article "Beyond Identification: The Use of Africans in Old Testament Poetry and Narratives," *Stony the Road We Trod: African American Biblical Interpretation* (ed. C. H. Felder; Minneapolis: Fortress Press, 1991) 165–84.

points out, is a Hebrew euphemism for the female sex organ.[22] Fearing that the lack of men will lead to their extinction, the two daughters, whom Lot so hospitably offered up to the men of Sodom (19:8),[23] devise a plan to get Lot drunk two nights in a row and to seduce him in order to get pregnant.[24] They successfully follow the plan—the older daughter on the first night and the younger daughter on the second night. Lot is so drunk both nights that he knows neither their lying down nor rising up (*wĕlô yāda' bĕšikbāh ûbĕqûmāh*). But he does perform!

They must have been truly sensitive to their cycles and the herd effect must have been in operation, for both women get pregnant after only one try each and both have sons. The narrative ends with the birth narrative formula *watahar, watēled, watîqrāh* (she became pregnant, gave birth, and named), followed by ethnological etiologies for the names of the two children, *mô'ab* (from my father, who is the progenitor of the Moabites), and *ben-'amî* (son of my people, who is the progenitor of the Ammonites). Thus, the incest is openly proclaimed in these names.

Though this narrative is commonly designated as coming from the hand of the Yahwist,[25] there are several indications that it comes rather from the hand of the Deuteronomistic school. First is the fact that with the exception of Ps 83:9, which refers to all Transjordanian and Mesopotamian nations as well as the Philistines as *benê lôṭ* (children of Lot), the only other mention of Lot outside of Genesis is in Deut 2:9 and 19. In these two passages there are injunctions against warring with the Moabites and Ammonites, who are called the descendants of Lot. No other canonical mention of these two nations connects them to this narrative in Genesis 19.[26]

Second, the term used for their place of settlement, *mĕ'ārāh* (a cave), is used in the Pentateuch only here and by P in reference to *mĕ'ārat hammahpēlāh,* the couples' cave, in which the patriarchs and matriarchs are said to be buried (see Genesis 24 and 49). All other references to this

---

22. D. M. Gunn, *The Fate of King Saul: An Interpretation of a Biblical Story* (Sheffield, England: Sheffield Academic, 1980) 93–94.

23. The extent to which some male commentators will go to exonerate Lot in this regard is seen in the pleas of both von Rad (*Genesis,* 218) and C. Westermann (*Genesis 12–36: A Commentary* [Minneapolis: Augsburg, 1985] 302) not to judge this by current-day standards, but rather to see the desperation in one seeking a way out of no way.

24. Jeansonne correctly notes, "These women, who have been passive throughout the narrative, now take action; they cleverly plan to obtain the means for changing their powerless existence. For the first time one of them speaks" (*The Women of Genesis,* 41).

25. See M. Noth, *A History of Pentateuchal Traditions* (Chico, Calif.: Scholars, 1981) 264; and N. K. Gottwald, *The Hebrew Bible: A Socio-Literary Introduction* (Philadelphia: Fortress Press, 1985) 151.

26. While Westermann notes the relationship between the double notice in Deuteronomy 2 and this unit, he does not explore the possibilities of source connection. Instead he argues that the notice in Deuteronomy is positive and should be used to support a positive view in Genesis 19 (*Genesis 12–36,* 315). On this point see my argument below.

term are found in the Deuteronomistic History. Joshua kills the kings of the southern coalition who are hiding in a *mě'ārāh* (Josh 10:16). In 1 Sam 22:1, while fleeing from Saul, David hides in a *mě'ārāh* in Adulam. Similarly, David could have killed Saul while defecating in a *mě'ārāh* (1 Sam 24:3-4). It is also while in a *mě'ārāh* that David requests water from a well in Bethlehem, his homeland (2 Sam 23:13).[27]

A third indication that this narrative is from the hand of the Deuteronomistic school is in the twice-used formula *běšikbāh ûběqûmāh* (her lying down and getting up). The only other place we find this formula in the canon is in Deut 6:7b and 11:19: "Keep these words that I am commanding you today in your heart. Recite them to your children and talk about them when you are at home and when you are away, when you lie down and when you rise [*běšākběkāh ûběqûmekāh*]."

Fourth, there is much attention given to the rights of birth in this narrative. As depicted, first the *běhîrāh* (the older daughter) and then the *ṣě'îrāh* (the younger daughter) act. As Deut 21:15-17 states, one must honor birth order in the right of male inheritance. In other patriarchal narratives this tradition is continuously subverted. In the giving of blessings, it is the younger son who receives them, by intention of the father, as with Abraham and Isaac, or by trickery of the mother, as with Jacob and Rebecca with Isaac. Similarly, in the Laban-Jacob cycle, it is only through trickery that Leah is the first to marry. In this narrative, however, there is scrupulous attention on the part of the narrator to observe birth order rights.

Finally, the concluding formula, *'ad hayyôm* (until today),[28] is a variation on the oft-used Deuteronomistic etiological formula, *'ad hayyôm hazeh* (until this day).[29] Thus, with all of these linguistic indicators, it seems safe to ascribe this unit, which most scholars argue as being a later addition to the Abraham-Lot cycle, to the Deuteronomistic school.

If our source designation is correct, how does this help us in understanding what is happening in this unit in terms of the polemical usage of sex? Why would the Deuteronomistic school go through so much trouble in adding such a narrative to this cycle of tradition? On the one hand, this narrative serves as an explanation of the harsh exclusion of members of these two nations, the Moabites and Ammonites, from the *qahal yhwh*, the assembly of the Lord, found in Deut 23:4. This passage offers the prohibition which states, "No Ammonite or Moabite

---

27. Perhaps Deuteronomy suffers from either a *mě'ārāh* complex or from *mě'ārāh* envy!

28. Again Westermann notes that this formula refers to the existence of the ethnos and not to the individual so named (*Genesis 12–36*, 314). In this regard he is following Van Seters, *Abraham in History and Tradition.*

29. See R. Polzin, *Moses and the Deuteronomist: A Literary Study of the Deuteronomistic History* (New York: Seabury, 1980); and M. Weinfeld, *Deuteronomy and the Deuteronomic School* (Oxford: Clarendon, 1972).

shall be admitted to the assembly of the LORD. Even to the tenth generation, none of their descendants shall be admitted to the assembly of the LORD." While this prohibition is followed by a motive clause referring to actions of these nations during the wilderness wandering period, the introduction of the unit is the general apodictic prohibition found in 23:2, "Those born of an illicit union [*mamzēr*] shall not be admitted." As von Rad has argued, within the Deuteronomic Code we have old laws that were elaborated upon by new laws for a new generation. Thus, the narrative in Gen 19:30-38 sets the background for labeling these two nations *mamzērîm* (bastards).[30]

The effect of both the narrative in Genesis 19 and the laws in Deuteronomy 23, therefore, is to label within the consciousness of the reader the view of these nations as nothing more than "incestuous bastards." Through the use of repetition in the narrative in Genesis 19 to depict the planning and carrying out of the seduction of Lot by his daughters two nights in a row, the narrator grinds home the notion of *mamzērîm*. First Lot is exonerated for his participation by the repetition of *wĕlō' yāda'* (he did not know) (vv. 33b and 35b).[31] The direct link to Abraham is not tarnished. It was Lot's daughters, children of the disobedient wife, who plotted.[32]

To further ensure this interpretation, the narrator has the women give the children names that unashamedly announce the incestuous circumstances of their conception. The narrative thus claims, in so many words: "Yes, Israel is ethnologically kin to the Ammonites and Moabites, but look where they came from. When we have the family reunion, they will be there, but we want nothing to do with these bastards."[33]

---

30. This is contrary to Westermann's argument that there is no ideological relationship between these two units (*Genesis 12–36*, 315).

31. R. Coote and D. Ord see this information functioning to exonerate Lot. As they state, "The children of Lot, cousins of Abram, were the Moabites and the Ammonites, two nations to the east subdued and ruled by David. They were under Israel's rule because they were born of incest, while Israel was born of a god. The result of incest though they may be, they were redeemed by the repetition of the phrase 'Lot did not know' (R. Coote and D. Ord, *The Bible's First History* [Philadelphia: Fortress Press, 1989] 132).

32. Jeansonne argues that the point of the narrative is to show him to be incompetent in many respects (*Women of Genesis*, 42).

33. Interestingly, Brueggemann looks at the same data *within* the text and arrives at the conclusion that "no stigma is attached to the action of the mothers in the narrative. In fact, they appear to be celebrated for their bold and heroic action, which surely stands beyond convention. In any case, the new children at least come of pure stock. Lot and his daughters are clearly treated as members of the family of promise. In an odd way, this is one more evidence of the inclusive attitude of Genesis toward other peoples" (*Genesis*, 176–77). Though he does state that in this narrative the two nations "are designated as bastards" (176), perhaps his not seeing the connection between the laws in Deuteronomy and this passage is what explains his viewing this as an example of Israelite "inclusiveness."

Once this dehumanization through graphic sexual innuendo is accomplished, one is then set to read the other narratives in the Deuteronomistic History, such as 2 Sam 8:2, where David lines up the Moabites and arbitrarily kills off two-thirds of them, and 2 Sam 12:26-31, where David ritually humiliates the Ammonites, and we are prone to accept this oppression as meritorious. Similarly, in depicting the move toward a monarchy, the Deuteronomistic Historian gives us three stories of the defeat of the Ammonites by Jephthah (Judges 11), Saul (1 Samuel 11), and David (2 Samuel 10 and 12). In all three of these narratives, the battle begins due to grotesque aggression on the part of the Ammonites, who are soundly defeated.[34] What else would one expect from such *mamzērîm?* Of course they should be ritually humiliated, since they are the very ones 'ad *hayyôm* (until today) who came from this incestuous union. In other words, once dehumanized through sexual innuendo, these nations are fair game for Israelite exploitation and oppression, as well as exclusion from the *qahal yhwh* (the assembly of the Lord).

Claus Westermann strongly objects to the polemical interpretation of this unit. He states:

> Moab and Ammon, as descendants of Lot, are described as Israel's kinsmen, distant though the relationship may be. It is viewed positively in Deut 2:9, 19. The later enmity toward the two people, which appears in Deut 23:3-6, can have led to the text being understood in a later period as showing contempt for Moab and Ammon; this, however, is not its purpose as such.[35]

In order to maintain his position, Westermann argues that the key to the interpretation of the narrative is found in the center, the concern of the women for continuation of the species after the destruction of Sodom. He interprets their actions within the framework of primeval events. Since there is nothing within the narratives, however, that draws this connection, namely, that they have returned to a situation of total depopulation of the world, this argument is not convincing. Similarly, since he views the etiologies at the end of the narrative to be secondary, he interprets the text as though they are not present. Thus, he ignores the final form in which the ending literarily overshadows the middle. Finally, he does not offer an alternative intention for the narrative. Thus, I would maintain that this narrative forms the bridge between the admission of Moabite/Ammonite/Israelite tribal relationship (Deuteronomy 2) and the curse upon them (Deuteronomy 23).

The final form of this narrative ends in the children being given names that openly attest to the incest. At the same time most of the refer-

---

34. See my discussion of these units and their similarities in *David in Love and War,* 64.

35. Westermann, *Genesis 12–36,* 315.

ences to Moab and Ammon in the Deuteronomistic History are negative. Thus, it appears that any ambivalence resulting from ethnic association between Israel and these nations is resolved by the contempt with which the polemical view presents these foreign nations.

"Look What He Did to Me!"

Now let us consider a postexilic narrative in which sexual innuendo is used polemically. Such a narrative is found in Gen 9:18-28, the end of the Noah cycle. Again we have a composite narrative as evidenced in the use of both divine names in verses 26-27. As the story goes, Noah's three sons, Shem, Ham, and Japheth, are reintroduced to the reader, with the additional information that Ham is the progenitor of Canaan and that these three sons of Noah are the ones who repopulate the earth after the flood. In addition, we are told that Noah is the first to plant a vineyard.

After this introductory material we are told of an incident that happened when Noah was drunk in his tent. The story is fraught with ambiguity as to what exactly happens.[36] We are told that Noah drank wine, got drunk, *wayitgal bĕtôk 'hālô* ("and he was 'uncovered' inside his tent" [v. 21b]). *Gālāh* (uncover) can connote the performance of a sexual act, but one wonders, especially since Noah is drunk, whether such is the case here; or is it merely a reference to self-exposure?[37]

As the narrative continues, Ham, who is once again designated by his parental relationship to Canaan, sees the nakedness (*'ervat*) of his father. Again, a question arises: Should this term be interpreted in line with the idioms "to uncover the nakedness" in Leviticus 18 and "to see the nakedness" in Leviticus 20, which both imply sexual misconduct, or in this narrative does the term refer to voyeurism?

Ham then goes and tells his brothers, who are outside. The problem of ambiguity[38] again arises, since there is no modifier to accompany *wayaged* (and he told [v. 22b]), as to what he actually tells them. In

---

36. See F. W. Bassett ("Noah's Nakedness and the Curse of Canaan: A Case of Incest?" *Vetus Testamentum* 21 [1971] 232–37) for a discussion of the varied interpretations of this text and a rebuttal to this article by Gene Rice, "The Curse That Never Was," *Journal of Religious Thought* 29 (1972) 5–27. Bassett argues that this narrative is about a sexual offense committed by Ham, whose line is cursed through Canaan. Rice argues that we have a composite narrative in which the curse is associated with a justification of Israelite conquest of Canaanite land in Davidic times, and that there is no relationship at all to Hamites in this. See my argument below in regard to this.

37. It is interesting that no other Hebrew Canon text speaks of one "uncovering oneself."

38. On the function of ambiguity in narrative see M. Sternberg, *The Poetics of Biblical Narrative: Ideological Literature and the Drama of Reading* (Bloomington: Indiana Univ. Press, 1985).

other words, it states neither "He told them what he saw," nor "He told them what he did."

At the same time, the narrative is fraught with reversal, in that while Noah is *bĕ'āhālô* (in his tent [v. 21]—which is generally associated with security),[39] and his other two sons, we are told, are *bahûṣ* (outside—which is generally associated with a location of trouble),[40] the trouble here is not outside but in the tent. To add to the ambiguity, the narrator then spends meticulous details in describing how carefully and awkwardly the other two sons place a robe on their shoulders (which is generally an idiom for burdens that only the deity can remove),[41] walk backward (which is generally associated with death),[42] and without seeing, cover their father. This causes the reader to think that maybe the suspicion of sexual innuendo is misdirected. It must have been only voyeurism on Ham's part.

The narrator then again muddies the water by telling us that Noah awoke from his sleep and knew (*wayēda'*) what his younger son had done *to him*. Does this now mean that the reader should refer back to the terms *wayitgal* (uncovered) and *wayērā' 'et 'erwat* (saw the nakedness)? Noah then proceeds to curse Canaan to be a slave to Shem and Japheth, who are called his brothers, not his uncles, and Shem and Japheth are blessed.[43]

For the purposes of this discussion, we shall not even attempt to resolve these knotty exegetical problems. The literature is replete with such attempts.[44] Rather, our concern is that the ambiguity leads the reader to resolve that something sexual has transpired, and, regardless of the act, it was enough to justify a curse of slavery upon at least one of the descendants of Ham.

While most exegetes assign this narrative to J, it appears to be a conflation of two sources, and the hand of the Priestly school is seen to be

---

39. See Gen 31:33, where Rachel is safe from Laban's search for his gods; Josh 7:21, where Achan places the *ḥerem* in his tent for safe keeping; 1 Sam 17:54, where David puts Goliath's head away for safekeeping; and 2 Sam 6:17, where the ark is placed within a tent. It should also be noted that, like our first example, the motif of trickery is found in Judg 4:17ff., where Jael tricks Sisera into her tent, a place he thinks is safe.

40. See 2 Kgs 10:24, where Jehu stations his men to catch any of the priests of Ba'al who might escape his slaughter, and Jer 6:11, Ezek 7:15, and Hos 7:1, where YHWH's punishment of the people is to take place outside.

41. See Job 31:36 and Isa 9:3, 5.

42. See 1 Sam 4:18, when Eli, hearing the news of his sons' death, falls backward to his death.

43. This point is very crucial to Rice's argument ("The Curse").

44. In addition to the previously cited works, see H. H. Cohen, *The Drunkenness of Noah* (Tuscaloosa: Univ. of Alabama Press, 1974); J. Hoftijzer, "Some Remarks on the Tale of Noah's Drunkenness," *Oudtestamentische Studiën* 12 (1958) 22–27; A. Phillips, "Uncovering the Father's Skirt," *Vetus Testamentum* 30 (1980) 38–43; and A. P. Ross, "Studies in the Book of Genesis. Part I: The Curse of Canaan," *Bibliotheca Sacra* 137 (1980) 223–40.

heavy in this narrative. In the first place, all of the terms in the narrative that open up the subject of sexual misconduct have their locus within the sexual prohibitions of the Holiness Code in Leviticus 18 and 20.

Further evidence for assigning the final form of this passage to the Priestly school is based on the fact that nowhere else in the flood narrative does J mention names for the sons of Noah. All such references to Shem, Ham, and Japheth are in P passages. When one looks at the Table of Nations in Genesis 10,[45] the J passages speak of Cush, Mizrayim, and Canaan as progenitors (10:8-19), which fits tenth-century BCE reality. J knows not Shem, Ham, and Japheth. Again, these names as progenitors are in the P recasting of the Table of Nations, with all of the above-mentioned J progenitors being subsumed under the P Hamite line (10:6-7, 20).

As Gene Rice has correctly noted, the function of the P recasting of the Table of Nations is to show the differentiation between these groupings and to show that Shem, the last mentioned, is the most important for the future line of Israel.[46] This interpretation is borne out by the delineation of the Shemite genealogy (ʾēleh tôlĕdôt šem) in Gen 11:10-20, which is then followed by the tôlĕdôt of Terah, the father of Abram in verses 27-32. Thus, it appears that the Priestly school has taken an old curse against Canaan and recast it within the context of Ham performing a suspicious sexual act.

Again, if our source analysis is correct, what is the purpose of the Priestly school giving us such a narrative in its current location? In other words, why not stop with the rainbow and the repopulation notice? A clue is seen when we look at the sexual misconduct laws in Leviticus 18 and 20. There we note that these sections of the code begin with "You shall not do as they do in the land of Egypt, where you lived, and you shall not do as they do in the land of Canaan, to which I am bringing you" (18:3). The implication is that the prohibition in verse 6, "None of you shall approach anyone near of kin to uncover nakedness," is the referent for "what the Egyptians and Canaanites do."[47]

Similarly, the section on sexual misconduct prohibitions in Leviticus 20 includes in its closing, "You shall not follow the practices of the nation that I am driving out before you. Because they did all these things, I abhorred them" (20:23).[48] Thus, the message is that these laws in Leviti-

---

45. For extensive treatment of this unit and attendant bibliography, see C. Westermann, *Genesis 1-11* (Minneapolis: Augsburg, 1984) 495-530.

46. See Rice, "The Curse."

47. As C. J. Wenham asserts, "Westermann is right to see the chief thrust of the story as blaming Ham for his improper, quite unfilial behavior....Now the Canaanites *are notorious* throughout the Old Testament for their *aberrant sexual practices*" (G. J. Wenham, *The Book of Leviticus* [Grand Rapids: Eerdmans, 1979]; emphasis added).

48. While Wenham notes that there is a polemical nature to these units in Leviticus, he accepts these statements as true presentations of the reality of Israel being different from

cus 18 and 20 should not be interpreted as an attempt to *stop* Israel from practicing taboo sexual activities. Rather, they should be interpreted as attempts to *keep* Israel from picking up such practices from the Hamite line, specifically Egypt and Canaan. Therefore, the narrative in Gen 9:18-20 polemically serves as the narrative backdrop that grounds these laws.

There is a second polemical purpose served in this use of sexual innuendo in Gen 9:18-29. One of the literary motifs used by some of the writers of ancient Israel in regard to African peoples is that of veneration of them or use of them as a standard of valuation for Israel.[49] Thus, the Queen of Sheba validates Solomon as wise on the basis of his passing her test of riddles (1 Kings 10). Similarly, Jeremiah, in an attempt to show Judah how locked-in to evil ways they are, raises the rhetorical question, "Would the Ethiopian change his/her skin?" In other words, Judah would be willing to repent and return to YHWH to the same extent an Ethiopian would be willing to be other than black, both possibilities being as ridiculous to Jeremiah and his hearers as a leopard wanting to look other than like a leopard. By the same token, when Deutero-Isaiah wants to prove to the exiles that YHWH is still their God and cares for them, he turns to the example of YHWH ransoming them with the Egyptians, Ethiopians, and Sabbeans (Isa 43:3b). Such rhetoric only makes sense in the light of extreme valuation of Africans by segments of ancient Israel.

The Priestly school was not in favor of such veneration of Africans.[50] Rather, the Priestly School consciously depicted members of the Hamite line, as they defined it in Genesis 10, with ridicule. The beginning of the polemicizing is found here in Gen 9:19-20. The Priestly writer gives us a depiction of Ham as violating some sort of sexual taboo, which legitimates his descendants being cursed to be slaves to the Shemites. The social order is to be Shemites over Canaanites/Hamites.[51]

Once this polemicizing is accomplished, the writer then gives us Genesis 10 with a clear delineation of nations into Japhethites, Hamites, and Shemites. Interestingly, the Arameans, whom the Deuteronomistic school associates with Israel's beginnings in Deut 26:5b, are associated

---

its neighbors in regard to the questions of sexuality (see Wenham, *Book of Leviticus,* 250ff.).

49. See my discussion of this motif in "Beyond Identification," 176–78.

50. Cf. my article "Is That Any Name for a Nice Hebrew Boy?: Exodus 2:1-10, The De-Africanization of an Israelite Hero," in *The Recovery of Black Presence: An Interdisciplinary Exploration* (Nashville: Abingdon, 1995), 25–35.

51. An integral part of Rice's ("The Curse") argument is that the curse on Canaan makes sense in tenth-century political terminology. Given the redaction of this curse by P to include not only Canaan but also Ham, since there are the repeated notices that Ham was Canaan's father, and the redaction of chaps. 10–11, one sees that in its final form, P makes no differentiation between Ham and Canaan. Thus, Rice's argument loses its force.

with the Shemite line. Thus, in Genesis 10 there is a clear distinction between Shemites (the proto-Israelites) and Hamites.

Next, in Gen 11:10-20 the Priestly school gives the genealogy of Shem, which leads directly to Abram. The Priestly school is thus saying that although the other pentateuchal sources might suggest different groupings that make up Israel, and although Hos 11:1 might even say, "When Israel was a child, I loved him, and out of Egypt I called my son" (with the verb *qārā'* [to call] being associated with formation and bringing into being), as far as this school is concerned, Israel is totally to be identified with Shem,[52] the one who took the lead in covering up Noah, the one to whom Canaan is to be a slave, the one whose God, YHWH, is to be blessed. This is the one who forms Israel. In effect, the Priestly school says: Why venerate Hamites? They're nothing but sexual deviants, destined to be slaves to Shemites. And if there is any question about it, listen to what YHWH has to say about them in Leviticus 18 and 20.

Conclusions

I have argued, first, that behind the use of sexual innuendo and the depiction of taboo sexual acts by non-Israelites within Hebrew Canon narratives, there is a polemic, which is carried out in other parts of the narratives given to us by the writer of the source. I have also argued that this polemic has as its agenda the discrediting of the people who are depicted as practicing taboo sexual acts, such that they are dehumanized in the process of labeling. Once this is done, other acts of Israelite oppression or devaluation of these people are readily sanctioned, condoned, and accepted by the reader, both ancient and modern. While not all such narratives have been explored, if my reading of these narratives is convincing, I have uncovered another literary motif that can be explored with other such narratives for liberative hermeneutics. In this regard, such a literary motif may lie behind the Deuteronomic label of "the uncircumcised ones" in referring to the Philistines (see 1 Sam 17:36), as well as behind the description of King Ahasuerus, who in Esth 5:1-4 is

---

52. It is interesting to see how this identification and polemicizing of "Shemites" as being the only stock to form ancient Israel and Judah have fed into and buttressed white supremacist notions, especially in the field of biblical studies. After all, many of our departments of biblical studies are found in Semitic studies departments. Similarly, the term "anti-Semite" is used almost exclusively to relate to what should be more appropriately termed "anti–Eurocentric-Jewish" discourse. In other words, even though Genesis 10 lists other nations within the line of Shem, the need for white supremacy to claim ancient Israel as totally separate and apart from its environment, in fact being "proto-Eurocentrist," has led to the embracing of the ideology of P in Genesis 10–11, with wholehearted appreciation.

depicted as being so sexually aroused that he offers half his kingdom to the "pretty woman" outside his window. Further, this polemical use of the motif may also function in the New Testament, especially in the labeling of the Gentiles and other opponents, such as in Eph 4:19-24 and Rom 1:24-27.

Second, I have argued that the use of the outsider/insider motif within the canon is a literary trap into which the reader can too easily fall. I am most surprised how often we oppressed people find ourselves identifying with the insiders in these texts, even though our own stories might be closer to those of the outsiders. Thus, indigenous people whose land has been stolen and who have been subjugated by others read Genesis 19 and do not see themselves depicted in the story of Lot's grandchildren. Rather, they identify with Lot. Oppressed people who have slavery in our "communal story" read Gen 9:19-28 and root for Shem and Japheth, instead of wondering why Ham and Canaan are being maligned. Perhaps this tendency bespeaks our own alienation from our own stories. Perhaps this speaks to an acculturation process whereby the oppressed adopt the ideology of the oppressor.

Finally, we are all aware of the struggle over and use of these texts, especially Gen 9:18-28, in sanctioning U.S. enslavement of African people and in being a cornerstone of South African apartheid. My exegesis could support the oppressive claims that have propped up racist utilization of these texts. Canaanites shall be slaves to Shemites forever. Even though this is a nationalist, as opposed to a racialist, claim (Canaanites and Shemites are of the same geographical and racial stock—that is, Northeastern African), the text does sanction one nation enslaving another. Thus, the appeal to "This isn't a curse on Ham, it's a curse on Canaan," offers no help to practitioners of liberation hermeneutics. By the same token, we have long seen such oppressive hermeneutics in the embracing of passages in Leviticus 18–20 that sanction the oppression of gay and lesbian individuals, all in the name of the "Bible says," which is somewhat ironic, since there is nothing about lesbian practices in these chapters. Such a hermeneutic of "holy hatred" is grounded in the polemical use of this literary motif. The problem is, thus, not only with these supremacist ideologies. Our problem is also with the biblical text itself. Thus, it is hoped this "subversive reading" will lead to liberative action.

7

Reading from My Bicultural Place: Acts 6:1-7

Justo L. González

I must have been six or seven years old. In a large Methodist church in Cuba, in rather broken Spanish, our missionary pastor was speaking of Peter's denial. "How was it that people knew that Peter was one of Jesus' followers?" he asked. And his answer was quite simple: "When you have been with Jesus, it shows on your face." It was a rather inspiring sermon, calling us all to closer fellowship with Jesus. The problem came later. After the service ended, I sat on a wall by the door, carefully looking at each parishioner as they filed out of the church, and deciding that not one of them had been with Jesus!

It was many years later that this text came to have a different meaning for me. The many turns and twists of life had brought me to the United States, and I had been asked to preach at a large and prestigious church. I was concerned that my Spanish accent might make it difficult for the congregation to understand me. I was to preach at a Lenten service, and the text that I had been assigned was Peter's denial, as it appears in the Gospel of Matthew (26:69-75). As I studied the text, verse 73 suddenly stood out: "After a little while the bystanders came up and said to Peter, 'Certainly you are also one of them, for your accent betrays you.'" The reason people knew that Peter was one of Jesus' followers was not because it showed in his face, but because it showed in his speech. He had an accent. He was a Galilean. He was an outsider.

Later, partly through the reflections of Virgil Elizondo, Orlando Costas,[1] and others, I have come to see that this is no incidental element in the gospel narrative, but rather that much of what is at stake in the passion narrative is the conflict between a periphery that has been visited by the Word of God (Galilee) and a center (Jerusalem) that sees its prestige and authority threatened by that very Word, and by the center's inability to control it.

---

1. V. Elizondo, *Galilean Journey: The Mexican-American Promise* (Maryknoll, N.Y.: Orbis Books, 1983); O. Costas, "Evangelism from the Periphery: A Galilean Model," *Apuntes* 2 (1982) 51–59; idem, "Evangelism from the Periphery: The Universality of Galilee," *Apuntes* 2 (1982) 75–84.

Out of these experiences and many long years of living in a society where many seem to think that speaking with a Spanish accent is a sign of ignorance or of sloppy thinking, I have come to read Scripture from a perspective that takes issues of language and culture quite seriously.

It is this perspective that I brought into my reading of the book of Acts, for a commentary on which I have been working for the last few years. It is a perspective that has provoked a number of interesting reflections. In the story of Pentecost, for instance, we are told that, while many were amazed at what was taking place, "Others sneered and said, 'They are filled with new wine.'" Who were those who mocked? I had often been puzzled by the question. How could anyone see so prodigious a miracle and still scoff? What is the image that the book of Acts is trying to convey here? Is it simply that some people are hard of heart—and, in this case, of hearing!—and no miracle will ever convince them? Or is it rather that there were some in the crowd who did not perceive the miracle and therefore laughed at the excitement and the antics of those who did? If so, how could anyone present not see what was taking place? Is Luke[2] so inept a storyteller that he simply introduces these mockers in order to give Peter opportunity for his speech, without realizing that he is thereby undermining his very description of the crucial events of Pentecost?

The matter puzzled me for years, until I came to the realization that the miracle of understanding is perceived as such only by those who do not expect to understand. I was in Istanbul, alone, on Christmas Day, 1957. All around me were sounds and signs I could not decipher. Then, as my gaze wandered to a newsstand, I suddenly noticed a newspaper I could understand. It was written in "Ladino," the sixteenth-century Spanish spoken by the descendants of Sephardic Jews expelled from Spain in 1492. I bought the paper and read it avidly, even though most of what it said was of no material interest to me. While I stood there, eagerly reading every word, several Turks walked up to the newsstand, bought a paper, folded it under their arms, and walked away as if they had done nothing special. They expected to understand; and precisely because they expected to understand, they did not share my joy at understanding.

The joy of unexpected understanding is a common experience among Hispanics in the United States, particularly in those areas where we are a small minority. We walk apprehensively into an office where we have never been before, and our ears pick up one or two words in Spanish. Suddenly the entire atmosphere seems friendlier.

---

2. No matter who the author of Acts may have been, there seems to be little doubt that he or she was also the author of the Third Gospel, and therefore here and in the rest of this essay I follow the convention of calling this unnamed author "Luke."

As I now look at the story of Pentecost through the lens of those experiences, I ask again: Could it be that in Luke's description of the events those who laughed did so because they did not perceive the miracle? And, if they did not perceive the miracle of understanding, could it be that they did not perceive because they expected to understand and therefore saw nothing extraordinary in being addressed in their own language? Had I been a native of Jerusalem and used to being addressed in my own language, I too would have seen nothing extraordinary in being able to understand what the disciples were saying. Could these be the scoffers in Luke's narrative of Pentecost, native Jews who expected to understand and therefore did not fully understand? If so, what we have here is one more case of a theme that appears repeatedly in Scripture: the insiders who are left out precisely because they expect to be insiders—those who are so ensconced in Jerusalem that they cannot see what is happening in Galilee.

That is one of many reflections on language and its use that the book of Acts elicits in me from my bicultural place. Other passages in Acts in which the issue of language may lead to interesting reflections are 14:8-18 and 21:37-40. In Acts 14, Paul and Barnabas stumble into a situation in which their lack of knowledge of the native language and of local traditions leads to a ridiculous misunderstanding.[3] Any bicultural person can tell a dozen stories, some of them funny and some of them tragic, where such misunderstanding took place. In Acts 21, the tribune takes for granted that Paul is a subversive character, until Paul shows that he can speak (rather cultured) Greek. That too parallels the experience of many a bicultural Hispanic in the United States.

For this essay, however, I propose to look more carefully at the story of the election of the seven, as it appears in Acts 6:1-7.

In order to understand my reading of this passage, a word must be said about the "place" from which I read it. I am a member of a denomination that has long prided itself for its pluralism and that has a significant number of Hispanics among its leadership—including one bishop. It is, however, a denomination whose very structure impedes the full participation of Hispanics and other minorities, as well as of the poor. The purpose of that structure is not to impede such participation; yet that is its net effect. It is a structure designed for middle-class congregations, in which any who do not fit that mould will be tolerated and even welcomed, but will never feel entirely at home.

It should also be noted that, although I know this particular denomination best, I work very closely with several others, from Roman Catholics to Pentecostals, and that the problems I find in my own United

---

3. See, for instance, the legend of Philemon and Baucis, as told by Ovid in *Met.* 8.611–724.

Methodist Church I find also in most other churches in the United States: not so much an overt, outright racism—although there is plenty of that too—as an unwillingness to adjust structures and procedures so that all may feel welcome.

The book of Acts begins with the account of Pentecost: the account of how the Holy Spirit was poured on all who were present, and they overcame the barriers of culture and language, and they gave witness to the mighty acts of God. It then moves on to describe the life of the early church, how they witnessed, how they broke bread together with joy, how they shared in all things.

But not everything is rosy. By the fifth chapter we come across the episode of Ananias and Sapphira, who lied to the church and paid dearly for it. Now, in the sixth chapter, we come to another difficult situation. There is "murmuring" in the church because the widows of the Hellenists are being neglected in the daily distribution.

In order to understand this passage, several things need to be clarified, however briefly.

First, the "Hellenists" and the "Hebrews." Actually, they are all Jews. But apparently some are Aramaic-speaking Jews from Palestine, and the others are Jews with connections with the diaspora, many of whom have picked up Hellenistic customs and language.[4] The Hellenists are looked upon with suspicion by many of the more orthodox Jews. Their faith and religious practice may not be entirely orthodox. And this has even political consequences, for it may be possible that the God who in ancient times responded to infidelity by turning the people over to the power of the Philistines is now responding to similar infidelity by supporting the power of Rome. One must remember that this was a time of increasing nationalism, which would eventually lead to the great rebellion and the destruction of Jerusalem, and that one of the great debates among Jews was precisely over the reasons God had allowed Rome to conquer them and over what should be done about it. In that debate, no matter what position various parties took, all were agreed that the main issue was faithfulness to God and to the traditions of their ancestors. Therefore, Hellenistic Jews were suspected not only of sympathies toward the foreign invader but also of being part of the cause for the continuing foreign presence. Perhaps if all Israel were strictly faithful and allowed no Hellenistic accretions to its traditional faith, God would intervene once again and free them from their oppressors.

---

4. H. J. Cadbury, "Note 7: The Hellenists," *The Beginnings of Christianity* (ed. F. J. F. Jackson and K. Lake; London: Macmillan, 1933) 5:59–74; E. C. Blackman, "The Hellenists of Acts 6:1," *Expository Times* 48 (1936–37) 524–25; W. Grundmann, "Das Problem des hellenistischen Christentums innerhalb der Jerusalemer Urgemeinde," *Zeitschrift für die neutestamentliche Wissenschaft* 38 (1939) 45–73; C. F. D. Moule, "Once More, Who Were the Hellenists?" *Expository Times* 70 (1958–59) 100–102.

Therefore, if regular Jewish Christians were regarded with suspicion by those whom Acts calls the "rulers" of Israel, Hellenistic Jewish Christians were doubly suspected.[5] Indeed, persecution will break out against them immediately after this particular text.

Then there are the Hebrews. Chief among these "Hebrews" were the twelve,[6] those who had come with Jesus from Galilee. They were the traditional leadership in the church. They had been with Jesus from the beginning. (At least, so they claimed at the time of the election of Matthias, although that is not what the Gospel of Luke says. That too is typical of the "old guard," which is often ready to apply to others tests that it cannot pass.) Some of them were related to each other: Was this the "cousin system" at work in the early church? They are in charge of the daily distribution. Actually, in Acts 4 we have been told that when people sold properties they brought the money and laid it at the feet of the apostles. So presumably the leaders of the distribution are not just any Hebrews but the twelve, the original leaders, the old guard.

Given such a situation, it is not surprising that the widows of the Hellenists were being neglected in the daily distribution—whatever that daily distribution may have been.[7]

So there is murmuring in the church. All is not well. The twelve, although they are Galileans and therefore are looked at askance by the Jews from Jerusalem, are "Hebrews," for they have grown up in Palestine and their language is Aramaic. Therefore, it is not surprising that their management of the church's resources did not seem fair from the perspective of the Hellenists.

At this point, the "Hebrew" leadership has a clear option, a most human and most natural option. They could say simply: "Who do these people think they are? They are latecomers. Let them be content with what they have. Take it or leave it. After all, we are already being sufficiently nice to them, and now they are creating problems for us."

Yet they cannot really say that. They cannot say it, first of all, because they themselves are Galileans, and from the point of view of the Jewish establishment a Galilean is just as much an outsider as a Hel-

---

5. An interesting interpretation of this passage, which has not been generally accepted but which takes into account the tension between "Hebrews" and "Hellenists" in Jewish society at large, is that of N. Walter, "Apostelgeschichte 6.1 und die Anfänge der Urgemeinde in Jerusalem," *New Testament Studies* 29 (1983) 370–93. According to Walter, the dispute did not take place within the church but in the wider community, and the response of the church in solidarity with the Hellenists was one of the reasons for its increasing appeal to the Hellenists.

6. This is the only passage where Acts refers to the apostles as the "twelve."

7. The phrase that the NRSV translates at "to wait at tables" may mean, as that translation implies, that food for the widows was actually served at tables. It could also have referred to a distribution of money, for the "tables" were also places where financial transactions took place; that would parallel usage in several modern European languages, where the words for "bank" and "bench" are the same.

lenist. But the real reason, the second reason, they cannot say it is that according to the narrative in Acts, the problem has not been created by the Hellenists and their widows. The problem has been created by the Holy Spirit, who on that day of Pentecost made the gospel be preached far and wide to all these strange people who were present in Jerusalem. The Hellenists are not in the church because they forced their way into it. These Hellenistic Jews, and soon Gentiles of every culture and background, are in the church because the Holy Spirit has this nasty habit of tearing down human barriers. Third, they cannot dismiss the murmuring of the Hellenists because the table at which the daily distribution is made is not theirs. Further, the money laid at the feet of the apostles is not the apostles' money. It is the money, it is the table, of the Lord. This has been made quite clear in the earlier story about Ananias and Sapphira. In their scheming, they were not lying only to the apostles. They were lying to the Spirit (Acts 5:3). Were the twelve to say, "This is our money, these are our resources, this is our table," they too would be lying and stealing from the Lord.

The problem is not created by the Hellenists. The problem is created by the Spirit, and either the church deals responsibly with it or it ignores the work of the Holy Spirit.

What that early church does is remarkable. If the twelve had been United Methodists or Presbyterians, they probably would have asked that a token Hellenist be named to help them with the distribution to the Hellenist widows. But they did much more than that. They created a new structure for the administration of the daily distribution. By the names of the seven whom they elected, it appears that they were all Hellenistic Jews. They all have Greek names. Indeed, we are told that one of them, Nicolaus, was not even a Jew by birth.[8]

This was a courageous and an unexpected thing to do. In fact, it was such a strange and unprecedented move that scholars have repeatedly tried to explain it away. When one analyzes their arguments, it is clear that they are not based on the text or on any historical or critical argument beyond the sheer improbability of the account. It is inconceivable to them that this community, where the majority were still "Hebrews," would put the management of its assets in the hands of a group of seven "Hellenists." Thus these scholars often argue that what took place is not what the text says, but rather that a parallel administrative system was established for the Hellenists, so that the seven would manage the affairs and resources of one group, and the twelve those of the other.[9]

8. On the possible later history of Nicolaus, see A. von Harnack, "The Sect of the Nicolaitans and Nicolaus, the Deacon in Jerusalem," *Journal of Religion* 3 (1923) 505–38; F. F. Bruce, *The Book of the Acts* (Grand Rapids: Eerdmans, 1954) 129–30.

9. Thus, for instance, J. Rius-Camps, *El camino de Pablo a la misión de los paganos: Comentario lingüístico y exegético a Hch 13–28* (Madrid: Cristiandad, 1984). Accord-

However, as one reads through the entire narrative of the early chapters of Acts, it is clear that the author is well aware of the difficulties that a decision such as that described in chapter 6 would bring about. In fact, immediately after the story of the election of the seven we are told that the witness of one of the seven (Stephen) led to persecution. Yet Luke also tells us that as a result of this bold decision, "the word of God continued to spread; and the number of the disciples increased greatly in Jerusalem" (Acts 6:7).

If this were all that Luke tells us, it would already be a remarkable sign of the strange way in which the Spirit works among us. But there is more.

The twelve decide that they will give to these seven the administrative tasks[10] and that they will reserve for themselves the ministry of the word. But even this is not enough for the Spirit, who has other ideas. Were we to continue reading the book of Acts, we would find that immediately after the passage read, we are told that Stephen, one of the seven elected to manage the financial resources of the church and not to preach, is giving witness, first with his speech, and then with his life.[11]

The longest "sermon" in Acts is the speech of Stephen, who is supposed to be "waiting at tables" and not preaching! Indeed, were we to read the sixth chapter of Acts without knowing what was coming next, the contrast between what Stephen is appointed to do and what he actually does would be so striking that we would probably think that he was being disobedient.

That, however, is precisely the point of the story, and even of the rest of Acts. In the next chapter, it is Philip, also one of the seven, who takes

ing to Rius-Camps, what was created in the events that Acts 6 describes was "a double administration.... The Twelve would continue, for the moment, to oversee the Hebrew community; the Seven ... would oversee those from the diaspora" (27). A similar "solution" is proposed by P. Gächter, *Petrus und seine Zeit* (Innsbruck: Tyrolia, 1958) 105–54. Gächter adds the conjecture that seven "Hebrews" were elected later and that these are the "elders" who appear in 11:30. This is probably due to the use of the verb *diakonēin* to refer to what the seven are to do and to refer to the fact that their responsibility is the daily *diakonía*. But it is also true that the function that the twelve reserve for themselves is the *diakonía* of the word. Furthermore, nowhere in the New Testament are any of the seven spoken of as deacons—indeed, of only two of them, Stephen and Philip, does the New Testament say another word.

10. Traditionally, the "seven" have been called "deacons," and it has been said that what we have here is the founding of the diaconate (see Irenaeus *Adv. haer.* 1.26; 3.12; 4.15; Cyprian, *Ep.* 3.3; Eusebius *HE* 6.43).

11. At this point, another reflection from my bicultural place may be in order. Those who made difficulties for Stephen were not the "Hebrews," but other Hellenists: "some of those who belonged to the synagogue of the Freedmen (as it was called), Cyreneans, Alexandrians, and others of those from Cilicia and Asia" (Acts 6:9). That too is a common experience in a marginalized bicultural community, where there are always some who, precisely because they do not wish to be considered outsiders, are quick to condemn those from among their own community who do not follow the strictest norms of the dominant culture.

up the ministry of the word. And then Acts turns to the conversion of Paul, who is neither one of the twelve nor one of the seven—and we are off on the mission to the Gentiles, and ultimately to us. In all that narrative, except for the story of Peter and Cornelius in chapter 10, and then other passing references, the twelve have been eclipsed by the seven and their spiritual descendants.

As one reads the entire narrative of Acts from this perspective, it appears that, without even intending to do so, the early church made the mission to the Gentiles possible by responding to the murmurings of the Hellenists in the original community in Jerusalem. By empowering the Greek-speaking element in the church, they opened the way for the mission first to other Greek-speaking Jews, then to the Gentiles, and ultimately to us.

When the book of Acts is read in this way, it appears that the function of the Spirit is not so much to create the structures and procedures by which the church must live forever, but rather to break open structures so that the church may be obedient as it faces each new challenge.

The twelve had a very limited vision of the mission of the church. They did not need a full vision of all that the Spirit would do in the future in order to be obedient in their own time. And yet because of their obedience in their own time, a new future that they did not even suspect was opened to the church and eventually to us. They knew that injustice was not to be tolerated in the community of the Spirit, and that was enough. But because they knew this and acted upon it, new horizons were opened to that community.

Time has passed, and we are constantly facing similar situations. Various groups are telling the church that it is not being entirely fair in today's equivalent of the "daily distribution." The church can ignore them, and often does. It can remind them that they are latecomers and that by all human standards they should be content with what they have. That too is often the practice with minorities in the United States. Or the church can make token gestures toward those who have reason to "murmur": it can set up an office for "ethnic minority issues"; it can develop a "national plan for Hispanic ministry" and then keep it marginal to the rest of the church; it can "elevate" a few token minorities to positions of bureaucratic responsibility. In other words, the church can find a dozen ways to tell ethnic minorities as well as other marginalized people that they are welcome in the church, but that their presence is a problem. The structures and practices are already set. They are set by the Holy Spirit. Those who come later have to adjust to those structures and practices.

Or, in contrast, the church can acknowledge that the problem is not with the latecomers. The problem is that as a church we live by a Spirit who has the uncomfortable habit of creating this sort of problem, of bringing in strange people, of making us sisters and brothers to such people, of inviting us to serve and to partake at a table that is not our own. And for that we are thankful, for were it not for that uncomfortable habit, that undescribable grace of our God, none of us would be here. We, all of us who are Gentile Christians, are here because the Spirit is inclusive, and we are here because long ago that early church was willing to do justice to the murmurings of the Hellenists. And if we will but be obedient to the Spirit today, only the Spirit knows what avenues of mission will be opened for the future.

__ 8 _____

"By the Rivers of Babylon":
Exile as a Way of Life

_____ Ada María Isasi-Díaz ____

It was the summer of 1961, in Santa Rosa, California, when I first read Psalm 137. I remember resonating with most of what the psalm says; I remember feeling it could appropriately voice the pain I was experiencing being away from my country against my will. After the Cuban Missile Crisis in 1962 I realized that my absence from Cuba was to be a long one. Shortly after there came the day when my visa status was changed from "tourist": I became a refugee. Psalm 137 became my refuge: "By the rivers of Babylon we sat and we wept when we remembered Jerusalem."[1]

I recall vividly the day I dared to mention to a friend how much I identified with Psalm 137. Jokingly she answered me, "Are you going to hang up your guitar from some palm tree?" I knew that though she and many others around me intended no harm, in reality they were incapable of understanding the sorrow of being away from *la tierra que me vió nacer* (the land that witnessed my birth). At times, trying to help me I am sure, my friends would ask me to talk about Cuba. Those around me could not figure out why I, who love to sing, always seemed reticent about singing "Guantanamera," the song that uses for its verses poems from the father of my country, José Martí. One of them says:

> Yo quiero cuando me muera
> Sin patria pero sin amo
> Tener en mi tumba
> Un ramo de flores
> Y una bandera.
>
> [I want when I die
> without country but without master

---

1. I do not know what translation was in the prayer book where I found Psalm 137. This and other verses of this psalm throughout this essay are the ones I learned by heart from that prayer book a long time ago.

149

> to have on my tomb
> a bouquet of flowers
> and a flag.]

So I kept saying to myself, "How can we sing Yahweh's song in a foreign land?"

During those early years in *el exilio*, as we Cubans continue to refer to our lives away from the island, circumstances beyond my control led me to live quite apart from my family and from the Cuban communities that were gathering in different parts of the United States and the world. And I struggled to find a way of being committed to what I was doing while, at the same time, always being ready to go back to Cuba as soon as it was possible. "If I forget you, oh Jerusalem, may my right hand wither! May my tongue cleave to my palate if I forgot you!"

Yes, I understand perfectly what the psalmist was trying to capture in the words of Psalm 137. Exile is a very complex way of life. The anguish of living away from one's country might seem to indicate how very much one remembers it. But then, an intrinsic part of the anguish is the fear that, because life does go on, one might forget one's country. "May my tongue cleave to my palate if I do not count Jerusalem the greatest of my joys!"

As years have gone by, it has become harder and harder to make others understand that though I am a U.S. citizen and have lived in the United States longer than the eighteen years I lived in Cuba, I continue to live in *el exilio*. It is today more difficult than ever to convince my friends that if I were allowed to do so by the Cuban government, I would move to Cuba immediately. It is much more challenging now than it was in 1960 to explain to those who love me that I would go back because *I want to*, and that part of the wanting to is having to do it to remain faithful to who I am. And I often continue to turn to Psalm 137 not to try to understand what exile meant for the Israelites and to learn from them, but to find someone who understands me!

Meeting Scientific Exegesis

Once I had discovered Psalm 137 I needed to study it, to find out as much as I could about the situation it was referring to, about the people whose sentiments it expressed and who understood me. I have been fortunate to have, like many of those who have studied the Bible in the second half of this century, a whole array of theories and tools of investigation at my disposal to find out about Psalm 137. I learned how to do scientific exegesis. But no matter how much I tried, I was not able to acquire that disinterested objectivity that seems to be required for this discipline. There are two things that always troubled me about this. First, as a *mujerista*[2] theologian, a Hispanic women's liberation theologian, my hermeneutics of suspicion led me to conclude that most of the time what is considered objectivity is the subjectivity of dominant groups who can impose their understandings on others. Much more important than trying to be objective, I believe, is to identify one's subjectivity, to make clear one's perspective and purpose when dealing with any biblical text. Second, the reason for disinterested objectivity is, supposedly, so that the scholar can come closer to the original meaning of a text. But this seems to me to ignore that the meaning of every text is found in the relationship that is created between the reader, the writer, and the text. It has always been obvious to me that the richness of Psalm 137 has to do as much with what it means to me as with what it meant to the Israelites in Babylon, while at the same time what it means to me is influenced by what it meant to them. This is true not only for me but for all who study and pray the Bible. The point of entry is precisely the reader: she is the one who frames the questions being posed about the text and to the text; her hermeneutics will ultimately influence what the text is understood to have meant and to mean today. Because scientific biblical studies ignore this, they cannot get at the real meaning of the Bible. Attempts to recover the original meaning in reality turn the biblical text into an undiscovered archaeological artifact.[3]

As I struggled doing scientific exegesis of Psalm 137, I discovered two other important considerations. First, knowing everything possible about Psalm 137 is not an end in itself. For us Christians, the important thing regarding this psalm, and all of the Bible, is that it gives voice to an authentic faith-experience. This psalm, precisely because it is an Israelite prayer, was "not inspired by any urge for scientific accuracy."[4] Second, during my exegetical study of Psalm 137, I needed to keep always in touch with the situation for which my studies were providing insight. Scientific exegesis, I believe, should "concern itself, not with the questions it raises, but with the questions that the common people are raising."[5]

---

2. For an amplification of *mujerista,* see my article *"Mujeristas:* A Name of Our Own," *The Future of Liberation Theology* (ed. M. H. Ellis and O. Maduro; Maryknoll, N.Y.: Orbis Books, 1989) 410–19. See also Ada María Isasi-Díaz and others, "Roundtable Discussion: *Mujeristas*—Who We Are and What We Are About," *Journal of Feminist Studies in Religion* 8/1 (Spring 1992) 105–25.

3. See E. Schüssler-Fiorenza, *Revelation: Vision of a Just World* (Minneapolis: Fortress Press, 1991) 1–5.

4. G. Gutiérrez, *The God of Life* (Maryknoll, N.Y.: Orbis Books, 1991) xvi.

5. C. Mesters, "The Use of the Bible in Christian Communities of the Common People," *The Bible and Liberation* (ed. N. K. Gottwald; Maryknoll, N.Y.: Orbis Books, 1983) 132. See also V. Wimbush, "Biblical Historical Study as Liberation: Toward an Afro-Christian Hermeneutic," *The Journal of Religious Thought* 42/2 (Fall-Winter 1985–1986) 9.

The exegetical questions I had about Psalm 137 had to do with its sociohistorical setting. I was interested in knowing about the parallels between the circumstances of the people who originally prayed this psalm and my own circumstances. I was interested in establishing a certain continuity of meaning for the text, in having a dialogue between the history of the people who first prayed Psalm 137 and my own history.[6] I knew they would have no problems understanding my love for my country; but I needed to know as thoroughly as possible if I could and would understand their relationship to their land.

I also needed to know what was behind the vengeful lines that close the psalm, a sentiment that often is also mine in regard to those who keep me from returning to my country. What was the theology regarding dealing with enemies that not only allowed the Israelites but made them pray to have the children of their enemies dashed against the stones? What kind of understanding of the divine allowed them to pray in such fashion?

Other Relevant Details of My Hermeneutics

Twenty years went by between my discovery of Psalm 137 and my exegetical study of it. Three key things happened to me during that time that have profoundly influenced my life and my perspective. First, I had the privilege of living for three years in Lima, Peru, and working there among the very poor. This was for me an "exodus," a formative and paradigmatic experience. For my biblical and theological hermeneutics, for my life perspective, the most important thing that happened to me there was that I, a middle-class white woman,[7] came in touch with *el pueblo,* the people—grassroots people who are mostly Amerindian and poor. Not only did I come in touch with *el pueblo* but I came to value and appreciate *lo popular. Lo popular* has to do with what is most central to the majority of the population, with its main traits.

> The term "popular" (*lo popular* in Spanish) summons images of inequality and subordination and directs attention to the poor conceived as "popular" groups or classes. References to *lo popular* also commonly evoke a sense of collective identity and a claim to group autonomy and self-governance, in particular with regard to choosing leaders, setting group agendas, and explicating the religious identity of all of this.[8]

---

6. Gutiérrez, *The God of Life,* xvi.

7. One of the most shocking things that I came to realize many years later was that when I came to the United States my race had changed from white to "Hispanic."

8. D. H. Levine, *Popular Voices in Latin American Catholicism* (Princeton, N.J.: Princeton Univ. Press, 1992) 6.

During my three years in Lima I came to have a preferential option for the poor, though this term was not being used at that time. I did so for my own sake, for once I lived daily among people who suffered injustice and came to understand how much injustice is an all-pervading system, I realized that only grassroots people who have nothing to gain from the present system can conceive of a different one.

The second thing that happened to me was that I was "born" a feminist. It was at the first "Women's Ordination Conference," celebrated in Detroit during Thanksgiving weekend 1975, that I became conscious of the injustice I was suffering simply because I am a woman. The fact that the Roman Catholic Church does not allow me to be ordained as a priest simply because I am a woman was the catalyst that started my process of conscientization as a feminist. I had lived among the oppressed in Lima; now I came to recognize the oppression in my own life. I went through all the different stages entailed in discovering one has been oppressed: disbelief, anger, compromise, and—eventually—praxis. Through it all, one suspicion was constant: what I was discovering about sexism and about the process of conscientization was familiar. I knew about it, but from where? Little by little I came to understand the connections between sexism and classism (a label for the exploitative system that causes poverty). Little by little I understood that what I had started to learn about the theology of liberation and liberation movements in Latin America could help me understand about sexism and how to struggle against it.

The third event in my life pertinent to my biblical hermeneutics had to do with coming to recognize that, as a Cuban living in the United States, I am part of the Hispanic community. This in turn led me to be aware of and to understand how and why in this country I am a "minority," how and why ethnic prejudice operates in this society and in my life, and how and why the specificity of ethnic prejudice is not necessarily included in the term *racism*. My process of conscientization from then on dealt with the role that racism/ethnic prejudice plays in oppression.[9]

---

9. These experiences and understandings have influenced my analysis of Cuban history, and I have come to believe that not all that has happened in the island since 1959 has necessarily been negative. Though the present devastated economic situation in the island has wiped out what I considered were accomplishments of the revolution, like advances in the delivery of medical assistance and in education, I still think that some good was accomplished. I admit that, though there has been a leveling and even deterioration of the standard of living for a certain sector of the society, there has been improvement for the poorer sectors. I, however, continue to question the cost at which all of this has been accomplished. I deplore the lack of freedom of expression and of self-determination of the people of Cuba, who have not been able to elect their leaders for over forty years. I denounce the creation of what is called "the new class," those in the higher echelons of the system who enjoy all sorts of privileges. And I condemn the preponderant influence that the now-defunct USSR has played in Cuba's history since 1959. Recently I have joined those who call for dialogue with Castro, who stand against the economic

My biblical hermeneutics, then, has as its central focus the binomial oppression-liberation. Central to it is the lived experience of Latinas, *lo popular*. Central to it is the multilayered oppression made possible and sustained in all aspects of our lives by sexism, ethnic prejudice, and classism.[10] Central to it is a liberative praxis that has our work to become agents of our own history—the challenge to be self-defining and self-actualizing women—as an intrinsic element. For this challenge to be met, we know that we have to develop and strengthen our moral agency. And that is one of the main perspectives from which we approach the Bible. For Hispanic women the interpretation, appropriation, and use of the Bible have to enable and enhance our moral agency. Finally, central to my biblical hermeneutics is the day-to-day struggle for survival of Latinas, a struggle made possible by hope in our ability to bring about a different future. Yes, hope makes our struggle possible, but, at the same time, our struggle makes hope possible.

A Scholarly Visit to Psalm 137

I do not intend to do an exhaustive review of the historical setting and circumstances that gave rise to the voices heard in Psalm 137. Suffice it to say four things. First, Psalm 137 "is the only unequivocal reference to the Babylonian exile in the Psalter."[11] But Psalm 137 is not a historical but rather a poetical view of Babylon. It is "a poetic picture, a general impression of nostalgia, of distress, and of a desire for vengeance."[12]

Second, the deportation of Israelites from their land was most probably partial, affecting mostly landed citizens, officials, and priests. Those who were able to stay in Judah, however, may well have been very few, given that many must have died in battle or of starvation and disease or fled away. It should be kept in mind that the deportation to Babylon did not affect the population of the northern state, that Israelites continued to live in Samaria, Galilee, and Transjordan. But though northern Israelites adhered to the religious practices centered in Jerusalem, their Yahwistic religion was highly syncretic. Besides, having been

---

blockade the United States imposed on Cuba some thirty years ago, who denounce any violent solution to the Cuban situation. I have actively joined those who oppose any intervention by foreign powers in Cuba, affirming that it is solely the responsibility of Cubans to resolve the crisis our country endures, and that it is particularly the Cubans in the islands who must map out the course that we are to follow.

10. Though I personally am not poor, the majority of Hispanic women with whom I stand in solidarity—those who are the heart and soul of *el pueblo hispano* (the Hispanic people) and whose lived experience together with my own is the source of my theological enterprise—are poor.

11. P. R. Ackroyd, *Exile and Restoration* (Philadelphia: Westminster, 1968) 225.

12. Ibid.

under foreign rule for 150 years left these Israelites with little nationalist zeal.[13]

The Babylonian exiles were most probably placed in settlements instead of being dispersed among the local population. Though the exiles did undergo hardship and humiliation, there is no evidence to indicate that they suffered unduly. "On the contrary, life in Babylon must have opened up for many of them opportunities that would have never been available in Palestine."[14]

Third, the biblical literature that refers to the Babylonian captivity as well as that written during that period (even though it is not about captivity) makes it possible to know how the exiled people felt about what was happening to them. Since it is hardly likely that they recorded their feelings and understandings of what was happening as it occurred, "an element of reflection and interpretation is surely present."[15]

Fourth, there is sufficient evidence in the Bible to have some understanding of the different reactions and interpretations of the Babylonian exiles as to what had happened to them. Some reacted to the disaster by turning to the worship of familiar Canaanite deities. Others turned to the religion of the conquerors, most probably concluding that the conquest of Judah indicated that the Babylonian gods had been victorious over Yahweh. A third group of the exiled people recognized what had happened to them as divine judgment and reacted with penance. This attitude helped them to accept the prophetic verdict and gave them the ability to look back and produce a significant amount of biblical material, while at the same time making it possible for them to maintain hope for liberation. A fourth and final group, not much different from the third one, saw the fall of Jerusalem as a suprahistorical event embodied in the disaster of 587 BCE—the Day of Yahweh. Because the Day of Yahweh is to be understood as a "cultic event," its historical embodiment draws together previous and subsequent experiences of the people of Israel and provides elements for those moments—including the day of final judgment—that originally belonged to the fall of Jerusalem.[16]

What was—is—the theology behind Psalm 137? First, to understand the Psalms one has to remember that Yahweh for Israel was a God who hearkened to the people in their oppression and often in spectacular ways gave them new opportunities for life. Then, one has to know that Psalm 137 is a psalm of lament in which the author not only was expressing personal grief but was also identifying with the affliction of Israel and grieving for the community. In the literature of Israel, as well as in that of the ancient Middle East, "laments" are a literary

---

13. J. Bright, *A History of Israel* (Philadelphia: Westminster, 1981) 344–45.
14. Ibid., 346.
15. Ackroyd, *Exile and Restoration*, 39.
16. Ibid., 40–49.

form with certain conventions, one of them being cries for vindication and vengeance that use stylized language.[17] Third, Walter Brueggemann points out that this literary form should be understood as "speech of disorientation or dislocation" pouring out laments and appeals for those for whom the orderly world has fallen apart, for those who doubt the meaning of their ordinary lives.[18] Norman Gottwald adds that this disorientation is not an individual matter in a neutral social situation. He insists that in the "laments" one meets "sharp tensions, crises, and ruptures in the social order that, while coming to very sharp expression in the lives of individual psalmists, nevertheless wrack the whole community."[19]

In order to understand the closing lines of Psalm 137, the reader must also be aware of who the Edomites were: neighbors to the Israelites to the east and the south and most probably racially related to them. When Saul (eleventh century BCE) defeated the Edomites, Joab, one of his generals, carried out a campaign of extermination against them. Edom remained in subjection for most of Israel's monarchical period, submitting quietly to the Babylonians in 604 BCE. When the Babylonians besieged and captured Jerusalem in 586, the Edomites joined their forces and were especially zealous against the Jews.[20] In 2 Kings 25:8-13 there is an indication that the Edomites were more zealous in the destruction of Jerusalem than the Babylonians.[21]

Brueggemann offers an insightful explanation of what he calls "venomous passages," such as the one at the end of Psalm 137. First, he contends, these passages need to be understood as cathartic—as bringing to consciousness and allowing expression of something that troubles one in an attempt to eliminate it. Second, it needs to be understood that when one is enraged, "words do not simply follow feelings. They lead them. It is speech which lets us discover the power, depth and intensity of the hurt." Third, vengeful speech is an attempt to make obvious unspoken feelings that, as long as they are not expressed, loom too large

---

17. For an explanation, interpretation, and amplification of the original classification of the Psalms by Mowinkle see B. W. Anderson, *Out of the Depths* (New York: Joint Commission of Education and Cultivation Board of Missions, United Methodist Church, 1970); N. K. Gottwald, *The Hebrew Bible: A Socio-Literary Introduction* (Philadelphia: Fortress Press, 1985); and W. Brueggemann, *Praying the Psalms* (Winona, Minn.: St. Mary's Press, 1982).

18. Brueggemann, *Praying the Psalms,* 21.

19. Gottwald, *Hebrew Bible,* 538.

20. S. Cohen, "Edom," *The Interpreter's Dictionary of the Bible* (ed. E. S. Buckes; Nashville: Abingdon, 1962).

21. See also Lam 41:2; Obadiah 10; Ezekiel 25. Some biblical commentators see the introduction of the phrase "O daughter of Babylon" in verse 8 as a later gloss, given that the Edomites were seen as the worst offenders. It was introduced most probably at a time when the share of the Edomites in the destruction of Jerusalem had been forgotten or at least blurred. See A. Maclaren, "The Psalms," *The Expositor's Bible* (ed. W. R. Nicoll; New York: A. C. Armstrong and Sons, 1908) 486.

for one to deal with. Fourth, we need to see that there is an abyss between speech of vengeance and acts of vengeance. The former is to be valued for "where there is no valued *speech of assault* for the powerless, the risk of *deathly action* is much higher from persons in despair." Finally, the language of vengeance is offered to God; it is for God to decide and to do, in matters not only of recompense but also of vengeance, as Deut 32:35 indicates. Thus there is distance between language and action in this matter of revenge.[22]

Reading Psalm 137 Today

I pray this psalm today for several reasons.[23] First, it is cathartic, helping me to deal with the ongoing pain and longing for my country that being *una exilada* brings me. Though I am not comfortable with its vengeful language at the end, knowing how this language functions in "laments" helps me to be more understanding with myself when I find myself wishing evil on those I hold responsible for my being in exile. This includes learning to be kind to myself, for, though I do not believe that at the time my family left Cuba I was capable of deciding to stay behind, I chide myself about not having been much more directly and aggressively involved over the years in working to resolve the political and economic situation in Cuba. I have come also to realize that the "speech of assault" of this psalm helps me to deal with being afraid that when the opportunity comes to return to Cuba, in spite of what I have always said, I will decide not to return. But as I have come to know the many groups of exiled Cubans working to change the political situation in the island—the great majority of whom constantly use this kind of "speech of assault," with but a few of them actually translating the speech into action—I have also come to realize that such speech can become the only means exiles use to express their feelings about that situation. Often denunciations and calls for vengeance seem to be all that many are willing to do.[24] The "speech of assault," I believe, often becomes not cathartic but rather a screen for the complicity (by omission if not by commission) of all of us in exile in what has happened in Cuba. The cries for vengeance can indeed function to absolve us falsely of all responsibility for the situation in our country.

---

22. Brueggemann, *Praying the Psalms,* 69–70.
23. I have been greatly inspired and helped in my appropriation and application of Psalm 137 by the work of W. Brueggemann. Three of his books have been specially important to me: *The Land* (Philadelphia: Fortress Press, 1977); *Israel in Exile* (Philadelphia: Fortress Press, 1977); and *Hopeful Imagination: Prophetic Voices in Exile* (Philadelphia: Fortress Press, 1986).
24. Polls have repeatedly shown that the vast majority of Cubans will not return to Cuba at the end of the Castro regime.

Second, Psalm 137 also helps to sustain me even when I do not see the possibility of change at hand: it helps me rekindle and sustain hope. Though many of us have become U.S. citizens, the majority of Cubans in exile do not think of ourselves as Americans.[25] It is not that we are not grateful for the opportunities we have had to work hard and make a life for ourselves in this country. Not considering ourselves Americans is part of a countercultural position that serves as a seedbed for hope and spurs us on to action. It is a matter not of chauvinism but of maintaining hope.

The third reason I continue to pray Psalm 137 is for the very reason that Brueggemann says it was written:

> It is important that generation after generation... remember... that the present arrangements are not right, not acceptable, and not finally to be accepted. Psalm 137 draws its power and authority out of another vision, marked by homecoming, which seems remote, but is not for one instant in doubt.... This psalm is the ongoing practice of that hope against enormous odds. It is always, "Lest we forget."[26]

The vehemence reflected in this psalm points to our pain, to our rejection of what makes it impossible for us to return to Cuba, to our love for Cuba—all of them passions that keep alive in us the hope for radical change. Without such passion, how would we be able to say to our children, "lest we forget"?[27] Psalm 137 has helped me maintain my identity as a Cuban so I can pass it on to our children.

Fourth, this psalm has helped me live my exilic existence as a vocation, affirming my exile but not allowing myself to be overcome by it, not giving in to despair and hate. If exile is a vocation, the pain one feels must birth new possibilities. Exile must be a time for radical questioning of the understandings and values that rooted and sustained pre-Castro Cuba. It has helped me, after many years, to be able to say, "There is no going back; when we return to Cuba things cannot be the way they used to be." Exile as a vocation means that we develop a new vision of Cuba, that we move into the future. But this future is not for those of us in exile to decide apart from those who have lived in the island while we were

---

25. Though the term "Cuban American" has begun to be used, it is but the tiniest minority of those of us born in Cuba or of our children born in the United States who identify with such a term. The majority of our teenage children born in this country usually say that they are Cubans born in the United States.

26. W. Brueggemann, *The Message of the Psalms* (Minneapolis: Augsburg, 1984) 75.

27. M. Buttenwieser, *The Psalms* (Chicago: Univ. of Chicago Press, 1938) 221. Buttenwieser notes that there are only three cases in the Hebrew Scripture where instead of the usual noncommittal clause, "So may God do unto me and even more," the writer by the nature of the case does not shrink from uttering a real oath. This is one of those three cases; the other two are Ps 7:4-6 and Job 31:5-40.

away.[28] The future does not rest with a fractured Cuban community, exile groups against each other, or exiles against those who stayed in Cuba. In order to be a unified community we must forgive even when there is no repentance, praying that our forgiveness may bring forth repentance. But we ourselves must also repent and humbly ask for forgiveness for not understanding from afar, for judging from afar. Those exiled from Cuba as well as those Cubans who chose exile must realize that the liberation and justice we all seek for our country cannot happen as long as there is hate and the desire for revenge. Justice and liberation demand forgiveness instead.[29]

Finally, Psalm 137 has taught me that injustice and oppression are also "places" of exile. It has helped me understand and deal with the situations of injustice I have encountered. For example, my "speech of assault" against sexism—against sexist people as well as sexist practices—helps me bring to the fore what oppresses me personally so that I can deal with it and, I hope, help to eliminate it.

Then, as I struggle to stand in solidarity with the poor in this country and in other parts of the world, Psalm 137 helps me sustain hope and maintain a countercultural posture while living in one of the richest countries in the world. This means, among many other things, not succumbing to consumerism, not caring so much about always having enough money that I am not generous in sharing what I have. It means that I have to influence other Christians, in whatever way I can, to understand and accept that we cannot call ourselves Christian if we do not avidly work so all can have what humans need in the struggle for fullness of life: food, shelter, health care, employment. Psalm 137 helps me to maintain a countercultural position by reminding me to "live simply so others can simply live."

A Modern Psalm 137

To close this essay, I want to offer a contemporary version of Psalm 137. I mentioned above how the meaning of any writing lies in the interconnections between the reader, the writer, and the text, and I have tried to

---

28. B. Torres, "Reflexiones de una cubana de visita en Miami," *Miami El Nuevo Heraldo,* August 1, 1992, 14A. This heartfelt article points out the differences between what the author perceives as necessary for Cuba now and in the future and what she learned regarding the positions and plans of the majority of Cubans in exile.

29. J. I. Rivero, "Relámpago," *Miami Diario de Las Américas,* July 19, 1992. In his column this well-known Cuban newspaperman refers to a radio program and congratulates one of the participants, Alberto Muller, for his stance. Muller, who was a political prisoner of Castro's regime for fifteen years, was the only one in the radio program who insisted that we must return to a liberated Cuba with a spirit not of vengeance but of forgiveness.

illumine how I as reader approached the situation and intention of the writer of this psalm and how I approached the text itself as a psalm of lament. Now I must return to the reader, to myself and what has become a new—but yet the same—Psalm 137 for me. This is no digression from Psalm 137. Indeed, I believe that this modern Cuban version of Psalm 137 completes the circle of meaning and helps us to understand the original Israelite version of the psalm.

One often hears Cubans claim that we need music as much as the air to breathe. And it is to a popular song that I wish to turn to offer a Cuban reading of Psalm 137 by those of us who are in exile. The song is "El Son de las Tres Décadas" (Song of the Three Decades), and the words, music, and original interpretation are by Marisela Verena. It was released in 1989, thirty years after the first Cubans had to leave the island.

> Yo vengo de un país privilegiado
> Con la naturaleza como aliada
> Con monopolio de sol
> Antepasado español
> Y gente con la sangre azucarada.

> > [I come from a privileged country
> > That has nature as its ally
> > With a monopoly of the sun
> > Spanish ancestry
> > And people with sweetness in their blood.]

> Yo pertenezco a una raza de risa fácil
> Que siempre pudo reírse de cada error
> Subía y bajaba el telón
> Gobiernos de quita y pon
> Jugando al que ríe último, ríe mejor.

> > [I belong to a race that laughs easily
> > That was always able to laugh off each mistake
> > The curtain would go up and down on
> > Governments of now-you-see-me-now-you-don't
> > Playing "whoever laughs last, laughs best."]

> Y entonces fui la heredera de los errores
> Y entonces tuve que irme de mi país
> Anémica de patria
> En toda soy extraña
> Luchando por no perder también mi raíz.

> > [Then I inherited all of the errors
> > And I had to leave my country

Anemic for my homeland
Everywhere I am a stranger
Struggling not to lose my roots.]

Chorus:
Trescientos sesenta meses de nostalgia
Son tres décadas de destierro y destrucción
Treinta años de duro exilio
De extranjero domicilio
¡Qué pena da el son que canta
Mi errante generación!

[360 months of nostalgia
3 decades of banishment and destruction
30 years of hard exile
Of foreign domicile
How sad is the song that sings
My wandering generation!]

Armados más de esperanza que de metralla
Allá en Girón
Confiados en la promesa de la potencia
Los armaron y embarcaron
Y embarcados se quedaron
Quedaron acorralados por la impotencia.

[Armed with hope more than with guns
Over there in Girón[30]
Trusting the promise of the Power[31]
They armed them and shipped them
And "shipped"[32] they stayed
They were left cornered by impotence.]

Salimos cientos de miles casi desnudos
Desnudos de justicia y libertad
Buscábamos refugio
Pidiendo sólo el lujo
De ganarnos el pan con dignidad.

[We left by the hundreds of thousands
Stripped of justice and liberty

---

30. Girón was one of the beaches in the area of the Bay of Pigs in Cuba where exiles landed and were defeated in 1962. The expedition was organized and financed by the CIA.

31. The United States.

32. This is a play on the word *embarcar*, which means "to ship," but which we also use as a slang term meaning "not to deliver," to "stand someone up."

We were seeking for refuge
Asking only for the luxury
Of earning our bread with dignity.]

Chorus:
Trescientos sesenta meses de andar prestados
Son tres décadas de trabajo y de tesón
Treinta años discriminados
Aunque naturalizados
¡Qué triste es el son que canta
Mi vagabunda generación!

[360 months of borrowed wandering
3 decades of labor and tenacity
30 years being discriminated against
Even though we are naturalized[33]
How sad is the song that sings
My errant generation.]

Mi tierra es hoy una jaula de gorriones
Pero un gorrión nunca se puede enjaular
Cuando vive en cautiverio
No le queda más remedio
Que escaparse de la jaula y emigrar.

[Today my land is a cage full of sparrows
But a sparrow cannot be kept in a cage
When in captivity
It can do nothing else
But flee from its cage and emigrate.]

No hay mal que por bien no venga
Dicen los sabios
No hay mal que dure 100 años
Dice el refrán
Nuestro mal son los intrusos
Los imperialistas rusos
Y un Judas que quiso a Cuba traicionar.

[There is no wrong that does not bring good
So say the wise
There is no wrong that lasts 100 years
So goes the saying
Our evil is the intruders

---

33. The majority of Cubans in the United States are U.S. citizens thanks to a law passed in the 1960s that makes it fairly easy to get citizenship.

The Russian imperialists
And a Judas who betrayed Cuba.]

Chorus:
Trescientos sesenta meses de humillaciones
Son tres décadas de censura y represión
Treinta años de dictadura
De cárceles y amarguras
¡Qué pena de el son que canta
Mi sometida generación!

[360 months of humiliations
3 decades of censorship and repression
30 years of dictatorship
Of prisons and sorrows
How sad is the song that sings
My subjugated generation!]

Treinta años desde que un déspota acorralado
Vendió mi sol a una tierra de poco sol
Y mi gente con firmeza
Sobresale a la cabeza
Dondequiera que establece el caracol.

[30 years since a cornered despot
Sold my sun to a sunless land
And my people in firmness
Stand out and ahead
Wherever they settle their shell.]

Chorus:
Son trescientos sesenta meses de idioma ajeno
Treinta años sin ver el sol que nacer me vio
Mi generación se aferra
A una raíz sin tierra
Qué largo es el son que canta
Mi desmembrada generación.

[360 months of a foreign language
Thirty years without seeing the sun that witnessed my
    birth
My generation clings on
To a root without soil
How long is the song that sings
My dismembered generation!]

9

Reading the Cornelius Story from an Asian Immigrant Perspective

_____ Chan-Hie Kim ___

The quest for understanding contextual/cultural interpretation of the Bible taking place recently in the United States as well as in other parts of the world is an indication that readers' cultural, historical, and social location is as important as the text itself in biblical hermeneutics.[1] One of the clear assumptions underlying the conviction that the reader's social location is as important as the text to be interpreted is that once a text is produced, what the author/redactor might have intended to communicate with his hearers/readers as well as what the original hearers might have heard and understood are not as important as what is appropriated by present readers. For once a document is produced, it becomes an independent entity, and even the author/redactor has no control over its "correct" interpretation and appropriation by readers. This position is also held by proponents of rhetorical and narrative criticism, where the focus is on the biblical text itself rather than on the theology and intentionality of the author/redactor, which is the major concern of redaction criticism. The historical-critical study of the Bible is important and has its merit in a biblical hermeneutic, but it is not sufficient for the Bible to be fully understood. It must be supplemented by other types of critical studies such as narrative criticism, rhetorical criticism, and the cultural anthropology of the biblical world. In narrative criticism, for example, the focus of interpretation is on how a narrative is constructed rather than on the author's theology. Since the way the plot, characters, and settings in a narrative are interwoven presents a

---

1. In 1990 the Society of Biblical Literature formed a group called Bible in Asia, Africa, and Latin America to investigate and understand what is going on in regard to biblical exegesis in the social and cultural settings of the developing countries. The Loyola Marymount University conference mentioned in n. 2 is another example of this trend in the American academy today. The articles and other writings in R. S. Sugirtharajah, ed., _Voices from the Margin: Interpreting the Bible in the Third World_ (Maryknoll, N.Y.: Orbis Books, 1991), are a good introduction to Third World hermeneutics.

strong emotive power, narrative criticism pays considerable attention to the text itself for its literary as well as for its religious appropriation.

It is my intention in this essay to read the Cornelius story from my own personal historical and social location in the United States. In appropriating the story I will take historical and redactional issues related to this pericope seriously. Without a clear understanding of adequate historical-critical data regarding given texts, one cannot appropriate many of the biblical books contextually. Particularly historical and narrative books require an adequate historical as well as redactional analysis in order for them to be heard clearly and understood. Historical circumstances that gave birth to a narrative and its redactional arrangement in a book are as important as my own historical and social location. If one wants to draw a historical analogy from a given text, an investigation of its historical background is an absolute necessity not only for understanding accurately the circumstances and truthfulness of the text but also for appropriating the text for one's own use.

The story of Cornelius in Acts 10:1—11:18 attracts the interest of persons from many different racial-minority groups in the United States as well as in non-Western countries.[2] The stories about interaction and encounter between the Jews and the non-Jews found in the Bible generally transmit significant messages to the believing communities. They help them understand their self-image vis-à-vis the dominant and/or different racial or cultural groups. Some of the texts of interest to these groups are the book of Esther, another story of a centurion in Q (Matt 8:5-13 || Luke 7:1-10), the legal code dealing with foreigners (Exod 12:19, 43-44; Lev 17:15; 19:10; and passim), and the stories about unclean or socially questionable persons (Luke 7:1-50). Peoples living on the margins of societies find in these texts paradigms for their self-understanding and motives for social actions.

One of the recurring questions about the Cornelius story has been whether the interaction between Peter and Cornelius was a historical event or a fabrication. If Luke did not fabricate this, is it then an early Christian tradition that Luke has merely inserted in the book of Acts? Is it probable that Luke created this narrative on the basis of the Cornelius tradition? If so, is it not possible that Peter's speeches and words are Luke's creation? If Peter's interaction with Cornelius was a true

---

2. On two occasions I have heard pastors, a Hispanic American and a Japanese American, speak on their community issues quoting the Cornelius story. Also, on March 20, 1992, Hisao Kayama of Meiji Gakuin University in Japan read an article entitled, "The Cornelius Story in the Japanese Cultural Context," at the Sixth Annual Casassa Conference. The conference, titled "Text and Experience: Toward a Cultural Exegesis of the Bible," was sponsored by Loyola Marymount University, Los Angeles. All three speakers had different exegetical approaches and interpretations. This phenomenon is certainly a proof that the biblical text can be appropriated from different perspectives depending on readers' historical and cultural contexts.

event, what is Luke's purpose in having this story at the beginning of his drama on the gentile Christian mission? Why does Luke use the Cornelius tradition in describing the beginning of the gentile mission when it is apparent that it was Paul who is to be given the credit for the success of that mission?

Adequate and satisfactory answers to these questions seem to have been given already by many exegetes. Ernst Haenchen gives an overview of the history of exegesis of the passage in his monumental *The Acts of the Apostles*.[3] This succinct summary of the exegetical work on the narrative notes that in an earlier stage of exegetical studies the question of historical authenticity was a key issue. However, subsequent exegetes made many other contributions in regard to other historical questions. These exegetical studies have been fruitful, and we can greatly benefit from them. There are, however, a few other items I would like to highlight and call to attention for further clarification and notation.

First, recent commentators generally agree that Luke did not fabricate this story. The narrative is more or less Luke's redactional work.[4] That is to say, Luke has constructed this narrative on the basis of Cornelius's conversion tradition and the tradition about Peter's vision regarding the Jewish dietary law.[5] The way the narrative is constructed supports this view. It is apparent that he added speeches to these traditions, or legends. Yet the question of the historical authenticity regarding these traditions is still unresolved even though Martin Dibelius and others have convincingly argued for its legendary nature. Perhaps we may not ever be able to solve it. Thus the important exegetical issue we should be concerned with is not authenticity but the redactor's intention in having this story in Acts. Haenchen is absolutely right when he says, "If we wish to gain firm ground in this jostling throng of opinions, we must first set aside all questions of historical authenticity or sources and seek to understand Luke's concern in reproducing the story of Cornelius."[6]

Second, what, then, is Luke's purpose for having this story in the book of Acts? It is very likely that Luke wants to show through the narrative that Jerusalem is the center of the gentile mission. The story fits

---

3. See E. Haenchen, *The Acts of the Apostles: A Commentary* (Oxford: Basil Blackwell, 1971) 355–63.

4. M. Dibelius, *Studies in the Acts of the Apostles* (ed. H. Greeven; New York: Scribner's, 1956) 109. See also Haenchen, *Acts*, 355–56. for further information on the subject. Dibelius argues here (120) that the original form of the story was "a straightforward legend of conversion, comparable in its simple beauty with the legend of the Ethiopian eunuch," if we delete Luke's additions such as Peter's speeches.

5. H. Conzelmann contends that Peter's vision originally "did not have to do with human relationship (Jews and Gentiles), but with foods" (*Acts of the Apostles* (Hermeneia; Philadelphia: Fortress Press, 1987) 80). Even if this is the case, the important point of our concern is to see how Luke has changed and edited the story to suit his theological need.

6. Haenchen, *Acts*, 357.

with Luke's contention that the gospel had spread out from the Jerusalem congregation, where Peter was a key leader. The Jerusalem Council described in Acts 15, particularly Peter's speech in verses 6-11, reflects this view very well. According to Luke, the gentile mission is not an independent work accomplished by Paul, nor was it initiated by Paul. As Hans Conzelmann has rightly pointed out, the story "reflects the Lukan view of history and Luke's concept of the church."[7] "Peter baptizes the Gentiles . . . without circumcising them. This is the presupposition of the related argument in Jerusalem. This account corresponds to the historical picture given in the book of Acts, according to which all initiative, even that for the non-law-observing mission, must issue from, and be sanctioned by, Jerusalem."[8] According to Luke, Jerusalem is the focal point from which the message of the Christian gospel spreads out to all the parts of the world, conquering finally the capital of the secular world, that is, Rome. Jerusalem is therefore the sacred city not only for the Jews but for the Christians as well. The Christian movement begins in the sacred city and moves into the secular cities. It is debatable whether the Ethiopian eunuch was a Jew or a Gentile and hence whether Philip was the first missionary to the Gentiles.[9] But at least one thing, mentioned above, is clear in the design of the book of Acts—that is, Paul is not the first missionary to the Gentiles, nor has he carried out his gentile mission independent of the Jerusalem church. This notion surely contradicts what we understand from Paul's own letters, particularly Galatians.[10]

Third, if we take Cornelius's conversion rather than the Ethiopian eunuch's as the first event of the gentile mission in the early church, then this narrative serves as a prelude to Paul's gentile mission in the composition of Acts. Contrary to what Conzelmann and ancient commentators have thought, this story does not only serve "as the preparation for chapter 15";[11] it functions further as an introduction to the whole gentile mission. By rendering a dramatic story of the origin of the gentile mission by Peter, Luke leads us into the next step of the unfolding drama, this time by Paul. He uses this story as a preface to the main

---

7. Conzelmann, *Acts*, 80.

8. H. Conzelmann, *History of Primitive Christianity* (Nashville: Abingdon, 1973) 58–59.

9. See Haenchen, *Acts*, 314. For a slightly different perspective on this issue, see C. H. Felder, "Race, Racism, and the Biblical Narratives," *Stony the Road We Trod* (ed. C. H. Felder; Minneapolis: Fortress Press, 1991) 141–42.

10. C. Talbert rightly observes that "in Acts 10-11, 15, Peter is portrayed as the initiator of the Gentile mission and the supporter of Paul in Jerusalem. One would hardly get this impression from Galatians" (*Literary Patterns, Theological Themes, and the Genre of Luke-Acts* (Society of Biblical Literature Monograph Series 20; Missoula, Mont.: Scholars Press, 1974) 101.

11. See Conzelmann, *Acts*, 80 and n. 6.

portion of the book of Acts. Luke gives here a story that in reality justifies Paul's action of accepting the Gentiles into the Christian fellowship without making them first Jews. It is generally assumed that Jewish-Christian leaders in Jerusalem, headed by James the brother of Jesus, were ultraconservatives who would never think that Gentiles could become Christians unless they abided by the Jewish laws and practices. Gal 2:3, 7 and Acts 15:1, 5-6 allude to this. In the first and second centuries of the common era, Judaism was very active in missionary work proselytizing Gentiles. It was natural, then, for the Jewish-Christian leaders to believe that Gentiles should become Jews first and then Christians.

Fourth, in this narrative Luke makes it clear that it is the Holy Spirit that is leading the gentile mission—that is, God is the one who initiates it and carries it on.[12] It is well known that the work of the Holy Spirit is the central theme of the Lukan theology in the books of Luke and Acts. Here again in redacting this story Luke is more concerned about the work of the Holy Spirit than about individuals involved in the missionary endeavor. This is also another reason why Luke has seemingly ignored Pauline primacy over against Peter in the gentile mission. Peter baptizes Cornelius and his party when he realizes "that the gift of the Holy Spirit had been poured out even on the Gentiles" (Acts 10:45).[13] Peter's challenge, "Can anyone withhold the water for baptizing these people who have received the Holy Spirit just as we have?" (Acts 10:47), well summarizes Luke's theology inherent in this narrative.

Fifth, it is to be noted that Peter does baptize Cornelius and his party without imposing on them his Jewish practices, because he heard the voice from heaven, "What God has made clean, you must not call profane" (Acts 10:15; 11:9). And his speeches in Acts 10:34-43 and 15:7-11 also give reasons for his action. The important point Luke is making here is that the "fear of God" rather than circumcision is the precondition of baptism and acceptance into the fellowship of the Christian community.

Sixth, there is yet another serious issue that many exegetes have failed to raise. In interpreting this narrative, commentators generally have focused their attention on the question of expansion of Christianity among

---

12. See U. Wilckens, *Die Missionsreden der Apostelgeschichte: Form- und Traditionsgeschichtliche Untersuchungen* (Wissenschaftliche Monographien zum Alten und Neuen Testament 5; 2d ed.; Neukirchen-Vluyn: Neukirchener Verlag, 1963) 64. Here he states, "The crossing over of the gospel also to the Gentiles is the work of neither Paul nor Peter, but rather an act of God, which he has accomplished independently of men as the fulfillment of his gracious will."

13. G. Lüdemann (*Early Christianity according to the Tradition in Acts: A Commentary* [Minneapolis: Fortress Press, 1989] 129) calls to our attention that "the account of the baptism after the receiving of the Spirit in vv. 47-48 only apparently contradicts Luke's theology, which suggests the bestowing of the Spirit after baptism (see 8.16; 19.5f.). Here as in 9.17f. (end) the bestowal of the Spirit comes before the baptism only for reasons of narrative technique."

the Gentiles, Cornelius being the first convert. The central character in this drama, however, is Peter, not Cornelius. The narrative is traditionally known as a story about the first gentile convert, but a closer look at it indicates that it is about the "conversion" of Peter instead of Cornelius's conversion to Christianity. The plot of the narrative shows us Peter's speech in verses 34-43 and his subsequent baptism of the Gentiles in verses 44-48 as the denouement of the narrative. Peter's confession beginning with the verses 34 through 43 is the highlight and climax of the whole episode in the narrative.[14] Peter, as a leader of the conservative Jerusalem church, could never have thought that Gentiles could become Christians unless they were first circumcised—that is, became Jews. But he is now, according to Luke (see Acts 15:7), a champion of the gentile mission. If that is the case, Luke's intention in utilizing the narrative has a meaning that has been so far unnoticed or neglected.

Seventh, even though the Cornelius tradition and Peter's vision may have been legends or historically untenable stories, the fact that Peter was a more lenient Jewish Christian toward the Gentiles cannot be denied. It is hard to say whether he took this position through the Cornelius incident, as Luke seems to suggest. As was mentioned above, there is no way we can verify the historical authenticity of the whole tradition.[15] However, we can say at least this much—Peter, unlike James the brother of Jesus, took a more liberal stance in the matters of keeping Torah, of circumcision, and of dietary law for the gentile Christians. He accepted Gentiles into the fellowship of the Christian community without imposing any Jewish practices. At least once in Antioch he was mingling with the Gentiles at the dinner table.[16] This is what we read also in the Cornelius story. It is apparent that Luke was somewhat knowledgeable about Peter's attitude toward the Gentiles.

What, then, does the story tell me, a person living in the United States as an Asian American in the second half of the twentieth century? What is the meaning I perceive from this text in light of my own social and cultural location here in the United States?

Before I seek to address this question, it is necessary to take a look at the historical background of the narrative once again. Data regarding the early Christian church acquired through research generally support the position that Luke's presentation in Acts is historically accurate.

---

14. Peter's speech in Acts 15:7-11 echoes the same idea.

15. If the narrative were a report on the factual event that actually took place, we could probably postulate that the event might have been the occasion for Peter's conversion from conservatism to leniency or laxity.

16. Paul testifies to this in Gal 2:11-14. M. Hengel argues that unlike the Jerusalem conservative leaders headed by James, Peter was fundamentally liberal in his dealing with gentile Christians. See Hengel's *Acts and the History of Earliest Christianity* (Philadelphia: Fortress Press, 1979) 97.

Before Peter was "converted," the only Christians he knew were Jewish Christians. But Paul's successful gentile mission changed his narrow conservative outlook. In fact, nobody expected that the gentile mission would turn out to be a success. Norman Perrin rightly analyzes the situation when he says:

> It should be emphasized that this success took everyone by surprise. Earliest Christians in general devoted their missionary activity toward their fellow Jews and expected that Gentiles would be brought into the divine plan by a direct act of God at the End itself. But the Christian mission to the Jews was largely a failure, whereas that to the Gentiles developed into an astonishing movement of vitality and power no one could have anticipated. This created a major problem, namely, how far the new gentile Christians should also become Jews: should it be demanded of them that they accept circumcision and Jewish dietary laws?[17]

The answer to this difficult question is given in the Cornelius story.

This story tells us that God accepts us as we are, and God does not impose any conditions for that. Becoming an American and also a Christian does not require that we should conform totally to the American way of life and cultural ethos. Nor does it ask us completely to absorb its lifestyles. Like the Gentiles we can live and remain free of "the law" of the dominant people. Peter's confession, "I truly understand that God shows no partiality, but in every nation anyone who fears him and does what is right is acceptable to him" (Acts 10:34-35), has a profound truth to this effect. Peter could not imagine that Gentiles could become Christians without first being circumcised. But the bestowal of the Holy Spirit on them even before they were baptized changed his whole outlook on the work of God, according to Luke. For the first time he was able to understand the profound will of God.

Despite the fact that Luke was preaching this message specifically to the Christian community through the mouth of Peter,[18] the U.S. Protestant establishment has turned a deaf ear to his message. A large number of Christian immigrants came to the United States from Asia because of the enactment of a new immigration law in 1965,[19] and they have built their own Christian communities and sought a fellowship with the existing U.S. Christian establishment by joining their denominations. However, because they are from cultures very different from

---

17. N. Perrin and D. C. Duling, *The New Testament: An Introduction* (2d ed.; New York: Harcourt Brace Jovanovich, 1982) 86–87.

18. Wilckens (*Die Missionsreden,* 67) argues that Peter's sermon in vv. 34ff. contains the phrase *humeis oidate,* which has no parallel in other sermons of Peter. He believes that the phrase is an indication that the sermon was addressed not to the general public but to the Christians.

19. The Immigration and Nationality Act (Public Law 89-236).

the dominant U.S. culture, they have received a very cool reception. Like the Jewish conservative Christian leaders, the U.S. establishment is not willing to accept culturally different new immigrants unless they are totally acculturated into American life. They seem to have forgotten the fact that right from the beginning, the Christian community has been as diverse as twentieth-century America in respect to its cultural mix and ethnic composition. This situation compelled the early Christian community to confront reality and live with it. The early Christian community accepted the cultural and ethnic diversity among its membership as a norm; it accepted ethnically as well as culturally diverse gentile Christians into its fellowship without asking them to follow the religious practice of a particular group. Peter realized that this was God's intention. The divine message was communicated to him through his vision.

Unlike earlier waves of immigrants who came to the United States from Europe, the majority of recent immigrants are from Third World countries. The U.S. churches have forgotten or ignored the fact that these Christian immigrants are products of their long-time missionary endeavors started in the late nineteenth century. Their overseas missionary work has been so successful in the past one hundred years that the membership of the Korean Presbyterian churches, for example, outnumbers that of the Presbyterian Church (U.S.A.), the mother church of Korean Presbyterianism. In the course of evangelizing Korea, it was inevitable that the American Protestant theology of the period and American Christian culture were introduced and transplanted on the soil, thus producing new indigenized forms of Christianity and Christian lifestyles. Recent Christian immigrants have been heavily influenced by American Christianity in their theology and Christian practices. Yet the mother church looks upon these immigrant Christian congregations as if they were its illegitimate children. For instance, the U.S. church ridicules immigrant Christians' evangelistic zeal and motives as stemming from ignorance of contemporary American social dynamics.[20] U.S. church leaders suspect that the hierarchical structure and management styles of immigrant pastors and elders are too authoritarian and against the democratic spirit. The hermeneutic of suspicion is an issue we need to deal with seriously.

Even in the midst of struggle for survival and settlement since the early 1970s, the new immigrants have kept their faith in the goodness of God and are determined to keep the Christian heritage they have brought with them. However, most of the mainline U.S. Protestant

---

20. The evangelistic zeal and very active missionary enterprises that the Korean churches are now engaged in are in fact what they have learned from the nineteenth-century American Protestant missionaries. They treasure this as one of the fundamental mandates of Christianity today.

churches do not seem to realize that these are the "gentile" Christians who do not know and are not willing to accept "Jewish" laws and practices. Perhaps U.S. society will condemn these people as an "unmeltable" minority, but we have to realize that the United States is not a monocultural country. Assimilation into the mainstream of U.S. life (which is an impossible task because of the physical differences) simply means a total loss of the immigrants' own identity in the society dominated by European cultures. Since the immigrants are unmeltable, the dominant society seems to have innumerable "headaches" and problems; but the headaches come from unwillingness to recognize the diversity of cultures within the Christian families.

Peter's conversion experience means, in a sense, a recognition of multiplicity of our cultures. As Hans Conzelmann says, "Peter...is instructed by means of a vision that the Jewish regulations about clean and unclean are not valid, indeed that they contradict the nature of God as the Creator of all living things."[21] Peter is convinced that the concrete expressions of the universal Christian faith are conditioned by diverse cultural traditions of different peoples and countries. We can express our Christian faith through our diverse cultural means. Consequently, we cannot claim the superiority of one culture over against another or insist that the European culture is the only norm for Christian faith and practice. Joseph C. Hough, Jr., and John B. Cobb, Jr., have rightly observed:

> As Christianity lost out to Islam in most of Asia and Africa, European Christians increasingly associated Christianity with their European culture and race. Although few altogether rejected the universalizing tendency of Christianity, many have thought of that as universalizing white Western Christianity without questioning the close connection of Christianity with whiteness and Western culture. Africans and Asians who became Christian were expected to adopt white, Western ways and even white, Western images of Jesus and of God. It is only as the victims of these partly unconscious habits of mind have forced attention to these distortions that white, Western Christians are beginning to rid themselves of this tribalization of their faith.[22]

Unfortunately, however, the recognition of this tribalizing tendency is very slow, and many cultural and racial minority persons in the United States are still suffering from the tardiness of its progress.

In a multicultural and multiethnic society like America, a dominant racial and cultural power group cannot demand that other groups

---

21. Conzelmann, *History of Primitive Christianity,* 58–59.
22. J. C. Hough, Jr., and J. B. Cobb, Jr., *Christian Identity and Theological Education* (Chico, Calif.: Scholars Press, 1985), 28.

follow or accept its religious ethos. Identifying Christianity with a particular cultural pattern and religiosity is a betrayal of the Christian gospel that is expressed in Peter's confession—"I truly understand that God shows no partiality, but in every nation anyone who fears him and does what is right is acceptable to him" (Acts 10:34-35).

10

"Hemmed in on Every Side": Jews and Women in the Book of Susanna

Amy-Jill Levine

I am a Jew. My interest in the origins of Christianity began when a neighbor accused me of "killing the Lord." As far as I knew, I hadn't killed anyone, so I told her she was wrong. "My priest said so," she replied. I knew priests didn't lie: if they did their special collars would choke them. I was seven years old, and I was very confused.

I am a woman. My awakening to what was only later labeled feminist consciousness occurred when my father died. I accompanied my mother to say Kaddish, and the men of my synagogue would not (initially) count either of us for the minyan. I was thirteen, and I was furious.

I am a student of religion. When I entered college, I naively believed that if I could understand the scriptural origins of anti-Semitism, I might help eliminate its modern recrudescence. Moreover, if I could understand how the canon marginalizes women and how women's history might be reconstructed, I could aid in countering sexism. I was eighteen, and I was optimistic.

I am a professor of religion. Twice as old now as when I began my formal studies of Scripture, I am still angry, still confused, but much less optimistic. I have seen how many of my teachers and colleagues in ostensibly secular settings interpreted the Psalms and the Prophets through ecclesiastical lenses; how the rabbis read these same texts was not often noted, and how the texts might be interpreted in light of their own time period alone was seen as insufficient. The Tanak had become the Old Testament. And I have encountered many feminist Christians who found the assertion that Jesus liberated women "to" their full potential was insufficient for both lectern and pulpit. They then claimed—either explicitly or implicitly—that Jesus liberated women "from" something, and that something was inevitably the repressive, patriarchal Jewish system. The perspective of the academy, although beginning to change, remains male and Christian, as well as white, Western, and heterosexual.

Subtle forms of disenfranchisement continue to afflict all those outside the dominant group. For example, although the proposal that

175

served as the basis for the present book speaks of "Jews and Christians," it also suggests that

> by using interpretations of the Bible as the basis for reflection on social location, a common text, read and studied by many diverse groups in many diverse ways, can be employed as the center of discourse, for while we may say many different things about the Bible, we are at least speaking about the same, publicly recognized text. All of these different voices, in one way or another, continue to look to the Bible for support and authority.

Nowhere does the proposal define "Bible," but the underlying presupposition is that the reference is to the Bible of the church, not the Bible of the synagogue. The talk of pluralism is a pluralism on Christian terms, and the public is the Christian one.

Yet Jews today often find that their own perceptions of marginalization are disregarded, attributed to paranoia, or seen as special pleading. "You are part of the establishment," we are told. "You are the oppressor, not the oppressed." Worse, we hear, "You are the occasion for your own oppression." Anti-Semitism remains, in many circles, a political bonus rather than a liability. I am writing these words while, in Philadelphia, signs from the "Lost-Found Nation of Islam" line the streets; they ask: "Are the Jews Hiding the Truth?" The stereotypes continue: of Jewish-American princesses; of wealthy, lustful, (im)potent businessmen; of covert political machinations; of clannishness; of Zionist racist conspirators.... Worse still, many within the Jewish community internalize these concerns and so fulfill the expectations of their gentile associates. Jewish men tell JAP jokes and so attempt to integrate into gentile society by distancing themselves from Jewish women, and Jewish women (and men) submit to rhinoplasty to conform to a WASP ideal. While Jewish identification remains strong, Jewish identity has been compromised by acculturation, assimilation, and ignorance of our own history and literature.

Thus I come to my project, which concerns the depiction of Jewish women in Hellenistic narratives. At first, my interest was in the reclamation of that which had been neglected on the *bima* and at the lectern. I desired both to remedy this lack and to contribute to a re-thinking of the history of Jews, both male and female, and of the history of women, both Christian and Jewish. That these texts have been ignored is no surprise. One might claim that Pseudepigrapha such as *The Marriage and Conversion of Aseneth* (*Joseph and Aseneth*) or the *Testament of Job* have been underrepresented because of their absence from modern religious canons and the (resulting) lack of manuscript availability. For the Apocrypha, however, the problem is more complex. In part, the relevant texts fail to address the academy's disciplinary desiderata. In biblical studies, theology has been privileged over narrative, canon over deuterocanonical texts (and so, consequently, Protestant concerns over Catholic), history over fiction. The narrative portions of the Apocrypha—Judith, Tobit, the Additions to Esther, the story of the Maccabean widow and her seven sons, the tale of Susanna—were rarely adduced in general, let alone for a study of women's history.

Here in the Greek texts, I thought, I could find female protagonists, worthy men, righteous behavior, and models of uncompromised diaspora existence. Susanna and the Elders seemed a gem in miniature: sixty-four verses depicting a righteous Jewish woman, the wisdom of Jewish youth, and an autonomous community unaffected by its Babylonian setting. But the Jewish men and Jewish women of Hellenistic narratives, like their biblical predecessors, are rarely ideal figures: they are morally ambiguous; not always clearly motivated; torn between divine and secular interests. As individual characters, metonymies of the community, or representatives for the deity, they continue to thwart the optimistic hopes of those seeking access to the history of Jewish women and their communities.

The reading of the character of Susanna in the modern academy and ecclesia is unequivocally positive: she "is cast in the role of the righteous one, condemned to death because of her obedience to God."[1] Descriptions of her social setting, however, while generally positivistic, are less positive. Some offer theological correctives to perceived social inequities: "In societies where a woman's word isn't worth much, the story says that God pays attention to the powerless, so the community should also."[2] Others address the extent of Jewish patriarchy: "Susanna also reflects the isolation of upper-class Jewish women in post-biblical times through virtual confinement to the home and the use of the veil in public."[3]

This distinction between Susanna, constructed as admirable, and her setting, constructed as repressive, dates to early Christian exegesis. Patristic writers viewed the lecherous elders as the twin threats of Ju-

---

1. G. W. E. Nickelsburg, *Jewish Literature between the Bible and the Mishnah* (Philadelphia: Fortress Press, 1981) 25; Nickelsburg's "Stories of Biblical and Early Post-Biblical Times," *Jewish Writings of the Second Temple Period* (ed. M. E. Stone; Compendia rerum iudaicarum ad novum testamentum 2; Assen: Van Gorcum, 1984) 38, equates her story with the persecution and vindication of the righteous in, for example, Genesis 34, Esther, Ahikar, and Wisdom of Solomon 2–5. See also C. A. Moore, *Daniel, Esther and Jeremiah, The Additions* (Anchor Bible 44; Garden City, N.Y.: Doubleday, 1977) 8–9; J. C. Dancey, *Shorter Books of the Apocrypha* (Cambridge Bible Commentary; Cambridge: Cambridge Univ. Press, 1972) 224.

2. C. A. Moore, "Susanna," *Bible Review* 8/3 (June 1992) 52.

3. D. W. Suter, "Susanna," *Harper's Bible Dictionary* (San Francisco: Harper and Row, 1985) 1001. The Apocryphon indicates neither isolation nor restriction. Rather, Susanna has a substantial entourage (Sus 30, Θ). She is also, contrary to Tobit's Sarah, apparently on good terms with her servants (Sus 27).

daism and paganism against Susanna the mother church. More recent commentaries parallel Susanna with the Christ of Matt 27:24;[4] the connection of the elders to the rabid Jerusalem crowd of the Matthean passion is unstated, but undeniable. Origen and Hippolytus even accused the Jews of deliberately removing Susanna from their Scriptures because of its negative portrayal of the community's leaders.[5] Continuing in this tradition, D. M. Kay concludes that "the story would not be popular with elders, and it was elders who fixed the canon. Susanna was useless for the polemical purposes of Judaism."[6]

But Susanna's sex and class impede any unambiguous reading of her character as a paradigm of righteousness or her setting as the epitome of patriarchy. Susanna, as character and as text, carries possibilities for condemnation as well as praise, for the recognition of women's social and religious freedom as well as their confinement, for the discovery of how Judaism survived challenges to its self-definition as well as the compromises it made in this process.

Nor is the reader in an unambiguous position. As Mieke Bal comments: "Although the unveiling is condemned, the visual feast is promised by the same token. Perniciously, the moral dimension of the tale

---

4. W. H. Daubney, *The Three Additions to Daniel* (Cambridge: Deighton, Bell, 1906) 161.

5. Susanna is absent from the Dead Sea Scrolls, the works of Josephus, and, except perhaps in vastly different formulation, the rabbinic texts. See R. Pfeiffer, *History of New Testament Times with an Introduction to the Apocrypha* (New York: Harper, 1949) 443; E. J. Bickerman, *The Jews in the Greek Age* (Cambridge, Mass.: Harvard Univ. Press, 1988) 95; A. LaCocque, *The Feminine Unconventional: Four Subversive Figures in Israel's Tradition* (Minneapolis: Fortress Press, 1990) 28. Origen also mentions a Jewish informant who added the following charming detail about the elders: they were in the habit of approaching respectable women and telling them that God had given them the power of fathering the messiah, and by this means they were able to seduce. See N. DeLange, *Apocrypha: Jewish Literature of the Hellenistic Age* (New York: Viking, 1978) 129; for further discussion of this motif see Bickerman, *Jews in the Greek Age,* 94.

6. D. M. Kay, "Susanna," *Apocrypha and Pseudepigrapha of the Old Testament* (ed. R. H. Charles; Oxford: Clarendon, 1913) 1:642; also cited by LaCocque, *Feminine Unconventional,* 28. Kay does not consider the "elders" who fixed the canon of the church. Moore (*Daniel,* 80, cf. 109) suggests, conversely, that "the story of Susanna was ultimately, and rightly, regarded by the Jews as a very unsuitable introduction to the materials in the canonical Daniel. Not only is the background of the Susanna story basically different from that of Daniel 1-6, but in 'Susanna' Daniel himself is poorly presented." By applauding the good taste of the Jews, Moore implies that the church, which canonized this text, lacked aesthetic sensibility. Consideration of canonical status thus devolves into ironic triumphalism. While the canonical placement of the narrative varies—the LXX and Old Latin have Susanna as the preface to the book of Daniel; the Vulgate makes it chap. 13; in the Jacobite Syriac it is placed with Judith, Ruth, and Esther—the book itself complements the Daniel tradition and therefore is not inappropriately included within the canon. Debates on canonicity might be better placed in the context of language and date rather than content, as Julius Africanus recognized in his letter on Susanna to Origen and as Porphyry (quoted by Jerome) also noted. See Pfeiffer, *History,* 442 and 443 n. 10.

absorbs the pornographic one and provides the innocent reader with an excuse to anticipate the pleasure sanctioned rather than countered by the moral indignation."[7] The text situates its readers as both accomplice and victim; the narrative renders us voyeurs, looking on with the elders at the naked Susanna at her bath and at her trial. Like Susanna, we cannot leave the garden without shame. Our task is to read without having the interpretation of social setting bleed over into anti-Semitism, the critique of the title character succumb to sexism, or the analysis of the narrative devolve into pornography.

My own social location raises the questions of Jewish history and women's history, and it sensitizes me to the dangers of viewing either as less than ideal. At the same time, it gives me a privilege less readily available to my gentile and male colleagues: committed to both feminism and Judaism, I am less likely to be charged with sexism or anti-Semitism should I point out less-than-ideal aspects of the subject matter. The death of objective history brings with it an inevitable but no less problematic privileging of some perspectives over others: those previously on the margins now appear to inhabit the moral high ground. To criticize a liberation-theological reading, for example, is apt to be viewed as a sign of the troglodyte. To be unconvinced is to be unsympathetic. But the true task of global interpretation means to me not merely the recognition of other perspectives, interests, and readings; it seeks a critical awareness of the problems as well as the benefits of such exercises.

Awareness of my own marginalized setting and the means by which I negotiate the twin tasks of self-affirmation and intercultural contact leads directly to my appreciation of Hellenistic Judaism. Like any product of a community facing the threats occasioned by diaspora and colonialism, the ancient texts indicate the mechanisms by which such groups achieve self-identity. Specifically, they address ethnic pride, personal piety, and class structure. And they locate their discussions, subtly but inexorably, on the bodies of women.

The conquest of the Near East by Alexander the Great in the fourth century BCE created a crisis for the Jewish population: Greek began to replace Hebrew as the language of Scripture and Aramaic as the language of trade. Biblical motifs, especially gender-coded ones, were then adapted to respond to such challenges to ethos and ethnos. The covenant community had traditionally represented itself as a woman: virgins (2 Kgs 19:12; Isa 37:22; Lam 1:15; 2:13; Jer 14:17); brides (Jer 2:2-3; Hos 2:15b); whores (Hosea 1–4; Ezekiel 16); and widows (Lam 1:1; Isa 54:4-8). The fracturing of the political unity is embod-

---

7. M. Bal, *Reading Rembrandt: Beyond the Word-Image Opposition* (Cambridge: Cambridge Univ. Press, 1991) 155.

ied by accounts of rape (Genesis 34; 2 Samuel 13).[8] In the so-called deuterocanonical materials, women continue to represent the covenant community, but Susanna, Judith, the various women of Tobit, and their sisters have more completely drawn personalities. This change is more than a formalistic move from metaphor to character or prophecy to narrative; the shift in representation appears to be the means by which the Jews, suddenly finding themselves part of an alien empire, worked through their disorientation and the threat to cultural cohesion.

Both to represent and to counter the challenge to communal self-identity, the Hellenistic texts employ three dominant motifs. First, women's bodies, like the community itself, become the surface upon which are inscribed the struggles between the adorned and the stripped, the safe and the endangered, the inviolate and the penetrated. As Susan R. Suleiman observes: "The cultural significance of the female body is not only (not even first and foremost) that of a flesh-and-blood entity, but of a symbolic construct."[9] Next, the women's husbands are depicted as inept, impaired, or simply stupid. Finally, the muddying of borders, both of body and society, is expressed through an emphasis on boundary-transgressive events: a focus on eating, defecating, burial, and sexual intercourse as well as a confusion between public and private, privileged and marginalized. The women characters in particular are, consequently, not primarily (if at all) windows into an anterior social world; rather, they are literary tropes. They tell us less about the lives of real women than about the social construction of "woman" by a particular community at a particular time. The women of the Apocrypha and Pseudepigrapha are the screen on which the fears of the (male) community—of impotence, assimilation, loss of structure—can be both displayed and, at least temporarily, allayed.

That women's bodies are threatened in ancient literature is hardly news to students of the Tanak. However, unlike their counterparts in Genesis and the Deuteronomistic History, the women of the Apocrypha and Pseudepigrapha retain both physical and moral integrity in the face of foreign or domestic foes. Esther makes clear only in the Additions her rejection of her doltish husband's culture: "I abhor the bed of the uncircumcised and of any alien.... I have not honored the king's feast or drunk the wine of any libation" (14:16). The Maccabean widow "threw herself on the fire so that no one would touch her body" (4 Macc 17:1). Judith's transformation from pious widow to forward seductress is only illusory; Holofernes, not Judith, loses his head and so his integrity. For Susanna, the enemies are domestic: she is threatened first with rape and

---

8. I thank Alice Keefe for calling my attention to this implication of the rape narratives.

9. S. R. Suleiman, introduction to *The Female Body in Western Culture* (ed. S. R. Suleiman; Cambridge, Mass.: Harvard Univ. Press, 1986) 2.

then, for refusing to submit, with death by the elders of her own community.[10] Her husband and father fail to protect her or even to come to her defense. Unlike Esther, the widow, and Judith, Susanna requires male intervention to resolve the threat; Daniel functions as the deity's proxy. Apparently, when the threat is external, women/the community can act; when the threat is internal—that is, when it threatens the very core of the community—a man, or, more precisely, the deity whom the man represents, must preserve the existence of the male-defined community and must reinstate its honor. Although she speaks, Susanna is not (first and foremost) subject, she is object. And she is abject.

Susanna is a projection of the threatened covenant community. Part of the diaspora whose (b)orders have been shattered, she faces the temptation to lose self-integrity, self-respect, and self: to submit to the elders is to be raped; to refuse will likely lead to a death sentence. Not only is she threatened, she is also threatening, as her iconographic reception (with the notable exception of the work of Artemisia Gentileschi) has suggested. No inexperienced child, she is a married woman with children of her own and with a husband occupied by affairs of state. Like Judith, her potential for illicit sex is clear. And this potential, this threat, is underscored by her story's setting, its intertextual references, and its forcing the reader into the voyeuristic role.

Although set in the Babylonian diaspora, the book of Susanna does not depict a lamenting community. The Jews possess wealth, autonomous governance, even the power of capital punishment.[11] They are comfortable, and the most comfortable of all is the wife of the wealthy Joachim. His home is the locus of communal administration, and thus he is, by implication, the wealthiest and most socially prominent Jew in Babylon. But this economic situation is one less admired than critiqued. And the critique comes in the form of a woman.

Initially, Susanna's description is entirely admirable: she is well married, very beautiful, pious, and educated: "Her parents were righteous, and had taught their daughter according to the Law of Moses" (Sus 3). And she participates in the lifestyle that accompanies such a social situation: free from domestic, juridical, and religious responsibilities, her one independent daily action is to walk in her husband's garden. However, the setting is redolent with negative or at best ambivalent references. First, Susanna represents unencumbered luxury: her walks

---

10. For very helpful observations on why the "attempted rape resists classification as such," see J. A. Glancy, "The Accused: Susanna and Her Readers," *Journal for the Study of the Old Testament* (forthcoming). While Glancy's article and my essay were written independently and reflect different methodological interests, they reach similar conclusions.

11. Bickerman (*Jews in the Greek Age,* 49–50) offers historical parallels but appropriately questions "how far the author was describing the institutions of his time and how much he was simply inventing" (96).

occur in counterpoint to the lawsuits argued in her husband's house. Second, although her Babylonian setting is emphasized in the first verse, neither she nor her family is suffering in exile. Rather than lamenting by the waters of Babylon, she bathes in them. Few could identify with her in terms of status.[12] Representing the threatened covenant community, she is already a warning to those who would enjoy social privileges in foreign settings: no garden is safe.

For the Apocrypha and Pseudepigrapha, communal integrity is located genealogically rather than geographically; the endogamous family, even if displaced, is the principle source of cultural cohesion.[13] Yet the family is continually at risk. And women, who define the borders of families and communities, are the source of that instability. According to Theodotion's version (Θ), Susanna's parents, children, and relatives are at the trial; the LXX mentions her parents and four children.[14] But her husband is absent.[15] Susanna's public shame is his shame,[16] and his shame is magnified by his failure to act. While the LXX locates the trial at the community synagogue, Theodotion places it at Joachim's house and so magnifies his silence. The flaws in the community leadership extend beyond the elders to Joachim himself. Only upon Susanna's exoneration do "Hilkiah and his wife praise God for their daughter Su-

---

12. Later versions of the story reinforce the status differential. The Samaritan text makes her the daughter of the high priest Amran. According to the Chronicles of Jerahmeel, she is the daughter of Shealtiel (see Ezra 3, 8) and the sister of Zerubabbel. Her husband becomes identified with the Judean king Jehoiachin, which then makes Susanna the bride of her grandfather (but cf. Lev 18:10). See M. Wurmbrand, "A Falasha Version of the Story of Susanna," *Biblica* 44 (1963) 34–36.

13. A.-J. Levine, "Diaspora as Metaphor: Bodies and Boundaries in the Book of Tobit," *Diaspora Jews and Judaism* (ed. J. A. Overman and R. S. MacLennan; Atlanta: Scholars Press, 1992) 105–17.

14. Theodotion (Θ) underlies the church's canon and hence modern English translations. The LXX survives in three manuscript traditions: the ninth-century papyrus codex Chisianus 88 rediscovered in 1783; the Ambrosian Syro-Hexaplar from Origen's edition; and the Kölner Papyrus 967 (ca. 150 CE). See Moore, *Daniel,* 33.

15. Also absent from the trial, and from the text, are other spouses: the wives of the elders; Daniel's wife. Comparable are the absent (dead) husbands of Judith and the Maccabean martyr; the deaths of Sarah's earlier husbands in Tobit; the fractious relationship between Tobit and Anna and between Job and his first wife in the *Testament of Job;* Esther's repulsion of her husband as well as her orphaned status; the war among the sons of Jacob in *Aseneth;* and so on.

16. M. D. Garrard ("Artemisia and Susanna," *Feminism and Art History: Questioning the Litany* [ed. N. Braude and M. D. Garrard; New York: Harper and Row, 1982] 152) notes that "Susanna herself is a personification of the good Israelite wife, whose sexuality was her husband's exclusive property, and Susanna's total fidelity to Joachim is demonstrated in her willingness to accept death rather than dishonor him by yielding to the Elders." Similarly, Glancy ("The Accused"): "I question the implicit narrative promotion of the idea that a virtuous woman prefers death to the dishonor a rape brings to a man's household." Yet Susanna's total fidelity is to the law of Israel, not to her husband. Her cry in the garden concerns "sin" (Sus 23), not marital honor. Further, his honor is in any case compromised: either his wife is an adulterer, or she is a victim of rape (which he does not stop), or she is brought to trial and humiliated.

sanna, *as did her husband Joachim* and all her relatives, because she was found innocent of any impropriety" (Sus 63). Failing, however, to acknowledge either Susanna's brave resistance or her religiosity, they appear simply to be thankful that she was not guilty.

Evoking the phenomenon contemporary feminists have labeled "blaming the victim" is one reading of Sus 7-8: "When the people left at noon, Susanna would go into her husband's garden to walk. Every day the two elders used to see her, entering and walking around, and they began to lust after her." According to Bal, "The sequence of the two sentences suggests... that it was because Susanna exposed herself unknowingly that they became inflamed."[17] Victims are not always innocent. While the repeated notices of Susanna's piety and fidelity reinforce her innocence, the references and the character are both compromised by the elders' desires. For the story to function, their desire must be comprehensible to the reader, and thus Susanna must be a figure of desire to us as well. And once we see her as desirable, we are trapped: either we are guilty of lust, or she is guilty of seduction.[18]

Multiple intertextual resonances of both the scene of bathing naked "in the garden" and the trial help to shift the onus from reader to Susanna. The bath, for example, is a known locus of seduction, and its association with Bathsheba is a likely antecedent to Susanna's story. Both women are married, and both have husbands occupied with political responsibilities; both are spied at their baths and then propositioned by the local authority (2 Samuel 11). Whereas Bathsheba submits to David's coercive courting, Susanna opts to take her chances in the divine court. Yet the intertextual connection alerts the reader to the possibility that Susanna, too, might have consented.

Jub 33:2-9 and *T. Reub.* 3:10-4:1 both employ the trope of the seductive naked bather in their depiction of Bilhah.[19] The former text reads: "And Reuben saw Bilhah, the attendant of Rachel (and) his father's concubine, washing in the water privately, and he desired her. And hiding at night, he entered Bilhah's house... and he lay with her.... And she lamented greatly concerning this matter. And she did not tell anyone at all." The *Testament of Reuben* extends the parallel by including a condemnation of the woman herself:

---

17. Bal, *Reading Rembrandt*, 149.

18. On the question of her "guilt," see now also Glancy, "The Accused." Readings informed by lesbian and gay men's critique would complicate even more the status of the reader. For example, Susanna must be desirable to women as well as to men. And Daniel, who prefigures and replaces Susanna as the object of desire, must be desirable to men as well as to women.

19. Noted by R. Doran, "The Additions to Daniel," *Harper's Bible Commentary* (San Francisco: Harper and Row, 1988) 866. *Jubilees* predates Susanna; the date of the *Testaments of the Twelve Patriarchs* remains uncertain.

Do not devote your attention to a woman's looks, nor live with a woman who is already married, nor become involved in affairs with women. For if I had not seen Bilhah bathing in a sheltered place, I would not have fallen into this great lawless act. For so absorbed were my senses by her naked femininity that I was not able to sleep until I had performed this revolting act.... Bilhah became drunk and was sound asleep, naked in her bedchamber.

Reuben blames the victim: even before he condemns Bilhah for drunkenness, he has already assigned her the burden of guilt—had she not bathed, had she not been so alluring, he would not have sinned. From this textual perspective, Susanna's ignorance of the elders does not excuse her: as a beautiful woman and therefore necessarily an object of desire, she is the occasion for sin.

Finally, the bath as well as Susanna's call for oil and cosmetics may be both compared and contrasted to parallel scenes in Esther and Judith. The former is "provided with her cosmetic treatments... and with seven chosen maids" (Esth 2:9) in order to "go in to King Ahasuerus" (Esth 2:12); the latter bathes and adorns herself in order to conquer Holofernes and so protect her community (Jdt 10:3). Esther is forced into sexual action; Judith is compelled by her sense of justice; Susanna simply pampers herself. Placed in juxtaposition to the juridical proceedings of the community, her luxuriating is a form of self-delusion: the problems of law and behavior cannot be washed away.

Beyond the bath is a second negative implication of the setting: the garden (*paradeisos*). In both classical[20] and biblical writings the garden symbolizes sensuality and seduction. The immediate comparison of Susanna to Eve uncovers much. Both are given impossible choices by cunning, explicitly or implicitly sexual figures. Both naked women come to recognize shame, both are humiliated before the male gaze, both are taken from the garden, both have husbands who fail to display loyalty. Like Eve, Susanna too is forced from her Edenic existence. Once accused of adultery, once displayed to the community, her innocence is lost. So too for women and for diaspora Jews: even when innocent of any crime, the accusations remain and thus do sexism and anti-Semitism prevail. As Susanne Kappeler states: "We also need to challenge the literalism of the argument of fiction experts that the victimization in pornographic representations is only make-believe, and that in fact the woman model

---

20. For example, Achilles Tatius 1.15.1; see R. Pervo, "Aseneth and Her Sisters: Women in Jewish Narrative and in the Greek Novel," *"Women Like This": New Perspectives on Jewish Women in the Greco-Roman World* (ed. A.-J. Levine; Early Judaism and Its Literature 1; Atlanta: Scholars Press, 1991) 148 and n. 21.

(usually) gets up unharmed after the photographic session, or does not really exist in the case of literature."[21]

The intertextual references then move from Eden to the patriarchal sagas, and again, the traditional representation of Susanna's innocence is compromised. Susanna's antecedents also include the story of Joseph and Potiphar's wife. Both Susanna and Joseph are chaste, beautiful, naked individuals displaced from their homeland. Both are propositioned by people in positions of authority, and both fail to confront their accusers. Both stories depict impotent husbands and leaders, and both require supernaturally inspired knowledge for redemption. Indeed, the story of Susanna deliberately draws from the Genesis text: "day by day" (Sus 12 ‖ Gen 39:10); "sin against the Lord" (Sus 23 ‖ Gen 39:9); mention of the household (Sus 26 ‖ Gen 39:14-15); and mention of a fleeing lover (Sus 39 ‖ Gen 39:18).[22] However, because Joseph may be assigned some responsibility for his unfortunate position, Susanna suffers guilt by association. A pampered son, a spy, and perhaps even a narcissist, the young man is sold by his jealous brothers into slavery. For those readers who sympathize with the less-loved brothers, Joseph's fate may be met with *Schadenfreude*. Conversely, the lack of closure to Mrs. Potiphar's story coupled with her husband's willingness to cede his authority to Joseph serves to mitigate the wife's negative reception.[23]

Joseph, the man, can parlay his connection to heaven for social advancement: he becomes master of Potiphar's house, of the prison, and of Egypt; he exacts retribution from his brothers. Susanna, unaccompanied by notices of divine favor, does not become a master by refusing to become a mistress. She is dependent on Daniel, who assumes Joseph's positive roles for her: Daniel, like Joseph, is the Jew in the foreign court, the interpreter of dreams, the dispenser of justice.

Susanna may also be compared to the sexually engaged woman of the Song of Songs.[24] Both are placed in the context of the fertile lushness of nature, and Susanna's name evokes the Song's natural setting:

---

21. S. Kappeler, *The Pornography of Representation* (Minneapolis: Univ. of Minnesota Press, 1986) 14–15.

22. Nickelsburg, *Jewish Literature*, 26 and 39 n. 19; idem, "Stories," 38; and, following Nickelsburg, LaCocque, *Feminine Unconventional*, 23. The parallel was noted as early as John Chrysostom, whose Sermon on Susanna asserted that she "endured a severe fight, more severe than that of Joseph. He, a man, contended with one woman, but Susanna, a woman, had to contend with two men, and was a spectacle to men and to angels" (cited by LaCocque, *Feminine Unconventional*, 23).

23. See discussion in LaCocque, *Feminine Unconventional*, 22–23; Pfeiffer, *History*, 453; Stith-Thompson 4:480–82 (the Genoveva motif). Pfeiffer suggests that the earliest occurrence of the motif is the story of Tamar and Judah (Genesis 38), yet here actual impropriety does take place: Tamar has sexual intercourse with someone other than her husband/betrothed. Judah exonerates her, and thus his word takes precedence over any external legal system. More comparable is the rabbinic tradition of Beruriah.

24. LaCocque, *Feminine Unconventional*, 24. The name appears in masculine form in 1 Chr 2:31, 34, 35; feminine form in 2 Chr 4:5; Hos 14:5. In Christian tradition, it is

Shoshanah, the lily, is in full bloom (for example, Song 2:1b); she entices us, and our response is to deflower her. Her name also creates a later parallel to *Leviticus Rabbah* 19: the account of Nebuchadnezzar's permitting the wife of Jehoiachin to have intercourse with her husband in prison and therefore to continue the Davidic line.[25] But she tells Jehoiachin, *c'shoshanah adumah ro'iti* ("I have seen something like a red lily"—that is, "I am menstruating"), and therefore he does not sleep with her.

Moving to the Ketuvim and beyond to the Apocrypha, one finds Susanna in the company of other sexually problematic women. André LaCocque expresses the point as follows: "Ruth allures Boaz, . . . Esther is wife to a pagan king, Susanna is accused of fornication and adultery, and Judith plays the harlot with Holofernes. The intent of such stories is clear. They want to drive home the idea that women can indeed become God's instruments, even when they use the most controversial resources of their femininity."[26] But Susanna has no resources, and she does not use her "femininity" to solve the problem. Conversely, one could argue that LaCocque's comparison of Susanna with the other three explicitly sexually active women, and women involved somehow with Gentiles at that, shows the perceived and received underlying sensuality as well as otherness of her character. Like Judith, Ruth, and Esther of the Additions, Susanna of Babylon needs to be reintegrated into the covenant community on both religious and ethnic levels. Further, her sexuality needs to be controlled. Judith returns to the isolation of her home; Esther emphasizes her distaste for the marriage bed; Ruth is domesticated through marriage and childbearing. And Susanna is, only at the conclusion of the trial, directly associated with her husband.

Among the sexually charged intertextual references of the trial are two long-recognized associations: the first with Solomon's judgment in 1 Kgs. 3:16-27; the second with the "suspected woman" of Num 5:11-31 and *m. Soṭa* 1:5.[27] Origen had already compared Daniel's wisdom to that of King Solomon, and the connection is acknowledged as well in relatively recent commentaries.[28] Yet these interpreters, by concentrating

---

the name of one of the followers of Jesus (Luke 8:3)—who is apparently unencumbered by domestic ties or responsibilities.

25. N. Bruell, "Das apokryphische Susannabuch," *Jahrbücher für Jüdische Geschichte und Literatur* 3 (1877) 1–69, followed *inter alia* by Wurmbrand, "Falasha," 35, and LaCocque, *Feminine Unconventional,* 25.

26. LaCocque, *Feminine Unconventional,* 2.

27. See, for example, F. Zimmerman, "The Story of Susanna and Its Original Language," *Jewish Quarterly Review* 48 (1957/58) 236–37 n. 2; Doran, "Additions," 867.

28. LaCocque, *Feminine Unconventional,* 22; see Pfeiffer, *History,* 449, and Daubney, *Three Additions,* 3, who also draws connections to the Johannine accounts of the woman caught in the act of adultery and to the sexually active Samaritan woman (124, 133).

on the relationship of Daniel to Solomon, do not comment directly on the further implications of the parallel: Solomon is judging a case between two prostitutes; Daniel is concerned with the charge of adultery. Male wisdom is required to harness the chaotic power of woman's sexuality. Although the "good prostitute" is proclaimed innocent and regains her child, she remains a prostitute. Although Susanna is exonerated, she is still shamed through her public humiliation.

According to the Mishnah, the accused woman who denies her guilt is to have her clothes torn by the priest "until he exposed her bosom" and to have her hair disheveled at her trial. "R. Judah says, 'if her bosom be beautiful, he does not expose it.' " The intent of the action is to present the woman in the state of just having left her adultery. While Theodotion has only Susanna's veil lifted (v. 32), the earlier LXX does not limit the accusers' voyeuristic intent to her face. Indeed, the treatment she is accorded at the trial is not just that of the dishonored wife but also that of the adulterer/prostitute, as Hos 2:3, 10 and Ezek 16:37-39 display.[29] Although the book ends with the reincorporation of Susanna into her family by her parents and husband, because she has been treated like the suspected adulteress, her life will always be suspect.

To avoid any such suggestions, later versions of the tale eliminate any possibility of Susanna's sexual complicity. The Samaritan account depicts her as a Nazirite on Mt. Gerizim. In the Falasha rendition, she is another Judith: "Her father, the king, said to his daughter, 'Come, get married.' But she refused and said to her father, 'I shall not marry after the death of my husband. I have devoted myself to the Lord, my Creator.' "[30] This revised Susanna returns to the deity, not to her husband; the silent, doubting figure of the earlier texts here fulfills his role: he is dead. And Susanna herself returns rewarded: already a queen in the Falasha version, she earns "a double reward for her faithfulness: queenship on earth and bliss in heaven."[31]

But the deuterocanonical Susanna can at best go back to her status quo. As metaphor for the community, she is ultimately an example of the protection that fidelity to the law of Moses provides: she is unpenetrated and unpenetrable. But her humiliation—as a character (before the elders and the entire community) and as a nation (before the world)—remains. The Jewish community, particularly that of the diaspora, is vulnerable: apart from its traditional religious leaders in court and temple, it can survive only with divine help. Charismatic figures, inspired by the holy spirit, can arouse the community and return them to the righteous path.

---

29. See Doran, "Additions," 867; and Moore, *Daniel*, 103.
30. Wurmbrand, "Falasha," 32. On her widowhood, see also H. Engel, *Die Susanna-Erzaehlung* (Göttingen: Vandenhoeck und Ruprecht, 1985).
31. Wurmbrand, "Falasha," 34.

While women serve as metonymies for the covenant community, they remain on the margins of human-divine interaction. The situation is similar in the text's apocryphal counterparts: women pray to the deity, and the deity responds with either silence or a male voice. Judith offers an impassioned prayer, but there is no direct mention of the deity's aiding her. The Maccabean mother dies a martyr. Tobit's Sarah prays for either death or salvation, but the angel Raphael, who does solve her problem, deliberately avoids her company. Predestined to be Tobias's bride, Sarah—like the married Susanna—cannot save herself.

Susanna's relationship to heaven is established in her garden speech: "I am completely trapped. For if I do this, it will mean death for me; if I do not, I cannot escape your hands. I choose not to do it; I will fall into your hands, rather than sin in the sight of the Lord" (Sus 22-23). Her mention of divine sight, however, is ironic: unlike the elders, unlike the reader, the deity is *not* looking at her nudity. Heavenly recognition comes only when she cries out at her trial (Sus 44); the deity is not a voyeur. Yet because her comment may be read as indicating that heaven will take notice of her *only* when she sins, the divine sight at first looks as wayward as that of the elders, who "turned away their eyes from looking to Heaven" (Sus 9).

At her trial, Susanna confirms both her faith and her impotence. "Then Susanna cried out with a loud voice and said, 'O Eternal God, you know what is secret and are aware of all things before they come to be; you know that these men have given false evidence against me. And now I am to die, though I have done none of the wicked things that they have charged against me!' And the Lord heard her cry" (Sus 42-44).[32] The people at the trial, however, are looking rather than listening: no one had sought Susanna's testimony; nor did she offer it.

Redemption comes therefore in the form of someone who can both speak to the importance of geographically based identity and speak against the Babylonian community's internal governance. Daniel represents the hope of the future: the pious (male) who can rescue fair, exiled Israel from her distress. Ethnic pride, not women's liberation, is at the heart of Daniel's speech. He "does not come to the rescue of the woman, but of the righteous (here identified with Judah)."[33] Indeed, no voyeur he, Daniel is never seen as looking at Susanna.[34]

The nationalistic concern is voiced by the narrator as early as verse 5 (Θ); in reference to the elders, "the Lord has said, 'Wickedness came forth from Babylon.'"[35] It is reinforced when Susanna first speaks: the

---

32. In the LXX, she prays when she is charged; in Θ she prays at her condemnation; the Syriac inserts the prayer at both points. See Moore, *Daniel,* 103.

33. LaCocque, *Feminine Unconventional,* 26.

34. Pointed out by Glancy, "The Accused."

35. The citation is Jer 29:21-23. Bruell ("Das apokryphische Susannabuch") proposes

LXX identifies her not by name but as "the Jewess" (*Ioudaia*). Daniel confirms the connection between exile and evil, ethnic pride and ethical behavior: "And he said to them, 'Why was your progeny corrupted like Sidon and not like Judah?' " (Sus [LXX] 56). Sidon, home to Jezebel (1 Kgs 16:31) and Athaliah (2 Chr 21:6; 22:10-12),[36] suggests that the elders have been corrupted by descent from promiscuous gentile women. Theodotion speaks of them as "offspring of Canaan" (cf. Gen 10:15, where the connection of Canaan to Sidon is explicit). Daniel confirms the narrator's ethnic interests by distinguishing Susanna, "this daughter of Judah," from the "daughters of Israel": "This is how you have been treating the daughters of Israel; and they were intimate with you through fear; but a daughter of Judah would not tolerate your wickedness" (Sus 57).[37] The distinction in this verse also explains the assignment of the title "daughter of Israel" to Susanna in verse 48: there, Daniel is referring to the judgment passed by the misguided people. They did not hesitate to "condemn a daughter of Israel without examination and without learning the facts." For the people, the woman is already other, already alien, and so already guilty. Only through Daniel's reclamation of her does Susanna regain her righteousness and her true ethnic identity.

How Daniel could know of the elders' past actions, just as how he could know what transpired in the garden, is explicable only by the divine "spirit of understanding" that overtakes him. His transformation confirms the impression that diaspora existence is unstable: the private sphere becomes public; the chaste Susanna is accused of adultery; judges commit crimes; and youth supplants the elders of the community. Even the plot hinges on instability: the young man in the garden is the pivot on which the story turns, but he does not exist. And this nonexistent figment is himself unable to consummate his tryst. Nothing is at it seems, or as it should be. Daniel resolves this instability by displacing, embodying, and redeeming the absent lover: this "young man" (*neōteros;* LXX 44, 52, 55, 60; Θ only 45), the disguised voice of heaven, substitutes for the "young man [*neaniskos*] [who] fled in disguise" (Sus [LXX] 39). The youth becomes the wise elder; Susanna the mother becomes his dependent. And thus the woman and the ethnos both enter safely into Daniel's

---

that the elders in Susanna are Ahab and Zedekiah, the two prophets condemned in Jer 29:22-23 for "committing adultery with their neighbors' wives."

36. See Moore, *Daniel,* 111–12; Zimmerman ("Story of Susanna," 237) points to examples of Phoenician bastardy in *Gen. Rab.* 37.

37. See Moore, *Daniel,* 112, on anti-Samaritanism. Bickerman (*Jews in the Greek Age,* 95) finds the contrast "curious." LaCocque, more sensitive to the political implications of the phrase, states that "such a characterization smacks of the ideology of the conservative party. Here, in the mouth of Daniel, it is unexpected" (*Feminine Unconventional,* 26). Read in the context of the Apocrypha, of Susanna as metaphor for the community, and in light of the tendency of threatened communities to circumscribe women's bodies, however, the line is neither curious nor unexpected.

charge. In turn, Daniel's case rests not on Susanna's protestation but on the elders' testimony.[38] Then the woman and the book are incorporated into the canonical version of Daniel and so safely tucked away into a story revolving around men's concerns.

But Susanna cannot be left to rest easily there. Susanna's exile from the peace and privacy of her own garden, the diaspora setting of the text, its problematic canonical history, and the marginalization of the modern Jewish woman engaged in analysis interweave around shifting borders. What may be celebrated from one perspective may be condemned from another. Susanna's freedom from domestic responsibilities may indicate to some the economic success of the diaspora community; to others it signals complacency and indolence. For some, she is a heroine whose righteousness is recognized by heaven; for others she is a weak figure unable or unwilling to protest her own innocence in the public sphere until seemingly too late. Recognition of class differences provokes an entry into the critique of Susanna-as-character and thereby allows exploration of intertextually negative associations. Recognition of her marginalized position as a woman leads to the discovery of the relationship between the constructs of gender and ethnicity in Hellenistic Jewish narratives. Recognition of the value of her education, her piety, and her prayer reinstates a more positive social role for Jewish women that is often overlooked by those wedded to Christian or select rabbinic reconstructions. I have asked questions that arise from my own various, marginalized situations. The explorations they generate and the tentative answers those explorations provide incorporate all fellow travelers across religious and sexual borders into the ongoing re-creation of Jewish history, of women's history, of human history.[39]

---

38. See Glancy, "The Accused."
39. Grants from the National Endowment for the Humanities and from the American Council of Learned Societies have enabled me to continue my analysis of the representations of Jewish women in Hellenistic literature. I also thank Jay Geller for his contributions to the substance and style of this article.

11

"And I Will Strike Her Children Dead": Death and the Deconstruction of Social Location

_____ Tina Pippin ____

Studies of the concept of death in the Apocalypse of John traditionally focus upon the theme of the martyrdom of the faithful witnesses of God and the Lamb. In this essay I intend to explore the concept by focusing upon the deaths of those who are perceived as witnesses of Satan, beginning with the death of the Jezebel figure and her "children" or followers in Apoc 2:20-25. The rhetoric of death continues through the ecological death of the earth accompanying the opening of the seven seals, the blowing of the trumpets, and the pouring of the seven bowls of wrath, and culminates with the death of the Whore and her followers and the eternal burning of the Whore and the eternal torture of Satan.

Before the utopian statement, "Death will be no more," is made in Apoc 21:4, the horror of death and punishment on both sides has occurred. How does the ideology of death figure into the literature of resistance? What are the political implications of death in the Apocalypse? What conclusions are gained by rereading the text for gender and sexuality codes? What are the ethical implications of the violent destruction of the earth and the majority of its inhabitants? What is our response and political responsibility as critics of this canonical text?

According to Terry Eagleton, the study of ideology is "a matter of discourse" and of power.[1] As discourse, ideology relates to the signification of "lived experience." In the Apocalypse death is governed by a political and gender-based discourse that is anticolonial (desiring the death of imperialism) and misogynist (desiring the death/eternal silencing of the female). The rhetoric of death is connected with the rhetoric

---

1. T. Eagleton, _Ideology: An Introduction_ (New York: Verso, 1991) 9, 5, following Foucault. Using Foucault's work on knowledge and power, M. Barrett points out the problem with the term "ideology." For Barrett ideology is mystification or misrepresentation, a partial truth (_The Politics of Truth: From Mary to Foucault_ [Stanford, Calif.: Stanford Univ. Press, 1991] 166–68).

of desire; Georges Bataille presents this connection as the link between death and sexual excitement.[2] The thanatos/eros syndrome is at work in the Apocalypse.

Death is also connected with life in the Apocalypse. Paul Ricoeur relates, "The desire for death does not speak, as does the desire for life. Death works in silence."[3] The silent earth, the silent women, the silent multitudes who die in the Apocalypse (for example, the seven thousand in 11:13) all serve as a metonymy—that is, parts representing the whole of what is perceived (and mimetically desired!) as evil. The social location of the text is deconstructed through the rhetoric of death, for death moves both the earth and its inhabitants to different places.[4] In particular, women are displaced and have no place in the heavenly city. The ideology of insider and outsider, the living and the dead, the sexually active and the chaste, and the pure and dangerous points to the multiplicity of voices in the discourse of the Apocalypse and the complexities involved in defining ideology in the text.

One main debate in recent studies on the Apocalypse is between those who want to retain a historical focus in reading the text and those who want to do narratology and poststructural readings, with certain sociological and political readings falling on either side or somewhere in between. The former group diligently searches for every crumb of historical and cultural evidence available; the latter group, although often accused of being ahistorical and apolitical, sees history and culture in a different way—as embedded in textual codes and in the social location of the interpreter. The shift from the former to the latter may be defined as a move away from the archaeological sites of the seven cities in western Anatolia to the credo that "all we have is the narrative itself"

---

2. G. Bataille, *Eroticism: Death and Sensuality* (San Francisco: City Lights, 1986) 11. The attraction of women to the Jezebel figure has homoerotic overtones. Jezebel seduces both men and women. Her body on the bed draws both her followers and her readers. Jezebel is one of the "idols of perversity," a term B. Bijkstra uses to describe the portrayal of women as evil at the end of the nineteenth century and beginning of the twentieth.

3. P. Ricoeur, *Freud and Philosophy* (New Haven: Yale Univ Press, 1970) 294.

4. V. Robbins defines social location as "the common structural position occupied by a number of individuals in relation to a larger social whole" ("The Social Location of the Implied Author of Luke-Acts," *The Social World of Luke-Acts: Models for Interpretation* (ed. J. H. Neyrey; Peabody: Hendrickson, 1991) 307). He further delineates: "If we can identify the arenas of the social system presupposed by various phenomena in the text, and if we can delineate the location, role, and competencies certain phenomena exhibit within different arenas of the social system, then we can make some progress toward identifying the social location of the thought within the entire document" (308). Robbins is relying on "intratextual functions" of implied author and reader to lead to the social location. My concern is less with the first-century Mediterranean social location and more with the cultural critique of the biblical text—different ways the text is received and interpreted. I do not think the trail of the implied author or reader will lead to the first-century communities of the Apocalypse. The legend of the city of Atlantis comes to mind.

(New Criticism). Or the difference may be defined as multiple readings of the archaeological site, with the one group wanting to trace and recover the "history" and the other reading the site as a material text. I think both these broadly described approaches are needed; maybe the model of the chorus in the Apocalypse is apt for the future discourse. By "chorus" I mean a multiplicity of voices (Bakhtin's heteroglossia), although I am not seeking harmony because I think the text pushes us toward disharmony. So what I want to explore here is one way to carry on the discourse between different methodological readings. I begin with an examination of the Jezebel of Apocalypse 2.

The Body on the Bed

Most commentators point to the general idolatry (= fornication) of turning toward pagan religions (= imperial cult) and eating food sacrificed to idols. This connection with the Jezebel of 1 and 2 Kings is in keeping with the general negative attitude and picture of Jezebel. The death scene in 2 Kgs 9:30-37 is vivid and grotesque; when the eunuchs throw Jezebel out of the window, nothing is left after the horses trample her and the dogs eat her but "the skull and the feet and the palms of her hands" (2 Kgs 9:35).[5] In the Apocalypse, Jezebel is thrown on a bed, and all who fornicate with her are thrown into distress and killed (2:22-23). The fate of Jezebel is held up as an example to avoid.

The Jezebel of Apoc 2:20-23 is interpreted figuratively by Elizabeth Cady Stanton as denoting "a company of persons, of the spirit and character of Jezebel, within the church under one principal deceiver."[6] Colin Hemer retraces the steps to ancient Thyatira and finds an unknown "Jezebel" who was an influential member of the church. He relates that for the hearers of the Apocalypse in this city, "It may have been a shock to hear this popular teacher equated with Jezebel." Jezebel represents all the syncretism of Judaism and Christianity and the indigenous religion. In particular, Hemer notes about Jezebel's teaching: "Presumably Jezebel argued that a Christian might join a guild and participate in its feasts without thereby compromising."[7]

Elisabeth Schüssler Fiorenza focuses on Jezebel as prophet. She summarizes:

---

5. A related example is Che Guevara's death and the demand for his hand by one of his enemies.

6. E. Cady Stanton, *The Women's Bible* (1895, 1898; reprint, Salem, N.H.: Ayer, 1986) 180.

7. C. J. Hemer, *The Letters to the Seven Churches of Asia in Their Setting* (Sheffield, England: JSOT, 1986) 123.

This reference to a leading woman indicates not only that women belonged to the target audience of Revelation but also that they were leading figures in the Christian communities of Asia Minor. Such influential leadership of women in the Asian churches is quite in keeping with the general religious and political positions as well as sociocultural influence women had in Asia Minor.[8]

Schüssler Fiorenza calls the prophet and her followers an "alternative Christian prophetic group" and adds that worship of the imperial cult was part of their practice.[9] Susan Garrett states that "probably the woman was a rival" prophet, maybe one of the Nicolaitans.[10] Whatever her group identity, the woman's real name has been changed. Schüssler Fiorenza rightly notes that this woman has been silenced and her real name forgotten.[11]

Hemer represents the traditional reading of this ritual murder of the female; the female body is ignored. All Jezebel's children/followers who follow/fornicate with her are struck dead. Hemer allows that "a problem here is that the judgment upon the children seems more severe than that upon Jezebel herself."[12] But the judgment on Jezebel is severe: to throw her on a bed because of her crime. What was the nature of her crime?

It is instructive to return to the death of Jezebel in 2 Kings 9. The other side of this reading of Jezebel deals with what is being condemned. The "idolatry" of the Jezebel of Hebrew Scriptures is her worship of the Canaanite goddess Asherah, the creatrix and mother goddess of the Canaanite pantheon. She killed the prophets of Yahweh and attempted to replace them with the prophets of Baal and Asherah. Jezebel was not an entirely virtuous woman and is admittedly an ambiguous character. But she does not deserve the completely negative portrayal she receives. To call a woman a "Jezebel" has always translated as a loose, whoring, conniving, evil woman. The other side of Jezebel is as a woman (and Phoenician princess) who was fighting to protect her indigenous religion and culture. Peter Ackroyd rightly acknowledges that Jezebel has been interpreted only as a negative type—"into her figure is projected in detail the hostility to what is believed to be alien practice."[13] But more than this, Ackroyd sees the face of the goddess in the adorned face of Jezebel looking out the window at Jehu: "It is almost as if she

8. E. Schüssler Fiorenza, *Revelation: Vision of a Just World* (Minneapolis: Fortress Press, 1991) 133; see A. Wire, *The Corinthian Women Prophets: A Reconstruction through Paul's Rhetoric* (Minneapolis: Fortress Press, 1990) 105.

9. Schüssler Fiorenza, *Revelation*, 133.

10. S. Garrett, "The Book of Revelation," *The Women's Bible Commentary* (ed. C. A. Newsom and S. H. Ringe; Louisville: Westminster, 1992) 3–4.

11. Schüssler Fiorenza, *Revelation*, 135.

12. Hemer, *Letters*, 121.

13. P. Ackroyd, "Goddesses, Women and Jezebel," *Images of Women in Antiquity* (ed. A. Cameron and A. Kuhrt; Detroit: Wayne State Univ. Press, 1983) 256.

is being presented, and rejected, as the goddess herself."[14] Merlin Stone agrees: "The murder of Jezebel...was actually a political assault upon the religion of the Goddess."[15]

Jezebel at the window in 2 Kings and the Jezebel in the bed of adultery/idolatry in the Apocalypse is the goddess and woman-power presented and killed. A difference is that the Jezebel of 2 Kings refuses to worship YHWH; the Jezebel of Apocalypse 2 refuses to repent as she attempts to hold a position of authority in the Christian church. The slaughter of "those who eat at Jezebel's table" in 1 Kgs 18:19 is echoed in the murder of Jezebel's "children"; both represent the ritual extinction of the indigenous religious practices of the local guilds. The destruction of pagan religions is the destruction of the goddess-centered rituals and the overturning of women-centered religion. The Apocalypse is a story of gender oppression.

In her writing on the Apocalypse, Mary Daly explains: "No one asks *who* are the agents of wickedness. It is enough to have a scapegoat, a victim for dismemberment."[16] Although there are both male and female victims in the Apocalypse, gender is ignored. The text is disembodied.

To the modern reader/observer this passage is a scene of horror and mass murder. The line between insiders and outsiders becomes clearer in the judgment of Jezebel and her children. The propaganda of death is strong; to resist is futile.

Undoing Death

The story of Jezebel in the letter to the church of Thyatira is a social text—a woman lying in a bed while her children are struck dead. Imagine a still photograph of this scene (the Flemish Apocalypse has Jezebel in bed with a fornicating follower). The bed of pleasure is an image reversed. Jezebel is thrown into the bed; she loses her freedom, her speech, her power. She is placed; she does not place herself.

In her book *Undoing the Social: Towards a Deconstructive Sociology*, Ann Game examines the themes of desire, memory and time, and the body. She summarizes her argument: "My concern has been to argue that the body provides the basis for a different conception of knowledge: we know with our bodies. In this regard, the authenticity of experience might be reclaimed; if there is any truth, it is the truth of the body." She also states: "We are written, our bodies are discursively produced; but

---

14. Ibid., 258.
15. M. Stone, *When God Was a Woman* (New York: Harcourt Brace Jovanovich, 1976) 57.
16. M. Daly, *Gyn/Ecology: The Metaethics of Radical Feminism* (Boston: Beacon) 105.

we also write, and in this writing, or practice of codes of the culture, there is a possibility of rewriting—rewriting ourselves."[17] Game's different reading of social theory includes a multiplicity of texts, theories, and images as a way of including the other (Lacan).[18]

The themes of desire, memory and time, and the body decenter traditional concerns of sociology (subject-object) for Game, and I find these themes helpful in rereading the Apocalypse. Questions occur: Who is telling this story of death? What does the storyteller desire? What is the function of women in this Christian community and in this polis? What do the women desire? How are the social roles of gender determined? Why is the prophet-teacher-leader woman Jezebel set up as an object of desire? Who is the monster responsible for the mass murder of Jezebel's children? And even more broadly, how did such a misogynist text make it into the Christian canon? At least the last question is readily apparent to the contemporary reader; the Apocalypse of John is part of the first-century version of the backlash against women. To get involved in the other questions, I want to tell several stories, several layers of stories:

> And to the angel of the church in Thyatira write: These are the words of the Son of God, who has eyes like a flame of fire, and whose feet are like burnished bronze: "I know your works—your love, faith, service, and patient endurance. I know that your last works are greater than the first. But I have this against you: you tolerate that woman Jezebel, who calls herself a prophet and is teaching and beguiling my servants to practice fornication and to eat meat sacrificed to idols. I gave her time to repent, but she refuses to repent of her fornication. Beware, I am throwing her on a bed, and those who commit adultery with her I am throwing into great distress, unless they repent of her doings; *and I will strike her children dead.* And all the churches will know that I am the one who searches minds and hearts, and I will give to each of you as your works deserve. But to the rest of you in Thyatira, who do not hold this teaching, who have not learned what some call 'the deep things of Satan,' to you I say, I do not lay on you any other burden; only hold fast to what you have until I come. To everyone who conquers and continues to do my works to the end,

---

17. A. Game, *Undoing the Social: Towards a Deconstructive Sociology* (Toronto: Univ. of Toronto Press, 1991) 192, 189.

18. For a discussion of the dialectic of same and other, see J. Butler's chapter entitled "Subversive Bodily Acts" (*Gender Trouble: Feminism and the Subversion of Identity* [New York: Routledge, 1990]). Jezebel is then a symbol for the libidinal. Butler's explanation of Irigaray is helpful: "Women are also a 'difference' that cannot be understood as the simple negation or 'Other' of the always-already-masculine subject.... They are neither the subject nor its Other, but a difference from the economy of binary opposition, itself a ruse for a monologic elaboration of the masculine" (18).

I will give authority over the nations;
to rule them with a iron rod,
as when clay pots are shattered—

even as I also received authority from my Father. To the one who conquers I will also give the morning star. Let anyone who has an ear listen to what the Spirit is saying to the churches." (Apoc 2:18-29)

•

Buttered, I lie on my single bed, flat, like a piece of toast. I can't sleep. In the semidark I stare up at the blind plaster eye in the middle of the ceiling, which stares back down at me, even though it can't see. There's no breeze, my white curtains are like gauze bandages, hanging limp, glimmering in the aura cast by the searchlight that illuminates this house at night, or is there a moon?

I fold back the sheet, get carefully up, on silent bare feet, in my nightgown, go to the window, like a child, I want to see. The moon on the breast of the new-fallen snow. The sky is clear but hard to make out, because of the searchlight; but yes, in the obscured sky a moon does float, newly, a wishing moon, a sliver of ancient rock, a goddess, a wink. The moon is a stone and the sky is full of deadly hardware, but oh God, how beautiful anyway.

I want Luke here so badly. I want to be held and told my name. I want to be valued, in ways that I am not; I want to be more than valuable. I repeat my former name, remind myself of what I once could do, how others saw me.

I want to steal something.[19]

•

Baby Suggs noticed who breathed and who did not and went straight to the boys lying in the dirt. The old man moved to the woman gazing and said, "Sethe. You take my armload and gimme yours."

She turned to him, and glancing at the baby he was holding, made a low sound in her throat as though she'd made a mistake, left the salt out of the bread or something.

"I'm going out here and send for a wagon," the sheriff said and got into the sunlight at last.

But neither Stamp Paid nor Baby Suggs could make her put her crawling-already girl down. Out of the shed, back in the house, she held on. Baby Suggs had got the boys inside and was bathing their heads, rubbing their hands, lifting their lids, whispering, "Beg your pardon, I beg your pardon," the whole time. She bound their

---

19. M. Atwood, *The Handmaid's Tale* (New York: Fawcett, 1986) 125-26.

wounds and made them breathe camphor before turning her attention to Sethe. She took the crying baby from Stamp Paid and carried it on her shoulder for a full two minutes, then stood in front of its mother.[20]

"We know with our bodies," and we know the text and its infinite meanings when we become embodied beings in our lived experience. Participating in the Apocalypse means saying no on many levels: no to this story as liberating for women; no to the violence to women's bodies; no to the sacrificial mass deaths. The stories of pain and violence and death and male desire ironically locate us in the same ideology of oppression as the Apocalypse. The wayward woman is always quickly marginalized, mainstreamed, or massacred. What women readers of this text know with their bodies is the history of abuse and violence and death of the body of the female. The clay pots are shattered. The iron rod[21] rules.

---

20. T. Morrison, *Beloved* (New York: Knopf, 1987) 151–52.

21. For Mary Daly this iron rod is a *god/rod:* "divine ruler of phallocrates possessed by penis envy, who obsessively compete, measuring/comparing their rods—e.g. guns, missiles, rockets" (*Webster's First New Intergalactic Wickedary of the English Language* [Boston: Beacon, 1987] 203). It is tempting here to play with the image of the pot as a womb.

12

Solidarity and Contextuality: Readings of Matthew 18:21-35

_____ Sharon H. Ringe ____

Publishing is a temptation to pride. When an author goes to press with an article or book, she would like to think that she has made a contribution of some lasting significance. If she is an exegete, she would like her study to play a role in opening the text in some striking new way for the understanding and enlightenment of the reading public, however that is defined for the work in question. Something published carries authority—is authoritative—and flirts with immortality, at least insofar as it will remain catalogued in research libraries.

Contextual readings—always in the plural, and by definition eschewing claims to universality or "objectivity"—seem more suited to a loose-leaf notebook or to a word processor, where additions, deletions, and other changes are always an option. Acknowledging that one's reading is contextual, and working self-consciously within the hermeneutical humility thus defined, quickly pricks the balloon of publishing hubris and sends it sputtering to the ground, brought back to the reality where it belongs in the first place. But the ground is a shifting landscape, by chance, by choice, and by "project." That shifting landscape as a vantage point from which to examine the teachings on forgiveness in Matt 18:21-35 is the locus of this study.

Context and Solidarity

At issue is the fact that no one's context stays put. Some factors seem to be fairly constant throughout a person's life: gender and race, for example. Others may change radically and obviously: economic class; local, national, or world-historical events; or the events of one's private experience, such as relationships beginning or ending, the birth and subsequent lives of one's children, or one's own or loved ones' health. Other factors in one's context and changes in them are more subtle: the quality and internal dynamics of significant relationships; events shaping the institutions on which one depends for livelihood, safety, and values; the organized and random threats that occur to one's livelihood, safety, and values. None of these factors is a neutral bit of information, but rather they all have concrete historical (that is, institutional and ideological) expressions and consequences that shape them from raw data into the meaning-bearing matrix that is one's "context."

But more than simply the data of one's own social location given meaningful shape, "context" is also a matter of one's active and deliberate engagement in the midst of that reality. It is thus possible for one's context to be affected—even transformed—by the realities and experiences of other persons and communities who "accompany" one and those with whom one, in turn, is in solidarity.[1] For example, I am a North American, white, middle-class, single woman, status-inconsistent by being part of the dominant race and class and from a powerful nation, but always marginal because of being a woman in a patriarchal society and being single in a world still ideologically (and in many ways institutionally) oriented to couples and nuclear families. I am "bi-lingual" in the sense of having learned the language and attendant worldview of patriarchy well enough to survive in its educational and ecclesial systems, and I now have a personal and professional investment in those same systems, however alien they may have felt initially and in many ways still do.

Those facts about myself cannot be erased at will, but they do not define the limits of my context, because others' realities have become part of it. For example, women and men from Central America with whom I have worked and lived struggle daily with the economic disasters caused by the debt owed by their countries to international banking institutions based in the Northern Hemisphere. These *compañeros/as* have taught me the immediate, human consequences of decisions that to me seemed distant, abstract, and—in principle—defensible. Similarly, I have never

---

1. "Accompanying," or *la pastoral de acompañamiento,* is the term used by many church workers in Central America to identify their style of identification with the persons in their communities, working with them to accomplish the community's goals and sharing the risks and hardships of their lives "from below," rather than ministering *to* them from a place of safety or of authority "from above." It is related to the following meaning of solidarity proposed by A. M. Isasi-Díaz ("Solidarity: Love of Neighbor in the 1980s," *Lift Every Voice: Constructing Christian Theologies from the Underside* [ed. S. Brooks Thistlethwaite and M. Potter Engel; San Francisco: Harper and Row, 1990] 32–33):

> Solidarity is *not* a matter of agreeing with, of being supportive of, of liking, or of being inspired by, the cause of a group of people. Though all these might be part of solidarity, solidarity goes beyond all of them. Solidarity has to do with understanding the interconnections among issues and the cohesiveness that needs to exist among the communities of struggle.

been abused by a spouse or a lover, but women who have lived with that reality have taught me their stories so thoroughly that the syndrome of domestic violence has become part of my own awareness and therefore my context—the meaning- and value-filled matrix out of which I live and view the world. Put another way, while neither set of experiences is part of my story, those stories are now part of my experience, and because of them, my world will never look the same.

When I interpret a text, therefore, I find myself "standing toward"[2] it in several postures, both because of my own status-inconsistency and because of others who have dared to "speak the language of their life."[3] The different angles of vision, not surprisingly, mean different starting points for the study, evoke different questions to the text, and consequently yield different results. Most telling is the shift from an abstract or idealist reading to material readings from particular contexts. That movement occurred for me in stages, which I have attempted to preserve in this essay, and not in a single shift—an experience itself probably attributable to the many laminae of my own reality. The two contexts of solidarity identified in my self-description in the previous paragraph—*la deuda* (the debt) as the defining reality of Central America, and domestic violence as the defining reality of its victims and survivors—provide specific grounding for this study and yield almost diametrically opposite results, "news" of death and of life.

Traditional Readings: The Text

The tools of literary and historical criticism focus one's gaze on the biblical text itself: its place in Matthew's Gospel, its literary form and structure, historical details to which it is transparent, the church context envisioned by the author, and its "theological" implications (that is, its contribution to doctrines of God, Christ, sin, grace, the church, and so forth). Those tools help us to recognize that the teachings and parable on forgiveness (Matt 18:21-22, 23-35) are part of a long section of teachings and advice to the Matthean church and that they themselves contribute to the emerging picture of the meaning and implication of the divine *basileia* (kingdom, realm, reign, or "project").[4]

---

2. S. H. Ringe, "Standing toward the Text," *Theology Today* 43 (1987) 552–57.

3. I am indebted to Holly Near's song "Sing to Me the Dream" for her expression of the experience of being taught another's language/life so powerfully that it becomes part of one's own "wonder," one's own dream, and thus the basis of solidarity.

4. Liberation theologians from Central America frequently use the dynamic phrase *el proyecto de Dios*—the "project" of God—instead of more static words such as "kingdom," "realm," or "reign" to translate the Greek word *basileia*. In so doing, they emphasize that God's will for justice and peace is as yet unrealized, and that it requires engagement and not merely assent or admiration.

Teachings for the Church

Beginning with Peter's first recognition of Jesus as the Christ (Matt 16:13-23) and continuing to the point of Jesus' entry into Jerusalem in chapter 21, the church (represented by the disciples and by the frequent references to *adelfos,* "brother")[5] is instructed on such matters as Christology, discipleship, eschatology, church authority and discipline, relations between Christians and the Jewish religious authorities, the dangers of leading astray the "little ones" of the community, marriage and divorce, wealth and wages, power and servanthood, and the dynamics of forgiveness. Though portions are strictly parenetic (for example, the carefully outlined "due process" for church discipline [18:15-18]), the teachings are eclectic in form—as often narrative as prescriptive.

Both in form and in content, this section of the Gospel sustains the tension between proclaiming the inclusive vision of God's *basileia* of justice and peace, and discerning practical implications for the church "household" that is fast becoming an institution of Hellenistic urban life.[6] Peace within the church seems to be of paramount concern—a peace ordered under the proper authorities (16:19; 18:15-18) and sustained by the members' willingness to forgive material debts as well as relational offenses standing between them. Their forgiveness is to be no pious show, but a forgiveness "from the heart" (18:35), modeled on the generosity of the divine Householder and mirroring the wholehearted love that they are to manifest for God (22:37). Failure to live out such an economy of grace within the community evokes (or should evoke) from the "brothers" the shock seen in the response of the other servants in the parable who witness their forgiven colleague's hard-heartedness (18:31).

The result of Matthew's concern for the proper management of the household of faith mirrors the compromises seen in the other New Testament guides for household management (Col 3:18—4:1; Eph 5:21—6:9; 1 Pet 2:18—3:7). Those more formal codes temper the

---

5. H. F. von Soden ("Adelfos, k.t.l.," *Theological Dictionary of the New Testament,* 1:145) cites Jewish usage of the term "brother" to refer not only to a male sibling, but also to a co-religionist (a greater degree of intimacy than a "neighbor," who might be simply someone from the same ethnic community but without religious ties). This usage appears to be the rule in Matthew's community as well (see Matt 5:22-24, 47; 7:3-5; 10:21; 12:46-50; 23:8; 25:40; 28:10, in addition to chap. 18; note especially the parallel usage in 18:5 and 25:40, where doing or not doing something to one of the *adelfoi* is equated with doing or not doing it to Jesus or to God). See also K. Stendahl, *The School of St. Matthew and Its Use of the Old Testament* (Philadelphia: Fortress Press, 1968) 28.

6. M. H. Crosby has identified "house" as Matthew's primary metaphor for the *basileia* of God. He suggests that Matthew's parenetic sections be seen as guidelines for management of the house-churches that are the basic units in Matthew's Christian praxis (*House of Disciples: Church, Economics, and Justice in Matthew* [Maryknoll, N.Y.: Orbis Books, 1988] 19).

one-sidedness of their parallels in Hellenistic philosophical writings by attributing responsibilities to husbands, masters, and parents as well as to wives, servants, and children. They do not, however, change in a fundamental way the distribution of power in those relationships. The more powerful are to love, treat fairly, and not aggravate the less powerful, who, in turn, are to obey or be submissive. Similarly, in Matthew's ideal,[7] the vision of inclusiveness and mutuality found in the traditions stemming from the Jesus movement is tempered so that the lifestyle of the house-church and of its constituent households would not shock or offend the imperial ethos by any fundamental change in existing hierarchical relationships. Those relationships are simply to be lived out more generously and tempered by "forgiveness."

Glimpses of God, Christ, and Human Vocation

The passage on forgiveness (18:21-35) begins as a follow-up question from Peter on the subject of church discipline: assuming the process is successful, how many chances does the offender get? Is there a limit to the recidivism that can be tolerated? The response (seen in the multiples of the numbers seven and ten, each of which symbolizes totality or completeness) is that there is no limit: Peter might as well stop counting![8]

The ensuing parable, linked closely to the teaching (*dia touto*) with no evidence of an editorial "seam," does not deal with a limitless number of pardons. It does, however, continue to call the reader toward consideration of transcendent concerns and ultimate values. The story is identified as a point of comparison for the divine *basileia*. The characters of the parable, a king and his servants, are stock allegorical representations for God and humankind. In addition, such details as the huge amount of the first debt,[9] its contrast with the second debt (which would be about five

---

7. Crosby (*House,* 71) identifies 17:24—18:4 as Matthew's "household code," but the whole section of teachings to the church—given the primacy of the metaphor of the "house" in Matthew's Gospel—might be seen in the same light.

8. One must be suspicious of the contrast suggested by M. D. Goulder between "the unending forgiveness demanded of the Christian apostle" and the vengefulness conveyed in the story of Cain and Able (Gen 4:24, LXX), simply on the basis of the common occurrence of the same numbers (*Midrash and Lection in Matthew* [London: SPCK, 1974] 402). Their symbolic use was far too common to substantiate such a connection and with it the implied contrast between Jewish and Christian patterns of human relationship.

9. The exact dollar amount is hard to calculate as well as to fathom, but comparative figures illustrate its immensity. According to court records, Herod's annual income was a mere nine hundred talents. In the middle of the first century, taxes collected each year in Galilee and Perea together amounted to only about two hundred talents. Clearly the size of the debt forgiven to the first servant resembled, in its day, the current U.S. national debt! (E. Schweizer, *The Good News according to Matthew* [Atlanta: John Knox, 1975] 377–78).

hundred thousand times less), the punishment of eternal torture (since the reinstated first debt could never be repaid), and the carefully constructed parallelism—both synonymous and antithetical—between the two encounters of creditor and debtor[10] support traditional readings of the parable as representing a contrast between divine generosity and human calculation, or, alternatively, a story about God and secondarily an imperative for human beings.[11]

To see the "debts" at issue in the story as moral or relational offenses has been the most common reading, and one that is variously given a christological, an ecclesial, or an existentialist accent. Built on the premise of original sin having resulted in alienation between God and humankind that God alone can overcome, this reading emphasizes the virtually infinite "debt" canceled by the God/king (an action often interpreted in the light of a christologically focused doctrine of atonement) as paradigmatic of divine grace. Any wrongs committed by one person against another are paltry by comparison, and clearly the only response possible is that people should forgive one another as God has forgiven them. That the sequence of divine and human forgiveness portrayed in the parable is the reverse of that implied by the Matthean version of the Lord's Prayer and the commentary that follows (6:12, 14-15) simply makes clearer what is already seen in the disproportionate "debts," namely, that God's forgiveness of us is a function of God's gracious nature and not of human merit. In an existentialist reading, God's initiative of forgiveness is what sustains human life even in the face of the recognized alienation at its heart, and in turn makes human social intercourse possible. In a recent variation of a more ecclesial bent, Daniel Patte expresses the motive of God's gracious action as the primacy of sustaining a relationship, which itself becomes constitutive of the church:

> By forgiving, one does not lose anything. On the contrary, one gains something, and indeed something very good: one gains a

---

10. The parallel sections are vv. 24-27 and 28-30. The description of the debtors' actions and words when confronted with the demand for payment is almost identical in both cases. Because of that, the contrasts in other details are striking. In addition to the different size of the debts, the first servant is brought to the king and given some semblance of due process (as unrealistic as it would have been that sale of all his possessions, plus the indentured servitude of his entire family, could ever hope to match the debt incurred), whereas the second is encountered by accident and seized with back-alley violence. The king, assumed to carry virtually limitless authority over the lives of subjects, acts with "compassion" (*splanchnistheis,* a word describing Jesus' own response to the two blind men in 20:34), whereas the first servant refused to acknowledge the more realistic plea for an extension of the loan by his peer (*syndoulos autou*). The first servant is "released" and the "loan forgiven to him," whereas the second is imprisoned and required to "pay the debt."

11. Goulder, *Midrash,* 50, 402–3.

brother and therefore the possibility of enjoying the presence of Jesus in their midst.[12]

Whether as a consequence of one's participation in the relationality of God known paradigmatically in the church, or in celebration of one's existential reconciliation with God, divine forgiveness becomes the basis for perseverance and the norm of conduct within the ambiguity of human nature and life.

In any event, the relationship between divine and human forgiveness conveyed by the parable is usually interpreted as being that of proclamation and commandment: God forgives, so human beings ought to forgive one another—a simple argument from the greater to the lesser. Another option is to recognize that what is at work is Matthew's affirmation of humankind as created in the divine image. That image is not an ideal from which humankind then fell away, but rather a germ or prototype defining the human being's potential and setting the human vocation. Here the "trait" or property is the capacity to forgive, whereas in 5:43-48 the divine quality toward which humankind is to grow to maturity is inclusive love.

The abstraction and generalization of the above comments are obvious. The assumption underlying them is that for any person, in any historical context, the meaning would be the same. However true and generally recognizable the values represented, they are like a plane that never lands. The spectacle, or in this case the rhetoric, may be impressive, but as "transportation"—conveyor of meaning—the vehicle is dysfunctional.

A "Woman's Reading"

When one examines the passage from the perspective of "women's experience" (as white, middle-class, North American or Western European women once imagined ourselves entitled to do), a fresh set of questions, problems, and possibilities of meaning emerges. As in the Bible generally, women's voices are not heard, nor are women's experiences reflected, in Matt 16:13—20:34.

In fact, this entire section of the Gospel has little to claim women's attention specifically *as* women. The church leaders prefigured in the disciples seem to be envisioned as male. Throughout the section, and in particular in the sayings and parable about forgiveness (18:21-35), members of the community are called "brothers." While it may be possible to see in that language the "generic" use of the masculine to include

---

12. D. Patte, *The Gospel according to Matthew: A Structural Commentary on Matthew's Faith* (Philadelphia: Fortress Press, 1987) 255.

both genders, the paternalism of that argument is obvious. Furthermore, it seems even more likely that such usage, particularly in Matthew's church, reflects the practice of counting only male participants as constituent of the gathered community, with women as the invisible, silent partners. The parable of the ungrateful servant (18:23-35) also is located in what was then (and for many still is) men's public world of finances, of the settling of accounts both fiscal and moral, and where physical or economic bullying is an acceptable way to resolve a dispute. Women are, at best, on the edges, needing to translate ourselves into a man's story, and into what is largely men's reality, if we are to be addressed at all.

Having done such a translation of ourselves into the reality envisioned by the parable and teachings, however, we can of course hear ourselves included in the general human category of "sinners" set free by God's gracious forgiveness, and we too can find comfort and strength for life in such a word, and a challenge to our petty human calculations. Unlike the various theories of atonement often used to interpret God's reconciling act of forgiveness, this parable at least offers no glorification of suffering—even of "divine child abuse" in the sacrifice of God's righteous "son" to cleanse the vast pollution of human sin[13]—that can be used to justify the continuation or "completion" of Christ's suffering in the lives of women and men without power to protect themselves.

But even such themes as human sinfulness and God's limitless generosity to forgive have often become weapons used against women, for the blame for human alienation and "original sin" has often been lodged at women's door. We most of all, the argument goes, should be grateful that even our very embodiment of sin is overcome by God! Shame on us! *Shame,* indeed, as a reinforcement of one of the most pervasive consequences of patriarchal values on women's psyches is driven home. The gospel word of "forgiveness," which in the abstract is a word of grace and promise, in the concreteness of women's lives secures our place lower on the "chain of being" than our "brothers," who by this bit of theological sleight-of-hand retain the upper hand in a landscape of power that remains unchanged. And, as the parable makes clear, those whose great debts have been canceled are obliged to be (even more?) forgiving of wrongs committed against them. Even the availability of protest is muted: Christians who have received God's gracious forgiveness in Christ *must* be forgiving in turn.

Once again, though, the analysis rings hollow. Just as in traditional readings the experience of men (at least of those men who also happened to be of the class, educational background, and general social

---

13. See the discussions in J. C. Brown and R. Parker, "For God So Loved the World?" *Christianity, Patriarchy, and Abuse: A Feminist Critique* (ed. J. C. Brown and C. R. Bohn; New York: Pilgrim, 1989) 1–30; and R. N. Brock, "And a Little Child Will Lead Us: Christology and Child Abuse," *Christianity, Patriarchy, and Abuse,* 42–61.

location to be writing formal theologies) was thought to suffice to encompass all of human reality, so "women's reality," as that term was used in earlier feminist writings, presumed the same about the experience of those few who made it into the ranks of academic theology. The abstraction labeled "women's experience" ignores the very different experiences and realities of women of color, poor women, women from the Two-Thirds World, women who are differently abled, or women who have been abused. Even when the writers of "feminist interpretation" or "feminist theology" shared in such specificities of experience, those factors were subsumed under the larger analytical category of "women." Such heuristic and hermeneutical imperialism serves to keep the theological plane in the air, while useful interpretation may be more in need of a local bus—one that makes many stops at the street corners and doorsteps of particular lives.

Forgiveness as a Death Sentence

Neglect and silence are never benign. Women[14] caught in the net of domestic violence have long been taught to keep their suffering secret. Family honor, personal shame at a broken relationship, and the suspicion (often reinforced by the abuser or abusers and other family members who are aware of what is happening) that the whole thing is her fault have colluded to keep the horror under wraps—sometimes literally under the clothing and makeup that hide the bruises, or behind stories of "clumsiness," frequent falls, and vague illnesses that keep one at home until the evidence disappears. Furthermore, many women (like virtually all children who are abused) have little or no possibility of escape. Such basic needs as shelter, food, and medical care (for themselves and for dependent children), and the fear of further and even worse violence, hold them hostage to the abuser who is often physically more powerful and economically dominant. Their captivity is enforced by the lack of adequate community resources such as shelters and safe houses to which they can go.

Christian theology and church teaching collude in terrifying and—to many people—surprising ways to perpetuate the abuse. Not all of those ways resemble the grotesque misreading of the household codes that allows one to say to a woman who has been abused that if she were a good wife, and if she were properly submissive, her husband would

---

14. In this discussion I have referred to the person who has been abused as a woman, since statistics indicate that women are far more likely than men to be abused by a family member, partner, or other intimate acquaintance. In the case of children, the statistical gap between males and females is smaller than it is for adults, underlining the fact that the syndrome of abuse feeds on unjust power relationships.

not have to beat her to show his love by "correcting" her! Supposedly benign doctrines fairly interpreted are also problematic. For example, anthropological dualism that negates the body or views it as the locus of evil (in contrast to the pure spirit within), atonement theology that identifies a redemptive value in suffering, or a view of human nature as inherently sinful and in need of God to set things right, all can work to convince a victim that her suffering is in some way deserved, or even not important.

A picture of God's limitless forgiveness, such as can be discerned in Matt 18:23-35, plays into her low self-esteem and sense of inherent unworthiness. Such a person is readily convinced that if God can be forgiving of so unworthy a creature, she must in turn forgive any wrongs done to her: it is the only possible Christian response! And so she forgives her abuser—the father she is instructed to honor (15:4) or the spouse to whom she is joined by God (19:6; ironically, teachings prohibiting divorce are found directly after the parable about forgiveness in Matthew's Gospel)—again, and again, and again.[15] And sometimes she dies at the abuser's hand, still articulating her own unworthiness and declaring forgiveness.

Abstract, idealist (nonmaterial), and noncontextual readings of such texts as the teachings on forgiveness are clearly not value-neutral, but can be profoundly dangerous. The danger stems from the interpreters' failure to take into account the economic, psychological, and religious matrix of the unjust power relationships into which those readings are set. For those teachings to be able to convey "good news" and not a death sentence, the economic framework and constellation of power that sustain the abusive relationship must be broken, so that the one or ones abused can have at least the material means of escape. For such teachings to convey "good news" at all, the physical, emotional, psychological, and theological wounds that were inflicted must first be tended and helped to heal. Then a word about forgiveness—offered from God's grace and spilling over into human relationships—can find a safe home.

Who's Who? Forgiveness as Unexpected "Good News"

Readings of the teachings and especially the parable on forgiveness that have a negative impact on victims and survivors of abuse, as well as

---

15. The destructiveness to the one abused caused by the requirement to forgive one's abuser is discussed in the following essays: S. A. Redmond, "Christian 'Virtues' and Recovery from Child Sexual Abuse," *Christianity, Patriarchy, and Abuse,* 70–88; idem, "Evil, Sin, and Violation of the Vulnerable," *Lift Every Voice,* 152–64; M. D. Pellauer with S. Brooks Thistlethwaite, "Conversation on Grace and Healing: Perspectives from the Movement to End Violence against Women," *Lift Every Voice,* 169–85.

traditional readings by theologians from Western Europe and North America, assume a moral or ethical meaning of "debts." While it is true that Semitic words for "debt" refer also to "trespasses" or even "transgressions" or "sins,"[16] the plain economic meaning cannot be ignored. To do so in fact is a reading so partial as to be false and dangerous.

Poor people in Central America (and elsewhere in the Two-Thirds World) and those in solidarity with them are little tempted to such a reading. In the first place, they have learned well the cost of an abstract reading of such teachings: as good Christians, they are obliged to be forgiving (without limit) of those whose wielding of power has kept them poor and sustained their suffering. Even more effective a teacher has been the economic reality with which they live. Every moment of their lives is shaped by the fact of *la deuda*—the debt. No further identification is needed to identify the economic agreements negotiated between their governments and banks in "the North." The loans ostensibly were to support projects of economic development leading toward greater economic stability in the region. In fact, however, the interest payments alone (and there is no possibility ever to repay the principal) continue to wreak havoc on their economies, sending inflation rates soaring, provoking ever higher unemployment, and widening the gap between the very small wealthy class and the destitute masses.[17] Informed by such a context, interpreters approaching the parable in Matt 18:23-35 recognize clearly that forgiveness of "debts" in the literal, economic sense is a necessary first step toward God's project (*basileia*) of justice and peace.

If one accepts that such forgiveness is part of the divine vision, then the implications of the parable for human involvement in the rhythms of forgiveness granted and passed on can be envisioned in different ways. First, one could engage in a hybrid reading of the reference to debts: God's forgiveness of the sin of humankind—an infinite gift—evokes the response of people's forgiveness of the various "debts" owed to them, including economic ones. Alternatively, one could derive the principle of unlimited forgiveness from the preceding teachings (18:21-22) and see both occurrences of the word "debts" in the parable as literal economic references. In that case, the king in the parable—the initiator of the large loan and the final authority in economic matters—becomes a stand-in for those controlling the centers of economic power in the North. Those holders of power, good Christian folk informed by the

---

16. See, for example, the discussion in Goulder, *Midrash,* 288.

17. See Crosby, *House,* 250–51; see also F. J. Hinkelammert, *La Deuda Externa de América Latina: El Automatismo de la Deuda* (San José, Costa Rica: Editorial D.E.I., 1989). For an analysis of the debt as part of a policy of "low-intensity warfare" against those nations, see J. Nelson-Pallmeyer, *War against the Poor: Low Intensity Conflict and Christian Faith* (Maryknoll, N.Y.: Orbis Books, 1990); and R. V. Meneses, *Centroamérica: La Guerra de Baja Intensidad* (San José, Costa Rica: Editorial D.E.I., 1989).

basileia vision and the teachings on forgiveness, would initiate the transformation of the landscape of power by forgiving the huge debts they control. The political leaders who had contracted the loans could then be held accountable for relaying throughout the internal economic systems of their countries the benefits accrued by the loans' cancellation. If they refused to do so, they, like the first servant in the parable, could be disciplined.

The latter reading is clearly outrageous by traditional standards of biblical interpretation as well as of economic practice. But the outrage may belong to the standards rather than the reading. The application of traditional fiscal and economic theories has so far served only to exacerbate the situation surrounding the international debt. The facts of the case suggest that unprecedented actions will be needed to avert the disaster now spinning toward its conclusion. Imaginations constrained by the institutions of the powerful may need to be set free by the wisdom of the poor, whose power to shape institutions is limited, but whose grasp of the truth about their reality is firm.

Similarly, exegetical methodologies governed by idealist, objectivist assumptions ignore crucial historical and theological dimensions of the text. Without a materialist analysis of the economic circumstances of first-century Palestine and other territories of the Roman Empire, interpreters have ignored the implications of the prevailing patterns of land ownership and tenant farming. With the concentration of land in the hands of a few wealthy landowners, most people found themselves lodged in some position of dependence or servitude, even if they were not literally held as slaves. They existed at subsistence levels, always on the edge of indebtedness that could overwhelm them. In that context, for a proclamation to be received as "good news," or (like this parable) a metaphor (*hōmoiōthē*) for the divine *basileia,* an economic dimension would have been essential.[18] Theologically and historically, as well as in the economic arena, possibilities that at first seem outrageous demonstrate their reasonableness.

The locus of indebtedness and the dynamics of forgiveness find yet another reading in the reflection on Matt 18:23-35 by Felipe, a Nicaraguan Christian from Solentiname:

> The one who owed those millions was rich, because a nobody doesn't owe that much money. It seems to me that Jesus gives the example of a rich person because he wants to give the example of an exploiter. Everything the rich have got they've stolen from us,

---

18. Crosby (*House,* 4) suggests such a connection between the parable and the life-setting in which it arose, when he points out that despite its obvious exaggeration of the size of the first debt, the proposed punishments, and other details, it nevertheless reflects underlying conditions.

because all their riches have been got with our labor; and now all their injustices are forgiven them, but they don't forgive us; they throw us into jail when we owe them a bit. Someday, it seems to me, God will settle accounts with them through the people and he'll collect the whole debt.[19]

In this reading, the identities of the characters shift, and so does the allocation of credit and debt. The rich are no longer represented by the king, but by the first debtor. The debt they owe is finally *to* the poor—the same ones the rich now dun for the repayment of their debts—on whose behalf the "king" acts.

The reading is both theologically and economically astute, and, if we acknowledge it, it should be frightening to those of us who are rich. In the global economy, it is clear that the wealth of the countries of the North rides on the backs of the poor of the Two-Thirds World. In the Americas, that unfathomably large debt has built up over five hundred years of military, political, and economic conquest, often with religious sanction. By now, it is a debt we could never repay. In Felipe's reading, that debt of injustice and exploitation in all their forms has been forgiven by none other than the God whose identity is "God of the Poor"[20] and whose generosity the poor celebrate. But in that affirmation, a question is planted: If the debt we have amassed has been canceled, does it not follow that we in turn forgive the recent and relatively puny monetary loans (most of them negotiated since the late 1960s) that we have made to our poorer neighbors? In this scenario, what will happen if we refuse and our loan is called in?

Felipe's analysis poses theological questions within a context—an economic reality—invisible to those of us who presume on its benefits. In that analysis, competing economic models vie for dominance. The traditional model of debt and repayment that appears on the surface to serve the needs of the rich, and that instinctively we support, pronounces our condemnation. The illogical and impractical economy of grace and generosity turns out to be the model that sustains life for rich and poor alike: everyone wins! And in the process the boundaries of our vision of God's project of justice and peace are broken open. The good news, like the forgiveness in which it is manifest, is without limits.

---

19. E. Cardenal, *The Gospel in Solentiname* (Maryknoll, N.Y.: Orbis Books, 1979) 3:165.

20. V. Araya, *El Dios de los Pobres: El Misterio de Dios en la Teología de la Liberación* (San José, Costa Rica: Editorial D.E.I., 1983); English trans.: *God of the Poor: The Mystery of God in Latin American Liberation Theology* (Maryknoll, N.Y.: Orbis Books, 1987).

Good News/Bad News/Other News

The varied results of contextual readings of Matt 18:23-35 seem to suggest the need for renewed reflection and conversation about such questions as the nature and basis of biblical authority, norms for biblical interpretation, and the meaning of truth. I want to suggest, though, that such a discussion is at least premature, and perhaps even impossible in those terms. For the questions themselves are framed in language that pulls any ensuing dialogue toward abstractions, absolutes, and eternal truths. They obscure the gulf separating affirmation of the historical, cultural, and otherwise contextual *relativity* of biblical texts and interpretations, from a *relativism* that denies the Bible's own recognition of the urgency and clarity of God's sovereign yearning for justice, peace, and integrity in all creation. Allowing the variety of contextual readings—especially those from the margins, which until now have rarely had a voice—to give new energy and focus to that longing of God's own heart may be the more urgent task of biblical interpretation.

13

A Second Step in African Biblical Interpretation: A Generic Reading Analysis of Acts 8:26-40

Abraham Smith

In his essay "Beyond Identification: The Use of Africans in Old Testament Poetry and Narratives," Randall Bailey both critiques traditional scholarship's dilution of African influence on the biblical text and challenges future biblical scholars to move beyond the mere identification of Africans in the Bible "to examine the significance of the presence of African individuals and nations within the text."[1] Similarly, Clarice Martin, after re-Africanizing and "reblackening" the Ethiopian official in Acts 8:26-40, moves beyond identification to an investigation of the official's narrative role as a black-skinned man from Ethiopia.[2] Cogently, she asserts that because Ethiopia was conventionally regarded by Luke's contemporaries as one of the ends of the earth, the conversion of a black man from Ethiopia would likely be viewed by Luke's readers as a "symbolic (and partial) fulfillment of Acts 1:8c."[3] In line with the common perspective of these two scholars (that is, a perspective focused on the literary function of African characters), I too wish to move beyond identification (while acknowledging that this first step in African interpretation is still and will always be necessary) and join them in a second step of African biblical interpretation by proffering this article as an experiment in clarifying other possible roles of the Ethiopian official in Luke's narrative.[4] Using a fairly specific reading model, then,

1. R. Bailey, "Beyond Identification: The Use of Africans in Old Testament Poetry and Narratives," *Stony the Road We Trod: African American Biblical Interpretation* (ed. C. H. Felder; Minneapolis: Fortress Press, 1991) 165–69.

2. C. Martin, "A Chamberlain's Journey and the Challenges of Interpretation for Liberation," *Semeia* 47 (1989) 105–20.

3. Ibid., 120.

4. Following the nomenclature of classicists, I will use the term "Ethiopian" when citing texts about this group from Greek, Roman, and early Christian literature. While Luke used the Septuagint, a text that translates the term "Kushite" as "Ethiopian," I

I propose that Acts 8:26-40 functions as a part of Luke's critique and transformation of conventional understandings of power.

Since all reading models reveal the particular stance and sociopolitical values of particular readers (over and against others),[5] it is important initially to state the methodological and hermeneutical parameters of my approach. Methodologically, my approach is consonant with audience-oriented criticism, giving primary attention to audiences and their actualization (or concretization) of textual stimuli, but with genre considerations posited as a basic point of entry through which modern readers may join the ranks of Luke's "authorial audience," that is, the hypothetical construct of the audience Luke was likely to have had in mind when composing Luke-Acts.[6]

Hermeneutically, my approach reflects an African liberationist perspective,[7] for it posits the historical contingency and ideological com-

---

will use the term "Kushite" when I cite First Testament texts. See F. Snowden, *Before Color Prejudice: The Ancient View of Blacks* (Cambridge, Mass.: Harvard Univ. Press, 1983) 3. On Luke's use of the Septuagint, see J. Fleming, "The N.T. Use of Isaiah," *Southwestern Journal of Theology* 11 (1968) 89–103.

5. It should be clear that any account of the past, using an explicit reading model or not, cannot be performed in a disinterested manner. Apparently "natural" methods of interpretation are free of neither recontextualization—not even the ancient interpretations—nor rhetorical strategy, for all critics (including Aristotle, who transformed real tragedies within his own teleological system of probable actions) are influenced by the cultural practices of their times and the strategic positioning of themselves among their peers. On the influence of cultural practices, see C. Martindale, "Redeeming the Text: The Validity of Comparisons of Classical and Postclassical Literature (A View from Britain)," *Arion* 1 (1991) 46–55. On the strategic character of critical interpretation, see Robert Fowler, *Let the Reader Understand: Reader Response Criticism and the Gospel of Mark* (Minneapolis: Fortress Press, 1991) 29.

6. Among the minefield of theoretical positions in literary criticism, I take a moderate, pragmatist position. That is, I understand meaning to be developed through an interaction between the text and the reader, and for this position, I am largely indebted to the critical discussions of audiences in the works of H. Jauss, W. Iser, and P. Rabinowitz. On audiences and their actualization, see W. Iser, *The Act of Reading: A Theory of Aesthetic Response* (Baltimore: Johns Hopkins Univ. Press, 1974). The term "authorial audience" was coined by P. Rabinowitz ("Truth in Fiction: A Reexamination of Audience," *Critical Inquiry* 4 [1977] 126). In line with his discussion on genre is the work of H. R. Jauss, "Literary History as a Challenge to Literary Theory," *Toward an Aesthetics of Reception* (Minneapolis: Univ. of Minnesota Press, 1982) 18–19, a work insisting on the reconstruction of the horizon of expectations in the original readers largely through a reconstruction of the literary environment "which the author could expect his contemporary public to know either explicitly or implicitly." My motive for reconstructing the past with texts from the past (though obviously not apart from modern theoretical discussions) is not to commit the "closed circle interpretive" fallacy of many classical historians (see Martindale, "Redeeming the Text," 46), but rather to indicate traditional biblical scholarship's failure to understand Greco-Roman aesthetics, a failure that, in the case of Luke at least, leads potentially, I think, to a marginalization of the Ethiopian.

7. That my hermeneutical stance is indebted to Cornel West is obvious. West adamantly opposes ahistorical interpretive approaches (either the precritical kind, positing biblical texts as verbally inspired revelation, or the critical but romanticist kind, designating texts as essentially moral, despite the glaring morally oppressive features

mitment of texts and interpreters and, then, gives prominence to a set of political and cultural textual stimuli virtually overlooked by traditional studies of Acts 8:26-40, that is, Luke's characterization of the Ethiopian as a man of power.[8]

With these prolegomena stated, the course of this article will develop as follows: (1) a generic reading of Luke-Acts; and (2) rhetorical readings of Acts 8:26-40 within the architectonic structure of its context in Acts.

A Generic Reading of Luke-Acts

While one may agree with Thomas L. Brodie that Luke-Acts cannot be cast into a single generic category, affinities between Luke-Acts and the ancient Greek novel (also known as "the ancient Greek romance") remain and cannot be dismissed.[9] Both Luke-Acts and the ancient novels depict familiarity with the same geographical setting, that is, the eastern Mediterranean;[10] both mediate the motifs and constitutive features of earlier genres for popular consumption;[11] both are full of religious

---

within them). See C. West, *Prophetic Fragments* (Grand Rapids: Eerdmans, 1988); see West's afterword in *Post-Analytic Philosophy* (ed. J. Rajchman and C. West; New York: Columbia, 1985) 259–75). See also *Stony the Road We Trod*; J. Grant, *White Women's Christ and Black Woman's Jesus* (Atlanta: Scholars Press, 1989).

8. As we shall soon see, however, the narrator has a paradoxical understanding of power, a perspective turning the conventional understanding of power on its head.

9. T. L. Brodie, "Luke the Literary Interpreter: Luke-Acts as a Systematic Rewriting and Updating of the Elijah-Elisha Narrative in 1 and 2 Kings" (Ph.D. diss., Pontifical Univ. of St. Thomas Aquinas, 1981) 100. A number of scholars view the ancient Greek novel as the prototype for the Gospels and Acts. On the ancient Greek novel as a prototype for the Gospels, see M. A. Tolbert, *Sowing the Gospel: Mark's World in Literary-Historical Perspective* (Minneapolis: Fortress Press, 1989) 59, 62. On the novel as a prototype for Acts, see R. Pervo, *Profit with Delight: The Literary Genre of the Acts of the Apostles* (Philadelphia: Fortress Press, 1987); S. M. Praeder, "Luke-Acts and the Ancient Novel," *SBL Seminar Papers 1981* (ed. K. Richards; Chico, Calif.: Scholars Press, 1981); D. R. Edwards, "Acts of the Apostles and Chariton's *Chaereas and Callirhoe*" (Ph.D. diss., Boston Univ., 1987); S. P. Schierling and M. J. Schierling, "The Influence of the Ancient Romances on the Acts of the Apostles," *Classical Bulletin* 54 (1978) 81–88; H. Koester, *Introduction to the New Testament*, vol. 2: *History and Literature of Early Christianity* (Philadelphia: Fortress Press, 1982) 51, 316. While some scholars classify Luke-Acts as history, I contend that that genre's consistent use of periodic subordination, hyperbaton, and atticized speeches does not reflect the generally popular character of all of the New Testament narratives, including Luke-Acts. For a generic reading that construes Luke-Acts within the conventions of political history, see D. Balch, "The Genre of Luke-Acts: Individual Biography, Adventure Novel, or Political History?" *Southwestern Journal of Theology* 33 (1990) 5–19.

10. B. P. Reardon, "The Greek Novel," *Phoenix* 23 (1969) 292–93; Praeder, "Luke-Acts," 284.

11. From historiographical literature, the ancient Greek novels drew their historiographical frames. See M. M. Bakhtin, *The Dialogic Imagination* (Austin: Univ. of Texas Press, 1981) 89. Of course, these frames need not be totally accurate. See Haegg, *The*

concerns and themes;[12] both feature a stylistically simple, yet intriguing plot;[13] both use "recognition scenes" (that is, scenes revealing the true identity or fate of characters);[14] both reflect the Greco-Roman patron-client reciprocity ethic through which powerful figures (gods, political rulers, and a variety of mediating brokers) were guaranteed praise from their clients in return for acts of beneficence;[15] both are heavily packed with irony;[16] and both are replete with paradigmatic or moralistic characterization.[17]

While a comprehensive generic reading of Luke-Acts would give considerable attention to several or all of these affinities, space and time limitations will allow sustained emphasis on only one, paradigmatic characterization. Paradigmatic characterization is particularly important because both volumes of Luke-Acts are replete with positive and nega-

Novel in Antiquity (Oxford: Basil Blackwell, 1983) 17. On the historiographical forms in Luke-Acts (for example, the historical prefaces and the genealogy), see D. Aune, *The New Testament and Its Literary Environment* (Philadelphia: Westminster, 1987) 120–31. From epic and drama, the ancient Greek novels drew their substance (journey motifs, episodic plot, turning points, and recognition scenes). See Haegg, *Novel in Antiquity,* 110–12; Tolbert, *Sowing the Gospel,* 67; Koester, *Introduction,* 137.

12. Haegg, *Novel in Antiquity,* 101–4; Pervo, *Profit,* 25.

13. See Schierling and Schierling, "Influence," 82; Pervo, *Profit,* 13. I am now speaking of the non-Sophistic Greek novels (Chariton, *Chaereas and Callirhoe,* and Xenophon of Ephesus, *An Ephesian Story*). The most likely dates for these works are the first century BCE and the first century CE, respectively. See also Haegg, *Novel in Antiquity,* 6, 20.

14. On recognition scenes, see Aristotle *Poetics* 11.4; Haegg, *Novel in Antiquity,* 75–76; see R. Tannehill, *The Narrative Unity of Luke-Acts: A Literary Interpretation* (Minneapolis: Fortress Press, 1986) 2:35; Tolbert, *Sowing the Gospel,* 75; Praeder, "Luke-Acts," 269.

15. On the patron-client system, see H. Moxnes, "Patron-Client Relations and the New Community in Luke-Acts," *The Social World of Luke-Acts: Models for Interpretation* (ed. J. Neyrey; Peabody, Mass.: Hendrickson, 1991) 244; P. Vanderbroeck, *Popular Leadership and Collective Behavior in the late Roman Republic (ca 80–50 BC)* (Amsterdam: J. C. Gieben, 1987) 50. On the reciprocity ethic, see P. Garnsey and R. Saller, "Social Relations," *From Augustus to Nero: The First Dynasty of Imperial Rome* (ed. R. Mellor; East Lansing: Michigan State Univ. Press, 1990) 347; R. Macmullen, "Personal Power in the Roman Empire," *American Journal of Philology* 107 (1986) 521; see Seneca *On Benefits* 1.10. On mediating brokers, see Moxnes, "Patron-Client Relations," 246; Garnsey and Saller, "Social Relations," 348.

16. G. L. Schmeling, *Xenophon of Ephesus* (Boston: Twayne, 1980) 120; B. E. Perry, "Chariton and His Romance," *American Journal of Philology* 51 (1930) 93–134; B. E. Perry, *The Ancient Romances: A Literary-Historical Account of Their Origin* (Berkeley: Univ. of California Press, 1967) 135; Pervo, *Profit,* 59–61.

17. In paradigmatic characterization, certain characters are constructed to solicit the audience's identification, empathy, and imitation. On paradigmatic characterization in the novels, see B. Egger, "Women in the Greek Novel: Constructing the Feminine" (Ph.D. diss., Univ. of California, 1990) 48; E. H. Haight, *Essays on the Greek Romances* (Port Washington, N.Y.: Kennikat, 1943) 5–6; C. Schlam, *The Metamorphoses of Apuleius: On Making an Ass of Oneself* (Chapel Hill: Univ. of North Carolina Press, 1992) 10; W. Kurz, "Narrative Models for Imitation in Luke-Acts," *Greeks, Romans, and Christians* (ed. David L. Balch, Everett Ferguson, and Wayne A. Meeks; Minneapolis: Fortress Press, 1990) 171, 176.

tive characters and, more importantly, because the two volumes, like the novels themselves, advance an audience's identification with particular characters by casting them as powerful, faithful, and idealized figures within a texture of strategically arranged journeys, thematically similar episodes, and rhetorically crafted typologies.

In the novels, leading characters are propelled throughout the *oikumene* (inhabited world)—often through a series of *agones* (conflict scenes)—among successively greater networks of power.[18] Their successful, albeit adventurous, journeys from private spheres to larger, more public arenas are strategically designed to demonstrate both the ultimate safe-keeping power of a particular deity and the extraordinary influence of that deity's representatives.[19] The net effect is that the authorial audience identifies with the protagonists because of their ability to impress powerful figures everywhere, and equally so because of their ultimate vindication, despite tests and trials.[20]

Relatedly, empathetic identification is advanced through thematically similar episodes about the protagonists' abiding fidelity, despite increasing instability and catastrophic reversals.[21] Plagued by a "real" world seemingly driven by change, chance, and coincidence, the authorial audience could take solace in a "literary" world that featured the

---

18. I am presently developing a longer study that treats the *agon* convention in tragedy, comedy, and ancient Greek novels as a key to understanding Luke-Acts. Following B. P. Reardon's lead (*Form of the Greek Romance* [Princeton, N.J.: Princeton Univ. Press, 1991] 104) that the ancient Greek novels adopted and extended the conventional *agon* of the earlier genres, I suggest that the contest between the devil and the Spirit-filled Jesus (Luke 4:1-13), a scene anticipating Jesus' later struggles with human opponents, is similar to the *agones* of tragedy and comedy, now mediated through the ancient novels for popular consumption. For more on the types and functions of *agones*, see P. D. Arnott, *Public and Performance in the Greek Theatre* (London: Routledge, 1989) 105–16. On the matter of the networks of power, see Edwards, "Acts of the Apostles," 123.

19. Ibid., 128.

20. As Egger has noted, "Each of the novelists, in his own particular way, attempts to engage the readers' interest in, and at best, succeeds in leading them to feel empathy or identify with, not only the main characters' final wellbeing and achievement of their goals (that is, the happy ending of the love plot), but also their many trials and tribulations until this end is reached" (Egger, "Women in the Greek Novel," 48).

21. According to R. F. Hock, the basic structure of the novels "entails humiliation of the novels' protagonists and then their exaltation at the end. A summary of the plot of these novels will point out their structure: hero and heroine come from aristocratic families but after they fall in love they lose their status and become slaves. In addition to the psychological humiliation of being treated as a slave they endure assorted physical hardship, usually as a result of their maintaining fidelity to their beloved. But in the end they are raised up to their former status by the aid of some gracious deity, after which they live happily ever after" (R. F. Hock, "The Greek Novel," *Greco-Roman Literature and the New Testament* [ed. D. E. Aune; Atlanta: Scholars Press, 1988] 134). See Pervo, *Profit*, 80; D. B. Martin, *Slavery as Salvation: The Metaphor of Slavery in Pauline Christianity* (New Haven: Yale Univ. Press, 1990) 35. On the novelists' fondness for reversals of all sorts, see S. Wiersma, "The Ancient Novel and its Heroine," *Mnemosyne* 43 (1990): 109–23.

indomitable faithfulness of characters facing a loss of power, means, position, and status.[22] Thus, the network of thematic correlation (for example, duplication, symmetry, and parallelism) forces the authorial audience to assume the protagonists' fate, to aspire to their level of fidelity, and to achieve their transcendence over circumstances, an achievement for which all persons in the Hellenistic world daily longed.[23] Moreover, the novels advance identification through repeated allusions to venerable stock figures and types in previous narrative worlds.[24] Through such allusions, the protagonists achieve validation and idealization because their speeches, actions, interactions, and fates are drawn from the scripts of familiar and well-respected figures from the past.[25]

In Luke-Acts, leading characters like Jesus, Stephen, Peter and Paul are strategically cast in a series of adventurous *agones* that herald their deity's claim to be the universal patron or benefactor. These positive and paradigmatic characters are repeatedly stylized in the patterns of the venerable Septuagint prophets, that is, as successful, albeit suffering, "cosmic power brokers"[26] vis-à-vis their stylized opponents (for example, rulers of synagogues, Pharisees, scribes, chief priests, and elders in the Gospel of Luke and a number of Jewish and Roman officials in Acts)

---

22. See Tolbert, *Sowing the Gospel,* 39, 40; and see C. Beye, *Ancient Greek Literature and Society* (Ithaca, N.Y.: Cornell Univ. Press, 1987) 197.

23. On duplication ("repetition of a similar event") and parallelism ("matching the experiences of one character to that of another") in the novels, see Pervo, *Profit,* 133. On symmetry in the novels, see Schmeling, *Xenophon,* 92. Also, note that all writings from the Greco-Roman world were strongly influenced by an oral/aural orientation. Writing was vocalized, and public or private readers (as in the case of the Ethiopian [Acts 8:28-30]) read aloud. For an excellent treatment of the oral/aural environment of late Western antiquity, see P. J. Achtemeier, "Omne Verbum Sonat: The New Testament and the Oral Environment of Late Western Antiquity," *Journal of Biblical Literature* 109 (1990) 3–27. On the other matters, see Beye, *Ancient Greek Literature.*

24. Much of modern characterization theory (for example, the oft-cited study of Shakespearean characters by A. C. Bradley, the popular study of "flat" and "round" characters by E. M. Forster, and the study of the range and depth of characters by W. J. Harvey) is firmly rooted in humanistic thinking and in moral psychology; I. Hunter ("Reading Character," *Southern Review* 16 [1983] 229) treats literary characters as autonomous human beings. Yet unlike some of their modern counterparts, ancient authors and auditors had no heightened conventional expectations about the personality or psychological motivations of characters (Schmeling, *Xenophon,* 76; B. P. Reardon, "Theme, Structure and Narrative in Chariton," *Yale Classical Studies* [ed. J. J. Winkler and G. Williams; Cambridge: Cambridge Univ. Press, 1982] 14). Characters in the novels were largely illustrative—not representative of real life—and thus the development of a character was contingent upon the contribution that it could make to the overall work (Tolbert, *Sowing the Gospel,* 76–77; C. Garton, "Characterization in Greek Tragedy," *Journal of Hellenic Studies* 77 [1957] 251; A. F. De Vito, "Characterization in Greek Tragedy" [Ph.D. diss., Univ. of Toronto, 1988] 336).

25. Beye, *Ancient Greek Literature,* 194; Edwards, "Acts of the Apostles" 123; Martin, *Slavery as Salvation,* 39; Praeder, "Luke-Acts," 280.

26. On the prophets as prototypes for the protagonists in Luke-Acts, see R. J. Miller, "Prophecy and Presentation in Luke-Acts" (Ph.D. diss., Claremont, 1986) 54–56. I owe the term "cosmic power brokers" to Doug Edwards.

who futilely seek to limit access to power to a select, exclusive few.[27] Through the journeys of the heroes, the good news of free access to God's power is taken beyond the exclusive control of the Jewish nationalistic power brokers to every region within reach. Moreover, the journeys provide settings for contact with increasingly more significant figures and for dramatic demonstrations of the deity's power and the protagonists' abiding fidelity.[28]

Rhetorical Readings of Acts 8:26-40

Among these significant figures in Luke-Acts stands the Ethiopian eunuch, who is strategically and thematically cast among other powerful figures in symmetrically similar episodes. Yet to see his strategic placement, we must initially assess the role of 8:26-40 within all of the rhetorical sense units of 8:1b—12:25, a missionary excursion illustrating the ever-enlightening and ever-expanding power of the deity. Then, we must raise specific questions about Luke's typological portrayal of the Ethiopian.

Luke's Strategic and Thematic Placement of the Ethiopian Episode

Within the series of *agones* in Luke-Acts, Acts 8:26-40 lies in the second of three missionary excursions (1:13—8:1a; 8:1b—12:25; 13:1—28:31) in Acts.[29] Whereas the first excursion vividly contrasts images of power

---

27. See Moxnes, "Patron-Client Relations," 256.
28. See Edwards, "Acts of the Apostles," 371, 372.
29. While I cannot give the full details of my overall analysis of Luke-Acts in this essay, I must give an abbreviated sketch of the movement of Acts, Luke's second volume, with respect to the first one. While the first volume features the *agones* of Jesus, along with his vindication through resurrection and exaltation, the second one (following a brief introduction [Acts 1:1-11]) places the witnesses in a series of missionary excursions, each of which builds intensely toward a climactic *agon*, that is, a death or a near-death escape. In the first excursion (limited to Jerusalem [1:12-8:1a]), the apostles are spared from the violent hands of the council, but Stephen, one of the seven and the one believer in all of the early chapters who speaks most vehemently against a parochial and nationalistic brand of Judaism, is stoned (5:33; cf. 7:54), thus bringing the first excursion and its escalating violence to a deadly end. In the second excursion (in and around Judea and Samaria [8:1b—12:25; cf. 1:8]), persecution abounds from beginning to end, but notice is given of the deity's ability to affect persons and places at all levels of society from all parts of the world (8:1b—11:26). Climactically, the excursion virtually ends with the daring angelic rescue of Peter near the Passover season and the equally angelic destruction of Herod Agrippa I—a stark contrast between the divine patron's response to the humility and supplication of some and to the hubris and self-aggrandizement of another (12:1-23). Finally, in the third excursion (13:1—28:31), Saul (Paul) takes over the leadership not only from Barnabas in the initial scenes but also from the Jerusalem hegemony in the rest of the story. Envious opponents dogging his steps cause Paul to suffer throughout Asia Minor, Europe, and Asia in ways similar to the other heroes

(for example, gifted, yet unassuming, disciples willing to pay any cost to share the good news of the deity's power versus inept, and tyrantlike, authorities incessantly seeking to muzzle the witnesses' paradoxical refrain of Jesus' death and resurrection),[30] its portrait of the protagonists' efforts is limited ethnically to Jews and geographically to Jerusalem. With 8:1b—12:25, however, the stakes are raised, a wider net of inclusion is cast, and before the excursion ends, important symmetrically structured reversals signal the power of the divine patron over a variety of mediating power brokers.

Architectonically, Acts 8:1b—12:25 is divided into two units (8:1b—11:26 and 11:27—12:25), and within the former, two smaller subunits (8:4-40 and 9:32—11:18) directly affect our interpretation of the Ethiopian episode. The first unit, 8:1b—11:26, casts the figure Saul in three pivotal sections of the second excursion—the beginning (8:1b-3), the middle (9:1-31), and the end (11:19-26), with the middle one featuring two recognition scenes (Saul's recognition of the true identity of Jesus [9:1-9, 17-19] and Ananias's recognition of Saul's true fate as a suffering witness to the people of Israel and the Gentiles [9:10-15]).[31]

Framing 9:1-31 are two similar series of episodes (8:4-40; 9:32—11:18).[32] Each series begins by casting a leading character (Philip or

---

(Jesus, Stephen, and Peter), and in the closing scenes that take him from Jerusalem to Rome, Paul is led by the hand of God from one adventure to another—imprisonment, trials, and even a shipwreck.

30. Note that the witnesses, despite their own participation in dramatic displays of power, quickly defer the honor, power, and responsibility to the Holy Spirit or Jesus, who, for the narrator at least, is the ultimate cosmic power broker (see Acts 2:22; 3:12; 5:3-4, 9). The inept nature of the authorities is demonstrated in the prison escape episode in 5:17-25. Moreover, the scene is highly ironic, for although the council's Sadducees do not believe in angels (see Acts 23:8), the narrator specifically indicates that an angel secured the deliverance for the apostles (5:19). On paradox as a theme throughout Luke-Acts, see R. Tannehill's discussion of authorial shifts ("Attitudinal Shifts in Synoptic Pronouncement Stories," *Orientation by Disorientation: Studies in Literary Criticism and Biblical Literary Criticism* [Pittsburgh: Pickwick, 1980], 183, 197); J. S. Lahurd's comments on narrative reversals ("The Author's Call to the Audience in the Acts of the Apostles: A Literary-Critical-Anthropological Reading" [Ph.D. diss., Univ. of Pittsburgh, 1987] 127); and J. O. York's identification of Luke's bipolar reversal, for example, in the Magnificat, the Beatitudes, Woes, and in a number of antithetic aphorisms ("The Rhetorical Function of Bipolar Reversal in Luke" [Ph.D. diss., Emory Univ., 1989] 101, 102).

31. We should note that in Luke's subsequent recountings of these earlier scenes (Acts 22:1-21; 26:1-23), Paul himself highlights his mission of bringing "light to the Gentiles" (22:21; 26:17, 20, 23), a role forecast by Isaiah (Isa 49:6) and previously linked to Jesus (Luke 2:32). For the authorial audience, however, even as early as the second excursion, Saul's role among the Gentiles is confirmed, and with the symmetrical reversal of his actions at the beginning and ending of this initial unit, the authorial audience is assured that the deity is powerful enough to change the heart and fate of the movement's most unrelenting opponent. For another confirmation of Paul's role as "a light to the Gentiles," see Acts 13:47.

32. Though Acts 8:4 continues to relate the scattering (*diasparentes*) of the disciples, the *men...de* construction holds both 8:4 and 8:5 together as the beginning of

Peter) on a journey away from Jerusalem (8:5; 9:32),[33] and each virtually ends with an allusion to Caesarea (8:40; 11:11ff.).[34] Furthermore, while each series begins with a report of a protagonist's mighty miracles (8:6-8; 9:32-41), each also treats prominent patrons or mediators, with the last patron being a foreign representative in the land of Israel. Moreover, the episodes featuring the foreign representatives give central attention to the theme of illumination: in 8:26-40, the illumination of a Gentile about the true identity and fate of Jesus; [35] and in 10:1—11:18, the illumination of Cornelius, Peter, and the Jerusalem hegemony about the true nature of the deity, that is, a nature of beneficence toward all, including Gentiles.[36]

---

a new section. See Acts 11:19, 20. Haegg, commenting on this type of construction in the ancient novels, asserts that "a *men* clause, usually summarizing retrospectively the preceding action, is coupled with a *de* clause, which starts the new action" (Haegg, *Narrative Technique in Ancient Greek Romances: Studies of Chariton, Xenophon Ephesius, and Achilles Tatius* [Stockholm: Acta Instituti Atheniensis Regni Sueciae, 1971] 314, 315). Moreover, we should remember the observation of Tolbert (drawn from Lucian in *De Conscribenda Historia, 55*) that ancient rhetorical sense-units often overlapped each other "at the edges." See Tolbert, *Sowing the Gospel,* 109.

33. It is curious that Luke places Peter in the story of the Samaritans' conversion, particularly to give them the Holy Spirit. It is more curious, however, that the narrator repeatedly links dramatic displays of the Spirit's involvement with reports of the Jerusalem hegemony's hearing about the new junctures of the mission. Accordingly, where they hear or will hear about a non-Jerusalem mission (8:14; 11:1), someone legitimated by the Jerusalem hegemony reports the Spirit's validation of the mission. Where they do not hear about it, no dramatic bestowals of the Holy Spirit are necessary. Thus, when the narrator does not narrate the gift of the Holy Spirit to the Ethiopian (8:26-40) or Lydia (16:14) or the Philippian jailer and his family (16:33-34) or the Athenians (17:4), the narrator is not denigrating their conversions. Instead, in the case of the Ethiopian's conversion, the narrator ironically is suggesting how the Jerusalem hegemony does not have as much power as it thinks. Jerusalem has no control over the conversion of the Ethiopian, and later, even before Peter finishes preaching and before Cornelius and his family are baptized, the Holy Spirit comes upon them (10:44-48).

34. In 8:40, Caesarea is the destination of Philip (whom the narrator mentions again only in 21:8). In 11:5-17, Peter recalls his earlier journey to Caesarea.

35. That illumination of the Ethiopian is a key issue in 8:26-40 is clearly signaled in the paronomasia or play on words in 8:28; 30-32: "And [the Ethiopian] was returning home; seated in his chariot, he was reading [*anaginoskontos*] the prophet Isaiah.... Philip ran up to it [the chariot] and heard him reading [*anaginoskontos*] the prophet Isaiah. He asked, 'Do you understand [*ginoskeis*] what you are reading [*anaginoskeis*]?' He replied: 'How can I unless someone explains it to me?' And he invited Philip to get in and sit beside him. Now the passage of the scripture he was reading [*aneginosken*] was this..." (NRSV). While the limitations of time restrict the purview of this study, I think the illumination theme could greatly enhance our understanding of every episode within the second excursion (Acts 8:1b— 12:25).

While some see the Ethiopian as a convert to Judaism, I agree with Tannehill (*Narrative Unity,* 2:109) that the audience would assume the Ethiopian to be a Gentile, not a Jew. We must remember, moreover, that worship in the temple (in the court of the Gentiles) was not limited to Jews or converted Jews alone. See H. J. Cadbury, "The Hellenists," *The Beginnings of Christianity: Part I: The Acts of the Apostles* (ed. F. J. Foakes Jackson and K. Lake; Grand Rapids: Baker Book House, 1966) 69.

36. On dreams or dream-oracles as a form of illumination in the ancient narratives, including the Greek novels, see G. L. Schmeling, *Chariton* (New York: Twayne, 1974)

The second unit, 11:27—12:25, though smaller, is not itself without symmetry and frames. Framed by episodes of Christian benefaction (the disciples' determination to send relief to Jerusalem [11:27-30] and the report of the completed mission [12:24-25]), a highly ironic middle section bespeaks the consequences of presumed greatness.[37] He who kills at the beginning dies ignominiously at the end; he who is imprisoned near the beginning escapes wonderfully near the end. The two fates, moreover, are not isolated incidents. An angel of the patron is involved in each case. Clearly, then, the second unit's radical reversals resound the deity's power over the feigned and presumed greatness of an imperially appointed ruler over all of the land of Israel, namely, Herod Agrippa I.[38]

Altogether, then, the various elements of the two units abound in illumination and recognition scenes, an emphasis on the inclusion of Gentiles, and an emphasis on the power of God's paradoxical order, an order capable of overcoming the most virulent and violent persecution, through the changed fate of Saul and the death of Herod Agrippa I. The effect on the authorial audience is that it is assured of the all-powerful nature of the Lukan deity, and it is prepared for a shift of focus toward Gentiles, a shift that will receive its greatest force in the next excursion by Paul (13:1—28:31). The two units of the second excursion, then, may be outlined as in table 1.

Since the Ethiopian episode falls within the first unit (8:1b—11:26), a more detailed reading of each series of episodes (8:4-40 and 9:32—11:18) in that unit could reveal both the function of the relatively similar images of Jesus given in each series and the force of each series' shift from Israelite to gentile patrons. In both the Isaiah quotation (8:32-34) and the speech of Peter to Cornelius, his family, and friends (10:34-43), the image of Jesus is given in the familiar paradoxical refrain previously echoed in the first excursion (Acts 1:12—8:1a), that is, the image

109; C. A. Anderson, "The Dream-Oracles of Athena, *Knights* 1090–95," *Transactions of the American Philological Association* 121 (1991) 149–55. Among the other parallels between the Ethiopian and Cornelius episodes are the emphases on divine intervention and on hindrance. In both 8:26-40 and 10:1—11:18, note how angels steer the plot—one angel, by directing Philip on the road to Gaza (8:26) and another, by instructing Cornelius to send for Peter (10:3; 11:13). Likewise, a voice offstage appears in both—the Holy Spirit, commanding Philip to join the Ethiopian's chariot (8:29) and the voice in Peter's dream-oracle, ordering Peter to go with Cornelius's envoys (10:19-20). With respect to the hindrance theme, note both how the Ethiopian episode virtually closes on this note (8:36) and how this theme connects Peter's speech in Caesarea (10:47) to his speech in Jerusalem (11:17). For more on divine intervention, see D. S. Dockery, "Acts 6–12: The Christian Mission beyond Jerusalem," *Review and Expositor* 87 (1990) 427–28.

37. R. Pervo, *Luke's Story of Paul* (Minneapolis: Fortress Press, 1990) 43.

38. That Herod Agrippa I ruled all of Palestine is noted by Josephus (*Jewish Antiquities* 19.274-75), and symbolically, Agrippa I's demise is likely a clue to the authorial audience that the narrative is shifting from a virtually exclusive Jewish front to provincial areas beyond.

TABLE I
OUTLINE OF THE TWO UNITS OF THE SECOND EXCURSION

8:1b—11:26

A	8:1b-3	Saul and the scattering of the church
B	8:4-40	Journeys to Samaria and Gaza
C	9:1-31	Saul's conversion and persecution
B'	9:32—11:18	Journeys to Joppa, Lydda, and Caesarea
A'	11:19-26	The scattering of the church and Saul

11:26—12:25

A	11:27-30	Saul and Barnabas sent on a mission
B	12:1-23	Persecutor Herod Agrippa I overpowered
A'	12:24-25	Saul and Barnabas return from mission

of a man of power who is humiliated in death and subsequently vindicated and raised to life by God.[39] As we have noted, similar images of status reversals provided the basic "structural form" for the whole of most ancient novels, and recapitulations of the image reminded the audiences of the novels of the indomitable fidelity of the protagonists and of the inevitable triumph of the protagonists' deities.[40] In the case of Luke, moreover, responses to the image, now just as before, relate the ideological position of a character or character-group for or against the Christian movement. That is, in the first excursion (1:12—8:1a), characters opposed to the paradoxical refrain of Jesus' death and resurrection are largely drawn in a dysphoric shade. They hoard power and authority; they are inhospitable and even violent; they are tied to conventional understandings of power. The Ethiopian and Cornelius, to whom the same refrain is given, however, remain receptive throughout their tenure with the witnesses.[41] Thus, both speeches function not only to signal the deity's inevitable control but also to relate the distance or

---

39. Here I follow Tannehill's translation of 8:33: "his condemnation was taken away." As Tannehill states, "In spite of some uncertainty in details, the quotation seems to fit the interpretation of Jesus' death and exaltation according to Scripture in the preceding speeches in Acts, broadening the base of Scripture quotations that support this interpretation" (Tannehill, *Narrative Unity*, 2:111–12). For a similar translation, see E. Haenchen, *The Acts of the Apostles: A Commentary* (Oxford: Blackwell, 1971) 312.

40. Hock, "The Greek Novel," 80.

41. Note that the hospitality of the Ethiopian, first demonstrated in his invitation for Philip to travel with him in his chariot (8:31b), does not stop once the Ethiopian learns the truth about Jesus. Instead, the two (and others) continue to travel together, and eventually, the powerful Ethiopian even submits himself to baptism (8:36-39). Likewise, Cornelius's hospitality, initially signaled by his gesture of deference (10:25), persists, for after Peter's speech, Cornelius and his household implore Peter to continue with them for a few days (10:48).

closeness that the authorial audience should have with certain characters. In the case of both the Ethiopian and Cornelius, then, the authorial
audience would easily identify with them because their submission to
the witnesses' order symbolically demonstrates their ideological acceptance of the witnesses' way of understanding power, that is, that true
power, far from being linked to conventional deference-entitlements,[42]
is linked rather to the recognition of one's ultimate dependence upon
the Lukan deity.

To see the force of each series' narrative shift from an Israelite patron
to a foreign one, we must carefully note Luke's comparison and contrast
between the two types of characters. For the authorial audience, the deity's ability to influence Simon Magus toward belief and repentance is
important because Simon is a man of means and power. In Samaria, he
is known for his power (*dynamis*) and for his ability to astonish others
(8:9), and yet through the deity's power broker (that is, Philip), even
Simon, the astonisher, is astonished (8:13).[43] The extent of the deity's
power, however, is not limited to a patron in Samaria, for the same
deity influencing Simon influences the Ethiopian *eunouchos,* a foreign
mediating broker, who, aside from being a man of means (as is attested
by his ability to travel great distances simply to worship, and in a chariot at that),[44] is acclaimed indeed as a *dynastes* in charge of all of the
Candace's treasury.[45] His prestige is not of a local variety; he is from a
distant land, Ethiopia (or Nubia), and is the power broker of a queen.[46]

Likewise for the authorial audience, the deity's ability to heal Ae-

---

42. For more on deference-entitlement properties in the ancient world, see L. Thompson, *Romans and Blacks* (Norman: Univ. of Oklahoma Press, 1989) 143.

43. Note, however, that the narrator draws Simon in dysphoric shades to show that
his conventional understanding of power (as something one can buy with money) is not
just inappropriate, but wicked and sinful (8:18-24).

44. Note also that the Ethiopian is riding in a servant-driven chariot (see 8:28, 38).
Also, note that the similarities and contrasts between Simon and the Ethiopian largely
form the basis of T. Brodie's analysis of Acts 8:9-40. Using the background of 2 Kings 5,
he suggests that both story complexes emphasize washing and money. Moreover, he contends that Naaman's desire for greatness and Gehazi's money-mindedness are fused into
one in Simon's character. On the other hand, he asserts that "the value of openmind-
edness, half-hidden in Naaman, comes to the fore in the figure of the Ethiopians" (T.
Brodie, "Towards Unraveling the Rhetorical Imitation of Sources in Acts: II Kings 5 as
One Component of Acts 8:9-40," *Biblica* 67 [1986] 41–67).

45. The term Candace is the Latin form of the Meroitic term Kandake (that is, queen
mother).

46. Ancient Nubia was composed of two parts, "Lower Nubia, extending from the
First to the Second Cataract [waterfall], and Upper Nubia, stretching southward from
the Second Cataract to the area in the vicinity of Meroe, situated about halfway between the Fifth Cataract and present-day Khartoum" (Snowden, *Before Color Prejudice,*
3). As L. Thompson has noted, "The powerful black eunuch and 'minister in charge
of all the treasures' of the Meroitic Candace (queen or queen mother) mentioned in
the Acts of the Apostles (8:27ff.) was admittedly a visitor of some distinction from
a foreign land, and not a resident in Roman social space, but he displayed some of
the symbols acknowledged in Roman society as symbols of high status: literacy (prob-

neas and to raise the charitable (*eleamosunon,* 9:36) patron Dorcas from the dead is a significant indication of the movement's power (9:32-43). Again, however, the parameters of the deity's power will not be limited. Even the charitable (*eleamosunas,* 10:2, 4, 31) and wealthy centurion,[47] a power broker of the emperor—indeed one whose network of power was more extensive than the little towns of Lydda and Joppa—is persuaded by the Christian movement.

These two observations suggest, then, that the development of both units is identical. The deity, while tied to Jerusalem, is seeking a much more extensive rule, not only over ostensibly powerful figures from within the land of Israel but over great foreigners as well. A wider net of inclusion is cast. The ante is raised even higher!

Luke's Typological Casting of the Ethiopian

From our previous discussions, we have concluded that Acts 8:26-40 is a small rhetorical subunit within a larger unit encompassing 8:1b—11:26. Juxtaposed to 8:1b-25, 8:26-40 functions to dramatize the power of the deity to influence not only powerful Simon, a native of Samaria, but even a powerful Ethiopian official. Our final rhetorical reading, then, must seek to add clarity to those conclusions by showing (1) Luke's motivation for selecting an Ethiopian among other foreigners and (2) the probable meaning of the term *eunouchos.*

Picked from any number of foreigners who could conceivably have been listed in this missionary excursion is a black-skinned African from Ethiopia, one of the ends of the earth. That Luke singles out this figure—and not another—could be based on the Greco-Roman proverbial ranking of the Ethiopians as wealthy, wise, and militarily mighty.[48] Of course, some may contend that the proverbial ranking may have been

---

ably in Greek), possession of a carriage and horses, attendance by personal servants" (Thompson, *Romans and Blacks,* 150).

47. That the centurion has a number of servants attests to his wealth. Moreover, at this time, centurions were well paid and highly respected. On their wealth, see J. B. Campbell, *The Emperor and the Roman Army, 31 BC–AD 235* (New York: Oxford Univ. Press, 1984) 102.

48. Nubia's great wealth was not a secret. J. De Weever asserts that its notoriety for gold mines extends "from Pharaonic times until the late Middle Ages" ("Candace in the Alexander Romances: Variations on the Portrait Theme," *Romance Philology* 43 [1990] 533); see also Snowden, *Before Color Prejudice,* 28; see Diodorus 1.37.5. Diodorus calls Meroe "the civilizers of ancient Egypt" (Diodorus 3.2.7; see Pliny *Naturalis Historia* 2.80.189), and Josephus asserts that the Queen of Sheba (whom he claims was ruler of both Egypt and Ethiopia) was "thoroughly trained in wisdom" (*Ant.* 8.165). Herodotus, Diodorus, and Pliny attest to the great military power of the Nubians. See Herodotus 7.69-70; Diodorus 3.2.4; 3.3.1; Pliny *Naturalis Historia* 6.35.182. While Heliodorus's *Aethiopika,* an ancient Greek novel, surely attests to the continuing significance of the Ethiopians, its late date (ca. fourth century CE) places it beyond the parameters of this essay.

based on an "intellectual wonderland vogue" or on educated Greeks and Romans' idealistic appreciation for the cultural benefactions of the Napata-Meroitic civilization[49] as opposed to the view of others that the proverbial ranking in some respect reflects reality,[50] but this debate among the classicists need not disturb our discussion. What adds weight to the acceptance of the proverbial image for Luke's authorial audience is that the Septuagint, the basic and venerable text from which Luke drew the typological mold for characters, also portrays Africans in general and Kushites (Ethiopians) in particular as wealthy, wise, and militarily mighty.

Repeatedly, the Septuagint casts the Kushites as wealthy. Isaiah (more specifically, Deutero-Isaiah) alludes to the "wealth of Egypt and the merchandise of Kush" (45:14), and the writer of Daniel refers to the "treasures of gold and silver, and all the precious things of Egypt and the Libyans and the Kushites" (11:43). The most memorable of such texts, however, is Ps 68:29-36, a text alluding to the tribute and worship brought to God in the Jerusalem sanctuary: "Egypt will bring bronze and Kush will stretch out her hands," that is, bring her possessions or the products of her hands, as Mitchell Dahood suggests.[51]

The veneration of African wisdom is quite evident in the visit of the Queen of Sheba in 1 Kings 10. As Randall Bailey has noted, the queen's validation of Solomon as wise would make sense to a reader only if Israel a priori considered the queen and African wisdom to be exceptional.[52] That Luke shares this evaluation of African wisdom is seen not only by the reference to the Queen of the South in Luke 11:31, where Luke casts her to validate the wisdom of Solomon and the even greater wisdom of Jesus, but also in Acts 6:8, where Stephen's wisdom proves to be too powerful for a number of foreign Jews, including those from Africa (Cyrene and Alexandria).

Similarly, the military prowess of the Kushites resounds in the Septuagint. A Kushite is found in David's army (2 Sam 18:21ff.), and in a text designed to show God's punishment of Israel with African warriors,[53] Kushite mercenaries are numbered among the troops of Shishak, the Egyptian pharaoh who invaded Judah during Rehoboam's reign (2 Chr 12:2-3 ‖ 1 Kgs 14:25). Zerah's army of a million men, though defeated, is nevertheless depicted as militarily powerful, indeed so powerful that

---

49. This is largely the position taken by Thompson, though he thinks that the military image is not a fixed one until "the middle of the 3rd century CE" (*Romans and Blacks*, 92–93).

50. Snowden, *Before Color Prejudice*, 57–58.

51. M. Dahood, *Psalms II: 51-100: Introduction, Translation, and Notes* (Anchor Bible; New York: Doubleday, 1983) 151.

52. Bailey, "Beyond Identification," 181–82. On Sheba as a part of Africa, see Bailey, "Beyond Identification," 172.

53. Ibid., 182.

the reader of 2 Chr 14:9-15 would have to regard the conquering power of God as even greater.[54] Isaiah acclaims the Kushites as "a nation tall and smooth, a people feared near and far, a nation mighty and conquering" (Isa 18:1, 2), and Nahum, looking back to years before, recalls Kush as the strength of Thebes, the fallen Egyptian city.[55]

Clearly, then, Luke's authorial audience, having at least a general knowledge of the Septuagint, would have based their view of the Kushites (and other Africans) on the consistent typological portrait of this nation as one to be revered for its wealth, wisdom, and military prowess.[56]

Before we conclude this analysis, however, some final remarks must be made about the term *eunouchos*, for its meaning has been the subject of debate. The issue is whether the term *eunouchos* indicates physical castration or some official capacity. If the authorial audience would have thought of Isaiah 56, as Robert Tannehill suggests, then the Ethiopian could have met two conditions of persons to receive the benefits of God's new order—a foreigner and a eunuch.[57] On the other hand, one need not limit the meaning of the term to castration, for in the Septuagint, it covered a variety of official capacities, including that of a military figure.[58] Accordingly, the audience's familiarity with the Septuagint, along with the text's inclusion of the Candace and the parallel episode about the centurion, could conceivably intimate a military designation for the *eunouchos*.[59]

---

54. Indeed as Bailey notes, the point of the story is to show that "belief and reliance upon YHWH are all that is needed" (ibid., 182–83).

55. Josephus likewise notes the military prowess of the Kushites, mentioning, among others, Shishak (Isokus), Zerah (Zaraios), and Tharsikes (Taharqua). See Snowden, *Before Color Prejudice*, 53–54. See Josephus *Ant.* 8.254, 292–94; 10.15–17.

56. The novels themselves have a favorable impression of the Ethiopians, for as B. Egger asserts: "Ethiopians never counted among the 'barbarians' in Greek thought. Since Homer and Herodotus they had been viewed as an ideal people, with even utopian qualities" (Egger, "Women in the Greek Novel," 154).

57. It is clear, of course, that there could be a number of other foreign "castrated" eunuchs besides those in Nubia. Thus, Tannehill's view that *eunouchos* means "castrated" obviates the narrator's interest in a specific kind of foreigner—a Nubian. For Tannehill's view, see *Narrative Unity*, 2:109; see H. Conzelmann, *Acts of the Apostles* (Hermeneia; Philadelphia: Fortress Press, 1987) 68.

58. See Haenchen, *Acts*, 311; see also W. H. Willimon, *Acts* (Interpretation: A Bible Commentary for Teaching and Preaching; Atlanta: John Knox, 1988) 71. The term *eunouchos* need not have exclusively or emphatically indicated castration. In the Septuagint, the word *eunouchos* was a designation for several roles (jailers [Gen 39:2]; chief bakers and cupbearers [Gen 40:2, 7]; chamberlains, keepers of harems [Esth 2:3]; and military officials [2 Kgs 25:19; Esth 2:3]).

59. Conzelmann's suggestion that the term *eunouchos* does not intimate the office because that role is assigned to the term *dynastes* (*Acts*, 68) is not solid because the term *eunouchos* in other literature could symbolize an office (for example, of a treasurer [Plutarch *Lives* (Demetrius 25.5)]), and the term *dynastes* sometimes replaces *eunouchos* as the translation for the Hebrew *saris* (see Jer 34:19 [LXX]), and at other times, simply indicates generally the great power of the person in question (see the cognate form

Perhaps too much attention has been paid to the testicles, however, and so I would like to offer a third interpretation, which transcends the debate between the contenders for the more conventional interpretations. What I think is overlooked is the extent to which both the *eunouchos* (regardless of the meaning) and the centurion are royal representatives: one, the servant of a queen, with a wide range of power; and the other, a servant of Caesar, whose power extends over the *oikumene*. Moreover, each belongs to a type of figure notoriously cast as one with better access to royal power than the average citizen.[60]

Thus, the larger issue for me is that these figures who already have access to power humble themselves before the Lukan deity's representatives and take on the quality of powerlessness, the same image associated with Jesus in the parallel speeches in 8:32-33 and 10:34-43. This image is the good news spoken to the *eunouchos* (8:35) and the words of instruction given to Cornelius (see 10:33). For in the narrator's understanding of power, God's paradoxical order demands submission of the ostensibly powerful in order that they might share in the truer powerful order of the ultimate patron. Moreover, for the authorial audience, if the deity can persuade such conventionally influential figures to leave their own networks of power to become a part of the deity's paradoxical order, then the members of the authorial audience are assured that the understanding of power represented in the narrative is surely the right one for them.

---

dynatoteros used to describe Artaxates, the eunuch, in Chariton *Chaereas and Callirhoe* 5.2.2).

60. J. B. Campbell asserts that soldiers were better able to get a rescript from Caesar than the average citizen (Campbell, *Emperor and the Roman Army*, 269–70). For an example of one of these rescripts, see Pliny *Epistles* 10.107. On the access of *eunouchoi* in Persian and Roman times, see K. Hopkins, "Eunuchs in Politics in the Later Roman Empire," *Proceedings of the Cambridge Philological Society* 9 (1963) 66, 77.

Part Three ─────────────────────────────

Social Location and Accountability

14

The Uninflected *Therefore* of Hosea 4:1-3

Walter Brueggemann

The crisis of contextualism affects a white, tenured male of upper middle age differently from the way it may touch a woman or a minority person. The difference is that the standpoint or perspective characteristically affirmed by a white male has been regnant. As a result, contextualism is more likely to be seen as a relativizing threat than as liberating localism, for it exposes so-called objectivity as a not disinterested standpoint. Most likely, as contextualism moves against so-called objectivity, it challenges confidence in historical-critical methods that have seemed disinterested but that in fact are allied with a certain rationality that in turn is allied with certain economic interests.[1] For a volume like the present one, this tenured, white male will not be able so directly to witness to the gain of contextualism. He will witness to a wholly new awareness of interpretive possibility, but the concreteness of liberation will not be so palpable. For that reason I have selected a topic that may seem remote from the issues of contextualism, but that in the end, I shall hope to show, is intimately connected to the justice questions present in a contextual hermeneutic.

I

It is no news to say that creation has not figured largely in discussions of Old Testament faith. (The most attention has been given by scholars interested in Near Eastern parallels and derivations, but those scholars have characteristically had a historical and not theological interest.) There are at least three reasons why creation has been marginal in Old Testament studies.

1. The influence of Gerhard von Rad in this regard can hardly be

---

1. See G. A. Phillips, "Exegesis as Critical Praxis: Reclaiming History and Text from a Post-Modern Perspective," *Semeia* 51 (1990) 7–49, esp. 13–14, and F. W. Burnett, "Post-Modern Exegesis: The Eve of Historical Criticism," *Semeia* 51 (1990) 51–80.

overstated.[2] His "credo hypothesis" in 1938 proposed that God's mighty deeds of rescue constitute the core of Old Testament faith; creation conversely is an *Aufbau* at the margin of the formation of both faith and text.[3] Indeed, creation is another "saving deed," so that the exodus model is pushed back and made cosmic. (The fact that in his last major book, *Wisdom in Israel,* von Rad moved toward a theology of creation has not been so influential for biblical theology, for Old Testament studies have been tempted to proceed with the notion that wisdom is in any case "not Israelite.")[4]

2. The programmatic strictures of the early Barth against "religion" have led to a singular focus on deeds of salvation.[5] This has been the case even though Barth exhaustively insisted that creation and covenant were the "external" and "internal" aspects of one faith.[6] There is no doubt that von Rad's thesis and Barth's strictures were related to each other. Both have as their formative *context* (*sic*) the capacity of Hitler to use "religion" for purposes of state ideology. The creation theme was expressed by National Socialism in the use of the swastika, an early and primitive symbol of fertility. As a result, even so conservative a scholar as Ernest Nicholson has made a sharp contrast between "the natural" and "the covenantal."[7] The emphasis of Barth and von Rad was heightened by G. Ernest Wright into a vigorous "againstness" between Canaanite religion and Israelite faith.[8] Moreover, the fact that Canaanite religion concerned fertility by default caused creation to be rejected as a theme of Israelite faith in a widespread rigorism.[9]

3. Where the accents of Barth and von Rad, intensified by Wright,

---

2. G. von Rad, "The Theological Problem of the Old Testament Doctrine of Creation," *The Problem of the Hexateuch and Other Essays* (London: Oliver and Boyd, 1965) 131–43; see also 63–67 in the same volume.

3. On the "irreducible core tradition," see W. Harrelson, "Life, Faith, and the Emergence of Tradition," *Tradition and Theology in the Old Testament* (ed. Douglas A. Knight; Philadelphia: Fortress Press, 1977) 11–30, and the phrase on 20.

4. G. von Rad, *Wisdom in Israel* (Nashville: Abingdon Press, 1972). A host of scholars, for example, G. E. Wright and H. D. Preuss, have questioned whether the wisdom materials are properly Israelite.

5. This is especially the way of Karl Barth in his early essays in *The Word of God and the Word of Man* (New York: Harper, 1957). G. Wingren has probed the cruciality of creation vis-à-vis the National Socialist regime in Germany.

6. K. Barth, *Church Dogmatics* (Edinburgh: T. and T. Clark, 1958) 3/1/41:42–329.

7. E. W. Nicholson, *God and His People: Covenant and Theology in the Old Testament* (Oxford: Clarendon, 1986) 191–217, esp. 195–96.

8. G. E. Wright, *The Old Testament against Its Environment* (Studies in Biblical Theology 2; London: SCM, 1950), and somewhat more nuanced, idem, *The Old Testament and Theology* (New York: Harper and Row, 1969).

9. This powerful "againstness" is echoed by E. Achtemeier, who continues to work with these interpretive categories that appear to many to have had much more credence in the context of a previous generation; see, for example, her "The Impossible Impossibility: Evaluating the Feminist Approach to Bible and Theology," *Interpretation* 42 (1988) 45–57.

became confident affirmation of the virile God of Israel who could "intrude,"[10] the way was prepared to turn creation over to the claims of Enlightenment science to exercise "mastery" over nature.[11] Thus as creation came to be "nature," so the human capacity to control by means of technological power permitted a model of *domination* to emerge as a way of thinking about the (male?) human person at the center of the natural world. I do not suggest that Barth, von Rad, or Wright intended such an anthropocentric mode of interpretation, but only that the end result of that mode of theological interpretation was the abandonment of serious theological thinking about creation in the face of the powerful claims of "objective" science.[12] What was left of creation as a category of faith was seized upon by frightened, defensive interpreters who, as an alternative to evolution, reduced creation to a question of "scientific origins," thus producing the odd phrase "creation science."[13]

This odd convergence of critical, political, scientific, and hermeneutical factors evoked a situation in which the claims of "creation faith" were largely muted or placed at the margin of reflection. As a result, my generation of theological students "missed the point" in the Bible. The church was largely silenced (and embarrassed) in the face of "science" and the force of a "developmental economy and its powerful technology." In such a sociopolitical *context* (*sic*), we have learned to interpret the Bible without risking the embarrassment of creation. As a result, biblical interpretation has handled creation largely through neglect or misreading. On the whole, even where creation was considered,

---

10. P. D. Miller ("The Sovereignty of God," *The Hermeneutical Quest: Essays in Honor of James Luther Mays on his Sixty-Fifth Birthday* [ed. D. G. Miller; Allison Park, Pa.: Pickwick, 1986] 129–44) has taken up some of the standard themes of Wright and shown how they may be given different nuance. More critically, see W. Brueggemann, "Israel's Social Criticism and Yahweh's Sexuality," *Journal of the American Academy of Religion* 45B (1977 Supp.) 739–72. In commenting upon the model of G. E. Wright, J. D. Levenson (*Creation and the Persistence of Evil: The Jewish Drama of Divine Omnipotence* [San Francisco: Harper and Row, 1988] 163 n. 8) comments: "It must be stressed that most of the time, God in the Hebrew Bible is doing nothing. The magnalia Dei are celebrated in part because of their rarity, in an effort to reactivate God's potential in times when he has allowed it to become sorely missed."

11. On the interface of the rise of science and "virile" metaphors, see S. Bordo, *The Flight to Objectivity: Essays on Cartesianism and Culture* (New York: State University of New York Press, 1987).

12. The dualisms of mind/matter and objective/subjective are not accidents of Cartesian thought but belong to its program; see Descartes's *Discourse on Method*. The well-known strictures of L. White, Jr. ("The Historical Roots of Our Ecologic Crisis," *Science* 155 [March 10, 1967] 1203–7; and 156 [May 12, 1967] 737–38), belong, in my judgment, not to Genesis 1 nor to biblical faith, but to the claims of modernity and its modes of scientific knowledge that is bent on control. To the extent that the church is allied with such a program, the church fully accommodates modernist categories of interpretation, both in progressive and reactionary postures.

13. On the subject, see L. Gilkey, *Creation on Trial: Evaluation and God at Little Rock* (Minneapolis: Winston, 1985).

a way was not found to make it structurally important to faith.[14] More philosophical theology was not silenced, but it often lacked access to the energy and authority of biblical faith and tended to make its concessions to modernism in a different but equally expensive way.[15]

II

In more recent times, with the waning influence of a theology of "mighty acts,"[16] Old Testament scholarship has begun to pay more attention to creation as a definitional element in Old Testament faith. We are in the midst of a major shift of interpretive categories, of the scope and significance to warrant Kuhn's term "paradigmatic shift."[17] Among the more important and influential efforts in this regard are the following.

1. The most important work is that of H. H. Schmid, who asserted, "The belief that God has created and is sustaining the order of the world in all its complexities, is not a peripheral theme of biblical theology but is plainly its fundamental theme."[18] Schmid has shown that righteousness as a moral requirement, so crucial to Old Testament ethics, is reflective of a governing principle for the world ordained by God that keeps the world coherent, healthy, and fruitful.[19] It is the ethical dimension of creation, grounded in a theological affirmation, that has made Schmid's themes cogent and crucial. Schmid has shown that creation faith has a nonnegotiable moral dimension that, when violated, produces chaos and death.

2. In a complementary piece, Rolf Knierim has argued that "the most universal aspect of Yahweh's domain is not human history. . . . It is the creation and sustenance of the world. . . . Creation does not depend upon

---

14. J. Sittler (*Essays on Nature and Grace* [Philadelphia: Fortress Press, 1972]) has shrewdly shown how "grace" belongs to an understanding of creation. My impression is that Sittler's work has been important for the development of the theme of "sustainable creation" in World Council of Churches circles.

15. See the helpful summary statement of H. P. Nebelsick, "God, Creation, Salvation and Modern Science," *Horizons in Biblical Theology* 9/2 (December 1987) 79–103. Nebelsick alludes to the large and helpful literature, including H. Butterfield, S. Jaki, J. Moltmann, A. Peacocke, and R. Torrence.

16. The so-called Biblical Theology Movement was especially critiqued by B. S. Childs, *Biblical Theology in Crisis* (Philadelphia: Westminster Press, 1970), and J. Barr, "The Old Testament and the New Crisis of Biblical Authority," *Interpretation* 25 (1971) 24–40.

17. T. Kuhn, *The Structure of Scientific Revolutions* (Chicago: Univ. of Chicago Press, 1962).

18. H. H. Schmid, "Creation, Righteousness, and Salvation: 'Creation Theology' as the Broad Horizon of Biblical Theology," *Creation in the Old Testament* (ed. B. W. Anderson; Philadelphia: Fortress Press, 1984) 102–17.

19. H. H. Schmid, *Gerechtigkeit als Weltordnung* (Beiträge zur historischen Theologie 40; Tübingen: Mohr/Siebeck, 1968).

history or existence, but history and existence depend on and are measured against creation."[20] Knierim takes then as the core theme of the Bible "the universal domain of Yahweh in justice and righteousness."[21] Thus Knierim echoes Schmid's accent on the ethical dimension of the productive, fruitful, life-giving order of creation.

3. Terence Fretheim has shown that acts of liberation, that is, the mighty acts of deliverance, are in fact interventions by God to reorder the creation in healthy, life-giving ways after the creation has been distorted and skewed.[22] In a stunning interpretive piece, Fretheim demonstrates that in Exodus 7–11, pharaoh not only is a social oppressor but is in fact the embodiment of chaos, whose abusive ways cause creation to be disrupted (the plagues) and turned into a system of deathliness.[23] Fretheim's is the most text-specific argument yet made concerning a rereading of "deliverance texts" with a different, larger horizon of creation.

4. In an influential article not directly concerned with creation, Klaus Koch has shown that for parts of the Old Testament witness, the world is understood to have "spheres of destiny," so that certain deeds operate to produce certain consequences without the direct intention of Yahweh.[24] The consequences that are produced are not initiated by a personal agent but proceed "automatically." That "automatic triggering of consequences" is because the righteous order ordained in creation has been violated. Thus Koch's construct of "deed-consequence" serves alongside the work of Schmid and Knierim to express the inalienable ethical dimension of the order of creation, as established and decreed by God.[25]

---

20. R. P. Knierim, "On the Task of Old Testament Theology," *Horizons in Biblical Theology* 62 (1984) 40.

21. Ibid., 43.

22. This is the programmatic thrust of Fretheim's splendid commentary, *Exodus* (Interpretation: A Bible Commentary for Teaching and Preaching; Louisville: John Knox, 1991).

23. T. E. Fretheim, "The Plagues as Ecological Signs of Historical Disaster," *Journal of Biblical Literature* 110/3 (1991) 385–96.

24. K. Koch, "Is There a Doctrine of Retribution in the Old Testament?" *Theodicy in the Old Testament* (ed. J. L. Crenshaw; Philadelphia: Fortress Press, 1983) 57–87. Koch's programmatic notions have been paralleled in several statements by Claus Westermann in his exposition of an alternative to mighty deeds. See C. Westermann, *What Does the Old Testament Say about God?* (Atlanta: John Knox, 1979); idem, *Elements of Old Testament Theology* (Atlanta: John Knox, 1978); and his suggestive essay, "Creation and History in the Old Testament," *The Gospel and Human Destiny* (ed. V. Vitja; Minneapolis: Augsburg, 1971) 11–38.

25. W. Zimmerli ("The Place and Limit of Wisdom in the Framework of the Old Testament Theology," *Scottish Journal of Theology* 17 [1964] 146–58) has served the same interest as Koch and Westermann by linking creation to wisdom thought, thus accenting the ethical dimension of creation. Zimmerli (316) writes, "Wisdom thinks resolutely within the framework of a theology of creation."

5. In a very different mode, Jon Levenson has explored the precarious way in which Yahweh's governance of creation is characterized in the text.[26] Levenson identifies two important facets of that precariousness. On the one hand, the powers of evil, which must be restrained in order for creation to be viable, are in fact not yet decisively defeated.[27] From time to time, they gather strength and reassert themselves. On the other hand, Yahweh's governance of creation depends upon the consent, support, and alliance of other gods, but the loyalty of other gods to the purposes of Yahweh is less than complete.[28] The alliance of Yahweh and the other gods is fragile and open to disruption. Thus on both counts, the ordering of the world is less than guaranteed. It depends upon the regular reassertion and reenactment of order through ritual drama to assure the well-being of the world. The world continues to be at risk and in the precarious process of formation.

III

These five scholarly contributions represent a decisive shift of categories that would have been unthinkable a generation earlier.[29] When we ask what has made this shift possible (or necessary), it is clear that the shift of interpretive categories is deeply affected by contextual factors, even though we do not yet fully understand them. I would identify four factors, which are closely related to one another, that have impacted in quite general ways the context in which scholars do their work. Thus while the shift of categories is an intellectual, methodological matter, such shifts in method are no doubt linked to context.[30]

1. The large epistemological map that gives us perspective has shifted with the loss of confidence in the claims of objective, positivistic science.[31] This of course is not a loss of confidence in which theological-

---

26. Levenson, *Creation.*

27. The emphasis of Levenson on the continuing ways in which evil threatens chaos is closely parallel to the work of Karl Barth on "Das Nichtige," *Church Dogmatics* (Edinburgh: T. and T. Clark, 1960) 3/3/50:289–368.

28. Levenson (*Creation,* 139) writes of "the consensual basis of the divinity of the God of Israel and the fragility of his reality in the world."

29. The shift of course did not come out of the blue; among the harbingers of the new accent is the work of von Rad, *Wisdom in Israel,* the works of Westermann cited in n. 24, and the work of B. Anderson, *Creation versus Chaos: The Reinterpretation of Mythical Symbolism in the Bible* (Philadelphia: Fortress Press, 1987). See Anderson's important bibliography on the subject in *Creation in the Old Testament,* 172.

30. The acknowledgment of context as a factor in shifting methods and perspectives is itself a post-Enlightenment recognition, for high forms of rationalism are committed to contextless objectivity.

31. On the epistemological shift away from objectivistic claims see, in addition to Kuhn (see n. 17), M. Polanyi, *Personal Knowledge: Towards a Post-Critical Philosophy* (Chicago: Univ. of Chicago Press, 1974); R. Rorty, *Philosophy and the Mirror of Nature*

biblical criticism of modernity has been decisive. It is in fact a much larger shift, as the whole claim of "objectivity" in science as well as in theological orthodoxy has largely failed. It has become clear that objective claims that describe settled reality are in fact "theory-laden," that is, interest-laden. Moreover, it is clear that one can no longer afford a scientific-technological enterprise that is indifferent to value, or that is narrowly anthropocentric. Human and environmental costs must be factored into new practices of knowledge. Thus the "softer" interpretive claims of humanistic thought (not very long ago readily dismissed as "romantic") become increasingly credible and urgent against the claims of "hard" science, which too easily becomes ideological-driven technology.

2. The climate of National Socialism that so influenced the categories of Barth and von Rad no longer sets the agenda or provides the categories for interpretation. (It is odd but correct that even the totalitarianism of Communism did not produce the hard either/or of Hitler, not even for Barth.) While there is no doubt an enduring, demanding either/or intrinsic to biblical faith, it does not often admit of so obvious an articulation as it did in Hitler's Germany. And at least in the United States, the travesty and shame of Vietnam have contributed to some lowering of strident voices that were too sure.[32] That is, the "West" will not again be so "innocent" in its massive claims to know best, and humanists will not again so easily turn the future over to scientists with their own guiding ideologies. The recent past introduces a reservation or suspicion concerning our capacity to "master" creation.

3. We have come to see that a "virile" religion, expressed through "mighty deeds," may be an offer of certitude and reassurance, but such a modeling of God is at the same time a high-risk venture. For it evokes human practitioners made in the image of that God who practice excessive theological certitude and who shamelessly intend control of the political, economic, and military enterprise.[33] Awareness of the devastating consequence of "macho" images of reality has both permitted and

_____

(Princeton, N.J.: Princeton Univ. Press, 1979); J.-F. Lyotard, *The Post-Modern Condition: A Report on Knowledge* (Minneapolis: Univ. of Minnesota Press, 1984); and L. Gilkey, *Society and the Sacred: Toward a Theology of Culture in Decline* (New York: Crossroad, 1981).

32. The Gulf War was perhaps the last sorry enactment of military technology shamelessly in the service of an uncritical ideology. The convenient and much-used fear of Munich-like appeasement is countered, or at least threatened, by the equally powerful scenario of adventurism in Vietnam. The high costs of adventurism might even on occasion chasten the use of appeasement as a justification for military action.

33. Three easy examples of "certitude" as crass control include: (1) the male sexual ethics of the Roman Catholic Church; (2) the alliance of patriotism and right-wing religion in the United States; and (3) strident liberalism that knows best and that allows for no room for interpretive alternative, slippage, or pause.

required a reconsideration of who God is and how God works. (The argument is not in fact about pronouns and inclusive language, though pronouns matter enormously, as is evident in the defense of masculine pronouns.)

4. These three elements—a loss of confidence in scientific "objectivity," a shift of the political landscape, and a theological rereading of God's virility—have together caused a shift in the categories of Old Testament interpretation. The most obvious point of the shift is the recognition that the wisdom materials provide a very different sort of theological discernment.[34] In the wisdom material we are able to see God less frontally discerned, as an orderer and maintainer of the structure and fabric of reality, and to see that violation of that order (foolishness as much as sin) cannot be undertaken without cost, for the fabric of life itself will respond in ways that punish, in defense of the delicate protection of life. This wisdom thought refuses our dominant model of creation as a machine to be serviced, driven, and repaired, and comes closer to the image of a web that is delicate, fragile, and lovely. The missing element in the image of a web is that this delicate fabric also contains within it the capacity to penalize those who threaten, diminish, or destroy parts of the web.

IV

This remarkable shift of categories not only permits fresh notice of texts that have been neglected, such as creation texts and wisdom texts.[35] It also permits us to reread texts through fresh categories, so that they are seen to have different meanings and intentions. I can think of no better case for contextualism than to recognize that the categories and perspectives through which a text is read yield very different outcomes. Here I will focus on a text from Hosea. I have selected this text, in the first instant, simply because it has occurred to me as suitable for our purposes. Beyond that, however, it is clear that Hosea, as much as any text in the

---

34. See von Rad, *Wisdom in Israel;* J. L. Crenshaw, *Old Testament Wisdom: An Introduction* (Atlanta: John Knox, 1981); and the work of R. E. Murphy, on which see the bibliography in Crenshaw, *Wisdom in Israel,* 269–70. In a very different way, S. Terrien (*The Elusive Presence: Toward a New Biblical Theology* [San Francisco: Harper and Row, 1978]) has also shown how wisdom functions differently as a mode of theological discourse in the Old Testament.

35. For my own efforts (now dated) on this subject, see W. Brueggemann, "Scripture and an Ecumenical Life-Style," *Interpretation* (1970) 3–19; idem, "The Triumphalist Tendency in Exegetical History," *Journal of the American Academy of Religion* 38 (1970) 367–80; and idem, *In Man We Trust: The Neglected Side of Biblical Faith* (Richmond: John Knox, 1972).

Old Testament, joins issue with "Canaanite religion" precisely through a willingness to utilize creation-fertility imagery.[36]

Hosea 4:1-3

This brief, self-contained unit stands as an introduction to the second, larger part of the book of Hosea (chaps. 4–14). The passage serves to announce the main themes of judgment that concern the book of Hosea. The structure of the passage is clear and without problems. It divides into three distinct elements.

1. In verse 1a, the people Israel is *summoned to a hearing* because Yahweh has filed a complaint against the inhabitants of "the land." The poem initiates an adversarial, judicial proceeding.

2. The substance of the complaint voiced by God (the prophet?) is stated in two ways (vv. 1b-2). First, there is a triad of words that indicates a fundamental disregard of Yahweh's covenantal intent. The first two terms, "faithfulness" and "loyalty," constitute a conventional word-pair, and refer to the basic requirement for covenant, the practice of fidelity. These two terms are reinforced by "knowledge of God," a favorite phrase of Hosea that refers to acknowledgment of Yahweh's governance and awareness of the substantive faith tradition of Israel.[37] These three terms indicate that Israel has disregarded the horizon of covenantal requirement in ordering its life.

These three programmatic terms are explicated by five specific items (v. 2). It is commonly recognized that this series refers to the Decalogue, even though the actual phrasing is something different. The complaint filed against Israel is that it has violated the Commandments in neighbor relations, which bespeaks a larger disregard of the defining relation of covenant.

3. Then follows the consequence of that disregard, introduced by the word "therefore," thus connecting deed and consequence (v. 3). The consequence of the violation of verses 1b-2 is that the land grieves, and its inhabitants are "enfeebled."[38] It is common to conclude that the words "mourn, languish" refer to a drought. The second half of the

---

36. For a convenient statement of the issue, see W. Harrelson, *From Fertility Cult to Worship* (Garden City, N.Y.: Doubleday, 1969). More currently and probingly, see P. D. Miller, Jr., et al., eds., *Ancient Israelite Religion: Essays in Honor of Frank Moore Cross* (Philadelphia: Fortress Press, 1987).

37. On the phrase "knowledge of God," see the recent discussion of D. R. Daniels, *Hosea and Salvation History: The Early Traditions of Israel in the Prophecy of Hosea* (Beihefte zur ZAR 191; Berlin: de Gruyter, 1990) 111–16.

38. F. I. Andersen and D. N. Freedman (*Hosea: A New Translation with Introduction and Commentary* [Anchor Bible 24; Garden City, N.Y.: Doubleday, 1980] 340) use the term "enfeebled."

verse, however, escalates the drought: the animals, birds, and fish are "gathered away"—that is, they disappear.

In the high season of form criticism, primary attention in this passage has been given to the "law-suit form," whereby God is prosecutor and judge who files a charge against Israel for breaking covenant.[39] The verdict of "guilty" is unstated but is assumed, for the poem moves directly to a devastating sentence. There is good reason why scholarship has seen in this text a clear example of the "law-suit form" and has been able to imagine the intended context of the courtroom. Moreover, as Herbert Huffmon reflects, "natural elements" figure as witness to the trial, or, he suggests, they may even participate as judges.[40] Scholarly preoccupation with the law-suit form, well evidenced in a series of splendid commentaries, reflects a rather rigid commitment to form-critical method and containment within the covenant treaty hypothesis articulated by George Mendenhall and Klaus Baltzer.[41] So far so good, but not so far!

With the shift of models of interpretation that I have suggested, with the emergence of "creation theology" as a lens for reading, we might reread to see what else is suggested by the text. Note well that the shifted model of reading reflects a shifted context, a large culture shift that currently is treated as "postmodernity."

The two parts of this small poetic unit are clear enough. On the one hand, there is massive disregard of Yahweh, signified in the violation of the Ten Commandments, Israel's most treasured and normative characterization of Yahweh's governance. On the other hand, the consequence is large and massive. The text focuses on the great triad of creation, animals, birds, fish. The staggering claim of this poem is to draw together *Decalogue* and *creation,* to assert that the disregard of *torah* leads to the collapse of *creation.* (The positive counterpoint is not stated but can be

39. C. Westermann (*Basic Forms of Prophetic Speech* [Philadelphia: Westminster, 1967] 199–200) discusses our passage among the law-suit passages. See also H. Huffmon, "The Covenant Lawsuit in the Prophets," *Journal of Biblical Literature* 78 (1959) 294–95; J. Harvey, "Le 'Rib-Pattern: Réquisitoire Prophétique sur law Rupteire de L'Alliance," *Biblica* 43 (1962) 172–96; W. E. March, "Prophecy," *Old Testament Form Criticism* (ed. J. H. Hayes; San Antonio: Trinity Univ. Press, 1974] 159–62); and H. W. Wolff, "Die Begründungen der prophetischen Heils—und Unheilsspruche," *Zeitschrift für die alttestamentliche Wissenschaft* 52 (1934) 1–22.

40. Huffmon, "The Covenant Lawsuit," 286, 292.

41. G. E. Mendenhall, "Ancient Oriental and Biblical Law," *Biblical Archaeologist* 17/2 (May 1954) 26–46; idem, "Covenant Forms in Israelite Tradition," *Biblical Archaeologist* 17 (September 1954) 50–76; K. Baltzer, *The Covenant Formulary in Old Testament, Jewish, and Early Christian Writings* (Philadelphia: Fortress Press, 1971). As concerns Hos 4:1-3 in relation to the treaty hypothesis, see Andersen and Freedman, *Hosea;* J. L. Mays, *Hosea: A Commentary* (Old Testament Library; Philadelphia: Westminster, 1969) 60–65; and H. W. Wolff, *A Commentary on the Book of the Prophet Hosea* (Hermeneia; Philadelphia: Fortress Press, 1974) 65–69.

imagined: honoring the Commandments leads to the maintenance and well-being of creation.)

As has been noted by many commentators, the term '*ereṣ* occurs in all three sections of the poem:

> summons: "inhabitants of the '*ereṣ*,"
> indictment: "no knowledge of God in the '*ereṣ*,"
> sentence: "the '*ereṣ* mourns."

The term '*ereṣ* permits reading either "land" (in this case the land of Israel) or "earth," that is, the whole of creation. We cannot determine which is intended, and the meaning may not be stable through the poem. It may indeed be that it is preferable to read "land" in verses 1-2, which concern the conduct of Israel, and "earth" in verse 3. If that is the case, then the abuse of '*ereṣ* locally leads to the death of '*ereṣ* cosmically.

The point that interests us here the most is the relationship between the indictment concerning the Decalogue (v. 2) and the sentence concerning creation (v. 3). How is it that *Decalogue* and *creation* are related to each other? Interpretation that follows the "law-suit" hypothesis says that this is the *sentence* of the judge (Yahweh) who rules in the case. Huffmon refers to verse 3 as "the crisis of covenant,"[42] and James Luther Mays refers to "Yahweh's coming punishment," "the effect of the divine curse and in this case for breach of covenant."[43] Even Koch, discussing this passage in his general argument concerning deeds-consequences, writes:

> It is in these circumstances that Yahweh intervenes. The battle which Yahweh instigates does not have the sole purpose of imposing upon the wicked person the corresponding consequence of one's action. Rather it is to protect the land from being utterly decimated by the destructive consequences of the Sin-Disaster Connection, so that the land could not be completely ruined.[44]

In broad stroke, this judgment of Koch is surely correct. But more specifically, his statement is odd for two reasons. First, there is in verse 3 no intervention or instigation by Yahweh. Second, there is no action to protect the land, for the verbs describe the disaster that is now happening to the land, or soon will. I suggest that while Koch has seen the matter of consequences, his comment is still under the rubric of "law-suit," in the service of the covenant form, a service which impedes use of his own categories for reading.

---

42. Huffmon, "The Covenant Lawsuit," 294.
43. Mays, *Hosea*, 65.
44. Koch, "Is There a Doctrine of Retribution?" 67.

The linkage between verse 2 and verse 3, between Decalogue and creation, is not stated in a way that yields a judicial sentence. There is only a "therefore" and three verbs. The first two verbs have *'ereṣ* and "inhabitants" as subject, and the third is a passive verb (*niph'al*), so that there is no active agent of punishment, not even Yahweh. I suggest that the poem carefully and deliberately mumbles over the relation between Decalogue and creation. It does not want to reduce this connection to a formula, and it does not want to identify an agent. It wants, however, to insist upon a crucial, devastating connection. Thus we are left with a connection that is not very well spelled out, but also is not left in any doubt.

It is this connection, I suggest, that can be reconsidered in terms of "creation theology" and the ecological crisis that is our immediate context for thinking about creation. In fact the "therefore" of this poem functions as a *parataxis,* that is, as a connection that is important but completely unspecified. Perhaps the device is used because the poet does not know what more precisely to say. More likely, I suggest, the device is used because the listener is invited into a moment of ominous awe before a profound mystery. That moment is filled with wonder and with threat, with sovereign insistence, with moral reprimand, with a jeopardy too deep to be spelled out with precision.

I submit that whereas our scientific propensity is to supply a series of secondary causes that link moral seriousness and practical outcome, this ancient poetry proceeds by an awesome phrasing that lets the connection soak in without articulation. Thus:

ancient poetry: violation...*poetic pause of awe*...consequence
between verse 2 and verse 3

scientific alternative: violation...*secondary cause*...consequence

The task of creation theology is to voice the connection between human action and the enhancement or diminishment of creation that is done in, by, and through human action. But how are human action and impact upon creation related? That is a great question of faith in the tradition of Hosea and, in a very different idiom, the great question of contemporary technological culture. The two, human action and the health or unhealth of creation, are related delicately, fragilely, precariously, but inescapably. How is Decalogue related to creation? For a long season of positivism, we imagined that the relation could be delineated without a moral dimension. Schmid, Koch, and Knierim now have noticed the inescapable moral dimension in this matter that we are learning, more practically, the hard way.

V

The rereading of Hos 4:1-3 points to the intractable connection between human conduct and the welfare of creation, a connection not at all diminished by an absence of secondary causes. The poetic-theological idiom of the Bible, not tamed by positivism, which seeks to explain, did not need secondary causes to fill in that connection. It needed only the large, unspecified affirmation of a moral dimension to creation wrought and guaranteed by the creator in order to recognize the unstated but decisive connection. In this essay I am claiming that our endangered environment, jeopardized by our disobedience, enables and requires us to reread texts that we have failed to hear. I note four vignettes in my experience that have taught me to read across the parataxis between verse 2 and verse 3 with a stunned recognition of our place in the law suit, just at the "therefore."

1. A strident young friend of mine, fresh from college, heard an outrageous radio preacher proclaim, "Human greed causes God to send a drought." The radio preacher was dismissed with a disdainful laugh. My educated, young friend could not entertain human acquisitiveness as the source of drought. I joined his dismissive laughter; but then I found myself with a continuing, in-depth reconsideration. While his laughter squared with my own "modernist" scorn of such an elemental religious connection, the laughter has become increasingly unconvincing and hollow.

2. Friends came to "bird-watch" in Britain in East Anglia. They went to the most noted bird sanctuaries, two of them, but they never saw a bird. Only late in their frustration were they told: "It's the drought. The birds had to leave." The languishing, enfeebled land caused the departure of one-third of the creatures named in Hos 4:3. (No news yet on animals or fish at the bird sanctuary.)

3. A month after the failed bird-watch, the headlines asserted: "Philippine flood caused by deforestation." The newspaper stated it as a certainty. The newspaper did not need to say much about the motivations for cutting down the rain forest. It happened because cleared land will produce more profits. The cycles of vegetation that nourish the atmosphere were seemingly dispensable and had to yield to the more important pursuit of profit.

4. The pictures of seemingly endless black smoke in Kuwait is summarized by the report that Kuwait has burned off 2.5 percent of its oil supply. The loss of course is not a "natural catastrophe" or "an act of God." Nobody thinks it is either of these. It is the result of a human invasion by Iraq. Behind that invasion, moreover, is long-term Western imperialism that arbitrarily made nation-states out of tribes. The "mother of all policies" for England was to keep the French out of trade

routes that ran through Palestine, all the way from India to Britain! And now U.S. technology, powered by U.S. ideology, keeps watch over the unfinished imperialism of France and Britain.

These four items are of course independent of one another. They move, in my growing awareness, in an order of increasing dismay, clear to the depth of dismay. The first is a religious affirmation that seems innocuous enough. The second may be a loss caused by a failure of rain. But the third ponders the failure of rain and its human provocation. It seems not far from the *deforestation* of the Philippines to the *de-oiling* of Kuwait.

The middle term in all these calculations,

> sin ... → drought,
>
> birds ... → drought,
>
> deforestation ... → drought,
>
> imperialism ... → loss of oil,

would seem to be acquisitiveness. That of course is a great deal to read into the uninflected "therefore" of Hos 4:3. The violation of commands (see Hos 4:2) regularly takes the form of greed and acquisitiveness, driven by fear and the yearning for security. The act of acquisitiveness, informed by ideology and implemented by technology, regards the created fabric of life as an available, usable resource, defined so by our Cartesian world of objective control. The slow, sustained processes of "fruitfulness" are disrupted for a "quick fix."[45] The quick fix works if one does not think about deeds-consequences but only thinks about control, mastery, and domination. Israel, and specifically Hosea, however, thinks about deeds-consequences, and the news is not good.

VI

Thus a tenured, white male rereads Hos 4:1-3, all of Hosea, and then the rest of the prophets. This reading is a long way removed from the eighth-century poet. Nonetheless, I will inevitably read with reference to my own context. I will read that way because the "early meaning" does not seem removed from the "present meaning." I will read that way because *'ereṣ* is again in crisis, apparently the same crisis.

---

45. The human "quick fix" that disrupts the long-term fruitfulness of creation evokes this comment from A. Quinlen ("Latest Weather Story Isn't Warmed Over," *Post-Dispatch*, July 31, 1991): "Once we believed that only God could make a heat wave; now we think that maybe we took creation into our own hands and fashioned a monster, a tent of gases that trap the warm air as surely as glass plates do."

My context is that of rural nurture, still working the fields with a team of horses, walking the fields in exhilarated rest on Sundays. It was not a romantic environment, but hard work in a context of belonging. But then has come, into those fields, agribusiness, fields too large to walk, crops to be turned to cash, cash to be turned to larger equipment, in order to farm more land. On the one hand, the outcome is the urban, absentee owners for whom farming is not a way of life but an "investment." On the other hand, the outcome is large farms, overextended farms with heavy mortgages, while believing the ill-kept promises of a market economy.

Wendell Berry contrasts "industrial economics" that uses the land and agriculture that cares for the land:

> Industrial economics has encouraged poor work on the farm. I believe that it has done so because poor work can be easily priced. Since poor work lasts only a short time, the money value of its whole life can be readily calculated. Good work, which in fact or influence endures beyond the foresight of economists, can be valued but not priced because its worth is incalculable. I am talking about the difference, say, between a wire fence and a stone wall, or between any gasoline engine and any good breed of livestock.[46]

With such a consideration, Berry helps us reread Hosea with its uncompromising "therefore."

And before Berry, John Steinbeck had seen the drastic turn of land vis-à-vis people in all its ugliness:

> And all their love was thinned with money, and all their fierceness dribbled away in interest until they were no longer farmers at all, but little manufacturers who must sell before they can make....
>
> Now farming became industry, and the owners followed Rome, although they did not know it. They imported slaves, although they did not call them slaves: Chinese, Japanese, Mexicans, Filipinos. They live on rice and beans, the businessmen said. They don't need much. They wouldn't know what to do with good wages....
>
> And all the time the farms grew larger and the owners fewer.
> ...The imported serfs were beaten and frightened and starved until some went home again and some grew fierce and were killed or driven from the country. And the farms grew larger and the owners fewer.

---

46. W. Berry, *The Gift of Good Land: Further Essays Cultural and Agricultural* (San Francisco: North Point, 1981) 124. See the entire collection by Berry, as well as *Home Economics: Fourteen Essays* (San Francisco: North Point, 1987).

And the crops changed. Fruit trees took the place of grain fields, and vegetables to feed the world spread out on the bottoms: lettuce, cauliflower, artichokes, potatoes—stoop crops. A man may stand to use a scythe, a plow, a pitchfork; but he must crawl like a bug between the rows of lettuce, he must bend his back and pull his long bag between the cotton rows, he must go on his knees like a penitent across a cauliflower patch.

And it came about that the owners no longer worked on their farms. They farmed on paper; and they forgot the land, the smell, the feel of it, and remembered only that they owned it, remembered only what they gained and lost by it.... And the owners not only did not work the farms anymore, many of them had never seen the farms they owned.[47]

Now we are more sophisticated than the poem of Hosea. We do not settle for a simple "therefore." Nonetheless, we can notice with even more analytical categories, the alienation of people from land, and both land and people end up being abused and displaced.[48] We are more sophisticated in our explanations, but the calculus is the same as that voiced by the prophet. The drive for more money leads to displacing people. As the people are displaced, the land goes untended, unloved, unrespected. A little at a time, the land forfeits its will to produce and to multiply, the earth ceases to be fruitful, and chaos comes (see Mic 3:12; Jer 4:23-26).[49]

My context is in that generation nurtured in cold war, fearful for our lives, with a passion for deterrence and a balance of terror, with endless dollars committed to "security systems." "The others" who threatened have now failed, and we end up as the "only superpower." My context is that of a superpower, addicted to its technology, believing its own advertisements, incapable of imagining alternative modes of life. The "more" of weapons and the "more" of consumer goods are all of a piece, and who with purchasing power can resist either? We end up fully armed, fully wired, but with an emptiness bespeaking fear and brutality.

The seizure of large tracts of land through credit arrangements and the development of massive security systems both require violation of covenantal modes of life. Those violations, however, in our recent past

---

47. J. Steinbeck, *The Grapes of Wrath* (New York: Penguin, 1967) 298–99.

48. W. Berry ("The Body and the Earth," *The Unsettling of American Culture and Agriculture* [New York: Avon, 1977] 97–140) has shown how disrespect for the earth leads to disrespect for persons, with particular reference to sexual exploitation. See also W. Brueggemann, "Land: Fertility and Justice," *Theology of the Land* (ed. B. F. Evans and G. D. Cusack; Collegeville, Minn.: Liturgical Press, 1987) 41–68.

49. The power of ideology to silence criticism and disclosure of destructive policy is evident in Jeremiah 26. In that trial narrative, it is not disputed that Jeremiah speaks the truth. All that counts is to keep the truth from being spoken. Thus abuse requires a conspiracy of silence by way of cover-up.

were seen to be not only necessary but bearable costs.[50] Now as a result of those "bearable costs" we are at the edge of the "therefore," and we wonder if the "enfeeblement" of creation is irreversible. We wonder what it would take to foreswear our disobedience so that creation may be fruitful again.

VII

These outcomes of my rumination on Hos 4:1-3 are of course perfectly obvious to any of us. What is worth noting is that those outcomes were not perfectly obvious to us a decade ago. They were not obvious to critical commentators who stayed with the "law-suit form" and the "treaty hypothesis." Nor were they obvious in our passion for "mighty acts". that distanced "creation" as "fertility." Partly we read differently now because our methods of reading have changed. Our methods are changing, however, because our old ways of reading were only congenial to our positivist, objectivist explanatory propensity.[51] So we read the form ("law suit"), rushed across the "therefore," and did not notice the convergence in the "therefore" of social criticism (pursuit of profit) and theological danger (nonnegotiable moral dimension to creation).

The reading I propose wants to jettison none of those learnings from older criticism. After that criticism, however, I propose a holy, awed pause between verse 2 and verse 3, just where critical reading was stopped by the silliness of the radio preacher who claimed too much, just where the commentaries become silent, because the "therefore" did not admit of decoding. One does not need "secondary causes" to discern afresh our crisis and the crisis of *'ereṣ*. One needs only a text that witnesses to the holy threat and the patience to attend to the resilience of the requirement of commandments and that threat arising from "deeds-consequences." Bringing such texts to our context, or better, submitting our context to the text, offers at least three gains.

1. The text that reperceives the world as a delicate, jeopardized creation invites us to *rediscern* our place in the world. Our place is not as operators of tanks in a pursuit of security or bulldozers in a chase for profits, but as *creatures under command,* upon which the future of *'ereṣ* depends. My place as a human being is repositioned. I am no longer invited, even in my male tenure, to domination. This rediscernment and potential threat are not an appeal to supernaturalism, for there

---

50. On bearable, necessary social costs, see the reasoning and conclusions of P. L. Berger, *Pyramids of Sacrifice: Political Ethics and Social Change* (New York: Basic Books, 1975).

51. On "objective" reading that is flagrantly interested, see the discussions cited in n. 1.

is nothing of supernaturalism in this poem. This is not a poem about the "intervention" of God. It is rather a practical, semi-Pelagian construal of reality that regards our acquisitiveness as more than a matter of indifference.[52]

2. The text that reperceives the world as a delicate, jeopardized creation invites us to *repent* of our policies, our fears, our hopes, and our cravings. My place as a citizen is repositioned, as I am no longer with innocence able to benefit from U.S. imperialism that lives from the wealth of "the colonies." Such repentance no doubt impinges upon "lifestyle." Much more, it concerns public policies that mask and enact shameless greed, driven by unreal hope, unacknowledged fear, and uncaring disregard of the neighbor.

3. The text that reperceives the world as a delicate, jeopardized creation invites to a *rereading* of the text. My place as teacher, pastor, and believer in this text is one directly in front of this text with its mumbling, hidden connection.[53] I understand the danger of setting the text too quickly into a contemporary context. This rereading can permit the text to be very ancient and yet help us to see that the ancient text had it recurringly right about command and creation, about duty and delight, about loyalty and productivity. This awareness leads the believer of the text to a greater treasuring of the text as fully present tense, and to a greater nerve in its explication, a greater confidence about the truth of this moral claim in a world exhausted with "enlightened," self-sufficient cynicism.

Our present context invites us to *rediscern as human beings,* to *repent as citizens,* to *reread as believers.* Probably... the text in Hosea did not have in purview agribusiness, U.S. superpower status, deforestation, or oil spills. The test of this contextual reading is finally whether it coheres with what the text in its early (I do not say "original") voicing intended. Did the text then concern a sense of autonomy and self-sufficiency that led to neighbor abuse, which in hidden but programmatic ways diminished *'ereṣ?* I conclude that this was precisely the issue in ancient Israel when the requirements of defense and of productivity caused a public distortion of covenantal reality.[54] The issues are unchanged in our

---

52. Reference to semi-Pelagian categories is of course an anachronism. I cite it only to point out that the human role in the maintenance of creation has been seriously retarded by a theology that refused the cruciality of human choice and human performance.

53. By speaking of "believer," I mean one who permits him- or herself to be addressed seriously by the claims of the text. I do not refer to any "larger package" of doctrinal, theological, or ethical claims.

54. Obviously a great deal has been written about "Canaanite religion" in contrast to the faith of Israel. Nonetheless, one can, as Gottwald has proposed, see "Canaanite religion" in the theological claims of the Old Testament as a coded reference to a social vision and a set of social relations that deny mutuality to the neighbor or to the earth. Thus I take "Canaanite religion" to refer to a set of legitimations for socio-

present-tense reading. A critique of positivism and its propensity to un-critical control and mastery of *'ereṣ* will let us see that the world is not settled and secure. It is, rather, enormously contingent and at risk.

I imagine, without having seen them, that other pieces in this book touch more immediately upon rereading texts in relation to sexual, racial, and economic justice. I have taken up the subject of the fruit-fulness and diminishment of *'ereṣ* because our transformations of eco-nomic, political, and interpersonal relations cannot lead to a revisioning of *'ereṣ* as "home" unless there is a repositioning of human power and human will vis-à-vis the creation. Without a break in our large-scale acquisitiveness that diminishes the earth, our closer agendas will fail.

Hosea's close partner, Deuteronomy, warned about autonomous in-difference:

Do not say to yourself, "My power and the might of my own hand have gotten me this wealth." (Deut 8:17)

That warning voice concluded:

I solemnly warn you today that you shall surely perish. (v. 19)

At the core of Mosaic faith is the claim that self-sufficiency leads to diminishment.

Hosea understood about the jeopardy and the potential of creation. The poet has the creator say:

Therefore [*sic*] I will take back
    my grain in its time,
    and my wine in its season;
and I will take away my wool and my flax,
    which were to uncover her nakedness. (Hos 2:9 [Heb. v. 11])

But then, in the generously restored world of righteousness, justice, faithfulness, mercy, and steadfast love (vv. 19-20 [Heb. vv. 21-22]), it is affirmed:

The earth [*'ereṣ*] shall answer the grain, the wine, and the oil. (Hos 2:22 [Heb. v. 24])

The enfeebled *'ereṣ* could again "bring forth."[55] Such fruitfulness, however, is on the other side of "knowing the Lord" (Hos 2:20 [Heb. v. 22]).

─────────────────────

economic, political practice. This assumption about "Canaanite religion" is behind the notion of "peasant revolt" in all its various forms as first (very differently) suggested by Mendenhall and Gottwald.

55. On Hosea 2 and the structural, intentional contrast between the two parts of the poem, see D. J. A. Clines, "Hosea 2: Structure and Interpretation," *Studia Biblica 1978* (Journal for the Study of the Old Testament—Supplement Series 11; Sheffield, England: JSOT Press, 1979) 83–103.

Framing Biblical Interpretation at New York Theological Seminary: A Student Self-Inventory on Biblical Hermeneutics

_____ Norman K. Gottwald ____

Critical study of the Bible in a theological seminary can be a disorienting and dispiriting experience for students, particularly if little or no attention is given to issues of biblical hermeneutics and biblical authority early on in their training.[1] At New York Theological Seminary, for the last eight years we have used an instrument called "Self-Inventory on Biblical Hermeneutics"[2] in order to stimulate our students' self-reflection on the ways they frame their biblical interpretation.

Our student body, composed of an ethnic mix of Blacks, whites, Hispanics, and Asians drawn from more than thirty denominations, brings a dizzying array of biblical hermeneutics to seminary. These ethnic groupings are of course not homogeneous blocs; for example, we have a growing number of Caribbean Blacks; Hispanics come from diverse Latin American backgrounds; and the perspectives of Koreans often vary between those born abroad and those born in the United States. When students land in "Introduction to Hebrew Bible," they encounter another set of frames with which many have had little or no previous acquaintance. We attempt to bring this kaleidoscope of divergent methodological and hermeneutical perspectives into sharp personal focus by use of the self-inventory.

The *praxis* goal of "Introduction to Hebrew Bible" is to equip students in knowledge of the contents of the Bible, in the exegesis of biblical texts, and in judgment and skills in uses of the Bible in the contemporary church. The *theory* goal of the course is to broaden and deepen understanding of alternative hermeneutical frames so that students will develop their own hermeneutics in a coherent and self-critical way.

---

1. This paper is an updated revision of a panel presentation at the Semiotics and Exegesis Group, AAR-SBL annual meeting, 1990, on the general topic: "Frames of Interpretation and the Production of Meaning."
2. The text of the self-inventory is given at the end of this essay.

At the outset of the course, students fill out the self-inventory, which aims at identifying the factors operative in the biblical interpretation they bring with them to seminary. The self-inventory is processed and discussed in small groups led by teaching assistants. At the end of "Introduction to New Testament," students reflect back over the inventory and report changes that have taken place in their hermeneutics as a result of their seminary studies.

I shall offer a few observations about the results of using this hermeneutical instrument at New York Theological Seminary over the past eight years.

I. Characteristically, students find some of the items much more difficult to address than others, generally in the following pattern:

A. Items 11–18, on personal and church uses of the Bible, are most easily answered.

B. Items 1–3, on church tradition, authority, and theology, often require some "digging" as many students for the first time try to articulate positions that they hold unreflectively or know little about, even though they may have been long active in church life. It has, in fact, been a surprise to discover how many students with strongly held views about the Bible are poorly informed about the history and theology of the denominations in which their views have been shaped.

C. Items 4–10, on ethnicity, gender, social class, education, community priorities, and political stance, occasion the greatest puzzlement and confusion. As expected, nonwhite students are on the whole more attuned to ethnicity and women to gender as hermeneutical factors. Many students, however, in all ethnic groups, fail to see—and sometimes deny—that these factors have much to do with their biblical interpretation. Community priorities are most often identifiable by students from inner-city churches, but in many instances the community concerns are cast largely in terms of immediate congregational needs with a minimum of attention to the broader community. Among all ethnic groups, political position is more often than not described as "neutral" or "above politics," or it is expressed in sweeping generalizations such as democracy, honesty in government, and so on. The follow-up item on "implicit political stance"—suggesting that being "nonpolitical" may have political implications—is for a fair number of students simply incomprehensible on first encounter. Social class is the greatest baffler. On initial exposure to the inventory, only a handful of students are able to answer this with confidence and specificity. Even those students who recognize ethnicity and/or gender as hermeneutically influential by and large do not readily relate these to social class. It is usual for students of all ethnic groups to see themselves as part of an amorphous "middle class," which seems often to be an expression of their aspiration to upward social mobility symbolized by their higher education status and commitment to ministry.

It is not uncommon for students to leave one or more of items 4–10 unanswered, requesting time to think more about matters that presently confound them. While we urge students to complete the inventory, we prefer to accept "blanks" on some items—following them up with conversation—rather than have students trump up answers that are not really their own. It is noteworthy that during their later years in seminary, many students report an "aha" experience in which these social and political factors in biblical interpretation gradually or suddenly become clear to them. This student sensitization to sociopolitical dimensions of biblical interpretation most often shows up at one or more of the following subsequent points in the curriculum: in biblical electives, in doing a community analysis centered on their local church, or in writing a credo in their senior year.

D. Responses to the concluding questions on mixing and prioritizing factors and on desired next steps are usually cautious and tentative. Many students do identify a central factor or cluster of factors in their hermeneutics (for example, authoritative church criteria, ethnicity or gender, life crises). A majority, however, are struck by a larger array of influences on their hermeneutics than they had previously recognized, and they are not so sure how all these factors work together. The result is that next steps are usually described as a desire to learn more about certain of the factors that represent "blind spots" in the understanding of their experience. They want to see how further study of the Bible in seminary will help to enlarge their self-awareness and offer interpretive tools and options that might do more justice to the complexity of their experience and understanding.

II. Our faculty and students have concluded that the self-inventory, although often initially disturbing, "spades up" soil for learning. It helps students understand that it is not the seminary faculty that is "inventing" problems in biblical interpretation, but rather it is the very nature of their own situations in church and world that generates hermeneutical issues. As students in "Introduction to Hebrew Bible" write weekly response papers to the textbook and discuss course content in small groups, they build upon the topics and insights opened up by the self-inventory. They possess a "map," however rudimentary, for locating issues that are not only "out there" in the biblical subject matter but, more crucially, "in here" within their own lives and communities. Moreover, by making the problematics of biblical interpretation an overt dimension of the seminary curriculum from the start, we ensure that students are not left to struggle with these issues isolated from one another but are drawn into an ongoing challenge shared with their peers and teachers and with the church at large.

III. Among the many configurations of hermeneutical issues that the self-inventory helps to lay bare, two are particularly important for our seminary context.

1. Nature and Authority of the Bible. If the Bible is a historical document with a history of interpretation, what does it say to our own history? How is the Bible related to various other sources of Christian authority?

Coming from a cross section of Protestant churches, many of our students carry with them naive understandings of the Bible and residues of fundamentalism. They would not be at our seminary if they were principled fundamentalists; nevertheless, a sizable number operate with traditions that minimize the historical character of the Bible and tend to elevate the Bible to the position of sole source of Christian authority. For such students, it becomes a seminary-long task "to take the measure" of the historicality of the Bible and its complex interweaving with tradition, reason, experience, and social location. In this project, "Introduction to Hebrew Bible" sets them on a course they will continue to pursue in church history, theology, ethics, and mission and ministry. The self-inventory introduces them in a concrete, relatively nonthreatening manner to a task that is theirs to work with in a supportive educational setting.

In the academic year 1992–93, New York Theological Seminary introduced a new curriculum that makes hermeneutics the linchpin of the entire course of studies, no longer the special province of biblical studies alone. Students begin their study with a single intensive course on critical interpretation, which explores the interrelationships of faith, experience, knowledge, analysis, and action. This course includes a sizable segment on biblical interpretation, presented in association with the modes of critical interpretation integral to history, theology, ethics, and ministry in church and world. Students next study Hebrew Bible and New Testament in tandem with foundations of ministry, followed by two "bridge" courses, one on sociology of religion and one on social history of formative Judaism and early Christianity, before moving on to church history, theology, and ethics.

One way of construing the new curriculum is to view it as an attempt to appropriate what we have learned from the biblical self-inventory for the benefit of all required seminary courses. The explicit aim of the entire curriculum becomes the development of a mature hermeneutic in approaching all subjects of study and all practices of ministry. The guiding presupposition is that similar issues and modes of dealing with them critically extend across the whole spectrum of theological studies and practices of ministry. The challenge will be to locate the shared hermeneutical thread running through all the particularities of the separate disciplines and the diverse ministerial practices.

2. *The Cultural and Social Task of the Churches.* If the Bible reflects a variety of cultural and social environments and assumptions, what does that mean for churches today? When we become aware of our own cultural and social situations, and of ways that we want to re-form them, what does the Bible—in conjunction with other theological, social, and psychological disciplines—have to contribute? What is its authority in the cultural and social mission of the churches?

Our students bring with them a societywide bias toward "possessive individualism" in secular matters and "privatization" in religion. Even those with a sense of social mission often see the task as a secondary "application" of a basically personal faith. Awareness of ethnic and gender oppression is not easily translated into its social-class and political implications. Beginning with the nexus of religion and society/politics in the Bible, our curriculum attempts to show the irreducible cultural and social correlates of particular ways of believing and practicing religion. Against the tide of our times, we seek to counter the social and political stupor that would keep us ignorant of what has shaped our corporate life and what can change it for the better.

I find that my use of the self-inventory outside of New York Theological Seminary has disclosed certain differences in sensibility on the social and political items. Since I have not used the inventory extramurally in any systematic way, and in any case have not kept records of the responses, I hesitate to make broad comparative generalizations. Nevertheless, I do find these perceived differences to be suggestive. Among clergy and lay leaders in the United States and Canada, there is generally an implicit recognition of the cultural and social embedment of the church and of the connection between political outlook and biblical hermeneutics. This appears to arise from years of firsthand experience in congregational leadership. Among clergy and students in Latin America and South Africa, the cultural and sociopolitical dimensions of biblical interpretation are even more clearly grasped, evidently because of the intense ethnic and class struggles in both those regions. In fact, when I entitled a course I offered at the University of Cape Town, "The Hebrew Bible and Social Spirituality," most of the students thought that the adjective "social" was a redundancy because it seemed to them a given that spirituality is a communal reality with inextricable social and political overtones.

IV. These hermeneutical issues concerning the nature of the Bible and the social mission of the church are joined in distinctive ways at New York Theological Seminary because the majority of our students are nonwhite. For the most part, fundamentalist residues among nonwhite students are less psychically entrenched and socially conservative than among white students. If the integrating and sustaining power of Christian faith can be shown to be viable, even strengthened, by a break with fundamentalist presuppositions, most of our students are open to taking that step. Furthermore, even when our nonwhite students—unlike their counterparts in Latin America and South Africa—have not as yet drawn structural connections between their marginality and "the way the system works," they have often had enough direct experience to know about cultural and sociopolitical domination in specific terms. They tend to harbor a diffuse "hermeneutic of suspicion" that seminary training clarifies and sharpens.

In fact, our students typically exhibit a hermeneutic of suspicion toward the intellectual disciplines of theology. The result is a certain tension and contradiction in teaching theological subject matters—especially biblical criticism, which, as historically conceived and shaped, comes from Enlightenment impulses more committed to intellectual freedom than to freedom from cultural, economic, and social oppression. In short, we are challenged to show that enlightening tools can serve liberative projects within the personal and communal horizons of our students. We are gambling that enlightenment and liberation are compatible and that, in the end, it is liberation that subsumes and actualizes enlightenment.

As a teacher in this situation, my primary goal is to empower and validate students in their quest for a biblical hermeneutic that is faithful and adequate to their situations in church and society. As I expose students to a range of hermeneutical options, I am completely "up front" about my own liberation hermeneutic, informed by political economy and process theology. At the same time, my colleagues and I repeatedly stress that students must work out their own hermeneutic since one's stance in ministry cannot be vital and effective if it is borrowed from someone else. In the process I am constantly learning new aspects of other hermeneutics so amply represented in our diverse student body, including, for example, fundamentalist, Pentecostal, dispensational, neo-evangelical, Jungian archetypal, feminist, Unitarian, Jewish, and Roman Catholic strains of thought. In my experience, our corporate struggle for a critically developed hermeneutic is New York Theological Seminary's most distinctive contribution to the churches we serve.

SELF-INVENTORY ON BIBLICAL HERMENEUTICS

Throughout the ages—and no less today—Christians have differed among themselves in their interpretation of the Bible, both with respect to particular passages and with respect to the meaning of the Bible as a whole. This can be explained only in part by the nature of the Bible itself.

How we construe the Bible is greatly affected by our experience and identity as interpreters. There appears to be a complex of factors at work in all of us as biblical interpreters, no matter how different our conclusions. We don't come "naked" to the Bible. Rather, the way we are "outfitted" with preunderstandings and pretexts shapes what we see and what we emphasize in the Bible.

As we come to see the hermeneutical factors at work in ourselves, we become more self-aware in our interpretation and more self-critical in a constructive sense. We are also able to see why differences of biblical interpretation arise among intelligent and sincere believers.

Your customary way of interpreting the Bible will of course profoundly affect your experience in this class. Some perspectives in the class are likely to be new to you and may seem silly or false at first acquaintance. As you study, you are encouraged to try to see why these perspectives on the Bible have arisen and to consider how they may be fruitful in clarifying and possibly enlarging your own perspective as it develops over time.

Several crucial factors in the preunderstanding of biblical interpreters are set out below in the form of questions that you ask yourself about your perspective on the Bible. You are asked to answer them thoughtfully and honestly with respect to your life. The "correct" answers are those that uncover as precisely as possible the mix of influences that have brought you to where you now are in your biblical understanding.

Please follow the instructions in submitting your completed self-inventory.

1. CHURCH HISTORY/TRADITION
   What is my denominational history and tradition regarding interpretation of the Bible?

2. AUTHORITATIVE CRITERIA
   What are the norms or standards beyond the Bible recognized in my tradition to indicate how and in what particulars the Bible is the word of God? This may include a founder of the denomination, a church body, a confession, a creed, a set of customs, a type of personal experience, a social commitment, as well as other possibilities.

3. WORKING THEOLOGY
   What is my actual working theology regarding interpretation of the Bible? To what extent is this the same or different from the official position of my denomination or the "average" viewpoint among my church associates? Is my working theology more or less the same as my formal theology, such as I might state in an application to a seminary or before a church body?

4. ETHNICITY

How does my ethnic history, culture, and consciousness influence my interpretation of the Bible? This may be somewhat easier for Blacks, Hispanics, and Asians to answer, but it is also a necessary question for Anglos to ponder.

5. GENDER

How does my gender history, culture, and consciousness influence my interpretation of the Bible? With the recent rise of feminist consciousness, this may be an easier question for women to confront, but it is also an important question for men.

6. SOCIAL CLASS

How does my social-class history, culture, and consciousness influence my interpretation of the Bible? Since the dominant ideology in our society tends to deny that social classes exist among us, or to belittle the significance of class, it may take considerable effort on your part to identify your class location. For starters, you can ask about work experience, inherited wealth, income, education, types of reading, news sources consulted, social and career aspirations, and so on, and you can ask these questions about yourself, your parents, your grandparents, your associates, your neighborhood, your church.

7. EDUCATION

How does my level and type of education influence my interpretation of the Bible? If I have had technical or professional training in nonreligious fields, how does this impact my way of reading the Bible?

8. COMMUNITY PRIORITIES

How do the values, welfare, and survival needs recognized or felt implicitly in my community/church influence my interpretation of the Bible?

9. EXPLICIT POLITICAL POSITION

How does my avowed political position influence my biblical interpretation? Politics is about as narrowly conceived in this country as is class. The term "political position" in this question refers to more than political party affiliation or location on a left-right political spectrum. It also takes into account how much impact one feels from society and government on one's own life and how much responsibility one takes for society and government, and in what concrete ways. Also involved is how one's immediate community/ church is oriented toward sociopolitical awareness.

10. IMPLICIT POLITICAL STANCE

Even if I am not very political in the usual sense, or consider myself neutral toward or "above" politics, how does this "nonpolitical" attitude and stance influence my biblical interpretation? What is the implicit political stance of my church and of other religious people with whom I associate?

11. CUSTOMARY EXPOSURES TO THE BIBLE

How does the mix of uses of the Bible to which I have been or am currently exposed influence my biblical interpretation? Such uses may include worship, preaching, church-school instruction, private study, Bible school training, ethical and theological resourcing, solitary or group devotions or spiritual exercises, and so on.

12. BIBLE TRANSLATION

How do the Bible translations and study Bibles I use influence my interpretation of the Bible? What translation(s) do I regularly or frequently use, and why? If I use a particular study Bible with explanatory essays and notes, what line of interpretation is expressed in it? Do I accept the study Bible interpretations without question or do I consult other sources of information to compare with them?

13. PUBLISHED RESOURCES

How do the published resources I regularly or sometimes consult influence my biblical interpretation? Among these resources may be one's private library, a church or seminary library, periodicals, church-school educational materials, sermon helps, and so on.

14. INTENT AND EFFECT OF BIBLICAL PREACHING

How do my church and pastor (or myself as pastor) understand the role of the Bible in preaching as an aspect of the mission of the church, and how does that understanding influence my own pattern of biblical interpretation?

15. ORIENTATION TO BIBLICAL SCHOLARS

How does my attitude toward and use or nonuse of biblical scholarship influence my biblical interpretation? Am I inclined automatically to accept or to reject whatever a biblical scholar claims? Does the biblical scholarship I am familiar with increase or decrease my sense of competence and satisfaction in Bible study?

16. FAMILY INFLUENCE

    What was the characteristic view of the Bible in my childhood home? Have I stayed in continuity with that view? Do I now see the Bible rather differently than my parents did (or do)? If there have been major changes in my view of the Bible, how did these come about? How do I feel about differences in biblical understanding within my current family setting?

17. LIFE CRISES

    Have I experienced crises in my life in which the Bible was a resource or in which I came to a deeper or different understanding of the Bible than I had held before? If so, what has been the lasting effect of the crisis on my biblical interpretation?

18. SPIRITUALITY OR DIVINE GUIDANCE

    What has been my experience of the role of the Bible in spiritual awareness or guidance from God? What biblical language and images play a part in my spiritual awareness and practice? How do I relate this "spiritual" use of the Bible to other ways of reading and interpreting the Bible? Do these different approaches to the Bible combine comfortably for me or are they in tension or even open conflict?

Learning from This Self-inventory

1. HOW DO I MIX AND PRIORITIZE THE FACTORS?

    Now that I have attended to each of these hermeneutical factors, is it possible to rank them in terms of the extent of their importance in my biblical interpretation? Do I recognize that some factors are "foundational" or "pivotal" for me? If that seems to be so, how are the less dominant factors related to and affected by the more dominant factors? Do I detect any factor at work in my biblical interpretation that is not identified in the self-inventory? Does it surprise me to find that some factors are apparently more influential in my biblical interpretation than I had previously realized?

2. WHAT NEXT STEPS DO I WANT TO TAKE?

    What new awareness do I gain from this self-inventory as to how I actually interpret the Bible as the particular person I am? Do I want to learn more about the workings of some of these hermeneutical factors in the way I interpret? Now that I am getting more aware of how these factors interplay in my interpretation, is there anything I may want to consider changing in my attitude or practice so that I may become a more adequate and self-consistent biblical interpreter?[3]

3. This self-inventory was first developed in an ongoing working group on the politics of biblical hermeneutics sponsored by New York Theological Seminary. The working group's membership included faculty from New York Theological Seminary, General Theological Seminary, and Union Theological Seminary, as well as pastors and denominational staff members. The self-inventory has gone through several revisions, and some of the hermeneutical factors listed have been contributed by students at New York Theological Seminary. Suggestions for improvement are always welcomed.

___ 16 _____

Reading for Liberation

_____ Mary Ann Tolbert ____

Over twenty years after the second wave of feminism swept ashore in
North America, patriarchy—with all its attendant dualistic hierarchies
of winners and losers, dominant and marginalized, powerful and powerless—continues to hold the beach against all comers. Although women,[1]
racial and ethnic minorities, the physically challenged, and to a lesser
extent openly gay men and lesbians have all won some access to the
upper reaches of the system, wage differentials, glass ceilings, and daily
harassment, even outright violence, maintain the line in the sand over
which they still may not cross. The hegemonic North American cultural values continue to privilege one who is male, white, of Anglo/
European descent, educated, middle- to upper-class (with attendant economic standing), heterosexual, married, healthy, physically fit, Christian/
Protestant, youngish, slim, attractive, and so on.

From television serials to advertisements, the dominant ideology of
the attractive, successful, wealthy white male as the one in control whom
we should all admire and trust is constantly reinforced. No matter how
hard we work or try, some of us by definition will never be able to attain
this hegemonic image, and that underscores its constructed nature and
the intent of those who construct it to preserve power and prestige in
the hands of only a few. And it _is_ only a few, for the majority of people,
perhaps even the vast majority of people, in the United States do not and
cannot embody these cultural values. Given the fact that the majority
deviate in some way from the hegemonic ideal, how and why does this
hegemony persist?

In this essay I want to explore the question of the persistence of patriarchal hegemony as a way of framing my growing concern that feminist

_____

1. To divide women from racial and ethnic minorities, the physically challenged, and
lesbians is of course extremely misleading, for all lesbians are women and half of the
racial and ethnic minority groups are women, and many of the physically challenged are
women. However, what this division does point out is that minority women, differently
abled women, and lesbians face a double jeopardy because they are marginalized by
race, physical challenge, or sexual orientation _in addition to gender._

biblical research, including my own, often seems ultimately to accommodate the status quo rather than challenging or undermining it. I want then to ask what it means to read the Bible for liberation and how one would do it. What are the dangers and what are the rewards of such reading? How must we liberate our reading of the Bible in order to read it for liberation?

Patriarchal Persistence

As a white, middle-class, educated, North American Protestant, I am profoundly privileged in relation to others across the globe and even others within the United States. However, as a middle-aged, nonmarried woman, I live a life continuously marked by social and economic oppression and personal harassment. Consequently, like many others in North American society, I occupy a variety of status positions vis-à-vis hegemonic culture, some dominant and some marginalized. Indeed, only a few people actually "fit" the norm totally—even for the wealthy, educated, physically able, Protestant, white male, the natural process of aging will eventually shift him into a marginalized position, a fact that may explain why in this culture the elite work with such fervor to remain "youthful." On the other side, even a smaller number do not "fit" hegemonic values in any way—to be completely disenfranchised by the present cultural system, one must identify with all the negative subject positions, being, for example, a non-Christian, lesbian, poor, unmarried, uneducated, non–English-speaking, obese, old, physically challenged, African-American, Native-American, Hispanic-American, or Asian-American, and so on.

Although the majority of people occupy a mix of status positions, most of us tend *not* to interpret our experience in that fashion. There are at least two reasons for this failure. First, Enlightenment philosophy bequeathed to modern Western society the concept of the unified self or subjectivity, the Cartesian thinking ego, as the foundation of our sense of being: *cogito ergo sum*. Thus, we describe our "self" as a unified entity with (or possibly seeking) a single identity. The illusory nature of that unified self has been forcefully pointed out in many postmodernist theories[2] as well as in the pragmatic negotiations required by a politics of difference. In the political sphere, an Asian-American lesbian, for instance, must decide at any given moment into which of her marginalized identity groups (women, homosexuals, or Asian Americans) she will channel her political efforts, realizing that no group will represent her

---

2. See, for example, all the essays in L. J. Nicholson, ed., *Feminism/Postmodernism* (New York: Routledge, 1990) but especially Nicholson's introduction, 1–16.

own best interests fully; indeed, given the politics of division encouraged by patriarchy, her various identity groups may be at war with each other, forcing her into painful and often untenable choices.

Second, our privileged locations in the hegemonic system seem right, normal, and unproblematic; hence, they tend to remain unmarked and generally unnoticed; indeed, they may even seem to be earned rewards rather than cultural privileges.[3] Only the negative positions of our mixed status are marked and draw our attention. The charge of focusing only upon victimization that is often brought against identity politics or liberation movements arises precisely from the origin of these groups in deviant hegemonic positions. We do not protest our privileges; we protest our pain.

Moreover, our fictional unified "self" tends to become identified with our marked condition, especially when that is the only condition that separates us from the hegemonic norm or when that condition is particularly disenfranchised by dominant society. I identify myself essentially as "woman," while ignoring or forgetting in the process that I am also white, educated, middle-class, and so on. Or an African-American male scholar may identify himself as "Black," forgetting that he is also male, middle-class, educated, and so on. Defining our essential identity as our marginalized status, while eclipsing our various privileged "identities," encourages identity groups to replicate almost unconsciously the exclusions of hegemonic culture in all but their one marginalized subject position. So the women's movement often draws the just criticism of being racist and homophobic, or the civil rights movement of being sexist and homophobic. Moreover, the marginalized status position by which the group focuses its identity is often proclaimed as the ultimate scandal of modern Western society, more odious than any other disenfranchised identity. Such rhetoric furthers the replication of hegemonic exclusions and sometimes degenerates into silly and sad debates over who is the most victimized.

To make sense of the mixed status most people experience requires

---

3. One of the major difficulties in recognizing our privileges as privileges is that some of them often require effort on our part to accomplish; thus, they may seem *earned* by us rather than given by the culture. For example, to be well educated certainly requires individual effort, but making that effort really fruitful depends on the schools one is able to attend, the economic comfort of one's family (so one can dedicate all of one's time to school without also working for pay), one's facility with English, the encouragement and attention one gets from teachers, one's daily nutrition, and so on. Yet, because I worked hard for my education, I may be inclined to say that I earned it and anyone else who works hard can do the same, ignoring how far ahead of the game I started by dint of race, economic standing, and so on. One of the best recent metaphors for privilege came in a comment by Texas Democratic governor Ann Richards about Republican former president George Bush: George Bush was born on third base, and all his life he has thought that he hit a triple. The careful analysis of privilege is a much needed study to which I hope to devote a future article.

recognizing that "I" am not a unified self with a single identity over time but instead a constantly shifting, fluid set of subjectivities, occupying a variety of status positions from moment to moment and context to context.[4] "My" status is both relative and highly contextual, for "I" participate in different discourses of power, take on different roles with different expectations for behavior, dress, proper relationships, and so on, continually throughout life. What complicates my awareness of this fluidity is that the variety of status positions I occupy are not separable like beads on a string but instead interpenetrate each other. Thus, for example, the experience of a Hispanic woman cannot be arrived at by adding the experience of a white woman to that of a Hispanic man. Gender, race, ethnicity, class, physical ability, and sexual orientation all conspire together to fashion qualitatively different experiences vis-à-vis hegemonic culture. Such interpenetration, besides confounding analysis, indicates the profound interconnections of the hegemonic system as a whole: no part is finally separable from any other, a crucial point for all liberation movements to recognize.

In relation to the overall hegemonic ideal, the mixed-status majority find themselves in a perpetual state of divided interests. My marginalized subject positions force me to experience the anomalies and negativities of the system and thus to see it as a cultural construction designed to privilege fully only a few. However, my dominant subject positions encourage me to naturalize and affirm the system, or at least part of it, because I have a personal investment in seeing it as a whole survive. Most people, then, are both disadvantaged by the culture and thus critical of it and, at the same time, also benefit from it and thus want it to prosper. In my view, such a divided situation inevitably encourages identity groups or liberation movements to adopt a moderating and narrowly reformative stance toward dominant culture rather than a revolutionary one. The goal all too often becomes not changing the system as a whole but reforming the one "unjust" element affecting me so that my essential marginalized identity will no longer be disenfranchised.

But is such piecemeal reformation really desirable or indeed even possible? I believe that it is not and, further, that the attempt to reform only one subject position ultimately serves to confirm and strengthen the status quo of the system in its entirety. Were it possible to recuperate one negative subject position, let us say for example women, by bringing it into the center of dominant cultural values (without at the same

---

4. For an excellent discussion of "positionality" as a feminist theory for understanding gendered subjectivity as historically fluid and contextual, thus avoiding essentialism and poststructural "free-play," see L. Alcoff, "Cultural Feminism versus Post-Structuralism: The Identity Crisis in Feminist Theory" *The Academy: Women's Education and Women Studies* (ed. E. Minnich, J. O'Barr, and R. Rosenfeld; Chicago: Univ. of Chicago Press, 1988) 257–88.

time expelling its "opposite" position, men), under the present cultural hegemony only a small minority of women would be fully franchised. Racially and ethnically diverse women, lesbians, physically challenged women, obese women, poor women, unmarried women, old women, lower-class women, and so on, would all continue to be marginalized. The interconnections between elements of the hegemonic system are too thorough for the reform of one position to exert much effect.

Moreover, given the foundation of the current ideological system on binary oppositions, the transfer of one subject position to the center would theoretically, and probably practically, require the delegation of its "opposite" to the margins. In fact, since from a dualistic perspective there can be no center without a "noncenter," the present hegemonic system as a whole demands that *some subject positions always be marginalized.* Under patriarchy some people must always be excluded, denigrated, and disenfranchised. Attempting to reform only one or two elements of the overall system leaves unchallenged its founding notions of dualism, hierarchical thinking, the necessity of exclusions to separate the few from the many, and the existence over time of a stable, unified self. Consequently, such attempts actually strengthen the hegemonic system by accepting uncritically its underlying construction of reality.

Nevertheless, many of the recent feminist studies of the Bible and early Christianity fall into this more reformative mode,[5] and while warnings about the potential of such readings to confirm rather than undermine the system have been sounded,[6] a mainly reformative stance continues to dominate Christian feminist circles. Since most feminist biblical critics clearly evince a mixed-status situation,[7] their divided interests, as suggested above, may encourage a more moderating approach. In addition, most feminist biblical researchers work in institutional contexts that have deeply vested concerns for the survival and growth of European/North American versions of the Christian church and thus the capitalistic, patriarchal system that undergirds it. But perhaps even more important than the institutional setting is the personal involve-

---

5. For a delineation of the reformative position in feminist biblical hermeneutics, see my earlier article, "Defining the Problem: Feminist Hermeneutics and the Bible," *Semeia* 28 (1983) 113–26.

6. For an analysis of the dangers of what she terms "neoorthodoxy" in feminist studies, see E. Schüssler Fiorenza, *In Memory of Her: A Feminist Theological Reconstruction of Christian Origins* (New York: Crossroad, 1983) 14–21. For more recent discussions of the moderating and reformative approach of much feminist work on the Bible, see S. Greeve Davaney, "Problems with Feminist Theory's Historicity and the Search for Sure Foundations," *Embodied Love: Sensuality and Relationship as Feminist Values* (ed. P. Cooey, S. Farmer, and M. Ross; San Francisco: Harper and Row, 1987) 79–95; and L. Fatum, "Women, Symbolic Universe and Structures of Silence: Challenges and Possibilities in Androcentric Texts," *Studia Theologica* 43 (1989) 61–80.

7. As many publicly recognize; see, for example, E. Schüssler Fiorenza, *But She Said: Feminist Practices of Biblical Interpretation* (Boston: Beacon, 1992) 8.

ment and commitment many Christian and Jewish feminists continue to experience for their faith communities. They find themselves in the deeply problematic position of struggling to remain faithful to their often admittedly destructive traditions while at the same time hoping to purge those traditions of their exclusive, hierarchical, and androcentric tendencies.

If one comes to believe, as I now have, that the destructiveness of the dominant patriarchal culture in the United States to human life and to the life of the world is profoundly *systemic,* then one is forced to recognize that liberation from that danger for any group or individual will come only through the demise of the system of hierarchical dualism as a whole. One's own privileges within the system and, I believe, even one's loyalties to communities of faith cannot be allowed to outweigh either one's own pain or that of the many others excluded, degraded, violated, or oppressed by current hegemonic values. Nor are piecemeal reforms, which leave the basic construction of reality intact, sufficient or effective. From such a radical perspective on the kind of thinking and action required for liberation, how are normative or influential cultural texts like the Bible to be read? What, in these terms, would constitute a liberative reading and what would not? To those issues I now turn.

Reading for Liberation: Reading as Cultural Treason

To some extent, it is clearly true to say if a reading of the Bible is done by a member of a marginalized group and is seriously regarded by hegemonic society, then it is liberative, for at the very least the legitimacy of a voice previously denied a hearing is recognized. Since the granting of such legitimacy questions the exclusive practices of the dominant discourse, the increasing presence of persons embodying negative subject positions in traditionally centrist institutions and publications cannot help but pose some challenge to hegemonic values. However, the mere presence of formerly unheard voices is generally insufficient to shake the hierarchical, dualistic foundations of patriarchy, as the limited accomplishments of the past twenty years of the women's and the civil rights movements demonstrate. While there are undoubtedly many reasons for this insufficiency, two readily come to mind.

First, since hegemonic society *grants* legitimacy to marginalized voices, it retains control over both who is allowed to speak and what they are allowed to say. The very common and generally well-founded charge of "tokenism" refers to this situation. Only a few well-groomed "outsiders" are permitted access to hegemonic institutions, and their legitimacy is *always* open to question. For women in academic settings, this questioning often takes the form of charges concerning the non-seriousness of feminist studies and the importance of establishing their credentials in other areas of "real" scholarship. Anxiety over their perpetually tentative legitimacy within the dominant discourse may be so great for some marginalized individuals that they actively seek to separate themselves and their work from anything related to their negative subject positions.

Second, when the quantity and quality of protest by marginalized voices become so intense that even those who enjoy the full privileges of hegemonic status begin to feel uncomfortable; when, in other words, the ideology of paternal care for the "naturally" inferior begins to sound like oppression and denigration even to the "naturally" superior, patriarchy tends to divert or co-opt the main themes of the protest in order to redirect and neutralize them. In contemporary U.S. society such a drive is well under way on many fronts. Three brief examples can illustrate the range of this ideological backlash.[8] In the academy, just as marginalized voices were starting to be heard in the mid-1980s, American deconstructionists and others began arguing that no voice had value or legitimacy in supplying meaning for a text. The right of anyone even to offer a textual reading is now often attacked as theoretically unsound, thus, of course, allowing the conventional interpretations of generations of elite male scholars to reign supreme by default.

On another front, as a response to the array of liberation movements, the so-called men's movement has developed in order to decry the alienation of men from their fathers and from their true mythic selves (predictably, according to the writings of some movement leaders, women are largely responsible for this alienation).[9] While billing itself as the *men's* movement, those participating are overwhelmingly white, of Anglo/European descent, and middle- to upper-class. Finally and outrageously, the language of victimization and its concomitant sympathetic regard are increasingly being extended to the aggressor and the oppressor as well as (and in some cases, instead of) the victim. In all forms of media, in scholarly writing, in sermons, and in conversation, people ranging from convicted rapists to respected senior male professors, preachers, and political officials are excusing their actions and their privileges by claiming themselves to be victims of the system. They even profess to be as oppressed by their role expectations as those they molest, kill, and exclude. When the rhetoric of suffering and victimization is stretched to describe those in power, the stinging cries of the less power-

8. For thorough documentation of the strategies of backlash in relation to the women's movement, see S. Faludi, *Backlash: The Undeclared War against American Women* (New York: Crown, 1991).

9. For a feminist response to the men's movement, see K. Leigh Hagan, *Women Respond to the Men's Movement: A Feminist Collection* (San Francisco: Pandora, 1992).

ful are effectively drowned out and well on the way to being completely neutralized.

If the mere presence of marginalized persons in dominant contexts, their claims of being victimized by hegemonic culture, and their attempts to reinterpret cultural artifacts can apparently be negotiated by current ideology without seriously disrupting the system as a whole, what kinds of actions are required to undermine this system? Although I cannot begin to answer the larger concerns raised by that question, I would like to consider the issue in the much more restricted arena of textual interpretation. What kinds of readings of texts, especially influential cultural texts like the Bible, might serve to unsettle the foundations of patriarchy?

Defining liberation as the demise, not the reform, of the present dualistic, hierarchical system of patriarchy, as I have done, requires that reading for liberation aim always at undercutting the status quo. Reading for liberation must employ reading as a form of cultural treason. However, such subversions may be accomplished in a wide variety of ways. For example, any interpretation that denies the naturalness of patriarchy by pointing out the constructed quality of its version of reality would challenge one of the foremost strategies of hegemonic culture. Readings that demonstrate the arbitrary nature of binary oppositions by showing, perhaps, that actual alternatives are generally more than two and not necessarily opposed would also be important. Moreover, liberative readings might analyze the differing consequences of recommended ethical acts for characters in relation to matters such as gender, race, ethnicity, class, and sexual orientation in order to exhibit their lack of universal applicability; they might reveal the gaps or silences in historical records to underscore the selective basis of history; or they might chart the variety of cultural constructions of power over the centuries to confirm the contextuality of social roles and thus undercut claims for normative archetypes.

Since most of the highly regarded texts of contemporary hegemonic culture (its literary "canon") and certainly the writings of the Bible are profoundly androcentric and hierarchical and deeply imbued with patriarchal values, they cannot be read simply as authoritative or normative visions of life as it should be. They may still prove useful for liberation purposes, however, for they can be read as resources for discerning and learning the characteristic strategies of patriarchal logic in order to name and refute them. For instance, patriarchal ideology generally attempts to hide or cover up the real sources of power in social situations in order either to show the male hero as above the fray or to further denigrate marginalized characters as the instigators of conflict or dishonor. In Luke 10:38-42, the friction between Martha and Mary occurs only because of the social privilege of the dominant male, Jesus, to transfer the servicing of his own needs onto any available woman, but the narrative contrasts the actions of the two women rather than suggesting any criticism of Jesus for not taking care of himself or at the least not excusing others from doing it for him. Likewise, in Genesis 21, the narrator places the onus on Sarah for casting out Hagar and Ishmael, depicting the conflict as one between the two women, all the while ignoring the fact that the entire situation is controlled by the desire of Abraham, the patriarch, to have a son and heir. Power and privilege reside in the hands of the dominant males, but the inevitable difficulties their privileges create are blamed on less powerful ones who are required to serve or obey them.

The killing of John the Baptist in Mark 6:14-29 is a quite blatant example of a similar "scapegoating" strategy. Herod is the only one who has the power to order John's death, and he, in fact, is the one who does just that. However, the narrator places the blame for his death on Herodias, who through her daughter merely makes a request that Herod decides for his own reasons to accept and act upon. In much the same way, Mark excuses Pilate, the Roman official, from his actual responsibility for ordering the death of Jesus (only the Romans could do that) by blaming the "envy" of the Jewish religious leaders (15:1-15) and the crowds. In both instances those possessing real power over life and death are shielded from responsibility for their actions by focusing on the desires of those who ultimately have no power. In order for hegemonic culture to maintain the positive image of the powerful few, those few must be consistently disconnected from the frightful consequences of systemic injustice.

Occasionally, hegemonic texts reflect rather openly and naively the culturally constructed nature of patriarchal reality. For example, in Hesiod's *Theogony*, the eighth-century BCE poem recounting the origins of the world and of the Greek gods, Aphrodite, the goddess of female sexual seductiveness, is created from the severed genitals of Sky, the father of the first generation of Greek gods, the Titans.[10] Later when Zeus, Sky's reigning grandson, is tricked by Prometheus into taking the poorer portion of meat at a feast with men, Zeus repays the insult by creating woman to be the bane of man's existence on earth.[11] In both stories, "woman" as man's sexual object and craved but hated wife is clearly presented as a *male* creation. Hesiod's story dramatizes, probably unintentionally, the cultural truth that men have created "woman" out of their own impulses and, in Aphrodite's case, out of their own sexual drives as the "other" they desire and need. "Woman" in patriarchy is a

---

10. Hesiod *Theogony* 154–210. For a comprehensive study of Hesiod's work as a whole, see M. L. West, *Hesiod's Theogony* (Oxford: Clarendon, 1966).

11. Hesiod *Theogony* 512–616.

culturally constructed gender role devised by and for men; it has little to do with who or what females may or may not be in their own right. This example of the creation of Aphrodite out of male flesh may illuminate the creation of woman out of man in Gen 2:21-25.[12] The construction of woman from the rib of *ha-'adam* is not a natural birth, in which all human beings, male and female, are born from women, but a cultural birth of the gender role "woman" as helper and companion for man. The Yahwist narrator seems to suggest something of the kind by providing only the man with a family heritage, a biological source (Gen 2:24); "woman" after all comes from male fantasy, not from biology.

Reading for Liberation: Reading from Multiple Perspectives

Besides analyzing texts in these and other culturally treasonable ways, readings for liberation can also emphasize the multiplicity of possible readings individuals and groups can construe for any one text. However, since the existence of multiple readings for texts has been a constant aspect of all textual interpretation,[13] as seen by the many controversies over which of the various proposed interpretations of a biblical text is the *right* one,[14] that existence alone does no harm to the status quo. These perpetual arguments over multiple readings arise from the fundamental ambiguity inherent in all textual interpretations. All texts, even prosaic ones such as toy assembly instructions, indeed all communications, have the potential of being construed in multiple ways. Further, since reading, like other communications, is always done within specific cultural, social, and historical contexts, those different contexts shape the reading process and form an important source of multiple interpretations. Thus, the assertion of having the *right* interpretation of a text should be understood as a claim about the cultural, social, and historical dominance of one context over all others. However, hegemonic culture has instigated and disputed such claims for centuries without difficulty. But what if the claims come from those occupying marginalized subject positions? Would that subvert patriarchy?

In some circles of biblical scholarship within the past few years, biblical interpretations presented by people identified with marginalized

12. For a very different feminist reading of this event that attempts to reappropriate the story for women, see P. Trible, *God and the Rhetoric of Sexuality* (Philadelphia: Fortress Press, 1978) 94–105.

13. For the Bible, see my earlier discussion of this issue in *Sowing the Gospel: Mark's World in Literary-Historical Perspective* (Minneapolis: Fortress Press, 1989) 7–13.

14. For a discussion of the problems raised for the Gospel of Mark when one searches for a right reading among its many conflicting interpretations, see R. Morgan with J. Barton, *Biblical Interpretation* (Oxford Bible Series; Oxford: Oxford Univ. Press, 1988) 230–38.

subject positions have gained a greater hearing. Feminist, womanist, lesbian, Hispanic, *mujerista,* African-American, Asian-American, as well as African, Asian, and Latin or South American interpretations of the Bible have grown in number and influence, as a glance at the program of the Society of Biblical Literature's annual meeting confirms. Since the increase in such work radically questions the exclusivity of hegemonic discourse, its overall effect is liberative. Nevertheless, there is a proverb I heard often in the early days of the women's movement: Be careful how you define your place, for you will very likely be told to stay in it.[15] The dangerous infiltration of patriarchal constructs can already be observed in responses to this work and also, unfortunately, within some of the work itself in the emerging tendency to essentialize and rigidify the perspectives coming from each marginalized subject position.

Even though in the last few years the women's movement has had to recognize that there is no "essential" woman, no one identity that all women share,[16] and that the attempt to enforce such a single experience is another example of hierarchical domination, some feminists and some critics of feminism continue to maintain that there is only one feminist point of view and that all women qua women must share it. Increasingly, interpreters closely identified with a specific context run the risk of being intellectually ghettoized by the dominant discourse. Everything a woman writes is from the "woman's" perspective. Everything an African American writes is from the "Black" perspective. Everything a lesbian writes is from the lesbian perspective. And so on. Furthermore, since patriarchy contends that these perspectives express the single, essential identity of those occupying each marginalized status position, their particular perspective is the *only* way they can view everything, and only they can view things that way. The logical result of such perspectivalism is readings of value only to the marginalized group involved (women write for women, Asians for Asians, and so on) and, therefore, most importantly, readings that can be dismissed by those of the dominant discourse.

But I would argue along with many other feminists that there is no one feminist perspective or feminist reading of a text, and since other liberation movements face similar issues, I would also want to argue that there is no one womanist perspective, no one Hispanic perspective, no one Asian perspective, no one lesbian perspective, and so on. Insisting that the many different people who identify with one marginalized subject position must share only one single experience of reality replicates anew the oppressiveness and exclusivity of hegemonic culture. More-

---

15. I am indebted to a conversation with T. S. Benny Liew, Ph.D. student in the Graduate Department of Religion of Vanderbilt University, for provoking my thinking on the dangers of rigidly defined identity politics.

16. See, for example, the excellent study on essentialism by E. Spelman, *Inessential Woman: Problems of Exclusion in Feminist Thought* (Boston: Beacon, 1988).

over, by confirming the us versus them, or dominant versus "other," binary opposition of patriarchal logic, such essentialism also serves to confirm the status quo!

One can see that rigid perspectivalism accommodates hegemonic values when one observes that some white, male, Anglo/European scholars are now also willing to agree that what they and their colleagues write and have written for generations is from a white, male, Anglo/European perspective, not a universal one. However, such confessions neither negate nor remove the hegemony which that perspective has been exercising for centuries. Indeed, in some cases such confessions may actually serve as the humble equivalent of the more common hegemonic boast that all Western culture is their creation and possession, once again causing all the women, racial and ethnic minorities, gay men and lesbians, and so on, who have contributed to the development and vitality of hegemonic culture, even when it failed to franchise them fully, to become silent and invisible.

To avoid the clear dangers of a rigid perspectivalism co-opted by dualistic, hierarchical structures, one must exorcise the illusion of the unified self with a single, essential identity and recognize instead that we all occupy a fluidity of subject positions vis-à-vis hegemonic culture. For most of us, some of those positions are marginalized, but some are also dominant. Consequently, most of us (though not all) have multiple *perspectives* from which we may interpret texts. As subjects of dominant cultural positions, we know and understand hegemonic perspectives, and as participants in marginalized cultural positions, we know and understand peripheral perspectives as well. We do not exist in one social context but in many. I contend that it is our very refusal to be definitively "placed" in either a superior or an inferior subject position or social context that will ultimately prove most disruptive to the status quo. Hence, it is not the production of multiple interpretations of a text in itself that is liberative, it is instead the reading of texts *with equal seriousness* from multiple perspectives that may subvert the designs of patriarchy. And such readings may be one of the special contributions of educated (a positive hegemonic value) individuals identified with marginalized subject positions (a negative hegemonic value).

Two important points need to be made about this contention that reading from multiple *perspectives* may prove liberative. First, whether the interpretation is carried out within the context of dominant discourses or within the context of marginal discourses, it must be presented with and accorded the same seriousness of regard. Since hierarchical dualism tends to view only dominant readings as serious and all others as trivial, insisting on the equally important role of both kinds of readings requires explicit argumentation. Feminist history is as important as hegemonic history; interpretations for popular consumption are as weighty as elite interpretations; minority insights are as comprehensive as majority insights. Moreover, free and constant movement among one's shifting perspectives should be encouraged, since the disruption of patriarchal conventions depends on the inability to fix individuals and groups into stable superior/inferior, winner/loser, elite/common, dominant/marginalized domains.

Second, since in the vast majority of cases educated readers identified with marginalized subject positions undergo their academic formation process in the profoundly hegemonic contexts of colleges, universities, and seminaries, it is far easier for them to read from a hegemonic perspective than from a peripheral one. Reading is, after all, a learned skill, taught according to conventional rules devised by the cultural elite of any literate society. It is thus a kind of socialization into the values and stereotypical roles expected by that society. Many people relegated to deviant subject positions are not taught to read at all or not taught to read well, and those few who do learn to read well are often so thoroughly socialized in the process that they cannot conceive of any alternative ways to read texts. Learning to recognize hegemonic "textual harassment"[17] and become "resisting readers"[18] of patriarchal texts is an additional task every interpreter from a marginalized perspective must undertake. The failure to accomplish this new learning may be yet another reason why many feminist readings of the Bible are less thoroughgoing and liberative than I would like them to be.

Not only do the "canonical" texts of Western culture communicate hierarchical values and androcentric worldviews, but the very conventions of good reading taught within the culture encourage their acceptance. For instance, readers are taught to suspend their disbelief in order to enter the narrative world of the text. That suspension generally includes a disconnection from the critical issues of a reader's own social environment, which may be ridiculed by the text (as is often the case for women) or confirmed by the text as natural (as is the case for slavery in some biblical texts). Moreover, readers are instructed to identify with the hero or with the ethical perspectives of the omniscient narrator/ implied author, even when those characters or viewpoints degrade and violate characters from the reader's own social locations. To be counted as good readers, individuals from marginalized groups often have to accept a whole book full of verbal abuse. Although no one in the present cultural situation can avoid learning these and other conventions, and indeed such learning must be used to produce textual interpretations

---

17. A phrase coined by M. Jacobus, "Is There a Woman in This Text?" *New Literary History* 14 (1982) 119.

18. For an early analysis of what this entails for women, see J. Fetterley, *The Resisting Reader: A Feminist Approach to American Literature* (Bloomington: Indiana Univ. Press, 1978).

that are convincing to other similarly trained readers, individuals from marginalized perspectives must learn to read both with *and against* such conventions in order to create compelling readings for liberation.

Reading for liberation is obviously no easy task, but the alternative for women, racial and ethnic minorities, gay men and lesbians, and all other subjects of marginalized status in contemporary society is, in my opinion, much worse.

The God of Jesus
in the Gospel Sayings Source

_____ Antoinette Clark Wire ___

The place from which I read the New Testament as a woman training Christian ministers in California at the end of the twentieth century
could be described in three ways. It is a place where churchgoing is as
little built-in to the culture as anywhere in the Americas, making the
new interest in everything spiritual stand out with particular sharpness.
People are eager for voices speaking of God at the very time that we
who teach religion have finally managed to reduce our claims to the
human. It is also a place after the second round of modern women's liberation where the male God still sits firmly on the throne in all major
religious communities, unperturbed by recurring loss of his male pronouns. Our ancient texts have themselves been exposed as products of
patriarchal power at the very time we have come to see that reform depends on reclaiming suppressed tradition. Finally, it is a place of wealth
in a world of poverty at a time when one superpower has risked becoming one among many nations while the remaining superpower plays
at world military empire, fostering luxury consumption by poverty and
debt at home and tribute from debtors abroad. This challenges all centers of learning in North America to envision new patterns of economic
and gender relations consonant with who God is and who we are, and
to rebuild the religious commitment and political alliances that can get
us from here to there.

To begin reading from this place of eagerness for God in a humanistic
world, of eagerness for new relations of women and men in a patriarchal
world, and of eagerness for justice in an imperial world, I turn as a historian of religion to another time and place. There the crisis in these ways
was no less great and people grappled with it, or—to speak from faith—
God sent prophets to interpret and judge and save. Specifically I turn to
the earliest major collection of Jesus' sayings, called variously the Gospel
Sayings Source, the Double Tradition, or Q (for *Quelle* or "source").
These sayings are usually held to be older than the first Gospel, Mark,

on the basis that the similarities in content and order in the first three Gospels are best explained by Matthew and Luke using Mark, and the material they share that is not in Mark must come from a second, by this time widely available, collection that is largely sayings of Jesus. This source cannot be fully reconstructed because we do not know how much of it Matthew or Luke omitted, but its minimal content can easily be found in the parallel passages of Matthew and Luke that are not taken from Mark, and its order is best taken from Luke because Matthew so actively reorders source materials.[1]

I differ from many interpreters in insisting that this source must be read as a whole. Recent efforts of scholars to distinguish early and late materials in the source are unconvincing.[2] On the one hand, the sages of our time see the historical Jesus as a sage and read the aphorisms and paradoxical sayings of this source to be Jesus' voice, but the judgment sayings they take to be voices of a later decade when the community was rejected and turned to gentile mission.[3] On the other hand, today's prophets see Jesus as a prophet of the social transformation of Israel, announcing a coming kingdom of justice.[4] They take the teachings that cannot have served that aim to be secondary. I do not want

---

1. I follow Luke's order with three exceptions: Luke 16:16 and 17:33 I put in Matthew's sequence after Luke 7:28 and 14:27, respectively, because Luke has quite clearly joined them with other materials. Also I follow Matthew and place Luke 11:52 after 11:46 for form-critical reasons. My analysis of the Sayings Source has been facilitated by the texts of Matthew and Luke in F. Neirynck's *Q-Synopsis: The Double Tradition Passages in Greek* (Louvain: Leuven Univ. Press, 1988), and J. S. Kloppenborg, *Q Parallels: Synopsis, Critical Notes and Concordance* (Sonoma, Calif.: Polebridge, 1988), the latter providing also an English translation of the Matthew and Luke texts that he considers the basis for Q.

2. Since E. Käsemann's proposal that Jewish-Christian apocalyptic fervor first shaped Christian theology from Jesus' nonapocalyptic sayings (*New Testament Questions of Today* [Philadelphia: Fortress Press, 1969] 66–139), multiple theories of the evolution of Q have developed, the most common projecting an early Jewish-Christian and one or more Hellenized redactions of the material (see S. Schulz, *Q: Die Spruch-quelle der Evanglisten* [Zurich: Theologischer Verlag, 1972]). The great difficulty of discerning layers through the way sayings were compiled and occasionally glossed and by comparison with Mark is also recognized by those who practice these methods (Schulz, *Q*, 40–44; J. S. Kloppenborg, *The Formation of Q: Trajectories in Ancient Wisdom Collections* [Philadelphia: Fortress Press, 1987] 96–100).

3. Kloppenborg sees the judgment material linked subsequently to wisdom sayings by catchwords and thematic associations (*Formation of Q*, 317–28). Other studies develop in different ways the depiction of Jesus as sage: B. Mack, *A Myth of Innocence: Mark and Christian Origins* (Philadelphia: Fortress Press, 1988) 53–97; M. Borg, *Jesus, A New Vision: Spirit, Culture and the Life of Discipleship* (San Francisco: Harper and Row, 1987).

4. P. Hoffmann, *Studien zur Theologie der Logienquelle* (Münster: Aschendorff, 1972); M. Sato, *Q und Prophetie: Studien zur Gattung und Traditionsgeschichte der Quelle Q* (Tübingen: J. C. B. Mohr, 1988); D. Batstone, *From Conquest to Struggle: Jesus of Nazareth in Latin America* (Albany: State Univ. of New York Press, 1991). Some studies that identify the prophetic-apocalyptic tradition as the earliest layer consider that wisdom sayings were integral to this purpose.

to deny possible development in the community that transmitted this tradition, but community history should not be built by projecting our struggle between sages and prophets into a time and place when wisdom and judgment sayings were not sharply distinguished from each other.[5] Better that we consider the Sayings Source as a whole and allow this Jesus—and we cannot get behind this community's Jesus—to share in his culture's mixtures.

The Sayings Source presents us with a theology that is surprising because it is different from twentieth-century theology. Following Paul and the early creeds, interpreters in our century have preferred to focus on Jesus' dying and rising as the heart of the Gospel, and more recently they have looked to Mark as the first written narrative of Jesus' life, or to the more church-oriented theologies of Matthew, Luke, and John. At the risk of sounding as though only this Sayings Source reflects the one true Jesus, I want to focus strictly on it and ask how Jesus depicts God in this early tradition. I see here a remarkable vision of God active for good in a human world of great injustice. In order to let these sayings speak for themselves, I have made a complete reconstruction of them in English in the indented passages below. In each of the three parts of this essay, the Sayings Source is presented in three sections, with introductions before each of the nine sections and comments from my place of reading at the end. I ask that you read them from your place and consider what they could mean in our world.

Part I: All Wisdom's Children

John and Jesus

The first third of the Sayings Source appears to be about John the Baptist and Jesus, beginning with John speaking of Jesus as the coming one, and ending with Jesus speaking of John as the greatest of the prophets. But a sharper look shows that neither one is focusing on the other but on what God is announcing through them both—as the intervening material known from the Sermon on the Mount highlights. If the two Jewish prophets and the question of their mutual relation frame this first third of the Sayings Source, then God and the people of Israel and their relation provoked by the prophetic announcements are its subjects.

---

5. The close ties of the aphoristic collections to judgments of the "divine Sophia" are demonstrated by R. A. Piper, *Wisdom in the Q Tradition: The Aphoristic Teaching of Jesus* (New York: Cambridge Univ. Press, 1989) 161–96. How wisdom and prophetic judgment sayings appeared together in this period is shown by E. E. Johnson, *The Function of Apocalyptic and Wisdom Traditions in Romans 9–11* (Atlanta: Scholars Press, 1989) 55–109, 123–39.

John's opening attack on those who come to be baptized ("Brood
of vipers, who warned you to flee from the coming wrath? Bear fruit
to match your repentance... ") shows that some hearers do not think
they need full repentance. John tells them that the axe is already set at
the root of the fruitless tree and needs only to be lifted to fell it and
consign it to the fire. Or, in another image, the shovel is in hand to
clear the threshing floor and heave the wheat into the barn and the chaff
into the fire. Though the Baptist names God explicitly only as the one
who can replace them "from these stones" if they rest on their laurels—
God the Life-giver at work—John's prophecy climaxes in the two images
of God the Life-taker with axe and shovel in hand ready to burn the
deadwood. This will be a baptism of spirit and fire to make John's words
and water look mild. Whether the agent of this firestorm is conceived as
divine or human is not clear. But the issue is the arrival of one who will
expose not so much the wicked and indifferent as the confident who
feign repentance without bearing its fruits.

Jesus is introduced by the story in which Satan tempts him with the
lure, "If you are God's son... " Only Satan calls Jesus "Son of God" in
the Sayings Source, and Jesus responds from Scripture very much in line
with John's preaching against presumption. He says human beings do
not live by bread alone; human beings are not to serve their own glory
but God only; human beings are not to test God's care for them. Jesus
defines himself as a human being, and Satan leaves him.[6]

Text: *John and Jesus (from Luke 3:7-9, 16-17; 4:1-13;*
and Matthew parallels)

He [John] said to those who came out to be baptized by him,
Brood of vipers, who warned you to flee from the coming wrath?
Bear fruit to match your repentance, and don't begin saying to
each other, We have Abraham for our father, for I tell you that
God can raise children of Abraham from these rocks. Already the
axe is set at the root of the trees, so every tree not bearing good
fruit is cut out and thrown into the fire.

I myself baptize you with water, but one stronger than I is coming whose sandals I am not worthy to carry. He will baptize you
with holy spirit and fire. His shovel is in his hand to clear off his

---

6. The references in the headings that precede the texts below are to Luke's version
of the common Sayings Source of Matthew and Luke, here reconstructed and translated.
Paragraph indents indicate transition from one reference to another, and blessings and
woes are also indented. Scriptural quotes are in bold type. I translate as literally as
possible except where noted, choosing between the synonyms and different syntax of
the two Gospel writers on the basis of the general usage of the Double Tradition over
against usage distinctive to each author.

threshing ground and gather the wheat into his barn, but the chaff he will burn with unquenchable fire.

Jesus was led in the spirit in the desert for forty days tested by the devil. He ate nothing and at the end he was hungry. And the devil said to him, If you are God's Son, tell this rock to become bread. But Jesus answered, It is written, **the human being does not live by bread alone.** Then he led him to Jerusalem and set him on the parapet of the temple and said to him, If you are God's Son, throw yourself down, for it is written, **He will command his angels concerning you and on their hands they will lift you up lest you trip on a rock.** Jesus said to him, It is said, **You shall not test the Lord your God.** Then the devil lead him up and showed him all the kingdoms of the world and their glory and said to him, All these I will give to you if you worship me. Jesus said to him, It is written, **You shall worship the Lord your God and him alone shall you serve.** Then the devil left him.

Jesus and the People When Satan leaves him, Jesus begins to tell the poor and abused that God's inheritance belongs to them and that they will be full and laugh and be rewarded with the prophets who were also abused. I translate "God's inheritance" rather than "God's kingdom" or "reign" because the phrase in these sayings is never associated with God's ruling or judging but always with God bestowing a kingdom or inheritance, as once upon David. By saying God's inheritance is theirs, Jesus assures the poor that the land or resources necessary for common livelihood and independence belong to them and to all who are incorporated into the family line of the prophets by their poverty or abuse. This includes those whose name is dirt on account of "the human being." I translate Jesus' self-designation as "the human being" rather than "Son of Man" since "daughter or son of" means being "one of that kind" in Semitic languages, and Hebrew uses this very phrase to signify the human species.

The woes that follow the Beatitudes explain that God's inheritance is not arbitrarily withheld from the rich but has already been given them in full: "Woe to you rich since you have what is coming to you." As the rich we may be relieved to be left out of the new dispensation when we hear what it is like: "To the one who slaps you on the cheek, turn the other cheek, and to the one who takes your coat, do not deny your shirt." It is this loving of enemies and praying for abusers that will show that the poor are "sons of the Highest, who raises his sun on evil and good and rains on just and unjust." Their generosity is made possible, and also necessary, by the unlimited generosity of this Father: "Be merciful," or translated more sharply, "Withhold nothing, even as your Father withholds nothing." Because their Father does not judge, they cannot judge others. Jesus' remaining words return to themes from the Baptist and favor Matthew's rendition of the same sentence, "Be perfect," or "Be whole, as your Father is whole." Be the good tree that produces good fruit, the whole person who not only hears but does what is right and so builds a house founded on rock.

The integrity of this life lived from within the inheritance of God is expressed in the language of a father-son relation. This reflects a social setting where the slave or servant—and one must add the daughter or wife—is seen to have limited access to the father's resources. But Jesus tells them that they are sons who can treat what is their Father's as their own (according to a saying later in this Source, no one knows father as son does, nor son as father), and it is bound to please this Father if his sons become like him. Because of the peculiar prodigal nature of their Father, the poor and abused can afford not to withhold anything asked of them, even the shirt off their backs. From our distant vantage point in time and social class we see that this could be used to legitimate their abuse (and it will be), but here they take up the claim to be like this God before they can be taken—and put to us the question whether or not God is like this, literally "withholding nothing."

Text: *Jesus and the People (from Luke 6:20-26, 27-36, 37-42, 43-49; and Matthew parallels)*

And he said,
    Blessed are you poor since God's inheritance belongs to you. Blessed are you who are hungry now, for you will be full. Blessed are you who are crying now, for you will laugh.
    Blessed are you when people hate you and insult you and treat your name as dirt on account of the human being. Rejoice and jump for joy since your reward in heaven is great, because that is how their fathers treated the prophets.
    But woe to you rich since you have what is coming to you.
    Woe to you who are full now, for you will be hungry.
    Woe to you who laugh now, for you will mourn and cry.
    Woe when all people speak well of you, because that is how their fathers treated the false prophets.[7]
    But I tell you, Love your enemies and pray for those who abuse you. To the one who slaps you on the cheek, turn the other cheek, and to the one who takes your coat, do not deny your shirt. To those who ask, give, and from those who take your things do not

---

7. I include the woes in Q although Matthew does not use them because the form mirrors the blessings so closely and because Matthew incorporates in his beatitudes the terms from the woes that I translate "what is coming to you," "mourn," and "speak [well] of you," making it probable that he knows the woes from the common source.

demand them back. Just as you want people to treat you, treat them the same. For if you love those who love you, what credit is that to you? Don't even tax collectors do the same? And if you do good to those who do you good, what credit is that to you? Don't even the Gentiles do the same? But be sons of the Highest, who raises his sun on evil and good and rains on just and unjust. Withhold nothing, as your Father withholds nothing.

Do not judge, so that you will not be judged. For the measure that you measure with will be used to measure you. A student is not above the teacher. It is enough that a student be like the teacher. The blind cannot lead the blind, can they? Will they not both fall into a pit? Why do you see the speck in your friend's eye but not notice the beam in your own eye? How can you say to your friend, Let me get the speck out of your eye, and, look, there is a beam in your own eye? Hypocrite, first take the beam out of your eye, and then you will see clearly to take the speck out of your friend's eye.[8]

A good tree does not make bad fruit, nor does a bad tree make good fruit. Every tree is known by its fruit. Are grapes gathered from thorn-bushes or figs from thistles? The good person from the heart's good storehouse produces good, and the evil from the evil produces evil. For the mouth speaks from the heart's overflow. But why do you call me, Master, master, and not do the things I say? Whoever hears my words and does them is like someone building a house on rock. The floodwater burst against that house, and it did not fall, because it was founded on rock. But whoever has heard and not acted is like someone who built a house on sand. The floodwater burst against it and it fell, and its fall was great.

Jesus and John The transition back to the issue of Jesus' relation to John the Baptist is provided by the story of Jesus healing the centurion's slave at a distance. Jesus praises the centurion's faith not because he is a gentile convert to Judaism, let alone to Christianity, but because his confidence in God's resources for his slave's well-being exposes all of those who know God and expect nothing. When John's disciples then ask whether Jesus is the one that is coming—the one with axe in hand to cut and burn the deadwood—Jesus answers by pointing to this slave and others just healed, and adds, "Blessed is the person not scandalized with me." Could we say that he sees the great discrepancy between himself and John's fire-baptizer, and yet he points to a certain complementarity?

---

8. I reverse Luke's order of the student saying and the blind saying for clarification and with slight support from Matthew's use in that order. I translate "brother" with "friend" in the teaching referring to the eye because neither the family member nor the fellow believer suggested by the English word "brother" is indicated.

As John said, God is gathering wheat into barns *and* burning chaff; good news for the disabled may be the flip side of bad news for the privileged.

This picture of John and Jesus as complementary is confirmed in what follows. Jesus asks his hearers why they went out to see John—surely not to see a king in soft robes but to see a prophet. Jesus calls him "more than a prophet" and the greatest of all "born of women"—yet, he adds, "the least in God's inheritance is greater." In this context Jesus cannot be presenting himself as the least who is greater than John because he goes on to say that ever since John's time people are *forcing* their way into God's inheritance, a verb that suggests mobs who will not be kept out. The least of this crowd must be greater than the greatest prophet because they are the ones who have heard and responded.

The first third of the Sayings Source ends here by substituting for the pseudodichotomy of John and Jesus the true dichotomy between those who hear them and those who do not. The tax collectors and prostitutes who vindicated God by accepting John's baptism become the basis for Jesus' attack on "this generation" who saw them repent and still were not moved. The people of "this generation" are compared to children who sit down at the crossroads and shout accusations at each other for not playing funeral *and* for not playing wedding. Jesus explains the parable, "For John came neither eating nor drinking and you say, He has a demon! The human being came eating and drinking and you say, Look, a freeloader and a drunk, a friend of tax collectors and sinners! Yet Wisdom is vindicated by all her children."

"This generation" takes John's stringency and Jesus' laxity in eating and drinking and plays them off against each other, yet Jesus says, "Wisdom is vindicated by all her children," or in a more homey translation, "All Wisdom's children do her proud."[9] "All" indicates a wider group than just Jesus and John, probably the crowd who do hear them and press into God's inheritance. God appears here not as the generous Father but as the unacknowledged Wisdom of God, a mother dependent on "all her children" to prove her right. She is attacked in the insults to her children, the prophets who are announcing God's inheritance. But she is also vindicated by her children who are rushing into God's inheritance when they hear and repent and begin to bear the fruits of a prodigal life.

In this first part of the Sayings Source two Jewish prophets have been juxtaposed, but it turns out that they are complementary in announcing God's inheritance. Two depictions of God have simply been juxtaposed, that of the Father who withholds nothing, and of Wisdom who claims vindication. The question is, are they also complementary?

---

9. The female characterization of God's Wisdom also has a long history (Prov 1:20-33; 8:1—9:18; Sirach 24; Wisdom 6–10; 1 Enoch 42).

Text: *Jesus and John (from Luke 7:1-10, 18-23, 24-28; 16:16
[in Matthew's order]; 7:29-35; and Matthew parallels)*

When he went into Capernaum a centurion approached and entreated him, My slave is sick and about to die. And he said to him, I will come and heal him. The centurion said, Master, I am not worthy for you to come under my roof. Only say a word and my boy will be healed. For I myself am a man under authority who has soldiers under me, and I say to one, Go, and he goes, and to another, Come, and he comes, and to my slave, Do this, and he does it. Hearing this, Jesus marveled and said to those following him, I say to you, not in Israel have I found such faith. And the boy was healed at that hour.

And hearing all these things, John sent his disciples saying, Are you the one who is coming or do we look for another? And Jesus answered them, Go tell John what you hear and see. Blind see again and lame walk, lepers are cleansed and deaf hear, dead are raised and poor tell good news, and blessed is the person not scandalized with me.[10]

When they went he began to speak to the crowds about John, What did you go out into the desert to see? A reed shaken by the wind? But what did you go out to see? A man dressed in soft clothes? Look, those are in palaces. But what did you go out to see? A prophet? Yes, I tell you, and more than a prophet. This is the one about whom it is written, **Look, I am sending my messenger before your face who will prepare your way before you.** I say to you, there is no one born of women greater than John, but the least in God's inheritance is greater than he.

The law and the prophets spoke until John. Since then the good news about God's inheritance is being announced, and everyone forces their way into it.

The tax collectors and prostitutes vindicated God by accepting John's baptism. But even when you saw this, you did not repent and believe him. What can I compare this generation to? It is like children sitting down in the marketplace and shouting at each other, We played the flute and you didn't dance! We mourned and you didn't cry! For John came neither eating nor drinking and you say, He has a demon! The human being came eating and drinking and you say, Look, a freeloader and a drunk, a friend of tax collectors and sinners! Yet Wisdom is vindicated by all her children.

---

10. The verb "telling good news" is read as middle voice. This sentence is quite different from Luke 4:18, where the passive form appears.

Part II: Representing God

Sent and Supplied

The central third of the Sayings Source can be called "Representing God." First we see those pressing into God's inheritance themselves sent out and supplied, then rejected, and finally assured. Jesus sends them throughout Galilee to heal and carry the news of God's inheritance, having warned them that the human being they follow, unlike fox or bird, has no place to sleep. Because they have nothing, every house they enter is challenged to care for them and thereby to welcome God's peace. The Sayings Source does not number them or name them, nor even call them disciples, that is, learners, since they are characterized strictly by their function to carry good news and to heal, and this defines who is one of them. Rejection cannot slow them down, and they apparently stir up a dust storm shaking off their sandals from town to town. Their constant rejection is shown by Jesus' lament over their own towns in Galilee that do not feed them. Capernaum and Bethsaida will outclass the great seaports of Tyre and Sidon in the sin-city category on judgment day— since, as Jesus puts it, whoever rejects his representatives rejects him, and whoever rejects him rejects the one who sent him.

Before he identifies this "one who sent me," Jesus returns to the "supply side" and praises God for these representatives: "You hid these things away from the wise and educated and revealed them to infants, yes, Father, just because you wanted to." And he blesses their eyes and ears since they are perceiving what prophets and kings longed to see and hear but never did. Whatever these "infants" want—bread supplied, debts canceled, rescue provided—they need only ask their Father, as Jesus' prayer teaches them. He concludes, "Ask and it will be given to you. . . . If you who are evil know to give good gifts to your children, how much more will the Father from heaven give good things to those who ask!"

Text: *Sent and Supplied (from Luke 9:57-62; 10:2-12, 13-15, 16, 21-24; 11:2-4, 9-13; and Matthew parallels)*

> And someone said to him, I will follow you wherever you go. And Jesus said to him, foxes have holes and the birds of the sky have nests, but the human being has no place to lay his head. Another said, Master, permit me to go and bury my father. But he said to him, Follow me and let the dead bury their own dead.
>
> He told them, The harvest is great but the workers are few. So beg the owner of the harvest to send workers out into his harvest. Look, I send you as sheep among wolves. Take no money bag, nor sack, nor sandals, nor greet anyone on the way. Whenever you

enter a house say, Peace to this house, and if the people there want peace your peace will rest on them, but if not it will return to you. Stay in the same house, eating and drinking what they do, since the worker is worth a wage. And if a town welcomes you, heal the sick and say to them, God's inheritance has come near you. But if the town does not welcome you, shake off your feet the dust of the town, because I tell you that it will be more bearable on judgment day for Sodom than for that town.

Woe to you, Chorazin! Woe to you, Bethsaida! For if the acts of power done in you were done in Tyre and Sidon, they would have long since repented in sackcloth and ashes. But in fact it will be more bearable for Tyre and Sidon in judgment than for you. And you, Capernaum, **you think you will be raised to heaven? You will go down to hell.**

Whoever hears you hears me, and whoever rejects you rejects me. But whoever rejects me rejects the one who sent me.

Jesus said at that hour, I praise you, Father, Master of Heaven and Earth, that you hid these things away from the wise and the educated and revealed them to infants, yes, Father, just because you wanted to. All things have been passed down to me by my Father, and no one knows the son the way the Father does or the Father the way the son does—and those to whom the son wants to make disclosure. Blessed are your eyes for seeing and your ears for hearing! For I tell you that many prophets and kings longed to see the things you see and never saw them, and to hear the things you hear and never heard them.

Pray like this: Father, your name be holy. Your inheritance come. Give us our daily bread each day. And forgive us what we owe as we also forgive those who owe us. And do not lead us into testing.

Ask and it will be given to you, seek and you will find, knock and the door will be opened for you. For everyone who asks receives, the one who seeks finds, and the one who knocks gets in the door. Or will any of you when your son asks for bread give him a stone, or when your daughter asks for a fish give her a snake? So if you who are evil know to give good gifts to your children, how much more will the Father from heaven give good things to those who ask![11]

11. I translate the second, unspecified example as "daughter" on the basis of the inclusive reference to "children" that follows.

Rejected

The central part of the Sayings Source reaches its climax in Jesus' two long retorts to those who reject him on religious grounds. To those who call his exorcism demonic he gives the choice of taking him either as the collapse of Satan's house by casting itself out or as the arrival of God's inheritance. His proverbs exclude any middle ground: those who do not gather are scattering; the house without a good spirit will have seven bad ones. For those who want a sign he summons the men of Nineveh and the Queen of Sheba to condemn "this generation" for not recognizing truth and wisdom.

With the warning to watch out lest the very light in them be darkness, he moves into a lament over the fate of the "separatists" and lawyers who are most exemplary in preserving the religious tradition. The care with which they are religious (keeping clean, tithing, appearing in public, holding people responsible to God, guarding God's inheritance, building memorials to the prophets) is contrasted step by step to the functional results of their conduct—extortion, injustice, people burdened, God's inheritance locked up, prophets killed and buried. The woes end in a judicial sentence: "Therefore God's Wisdom said, I will send them prophets and the wise, and they will kill some of them, so that the blood of all the prophets poured out on the earth might be charged to this generation."

Now we hear the name of the one who sends the prophets, the Wisdom of God, and can understand Jesus' threat: "Whoever rejects you rejects me. But whoever rejects me rejects the one who sent me." Wisdom is the one who sends the prophets and the wise to bring the world to accountability.

Due to the long and lethal history of the use of this verdict of Wisdom about the blood of the prophets, I must state what should be obvious: that it was not directed at an ethnic group or religion but was spoken by a prophet to certain exemplary practitioners within his own religious tradition. Christians who have aimed this against Jews, or we who allow others to do so, are in fact trying to evade the force of its judgment against ourselves as the religious practitioners whose tradition it became. In this way we confirm its truth—as a verdict of exclusion and murder against ourselves. We caution Jesus that our quality-control is not meant to be exclusion, and our building memorials is in no way killing prophets, but Wisdom is unmoved. Her voice that Jesus quotes, "I will send them prophets and the wise, and they will kill some of them, so that the blood of all the prophets...might be charged to this generation," vindicates every person who has been burdened or locked out or killed—especially when it was done under legal or religious cover—and makes the latest generation of gatekeepers, however mild, responsible for all the victims of such "virtue." The converse truth is that those whom Wisdom sends out to be news-carriers of God's inheritance in every time and tradition bear no responsibility for their own rejections or deaths but stand vindicated by Wisdom's verdict against their abusers.

Text: *Rejected (from Luke 11:14-26, 29-32, 33-35, 39-46, 52 [in Matthew's order], 47-48, 49-51; and Matthew parallels)*

When a mute demon was cast out, the mute person spoke and the crowd was astounded, yet some said, It is by Beelzebul the prince of demons that he casts out demons. But knowing their thoughts he told them, Every kingdom divided against itself is laid waste, and if Satan is divided against himself how can his kingdom stand? If I cast out demons by Beelzebul, by whom do your sons cast out?—so they will be your judges. But if it is by God's finger that I cast out demons, then God's inheritance has overtaken you. Whoever is not with me is against me and whoever does not gather with me scatters. When the unclean spirit has come out of a person, it wanders through places with no water seeking rest and not finding any. Then it says, I will go back into my house where I came from. And when it comes it finds everything swept and in order. Then it goes and brings along seven other spirits more evil than itself, and the last state of that person is worse than the first.

Others wanted a sign from him and he said, An evil generation seeks a sign, but no sign will be given it but Jonah's sign. For just as Jonah was, so the human being will be. The Queen of the South will be raised in the judgment with this generation and will condemn it, for she came from the other side of the earth to hear Solomon's wisdom, and, look, something greater than Solomon is here. The men of Nineveh will rise up in the judgment with this generation and condemn it because they repented at Jonah's announcement, and, look, something greater than Jonah is here.

No one lighting a lamp puts it under a bucket but on a lampstand to give everyone in the house light. The eye is the body's lamp. If your eye is sharp, your whole body is lit up. But if it is evil, your body is dark. Look whether the light in you is darkness.

You separatists, you clean the outside of the cup, but the inside is full of extortion. First clean the inside so the outside might be clean.

Woe to you separatists, for you tithe mint and ignore justice. You were expected to do these without ignoring those.

Woe to you. You love the front seat in the synagogues and greetings in the marketplaces.

Woe to you, for you are like disguised graves.

Woe to you lawyers too, for you give people heavy burdens and you do not move them with a finger.

Woe to you lawyers, for you lock up God's inheritance. You don't come in and you don't let people come in.

Woe to you, for you build the tombs of the prophets, but your fathers killed them. So you witness that you are children of your fathers, for they killed them and you build on it.

Therefore God's Wisdom said, I will send them prophets and the wise, and they will kill some of them, so that the blood of all the prophets poured out on the earth might be charged to this generation, from the blood of Abel to the blood of Zechariah who perished between the altar and the temple. Yes, I say to you, it will be charged to this generation.

Afraid and Assured

Though Wisdom's verdict has been pronounced, those she sends out are understandably afraid, and the central part closes with two kinds of assurance for those who represent God. The first comes from the verdict of Wisdom and the impending reversals that will bring to light everything that is hidden. Therefore, it is safer to fear ultimate judgment than death, which is all that people can deliver. Other than the single verdict of Wisdom against those who kill prophets, which I quoted, there is no clear image of God in a judging role in the Sayings Source. Euphemisms are preferred, as in the claim that those who acknowledge the human being will be acknowledged before God's angels, and those who deny will be denied. Even this denying is said to be forgivable, whereas speaking against the Holy Spirit will not be forgiven. The Holy Spirit, who appeared once before with fire in the Baptist's preaching as the instrument of an ultimate baptism or judgment, may signify God as justice. This is also suggested by the feminine gender of both Spirit and Wisdom in the probable earlier Aramaic forms of these sayings. It may be that only the female face of God is able to represent judgment directly because she is seen not as enthroned but as herself abused in every instance of abuse of her children. Speaking against the Holy Spirit may not be forgiven because, as mother of "all her children," the Spirit or Wisdom is the ultimate appeal of the abused and so cannot finally be mocked.

God's other face gives the second kind of assurance, which comes not from judgment but from nature—assurance from sparrows the Father guards and crows the Father feeds, assurance from the lilies dressed by God more finely than Solomon, though they are here today and gone tomorrow. Although no excuse is possible for abusing the Holy Spirit, one can seek God's inheritance without fear because "your Father knows [what] you need." Even the storehouse in heaven is not introduced as useful in time of judgment but as anchor for the heart, "Make heaven your storehouse..., for where your stores are, there will your heart be also."

There is a single message from both nature and justice for those who represent God: do not be afraid. The reason is doubly spoken: your Father will provide; Wisdom's children will vindicate her.

Text: *Afraid and Assured (from Luke 12:2-3, 4-7, 8-12, 22-31, 33-34; and Matthew parallels)*

Nothing is covered which will not be uncovered or hidden which will not be made known. Whatever you said in the dark will be heard in the light, and what you whispered in storerooms will be proclaimed on the roofs.

Do not fear those who kill the body and after this can do nothing more. But fear the one who after killing has power to throw into hell. Are sparrows not sold for two coins?—and not one of them falls to the ground without your Father's knowledge. But even the hairs of your head are all counted. Don't be afraid. You are worth more than many sparrows.

Each one who acknowledges me before human beings the human being will acknowledge before God's angels. But whoever denies me before human beings will be denied before God's angels. And whoever will speak against the human being will be forgiven. But whoever says anything against the Holy Spirit will not be forgiven. When they turn you in, don't worry how or what you should speak, because in that hour what you should speak will be given to you.

Therefore I tell you, Don't worry about your life and what you will eat, nor about your body and what you will wear. Is life not more than food and body more than clothing? Look at the crows, since they neither sow nor harvest nor gather into barns, and God feeds them. Are you not worth more than they? Which of you by worry can add one inch to your life span? And why worry about other things? Notice the lilies how they grow—they neither labor nor spin, but I tell you, Solomon in all his glory was not dressed up like one of these. If God so clothes the grass in the field—here today and tomorrow thrown into the fire—how much more you, you faithless ones. So don't ask what you should eat or what you should drink, since all the world's nations seek these things and your Father knows you need them. But seek God's inheritance and these will come as a bonus.

Make heaven your storehouse where thieves do not encroach nor rust decay, for where your stores are, there will your heart be also.

Part III: The Shock of God's Inheritance

Warnings

If we expect in the final third of the Sayings Source a simple resolution of this double speech, we will be disappointed. Neither the Father nor Wisdom is named again, being eclipsed in a final demonstration of the shock of God's inheritance. Yet each does make a brief appearance that shows how God's giving and God's accounting take place in the arrival of God's inheritance.

This part of the Sayings Source is framed by warnings, and those at the beginning are parabolic: "If the owner had realized at what hour the thief were coming..."; "If that slave...begins to beat his fellow servants and to eat and drink and get drunk..."; "Settle with your accuser on the *way* to court...." The point in each case is that if you don't act now before you face the thief, master, or judge, you will take a great loss. This shows Jesus is talking in this third part to people with something to lose.

The story of the thief ends, "You have no idea what time the human being is coming." Since Jesus is already present, this sounds as if he is announcing another human being such as the apocalyptic human being who comes to judge in Dan 7:13. Or is this rather a later voice-over of someone awaiting Jesus' return? In the context of the Sayings Source it at least remains part of Jesus' own self-naming. Jesus first defines himself in contrast to John the Baptist as a garden-variety human being "eating and drinking" like everyone else, but the name comes to include a sharp realism—"The human being has no where to lay his head." It then takes on some representative meaning (whoever acknowledges him before human beings the human being will acknowledge before God), and now, without letting anything go, it reclaims, through the story of a night thief, John the Baptist's threat of one who is coming—as Jesus says, "You have no idea when the human being is coming." The warning culminates, "Do not think I came to cast peace on the earth. I came not to cast peace but a sword. For in one house they will be divided son against father, daughter against mother, and daughter-in-law against mother-in-law."

Text: *Warnings (from Luke 12:39-40, 42-46, 49-56, 57-59; and Matthew parallels)*

But know this, that if the owner had realized at what hour the thief were coming, he would not have let his house be broken into. And become ready yourselves, for you have no idea what time the human being is coming.

Who is the faithful and wise slave that the master appoints over his servants to give them their food on time? Blessed is the slave whom this master finds doing so when he comes. I tell you the truth, he will appoint him to be responsible over all his possessions. But if that slave says in his heart, My master is delayed, and begins to beat his fellow servants and to eat and drink and get drunk, that slave's master will come on a day when he does not expect him and in an hour he does not know and will cut him off, and his fate will be with the unfaithful.

Do not think I came to cast peace on the earth. I came not to cast peace but a sword. For in one house they will be divided son against father, daughter against mother, and daughter-in-law against mother-in-law. Evenings you say: A good day, the sky is fiery. And mornings: Storm today, the sky is dark and firey. You know how to read the look of the sky, but you cannot read this time.

Settle with your accuser on the way to court, lest he deliver you to the judge, and the judge to the guard, and he throw you into prison. I tell you, you will not get out of there until you have paid your last coin.

The Shock of God's Inheritance

The sword cast by the human being that cuts to the heart of the patriarchal family—where the mother and the daughter-in-law hold everything together—turns out to be God's inheritance. It begins innocently enough. But the mustard seed thrown out in the yard makes a nesting tree in months, and yeast hidden in fifty pounds of flour fills the room in hours. This inheritance, which cannot even be thrown out or hid and is wide open to the poor who have broken in once-closed doors, is experienced by others as a narrow gate or a locked door. Familiar voices call out, "Lord, open up for us!... We ate and drank with you, and you taught in our streets!" The answer comes, "I don't know you.... Get away from me, all of you that do injustice." Jesus explains, "Outside there will be weeping and gnashing of teeth when you see Abraham and Isaac and Jacob and all the prophets in God's inheritance, but you are thrown out." It is not said that ethnic Gentiles replace

Jews in God's favor, as we often read the New Testament, but that outsiders replace insiders among those who ate with Jesus, and every expectation is undermined in the multiple reversals set off by God's inheritance. This is reinforced: "Look, the last will be first and the first last," and, "All who exalt themselves will be humbled, and those who humble themselves will be exalted."

When someone shouts, "Blessed is the one who will eat in God's inheritance," this enthusiasm is met with an account of a great party where no one invited shows up, so that the poor and blind and lame must be impressed to fill the house. This is the shock of God's inheritance, both who is not there and who is there. Luke later turns the story into a model of Christian hospitality, "When you give a banquet, invite the poor" (Luke 14:13), and Matthew makes it an allegory of the church where bad and good are mixed until the host checks for proper wedding garments (Matt 22:1-14). But in the Sayings Source we have only the guests excusing themselves and the street people piling in—crutches, canes, grocery carts and all.

If this is God's inheritance, what does it tell us about the God of Jesus? When "reasonable" excuses are not accepted and being an insider gets no respect, one looks around for Wisdom. Midway in announcing the shock, Jesus begins to lament the holy city itself: "Jerusalem, Jerusalem, killing the prophets and stoning those sent to her! How often I wanted to gather your children the way a hen gathers her brood under her wings, and you were not willing." Jesus in the metaphor of the hen takes on the persona of Wisdom, who has appealed over and over through her prophets and the wise. The verdict that follows is not a curse on the temple but seems to be Wisdom's familiar threat to withdraw: "Look, your house is left for you," or perhaps caustically, "Look, you can have your house! But I tell you, you will not see me until you say, Blessed is the one who comes in the Lord's name." At the heart of holiness, wherever people most expect the in-gathering of God's people, she most continually finds herself put off by people who have no time for her invitation.

The Father who is generous to a fault also makes an appearance in the story of a shepherd who is fool enough to risk his whole flock for one sheep. His satisfaction stated in the last line—"Just so there is more joy in heaven over this one than over the ninety-nine who are not lost"—contrasts sharply with the frustration of Wisdom as the hen without her chicks. The Father reaches out, withholding nothing, in order to overcome loss in joy, whereas Wisdom exposes her prophets to abuse and stoning in order to make the truth plain that no one will see her until her children are welcomed. I will come back to that disparity.

Text: *The Shock of God's Inheritance (from Luke 13:18-21, 24-30, 34-35; 14:11, 15-24, 26-27 with 17:33 [in Matthew's order]; 14:34-35; 15:4-7; and Matthew parallels)*

God's inheritance is like a mustard seed that a man threw in his garden, and it grew and became a tree, and **the birds of the sky sheltered in its branches.** God's inheritance is like yeast that a woman took and hid in fifty pounds of flour until it was completely leavened.

Enter through the narrow door, for many try to enter and cannot. Once the owner has locked the door you will say, Lord, open up for us! He will answer, I don't know you. You will say, We ate and drank with you, and you taught in our streets! And he will say, I don't know you. **Get away from me, all of you that do injustice.** Outside there will be weeping and gnashing of teeth when you see Abraham and Isaac and Jacob and all the prophets in God's inheritance, but you are thrown out. And they will come from east and west and will sit to eat in God's inheritance. And, look, the last will be first and the first last.

Jerusalem, Jerusalem, killing the prophets and stoning those sent to her! How often I wanted to gather your children the way a hen gathers her brood under her wings, and you were not willing. Look, you can have your house![12] But I tell you, you will not see me until you say, **Blessed is the one who comes in the Lord's name.**

All who exalt themselves will be humbled, and those who humble themselves will be exalted.

Someone said, Blessed is the one who will eat in God's inheritance.[13] But he said to him, A certain person made a great feast and invited many people, and sent his servant at the hour of the meal to say to those invited, Come for it is already prepared. But they went away excusing themselves, one to his own field, one to his business, and another to his wife. Then the host was angry and said to his servant, Go quickly to the streets and gather here the poor and crippled and blind and lame. Go out into the roads and alleys and force them to come so that my house might be filled.

If any come to me and do not hate their own father and mother and brothers and sisters, they cannot be my followers. Those who do not carry their own cross and come after me cannot be my

---

12. My translation of the literal "Your house is left for you" tries to make sense both of it and the adversative that follows.

13. Both Luke and Matthew refer to this story as one about God's inheritance. I adapt Luke's opening to show this.

followers. Those who seek to preserve their life will lose it, but those who lose their life will keep it.

If salt has become tasteless, what can it be salted with? It is good for nothing. They throw it out.

Which one of you who has a hundred sheep and loses one of them does not leave the ninety-nine and go after the lost until it is found? I tell you that when you find it you rejoice! Just so there is more joy in heaven over this one than over the ninety-nine who are not lost.

Warnings

The Sayings Source ends with warnings to those who seem bent on losing God's inheritance. They appear in the last act not killing and looting but very respectably trying to serve God *and* Mammon, thinking to evade God's law against adultery through divorce, rationing forgiveness and tripping up the vulnerable, pursuing business as usual as if fire and brimstone were not falling from heaven, and burying God's gift in the ground for fear of losing it. Here are those of us who hedge our bets concerning God's inheritance, and the last third of the Sayings Source is intent on giving us its shock. Each of these final warnings works not by threat of divine reprisal but by exposure to reality. Jesus says: you simply cannot serve two masters at once; God's uniting two people does not pass away; better for *you* if you drown than to harm these little ones; your business as usual and secret knowledge will be exposed on the human being's day as when lightning lights the whole sky or vultures circle over a corpse; and about money, simply a folk proverb: those who have (and use it) will be given more, but those who do not will have it taken away.

After these warnings about the consequences of a double life, Jesus speaks the last sentences in the Sayings Source to those around him, "You are those who have continued with me. And you will sit on thrones judging the twelve tribes of Israel." The recognized rulers will not judge God's people, but judgment, he claims, will fall to "those who have stuck it out with me," which in the context of the Sayings Source are the last and least of Israel, who God takes to be first and greatest. Since judging is the identifying role of rulers in the ancient Near East, this final saying pronounces that the poor and abused, to whom Jesus' blessings first conceded God's inheritance, are also its rulers. It is, if you will, the day of the human being.

Text: *Warnings (from Luke 16:13, 17-18; 17:1-4, 6, 23-24, 26-30, 34-35, 37; 19:12-27; 22:28, 30; and Matthew parallels)*

No one is able to serve two masters, for you will either hate the one and love the other, or you will cling to the one and despise the other. You cannot serve God and wealth.

It is easier for heaven and earth to pass away than for one dot of the law to collapse. Every man who divorces his wife and marries another commits adultery, and the man who marries a divorced woman commits adultery.

People are bound to stumble, but woe to the person that causes it. It would be better for that one to have a millstone put around the neck and be thrown into the sea than for one of these little ones to be made to stumble. If your brother sins, point it out to him, and if he repents, forgive him. And if he sins against you seven times a day and turns to you seven times saying, I repent, you will forgive him.

If you have faith like a mustard seed, say to this sycamore, be uprooted and planted in the sea, and it would obey you.

They tell you, Look in the desert! Don't go off. Look in the storeroom! Don't trust them. For as the lightning comes from the east and shines to the west, so will the human being's day be. Just as it was in the days of Noah, so it will be in the human being's days.

They were eating and drinking, marrying and being married—until the day Noah went into the ark and the flood came and destroyed them all. It was the same in the days of Lot. They were eating, drinking, buying, selling, planting, building. But on the day Lot went out of Sodom, it rained fire and brimstone from heaven and destroyed them all.[14] So will the human being's day be.

Two will be on one bed, one taken and the other left. Two will be grinding at one mill, one taken and the other left.

Where the body is, there the eagles will gather.

A certain man going on a journey called his slaves and gave them each a hundred-drachma coin and said, Trade until I come. When he came he made an accounting. The first came and said, Master, your coin made ten coins. And he said, Well done, good servant, you were faithful in the least thing, take power over ten cities. The second said, Your coin, master, made five coins. And he said to this one, You will be over five cities. And the other one came saying, Lord, look at your coin which I laid away in a napkin. For I feared you because you are a harsh man, harvesting what

---

14. Lot's story is so similar to Noah's that Matthew's dropping a doublet is more likely than Luke's adding it to the source.

you have not sown. He said to him, Evil servant, you know I am a man harvesting what I have not sown. Why did you not deposit my money and when I came I would get it with interest? Take his coin away and give it to the one who has ten. To each who has it will be given, but from the one who does not have, what he has will be taken.

You are those who have continued with me.

And you will sit on thrones judging the twelve tribes of Israel.

Conclusion

In closing I return explicitly to my place of reading, which I have identified as a place of longing for God in a humanistic world, of longing for new relations of women and men in a patriarchal world, and of longing for justice in an imperial world. Have I begun to read Jesus' sayings from this place?

The search for God points me to the final words of the Sayings Source announcing that Israel's least will sit on thrones judging the twelve tribes. This introduces a new politics. Speaking of God is the oldest way of talking politics, but where tradition conceded to God all power over human creation, here God abdicates this inheritance in favor of the least, and the least in the demographics of an advanced agricultural society are the great majority of people whose labor feeds a small ruling group.

Looking for God in a humanistic world today, I am struck by the assertion of the human responsibility to rule, to take care of oneself and others. This God will not appear with power to rescue people who meditate on divine things. And if God's inheritance is ceded to the least, those of us with privilege no longer have a divine "friend at the top" through whom we can maintain leverage and hope to recover our dominance. At best we can take our place as human beings and learn to carry our own weight alongside other people. Because this happens in a world where the great wealth of industrial production serves a tiny circle of managers and those who legitimate them, claiming the gift of God's inheritance today is a constant struggle.

Is the God who has abdicated the ruling inheritance effectively absent in this struggle? These sayings of Jesus assert God's active presence in two essential ways. On the one hand, God is present to provide what people ask, so that they can live and rule themselves wisely. Granted that human beings often transmit to each other what God provides, this Father's provision exceeds that of the best human parent. Because God is not manipulative, rain falls on just and unjust, and wisdom is given to the untaught. God withholds nothing, even God's own inheritance, so people become able not to withhold from each other.

God is also expected in a very different way, challenging people. Wisdom does not stop sending out representatives to provoke the world to feed the hungry, to hear the good news of God's inheritance, and to be healed—though they may be called journalists or peace activists or teacher's aids rather than prophets and miracle workers. When they and the people they serve are rejected, Wisdom herself is scorned, but when they and their people are received, she is vindicated and God's righteousness is revealed. This unrelenting demand of Wisdom, along with the boundless supply of the Father, is what keeps the human struggle to realize God's inheritance going. We could begin to celebrate this in a world where people are alternately obsessive and resigned but seldom confident that their human labors have God's judgment and blessing and will bear fruit.

I also read these sayings in a place where people long for new ways that women and men can relate in a patriarchal world. Here we must ask whether the images of abused Wisdom and the generous Father reinforce gender stereotypes that are destructive for us. Should we resist "Father" and "Wisdom" as names for God, knowing as we do that, while sexual difference is natural, gender expectations are socially constructed, religiously legitimated, and tend to maintain power structures? There is no denying that these two ways of naming God reflect people's social experiences of father and mother in a society where males had the resources to give and women had to learn endurance. Yet at present I find the value of these names for God to be greater than their danger, *if* they can be understood as they were within their own religious context, where I believe they worked largely as counterweights to the dominant gender stereotypes.

The dominant paternal image was, and probably is, the father who takes care of his own in order to increase his relative strength in the world. In contrast to this, many rabbinical stories tell about God the indulgent Father who ignores with no difficulty the schemes of the wise and the powerful who would make alliance with him, but he simply cannot say no to children, nor to people of childlike faith who pray fervently for rain or for healing, nor even to the commonest person who does one good deed from the heart:

> Hanan ha-Nehba was the son of the daughter of Honi the Circle-Drawer. When the world was in need of rain the Rabbis would send to him school children and they would take hold of the hem of his garment and say to him, Father, Father, give us rain. Thereupon he would plead with the Holy One, Blessed be He, "Master of the Universe, do it for the sake of these who are unable to distin-

guish between the Father who gives rain and the father who does not."[15]

Rab Judah said in the name of Rab: Every day a Heavenly Voice is heard declaring, The whole world draws its sustenance because of Hanina my son, and Hanina my son suffices himself with a kab of carobs from one Sabbath eve to another. Every Friday his wife would light the oven and throw twigs into it so as not to be put to shame. She had a bad neighbour who said, I know that these people have nothing, what then is the meaning of all this [smoke]? She went and knocked at the door, [and the wife], feeling humiliated, retired into a room. A miracle happened and [her neighbour] saw the oven filled with loaves of bread and the kneading trough full of dough; she called out to her: You, you, bring your shovel, for your bread is getting charred; and she replied, I just went to fetch it.[16]

This God is Jesus' Father in the Sayings Source, never beholden to the powerful to increase divine power, but giving sun and rain to all, and supplying those whom Wisdom sends out as lambs among wolves with whatever they ask.

Wisdom's tradition shows she is equally distinctive among neglected mothers and wronged women. In Proverbs 1–9 she appears on the street shouting for attention, making the same preparations of her home and using the same call as the prostitute (9:1-6, 13-18), but she alone is not welcomed. Yet her authority is secure from before the world's creation (8:22-31), and she can say, "Because I have called and you refused, have stretched out my hand and no one heeded . . . , I also will laugh at your calamity; I will mock when panic strikes you" (1:24-26). It is not weakness when Wisdom in 1 Enoch 42 returns to heaven to live because no one will receive her on earth. The Sayings Source shows that her power base is sure, her withdrawals rhetorical, her outreach unrelenting. She is the rejected woman we would all like to be in her strength. Who can doubt that she will in due time be vindicated by all her children?

So although divine images of the generous man and the abused woman could be used to confirm the worst gender stereotypes, the Jewish traditions where Jesus found them do not do so. They begin with these basic experiences of men and women in patriarchal society in order to counteract them. In Jesus' sayings the generous man who is the divine Father cannot resist the weak and becomes their sure resource; the abused woman who is the Wisdom of God outlasts the powerful until all

_____

15. *b Ta'anit* 23b, trans. I. Epstein, *The Babylonian Talmud* (London: Soncino Press, 1935–52).

16. *b Ta'anit* 24b–25a, trans. Epstein, *The Babylonian Talmud.*

the abused in the world are vindicated. This may suggest that we need not wait to build new gender relations until we can start from scratch. We can begin where we are and move in unexpected ways. The one who has received or accumulated can discover the vulnerability of great giving, and the one from whom so much has been taken can claim justice until she—or he—is vindicated. It does disorient our gender stereotypes to see God's caring face as male and God's demanding face as female.

Finally, I read these sayings of Jesus from a place of thirst for justice in an imperial world. We in the church cannot speak about justice to others without first facing the truth of how much we have contributed to injustice by allowing Wisdom to be forgotten among us and the Father to be enthroned so that neither one is able to function.

John's Gospel is a poignant window into this transition. Wisdom is the one with whom the Gospel begins at the moment of creation itself, renamed the Word of God for Greek readers but still the one who is with God and is God, the one who is Life and Light. And as we have seen before, she comes to her own world and it does not receive her. Yet "the Word became flesh and lived among us." Jesus is identified as Wisdom in the flesh, and at the end of the Prologue is named the only-begotten God who makes the Father known (John 1:1-18). This both narrows and extends Wisdom's identification with her prophets in the Sayings Source. Now only one prophet is named as her representative, but he is taken as the very Wisdom of God. Jesus' death may be seen in this Gospel as the culminating rejection of Wisdom, and his resurrection as the mutual vindication or glorification of Jesus (Wisdom) and the Father. What is more, when Jesus leaves the world, the Spirit of Truth will be sent by the Father as "another Advocate"—Wisdom again?—coming to extend Jesus' teaching and to expose evil and righteousness, so that others can do greater works than Jesus (John 13:31—16:15). Yet in the process of Jesus' being identified with Wisdom, her sending of the prophets including Jesus to challenge the world is supplanted by the Father's sending the only Son to reveal his glory. And at the end of the Gospel the Father is predictably on the throne, with Jesus settled on his right. Most alarming, this entire rich, Jewish-rooted Wisdom theology is being used by the writing community to claim exclusive access to the Father through the Son over against those it calls "the Jews." The Father is no longer himself, having been domesticated and exalted in order to provide vindication for one circle at the cost of violating those outside it.

As long as this is the church's theology, we are in no position to be teaching about justice. The very different theological vision in Jesus' sayings can draw the world toward justice only if we can learn to live in its light. This is the vision of God who is at the same time Wisdom that exposes all abuse and the Father of all mercies, at the same time the one who demands all that is just and the one who supplies all that is needed. The question, both conceptually and practically, is: What holds these two together? In terms of this essay, if these two images cannot refer to the same God, then the Sayings Source cannot be read as a whole, and we must ask which was the God of Jesus and which the God of those who refashioned his sayings. In terms of our human commitment, if these two images cannot refer to the same God, then the Father who withholds nothing is subject to our endless manipulation, or Wisdom who sends us out without resources will never be vindicated nor justice attained. Nonetheless, I hesitate to inquire about God's nature, because who can know about these things? Even with our own parents we learn to stay at a respectful distance and not ask how they have been able to get along with each other all these years—and that distance is far, far greater when it comes to asking questions of God.

Yet multiple images of God have not been seen as a problem historically. The Jesus of the Sayings Source shows no unease about speaking of God in different ways. His Jewish theological tradition integrated many different names for God. The Father was invoked in prayer and personal claims on God, Wisdom in teaching and theodicy, and God's inheritance in hopes of communal restoration. One or another address for God might be favored by different groups, but the wholeness of Israel always meant a fullness—if not a neatness—in the one God. The church has also been rich in experience of God. Its dogmatic periods can be seen as efforts to catch up with this experience, if sometimes in misguided ways.

Nor is the problem conceptual. We need not think of two competing Gods, nor of a divine couple. Nor are there two conflicting values being personified, between which we must seek to find the golden mean. It is closer to the truth to say that Wisdom and the Father are the presence of the single Holy One, always fully extended on this world's behalf, whether in supply or in demand.

Our imperial world suggests that the real problem of being faithful to this one God is practical. By this I do not mean the practical problem of how to pray—prayer speaks every human language and more—nor even of how to deal with people who insist on traditional formulations. The practical question in the union of Wisdom and the Father is our position as the privileged in an unjust world. We want to know without asking: Is the Father's storehouse without limit? Is Wisdom's patience without end? And the answer from the sayings of Jesus is, "Don't count on it." To the rich Jesus says, "You have what is coming to you," and in Wisdom's voice, "You will not see me until you say, Blessed is the one who comes in God's name."

Our world is a close replay of the early Roman Empire, where one nation's laws and arms assured the flow of wealth from poor to rich. Of that we are the beneficiaries. Few of us will find ourselves propelled into the banquet of God's inheritance with the poor and hungry and crying and abused. For us there is only the narrow gate that is entered by shock and repentance, repentance not in words but in life. Jesus taught that if we should join the world ruled by the last and the least, then the Father will give whatever we ask when Wisdom sends us out with the news and signs of God's inheritance. And the word is that she will be vindicated by all her children.

The Politics and Poetics of Location

_____ Mary Ann Tolbert _____

> The hegemony of patriarchal thought in Western civilization is not
> due to its superiority in content, form and achievement over all
> other thought; it is built upon the systematic silencing of other
> voices. —Gerda Lerner, *The Creation of Feminist Consciousness*

On January 22–24, 1993, most of the people whose essays appear in
this volume met together at Vanderbilt University to discuss drafts of
their papers with each other and an eager audience. In addition, on the
final morning of the Vanderbilt meeting, Professor Rebecca Chopp of
Emory University and Professor Peter Hodgson of Vanderbilt University
presented overall responses to the paper presentations and discussions,
which had occupied the three-day event. The purpose of the conference
was not only to encourage the active engagement of the authors with
each other, a process that essay volumes rarely permit, but also to push
the debate on social location and biblical interpretation farther in order
to begin to surface some of the possibilities and difficulties such debate
must inevitably pose.

In these "Afterwords" I would like to voice my own reflections on
some of the issues raised during the conference discussions and indicate where I, as one participant in the process, see new constructions
of discourse forming. However, just as the Vanderbilt conference in no
way intended to provide closure to the discussion of social location and
interpretation, these "Afterwords" do not stand as a "conclusion" to
this volume. The desire for a nicely turned ending that wraps the effort up in ribbon and presents it as finished gift to a waiting public,
who will consume the thought-package in silence, owes its existence
to the very structures of hegemonic discourse that most of these essays
have attempted to displace. Taking difference seriously requires the continuing interaction of many voices and many perspectives without any
assurance that a final unified perspective for the "common good" can
or will emerge. Indeed, the quest for unity itself has often been used to
enforce the reign of silence upon which patriarchal discourse as a whole
depends. All participants or observers of the conference would undoubt-

edly cast their reflections on the event in a manner different from the following, and I would encourage them to do so.

In the papers themselves and in the discussions among the participants, I heard the complex relations between modernism and postmodernism emerge as one of the primary sites of contention in assessing the effects of social location on biblical interpretation. Consequently, I would like to begin my own reflections by examining those relations, especially in regard to their political potential, and then move from that examination to a discussion of the factors involved in a "politics of location."[1] While a politics of location may inform the sensibilities of those who read texts, the historically specific process of reading itself, and the critical and educational practices upon which it rests, requires a shift of focus from a politics of location to a "poetics of location,"[2] a newly unfolding field of exploration. Thus, what a poetics of location might mean for readings of biblical texts is the final consideration of these "Afterwords."

Modernism versus Postmodernism

In her closing response to the Vanderbilt conference, Rebecca Chopp described the entire agenda of papers and discussions as the attempt to "develop a discourse of postmodernity," and she also raised the issue of what it might mean politically to strategize self-consciously out of such a discourse. Peter Hodgson, in his comments, portrayed himself and some of the other participants as clearly on a bridge between the Enlightenment and liberation, the modern and the postmodern. Modernism, rooted in the Enlightenment exaltation of reason and its manipulation by a unified thinking self on a world of objects, has been under a many-sided theoretical siege in the Western world since the 1960s. Beginning in architecture, linguistics, and philosophy, and spreading to art, history, literary theory, anthropology, and the physical sciences, spurred in great measure by the challenges of feminism and other liberation perspectives, a far-reaching critique of Enlightenment thinking and values now goes under the banner of postmodernism.[3]

---

1. The phrase was developed in feminist work by A. Rich, "Blood, Bread, and Poetry: The Location of the Poet (1984)," 167–87, and "Notes toward a Politics of Location (1984)," 210–31, in *Blood, Bread, and Poetry: Selected Prose 1979-1985* (New York: W. W. Norton, 1986).

2. The phrase was developed in feminist work by N. K. Miller, *Subject to Change: Reading Feminist Writing* (New York: Columbia Univ. Press, 1988) 4.

3. There are numerous introductions and discussions of postmodernism. Some of the most important for this essay are the following: L. J. Nicholson, ed., *Feminism/Postmodernism* (New York: Routledge, 1990); Hal Foster, ed., *The Anti-Aesthetic: Essays on Postmodern Culture* (Port Townsend, Wash.: Bay Press, 1983); A. Huyssen,

Postmodernism is not, however, merely an *anti*modernism, a rejection of the tradition of Enlightenment thinking. Instead, it is an ironic critique that always acknowledges its own embeddedness in the tradition it is undercutting. In the words of Linda Hutcheon, postmodernism is "complicitous critique."[4] It must be so, since one of its most cogent arguments concerns the mistaken dichotomizing of subject and object, so central to positivistic logic. If, as postmodernists argue, an "object" is always subjectively framed, always seen through a particular methodological, theoretical, or cultural lens, the "subject's" own perspective is always written into the "object" under analysis. Hence, subject and object must always be functions of one another rather than distinct and separable entities. Since the proponents of postmodernism, no less than the defenders of modernism, are the heirs of Enlightenment thinking, that thinking inevitably shapes their analyses. Postmodernism, thus, is—and must be—a critique from within, ironically affirming the tradition it at the same time subverts.

Indeed, part of the postmodern trajectory might be helpfully characterized for biblical scholars as an affirmation of radical historicity, which extends the historical consciousness of the Enlightenment to its logical end for those living in the present. If history makes us conscious that people and groups in past ages were fully situated within the cultural assumptions and conditions of their own age and were influenced in their thoughts and actions by their own distinctive social circumstances and power relations, then those same realities must of necessity condition people in contemporary societies. Present patterns of thought, even the patterns of postmodern thought, are as thoroughly imbued with distinctive contemporary notions of value and truth as those of any past period. No individuals—past *or present*—can transcend their own historical moment. We, no less than those we historically reconstruct, are socially located and culturally constrained.

Moreover, the very fact that present cultures and those of the past appear so distinctive and so different from each other questions any claim that cultural configurations are founded upon eternal mandates or inevitable natural laws. For postmodernism, cultures are clearly and fully human constructions. Consequently, postmodernists are concerned "to de-naturalize some of the dominant features of our way of life; to point out that those entities that we unthinkingly experience as 'natural' (they might even include capitalism, patriarchy, liberal humanism)

After the Great Divide: Modernism, Mass Culture, Postmodernism (Bloomington: Indiana Univ. Press, 1986); L. Hutcheon, *The Politics of Postmodernism* (New York: Routledge, 1989).

4. Hutcheon, *Politics of Postmodernism*, 2.

are in fact 'cultural'; made by us, not given to us."[5] Those cultural
entities that a given period "naturalizes" are instead created by the distinctive social and linguistic systems developed in and by that human
community.

While modernism tends to view language as representative of some
utterly separate, nonlinguistic reality "out there," for postmodernism
language is *constitutive* of reality; it constructs the "reality" in which
we live, the "truth" we subscribe to, and the "future" we envision.
Modernism, in order to support its metalinguistic belief system, depends
heavily on the dualistic patterns of Enlightenment thought, offering in
any cultural situation only two "opposite" categories of analysis (for example, better or worse, right or wrong, public or private, rich or poor,
inside or outside, male or female, free or slave, order or chaos, whole
or disabled, and so on). For postmodernists, such dualism perpetrates a
stunning reduction of the manifold differences found even within modern human experience, not to mention the experiences of past cultures
and epochs. Taking those lived differences seriously demands the displacement of dualistic thinking by other, multiple categories of analysis
and, perhaps most importantly of all, the willingness to tolerate endless
ambiguity, an almost impossible demand for the closure-seeking modernist, who tries to push every agenda toward a universal or totalizing
conclusion.

Some of the reasons for the appeal of postmodern thought to feminism and other liberation movements should be clear at this point:
oppressive "natural" conditions (like the subordination of women to
men or the "inferiority" of people of color) are in fact cultural constructions imposed by dualistic thinking that requires one "opposite"
to be valued over another and that determines the hierarchical relations of those "opposites" on the basis of who has the most power
in society at a given moment. Indeed, the insistence that such dualistic categories are "natural" always serves to perpetuate the power of
those presently in power and thus must always be seen as a political act,
whatever other claim it may make. However, as cultural constructions,
those conditions and the hierarchical relations upon which they stand
may be deconstructed and displaced by alternative systems, which take
the rich diversity of human experience more seriously and provide more
equitable access to power. Or so one might hope. Yet it is at the point
of actual social change where the promise of postmodernism appears
to falter.

---

5. Ibid., 2.

The Political Limits of Postmodernism

Two obstacles to the political application of postmodern thought are often cited.[6] First, postmodernism as "complicitous critique" insists on the radical acknowledgment of one's own collusion in the very structures of power one is attempting to dislocate. Recognition of such collusion leads many postmodernists to limit their praxis to the analysis and critique of culture as construction without any real sense of human agency capable of altering that construction.

American postmodernism has been encouraged in its nonactivist tendencies by its, in my view, unfortunate affiliation with poststructuralism, especially in its American version.[7] American poststructuralists have often tended to mold Jacques Derrida's devastating critique of Western metaphysics into a joyful, elitist nihilism that invokes the "free play of difference" to trample over every assertion of voice, standpoint, or "rights," whether from those defending the status quo or, more likely in recent years, from those demanding an end to oppressive structures. They argue that since no transcultural, metalinguistic "realities" exist to ground claims for "truth," "meaning," or "justice," all such claims are illegitimate attempts to assert a new "universalism." The only work generally excused from rigorous interrogation of its implicit "totalizing" claims is, not surprisingly, poststructuralism itself. What the radically aesthetic position of many American poststructuralists ignores, or perhaps actually intends to hide, is that present social structures are already profoundly encoded with claims about "truth," "meaning," and "justice," regardless of how little warranted theoretically, that serve to protect those in power from losing that power or having to share it.

To voice alternative visions of social structure does not require the assertion of transcendent "truth" or "universal" human needs but only the historically transitory assessment that contemporary structures evince oppressive relations impossible to justify even within the constraints of current cultural ideals. The limitation of this response to the poststructuralist position is that it seems to imply that cultural systems whose ideals embrace inequality and oppression offer no standpoint from which to argue for equality and liberation. For example, since de-

---

6. See, for example, the entire discussion in ibid.; and also bell hooks, *Yearning: Race, Gender, and Cultural Politics* (Boston: South End Press, 1990) 15–31; F. Jameson, "The Politics of Theory: Ideological Positions in the Postmodernism Debate," *New German Critique* 33 (1984) 53–66; and L. Alcoff, "Cultural Feminism versus Post-Structuralism: The Identity Crisis in Feminist Theory," *Reconstructing the Academy: Women's Education and Women's Studies* (ed. E. Minnich, J. O'Barr, and R. Rosenfeld; Chicago: Univ. of Chicago Press, 1988) 257–88.

7. For a discussion of the history of postmodernism in America and its relations with poststructuralism, see the helpful discussion in Huyssen, "Mapping the Postmodern," *Feminism/Postmodernism*, 234–77.

mocracy and equality are clearly valued in the founding documents of the United States, no matter how unfairly applied, liberation movements in this country have culturally approved grounds for their demands. However, in some strict Arab countries, for instance, inequality and class privilege are divinely sanctioned norms. Should calls for liberation and equality in those cultures or even the judgment that their present practices are oppressive be considered illegitimate? Very few feminists, womanists, or members of other liberation movements would want to agree to such a limitation, I would imagine, although they would certainly agree that those within the culture itself must be the ones to guide and develop movements for change. Some further response to the poststructuralist position seems called for.

The second obstacle to the political appropriation of postmodernism revolves around its challenge to the notions of self that have served as the basis of recent identity politics. Postmodernism has countered the Enlightenment notion of the unified self with a fluid "self," drawn from the data of human experience. For example, my sense of "who I am" shifts over time and varies in different contexts (for example, daughter to my parents, teacher to my students, woman in group of men, white in group of people of color, and so on) with each different subjective "identity" position requiring distinctive behavior, language usage, dress, and so on. My "identity," then, is not static, essential, and clearly defined but, instead, a fluid, shifting perspective, which is generally context-dependent.[8] Many contemporary liberation movements in the United States, including feminism, the civil rights movement, and movements among various ethnic groups, have proclaimed a common "essence" of identity, which unites all of their constituents and distinguishes them from society at large, as the basis for political action. Suggesting that such an "essence" does not exist appears to some to undermine the cohesion necessary for political survival and collective voice.

While some have seen the postmodern critique as threatening political unity, others have welcomed the attack on "essence" as a liberating force *within* these movements. For the past decade, most thoroughly in feminism, but with growing vigor in black liberation and ethnic movements, voices from within have been protesting that the announced "essence" does not represent their own experience.[9] In feminism, the "essence" of woman seemed mainly to describe only the ones talking the loudest— middle-class, white, heterosexual women—and not the vast majority of women oppressed in the United States. Narrow and rigid determinations

---

8. See my earlier article in this volume, "Reading for Liberation," for a fuller discussion of this issue.

9. In feminism, for example, see the extended discussion of this issue in E. V. Spelman, *Inessential Woman: Problems of Exclusion in Feminist Thought* (Boston: Beacon, 1988); for black liberation, see, for example, hooks, *Yearning,* 28–31.

of "essence" have also been used to exclude those whose views contrasted with movement leaders and to test one's loyalty to the political group, practices inimical to the very goals of liberation the movements are actually seeking.

Nevertheless, political solidarity in the face of the racist, patriarchal construction of modern Western society does seem to demand some attention to identity issues. Perhaps as Diana Fuss, among others, has argued, women for political ends need "to consider a possible strategic deployment of essence."[10] To avoid the exclusionary tendencies of constricted definitions of essence, however, even a strategic use of such rhetoric must be constantly deconstructing itself. If the postmodern rejection of a rigid essentialism actually conforms to the lived experience of many persons structurally disadvantaged by the hierarchical values of patriarchy, but some bonds of cohesion are deemed necessary to fight collectively the inequity of present power relations, then one solution might be to move from a politics of identity to a politics of location, defined precisely in light of the modernism–postmodernism debate.

A Politics of Location

Adrienne Rich in a 1984 essay on the political impact of the poet in a sexist, racist society suggested that the poet was located by "the facts of blood and bread."[11] The "facts of blood" referred to general areas of social, personal, and familial alignments while the "facts of bread" pointed to national, economic, and political standing. One is "located" in relation to the rest of world society at any one moment by all of these factors together. Without, I hope, damaging Rich's ideas too much, I would like to adapt the metaphors of "blood" and "bread" to describe a politics of location that both affirms some "essential" ties of identity but also reflects the complexity and fluidity of lived experience.

The "facts of blood" connote the broad areas of physical and mental integrity, race, gender, ethnicity, sexual orientation, familial affiliation, etc, which individually have often formed the basis of definitions of "essence" and the grounds for developing a politics of identity. But for each person, the "facts of blood" include *all* of these profoundly interrelated factors, a social and personal complexity that narrow descriptions of "essence" ignore or denigrate. The "facts of blood" constitute the shifting complexity of the one who speaks. The "facts of bread," on the other hand, situate where one speaks, the grounds of authority, national

---

10. D. Fuss, " 'Essentially Speaking': Luce Irigaray's Language of Essence," *Revaluing French Feminism: Critical Essays on Difference, Agency, and Culture* (ed. N. Fraser and S. Bartky; Bloomington: Indiana Univ. Press, 1992) 94.
11. Rich, "Blood, Bread, and Poetry," 171.

and institutional context, economic and educational status that shape each utterance we make and often determine who will listen to what we say and who will not. The "facts of blood and bread" together locate each person politically in relation to access to power, freedom from oppression, and human dignity and integrity, and they indicate the possible options for political coalition of interest to each person.

At the Vanderbilt conference, while the "facts of blood" separated us along gender, racial, and ethnic lines, I was often struck by how similar our language, views, and hopes were. What I failed to recognize as fully was that we all spoke from the same national (U.S.), institutional (university or seminary), and educational (M.Div./M.A. or Ph.D.) settings, regardless of our "blood" differences. One or two participants tried to point out these similarities and make us reflect upon them without great success. I now think that our reluctance to notice or discuss these "agreements" stemmed from the concentration of many of us on the "facts of blood," ignoring the equally vital connections of the "facts of bread." Indeed, in discussing the conference with two international students after the event, I was struck by their response that regardless of how much the language of difference was employed by conference participants, what they saw and what they heard was all "First World." And, in truth, it was.

Acknowledging the multiple alliances and fluctuating boundaries between people obviously supports the postmodernist affirmation of a fluid "self" and its rejection of rigid definitions of "essence." However, can a politics of location that takes account of all the factors circumscribing personal, social, and political existence provide some basis for group solidarity? After all, the ultimate goal of all liberation movements is to change the world, and any notion, no matter how theoretically praiseworthy, that does not promote that end is useless. Everyone, whether advantaged by the present hierarchical structure of patriarchy or disadvantaged by it—or, more likely, some of both—is located by the "facts of blood and bread." Everyone, in other words, is involved in the politics of location; everyone speaks out of their particular complex situation of social and personal affiliation and institutional and political status; all perspectives are constituted out of these same ingredients.

What differentiates these perspectives is that in this particular cultural and historical period some "ingredients" are deemed more worthy of trust, reward, power, and prestige than others. Please note that it is not, initially, some *people* who are deemed more worthy by reason of their special actions and thoughts, but instead some small selection of *"ingredients" or traits* (for example, male, white, wealthy, First World, physically sound, heterosexual, Christian, middle- to upper-class). People who embody any of these valued traits are privileged, begin ahead of the game, with more and easier access to power and prestige—not necessarily on the basis of the quality of their minds or hearts but on the basis of the traits they by birth or by place inherit.

Those who embody less culturally valued traits find their access to power, prestige, or human dignity blocked, not initially by their actions or quality of life, but simply by their subordinate location in the patriarchal economy. Whatever the point(s) at which that blockage occurs, it creates a sense of outrage (or just rage) and alienation that gives rise to a yearning for a different reality, a reality in which one's actions and quality of heart, spirit, and mind matter more than the "facts of blood and bread," a reality in which no one would cavalierly treat others in ways they would never tolerate for themselves or ones they love. And I submit that it is this yearning that can form the basis of group solidarity and political action. In the words of bell hooks:

> Many other groups now share with black folks a sense of deep alienation, despair, uncertainty, loss of a sense of grounding even if it is not informed by shared circumstance. Radical postmodernism calls attention to those shared sensibilities which cross the boundaries of class, gender, race, etc., that could be fertile ground for the construction of empathy—ties that would promote recognition of common commitments, and serve as a base for solidarity and coalition.[12]

In a politics of location, solidarity may be founded upon the affective experience of oppression rather than solely upon narrow definitions of "essence" or particular collective circumstances, and cohesion would result from this shared yearning for a different reality, rather than from the duplication of "identity." It is this sensibility of yearning or the empathy created by this sensibility that undergirds the creation of political coalitions.

The coalitions informed by a politics of location would, like the postmodern view of "self," be fluid and shifting. Political coalitions would be a matter of choice, not a matter of "blood" or "bread" alone. Since no group could represent the full complexity of one's location, one might choose to align with different groups over different sets of issues at different times, and these shifting alliances would *not* be perceived as disloyalty to one's "nature," an all too common charge in the realm of identity politics. Furthermore, such shifting alliances would mirror more accurately the profound interconnections of race, gender, ethnicity, class, national origin, and so on, than is often recognized in present alignments, and they would also work to prevent such total absorption in one issue of difference that one risks becoming indifferent to all else.

---

12. hooks, *Yearning*, 27.

In the end, the success of every coalition in subverting the status quo on whatever particular set of issues would be seen as a gain for everyone.

In many institutions, individuals and groups, often associated with distinct "marginalities," are already forming such shifting coalitions around collectively important issues. Especially given the relatively limited number of such people in most institutions, collective effort is essential for success. If such coalitions were the rule rather than the exception, the cumulative power of their protests would increase dramatically. Too often under a politics of identity coalitions exist in a kind of barter economy where one group "helps out" another, hoping for a similar hand in the future, or refuses to "help out" because past support for "their" causes was lacking. The fact that people within the "identity" group may be crucially affected by the issues being addressed by other groups becomes less important than the options for bartering.

Hence, a politics of location, as distinct from a politics of identity, attempts to acknowledge both the complexity and mutability of each person's relation to world society by carefully analyzing the "facts of blood and bread" and also the highly contextual nature in which those "facts" are lived out in daily experience. We all create "reality" from a particular perspective, but that perspective itself changes and shifts as we move from one context to another, as we focus on one aspect or another of our very fluid and multiple "selves."

While the value of a politics of location for the practical tasks of coalition building may be maintained, how would such a sensibility apply to the reflective tasks of reading texts or developing theory? What, in other words, would it mean to move from a politics of location to a poetics of location?

A Poetics of Location

Since a politics of location, as I have just tried to sketch it, emphasizes the multiplicity, complexity, and contextuality of human experience, any kind of poetics coming out of such a sensibility must also be marked by fluidity, shifting perspectives, and situational specificity. The insistence on fluidity does *not* mean that all perspectives are applicable at all times to all subjects. Indeed, just as the particular context influences which of my multiple "selves" I am at any one time or place, just so would the site of reflection, its specificities, power dynamics, and goals, invite appropriate perspectives and dismiss others. A poetics of location must be profoundly involved in analyzing each site of writing, reading, or theorizing by carefully investigating the specific historical, cultural, political, and social matrix that grounds it.

In discussing her sense of what a poetics of location might be,

Nancy K. Miller argues that it "would acknowledge both the geographics of the writing it reads and the limits of its own project." For her, it is first and foremost "a more historicized poetics,"[13] one that concentrates on the local particularities of text and reader, the "realities" they create and have been created by, the intricate relations of power and knowledge they embody and wield. As a more historicized poetics, a poetics of location would explore not only the possible historical scenarios, which might be reconstructed through the content of a text, the primary concern of traditional biblical historical criticism, but also the historical production of the text itself, its material and economic base, its relation to other texts, to language usage generally, and to other cultural constructs. But just as importantly as all this, a poetics of location must acknowledge its own boundaries in the "facts of blood and bread" that shape the perspectives of every reader.

In addition to these connections to the radical historicity of postmodernism, a poetics of location should reflect the postmodern understanding of language as constitutive of reality, rather than merely reflective of it. In so doing, the interpretive task of a poetics of location properly shifts from hermeneutics to rhetoric, a shift defined and called for by Rebecca Chopp at the close of the Vanderbilt conference. Under the Enlightenment paradigm, hermeneutics implied the existence of an object in the past that could be apprehended "objectively" by a later interpreter and restated in the terms of her/his present cultural idiom. Such hermeneutical endeavors were then judged by how closely or adequately the restatement copied the original object.

For at least the last fifty years, even most biblical scholars have not subscribed to such a rigid understanding of hermeneutics, recognizing that the "hermeneutical circle," that necessary interrelationship of text and reader, qualified the objectivity of all readings. Still, the search for a more "objective" (or "right") reading and the judgment of the adequacy of the interpretation to the original remain the primary critical concerns of contemporary biblical scholarship–spuriously and misleadingly so, in my view. Since the very admission of a "hermeneutical circle" reveals the inseparability of subject and object, a "right" or "objective" reading is finally impossible, for every reading will bear the stamp of the one who makes it. What, then, is involved in the continuing claims for "objective" readings? I think Robert Morgan's recent discussion of biblical interpretation provides a clue. About the many different, recent interpretations of the Gospel of Mark, Morgan writes:

> But Christian interpreters have good reasons for maintaining their
> hope that what they say about Mark is what Mark intended, however mistaken the great majority of them must be. Without this

---

13. Miller, *Subject to Change,* 4.

claim that their interpretations represent the author's intention, theologians cannot usually persuade others in the religious community to listen. What the latest professors say about God on their own authority has less claim upon the community's attention than what they say (with whatever authority their scholarship bestows) that Mark or Jesus were saying about God.[14]

Hence, for Morgan the importance of claims to "objective" knowledge of the past resides in their value as *persuasion* in the present. The ultimate goal of interpretation, Morgan suggests, is to persuade others to listen to the religious views you wish to express. Would it not be considerably more honest to call this process what it actually is—rhetoric?

In a poetics of location, where language is clearly understood as constitutive of reality, interpretation is just as openly recognized as the practice of rhetoric. Defining interpretation as rhetoric has several important ramifications. First, both the postmodern view of language itself and the delineation of interpretation as rhetoric disclose language as power. Language can create—or destroy—worlds; it is a force acting on society to perpetuate current ideologies, establish structural relations, generate visions of the future, spread fear and hatred, attack oppression, and so on. Language constructs our vision of "the good, the true, and the beautiful."

Second, because language is power, a poetics of location must be situated in communities of accountability and structures of responsibility. Since the sites of writing, reading, and theorizing are diverse, those communities and structures may be so as well. The academy, churches, coalitions, national and international forums are all possible communities of accountability. However, one is not accountable solely to one's own "blood" or "bread" grouping. Since a common sensibility of yearning underlies many possible communities, one can submit one's rhetoric to critical scrutiny across many lines. Such a practice is important in assisting each interpreter in analyzing more fully his/her own distinctive contexts and constraints. Because one tends to be most conscious of the pain of one's own particular circumstances, it is often possible to ignore in one's life and in one's rhetoric those areas where one's privileges are complicitous in the oppression of others. At the Vanderbilt conference we learned, occasionally in upsetting ways, where our rhetoric "unconsciously" perpetuated destructive stereotypes of others. Such learning is essential to a poetics of location.

The mention of critical scrutiny raises a third ramification of interpretation as rhetoric: the development of critical languages and critical

---

14. Morgan with J. Barton, *Biblical Interpretation* (Oxford Bible Series; Oxford: Oxford Univ. Press, 1988) 235–36.

practices. In general, critical judgments are based on publicly shared standards, values, and sensibilities. This is the case in academic communities, in which reason, logic, and critical thinking are valued and rewarded. While those who experience rage and alienation within the present structures of Western patriarchy may share a common sensibility, the complexity of location suggests that no one critical standard could adequately address the multiple contexts encountered by everyone. Consequently, a poetics of location should recognize a variety of critical languages, depending on the context and the concerns of those involved. Nevertheless, since language is power, the relevant categories of critical analysis will probably tend to be the persuasiveness, the dangerousness, the subversiveness, the insightfulness, the usefulness, and so on, of the interpretation rather than its "rightness" or "wrongness." However, whatever the categories of analysis, there are two prerequisites for employing any critical language: one must learn to listen to others carefully and fully, and one must always analyze one's own self-interests thoroughly before critiquing those of others.

A poetics of location maintains the radical historicity of texts and interpreters, their creative and multiple interconnections, and their powerful constructions of "reality," "truth," and "justice," in the hopes of persuading the world that those yearning for a better way finally need to be heard.

Index of Names ———————————————